Edexcel GCSE (9–1)

BUSINESS

SECOND EDITION

Ian Marcousé

HODDER
EDUCATION
AN HACHETTE UK COMPANY

In order to ensure that this resource offers high-quality support for the associated Pearson qualification, it has been through a review process by the awarding body. This process confirms that this resource fully covers the teaching and learning content of the specification or part of a specification at which it is aimed. It also confirms that it demonstrates an appropriate balance between the development of subject skills, knowledge and understanding, in addition to preparation for assessment.

Endorsement does not cover any guidance on assessment activities or processes (e.g. practice questions or advice on how to answer assessment questions), included in the resource nor does it prescribe any particular approach to the teaching or delivery of a related course.

While the publishers have made every attempt to ensure that advice on the qualification and its assessment is accurate, the official specification and associated assessment guidance materials are the only authoritative source of information and should always be referred to for definitive guidance.

Pearson examiners have not contributed to any sections in this resource relevant to examination papers for which they have responsibility.

Examiners will not use endorsed resources as a source of material for any assessment set by Pearson.

Endorsement of a resource does not mean that the resource is required to achieve this Pearson qualification, nor does it mean that it is the only suitable material available to support the qualification, and any resource lists produced by the awarding body shall include this and other appropriate resources.

The Publishers would like to thank the following for permission to reproduce copyright material. Photo credits can be found on page 290.

Acknowledgements

Pg. 112, Top tips for writing a business plan. © The Prince's Trust. The original version can be found at *https://www.princes-trust.org.uk/help-for-young-people/tools-resources/business-tools/business-plans*; **pg. 119**, extract from *The Guardian*, 12 March 2015, © Guardian News & Media Ltd 2016; **pg. 145**, extract from *The Guardian*, 3 August 2016, © Guardian News & Media Ltd 2016; **pg. 190**, extract from *The Guardian*, 26 January 2016, © Guardian News & Media Ltd 2016; **pg. 258**, extract from *The Guardian*, 11 August, 2016, © Guardian News & Media Ltd 2016.

Every effort has been made to trace all copyright holders, but if any have been inadvertently overlooked, the Publishers will be pleased to make the necessary arrangements at the first opportunity.

Although every effort has been made to ensure that website addresses are correct at time of going to press, Hodder Education cannot be held responsible for the content of any website mentioned in this book. It is sometimes possible to find a relocated web page by typing in the address of the home page for a website in the URL window of your browser.

Hachette UK's policy is to use papers that are natural, renewable and recyclable products and made from wood grown in sustainable forests. The logging and manufacturing processes are expected to conform to the environmental regulations of the country of origin.

Orders: please contact Bookpoint Ltd, 130 Milton Park, Abingdon, Oxon OX14 4SE. Telephone: +44 (0)1235 827720. Fax: +44 (0)1235 400454. Email education@bookpoint.co.uk Lines are open from 9 a.m. to 5 p.m., Monday to Saturday, with a 24-hour message answering service. You can also order through our website: www.hoddereducation.co.uk

ISBN: 978 1 4718 9935 5

© Ian Marcousé 2017

First edition published in 2009

This edition published in 2017 by

Hodder Education,
An Hachette UK Company
Carmelite House
50 Victoria Embankment
London EC4Y 0DZ

www.hoddereducation.co.uk

Impression number 10 9 8 7 6

Year   2022 2021 2020 2019

Cover photo © VLADGRIN/iStock/Getty Images/

Illustrations by Peter Lubach and Integra Software Services Services, Ltd.

Typeset in India by Integra Software Services, Ltd.

Printed in Dubai

A catalogue record for this title is available from the British Library.

Contents

Theme 2: Building a business

Introduction

Acknowledgements

Many thanks to all the people involved along the way in making this GCSE course a success – and therefore helping the book. Key figures include the team of entrepreneurs who helped me devise the original course, plus the modern driving force of Isla Billett and Colin Leith. For the book itself, many thanks to Michelle Billington and Louise Stubbs, plus the Hodder input from Beth Cleall and Melissa Richards.

Personally, the most important input came from my 3-year-old grandson James, whose question: 'Why do shops die?' deserves a 12-mark exam question of its own. For him, my wife Maureen and the rest of my family, writing books means time locked away – so my love, thanks and apologies to them all.

Dedication

This book is dedicated to Marcousés: Carly, James, Lily, Owen, Scarlett, Skye and Tilly

Using this book

There are five main ways to use this book. The very best students might use all of them, but using any one of the five will help towards exam success.

Read it. The chapters are written to be read. They're not too long, and are packed with real-life examples to help make the theory more understandable. A classroom lesson plus a read through the relevant chapter will put you in control. If you can find the time, test yourself on the 'End of chapter exercises'.

Look it up. The index at the back of the book helps you find the precise topic your homework is about – or the topic you've been told is coming up in tomorrow's test. That means you only need to read what you need. Make sure to check whether there are relevant definitions given in the 'Revision essentials' boxes.

Build on it. At the end of each chapter are exam-style 'Practice questions'. Each question gives you some text about a real business, then exam-style questions. Each one is a mini-mock exam. Have a go and then ask your teacher for a copy of the author's answers (available in the Answer Guide). This will be a very useful way of preparing for the exams.

Revise it. At the end of each section of the book are multiple choice questions that enable you to test yourself quite quickly (and without much writing). These sections of the book mirror the specification and are therefore helpful for exam preparation. Your teachers have the answers in their Answer Guide.

Key revision terms. Towards the end of the book is a very full Glossary. It covers every term set out in the Specification – and is therefore crucial to your exam revision.

Teachers will be pleased to know that an Answer Guide is available for this book: Edexcel GCSE (9-1) Business Answer Guide, ISBN 978-1510405288.

Theme 1

Investigating small business

1 The dynamic nature of business

Business enterprise is about starting something of your own. It would probably be a business, but it might also be a charity or a sports club. The key is that *you* want to do it, and that it proves to be a success. However, changes in technology, in fashion and in the economy mean that success can never be taken for granted. These changes represent the **dynamic nature of business**, and are illustrated by the following story.

In 2011, Evan Spiegel made a presentation to his university class about an app idea called Picaboo. He demonstrated photos being taken and sent by phone, and then disappearing. His classmates weren't impressed. Convinced he was on to something, Spiegel kept working on the idea with two friends. A couple of months later, a renamed Snapchat got a low-key launch. Student take-up in California enabled the new business to raise $13.5 million in **venture capital** in early 2013. Such was Snapchat's

growth that, by late 2013, Facebook offered to buy the business for $3 billion. In 2016, Snapchat overtook Twitter to become one of the biggest social media outlets in the world, with 150 million users daily. The company's value hit $18 billion, with Spiegel becoming a multi-billionaire in five years.

The dynamic nature of business arises because of changing customer tastes and needs, which are driven by changes in technology and in other factors outside the business' control. The unexpected 'out' vote in the 2016 European referendum was a case in point. Suddenly companies had to rethink their plans in the light of a new economic reality. Successful businesses are the ones that can adapt quickly to new circumstances.

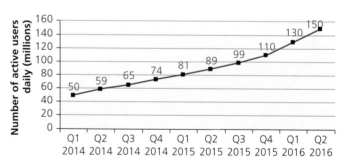

Figure 1.1 Growth in Snapchat usage worldwide

> Every teenager who wants to be an entrepreneur is a rescue from wanting to be on *The X Factor* or *Big Brother*.
>
> *Duncan Bannatyne, entrepreneur and 'dragon' on Dragons' Den*

When starting a new business, all the challenges speed up. Decisions that a big company has months to think about must be decided immediately. Should the new burger bar buy one milkshake machine or two?

Evan Spiegel first presented his idea for Snapchat to his classmates in 2011

Quickly, decide! Should it sign up to Just Eat or create its own e-commerce website and app? Decide! In business, virtually every decision costs money and, because most start-up businesses are short of cash, the personal pressure involved in each decision gets ever-greater.

The three main questions to ask about start-ups are:

1 Why?
2 Who?
3 How?

Why?

The main motive for starting up something new is desire. People want satisfaction from a sense of achievement. If they could get it from their normal workplace, they might not take the risk of starting on their own.

The next most important motivator is the wish to be your own boss. Independent decision making allows the individual to do things the way that they think is best. Most jobs involve a degree of compromise. When you are running something for yourself you may not be able to afford the best, but at least you know that you will get the best you can afford. So, the chef who hates working in a cramped kitchen with second-rate ingredients may long to be in a position to make all the decisions.

Then, of course, there is money. A person may start a burger bar because of their conviction that they will make a fortune. Such a person may dream of retiring early, with a beachfront house and a huge fridge packed with beer. The typical business to go for would be a franchise, in which the individual buys the rights to open a local branch of a business that already exists (and makes good profits). The Subway sandwich chain works in this way.

> The common question that gets asked in business is, *why*? That's a good question, but an equally valid question is, *why not*?
>
> *Jeff Bezos, founder of Amazon*

Who?

A successful start-up requires a huge list of qualities and skills, especially if starting up on your own. Among these are:

- personal qualities: determination, resilience (can bounce back from setbacks), enthusiasm, hard-working, decisive, willing to take risks
- skills: can listen as well as speak, can plan and organise, can persuade, can manage others
- resources: can find help when needed (finance or advice), may have exceptional knowledge of a special topic (for example, building a website).

Of course, few entrepreneurs (business risk-takers) have *all* these qualities, but without quite a number of them it will be hard to succeed.

How?

The most common way to start a new enterprise is to trial a business idea while still working, often from your own home. It is tried out in a limited way before committing too much money and time.

Duncan Goose, however, started bottled water brand One as a social enterprise by giving up his regular job. The water is bottled in Wales and sold throughout Britain, with the profits going to the One Foundations, a UK-registered charity funding water projects in Africa. It took him six months, without pay, to get the enterprise going.

When people need to raise capital to help them start a business, they write a business plan. This sets out the aims, the strategy, the financial forecasts and financial requirements. If carried out professionally, a good business plan greatly increases the chances of getting funding. Crucial to a good business plan is a sensible sales forecast based on independent market research.

> Ideas are easy. Implementation is hard.
>
> *Guy Kawasaki, marketing specialist and venture capitalist*

One works to provide clean water in Africa

Talking point

Which of the 'who?' qualities are strengths of yours? Which are weaknesses?

⬤ Drawing the right conclusions

Business is exciting because of its dynamic nature. A business may seem to be unstoppable one year. Every decision works out well. The next year, nothing is quite the same. A best-selling business book called *In Search of Excellence* was written to explain why 43 companies were excellent. Famously, by the time the book was published even some of those companies were struggling. The dynamic nature of business is such that today's star can be tomorrow's fall guy.

If there is one general point that can be made about business, it is that sustained business success comes to companies that keep talking to customers and keep adjusting to their new needs and wants.

> A man is a success if he gets up in the morning and gets to bed at night, and in between he does what he wants to do.
>
> *Bob Dylan, musician*

Revision essentials

Dynamic nature of business: the idea that business is ever-changing because external factors, such as technology, are always changing.

Venture capital: risk capital provided by an investor willing to take a risk in return for a share in any later profits; the venture capital provider will take a share stake in the business.

End of chapter exercises

1 Outline two dynamic forces currently putting pressure on companies in the market for:

   (a) potato crisps

   (b) takeaway pizza.

2 Look at Figure 1.1 on page 2 and calculate the percentage increase in active users between the second quarter of 2015 and the second quarter of 2016.

3 Why might a young entrepreneur prefer to start a franchise, such as Subway, than a wholly independent business?

4 Without looking back at the text, briefly write down what you understand by the 'why', 'who' and 'how' of starting a business.

5 Read the following extract. Why might the figures 'explain the huge amount of interest in business start-up among women and non-white people'?

Although women make up 50 per cent of the working population, only 5.2 per cent of executive directors of big businesses are women. About 15 per cent of the UK population is non-white but only 1.5 per cent of executive directors are non-white. This apparent ceiling on career prospects may explain the huge amount of interest in business start-up among women and non-white people. Unfortunately, even then discrimination may apply. A recent survey suggested that banks charge businesswomen a one per cent higher interest rate than businessmen.

6 Outline two possible reasons why a bank might charge businesswomen a higher rate of interest than men.

Practice questions

The big day was 9 December 2013. The first ever Cuckoo Foods muesli yoghurt pot was sold in Selfridges, London. For friends-since-13 Anna Mackenzie and Lucy Wright it was both the start of something exciting and the result of 18 months' work. Anna's mum's recipes for muesli were a starting point, when Anna realised they'd make a really good on-the-go breakfast. Having just finished university, she and Lucy started working on recipes, ingredients and learning about the market. Eventually they came up with a range of bold tastes: mango and coconut, elderflower and cranberry, and many others. The target market was always clear: young, busy, foodie people.

They got in touch with other foodie entrepreneurs, such as the former boss of Rachel's Organic. He gave advice on pitching successfully to supermarket buyers, and in basics such as shelf-life. Anna's mum wanted fresh fruit, but an agreed shelf-life of 20 days made that impossible.

After Selfridges, further success came from distribution deals with Waitrose, Ocado and AMT, a coffee-shop chain with 50 outlets in railway stations – perfect for busy commuters. Helped by astute PR (free publicity in newspapers and magazines), Anna and Lucy were able to double sales turnover to £400,000 in 2016. They seem very keen to push far beyond that in the coming years.

When asked about the single most important quality needed in an entrepreneur, both answered 'resilience'. For continued business growth, they'll need that and more.

➡

Cuckoo Foods sold its first product in Selfridges in 2013

Total: 15 marks

1 Look up the word 'resilience' and outline why it might be important in a start-up such as Cuckoo Foods. (2)

2 State two more entrepreneurial qualities that Anna and Lucy will need in the future. (2)

3 Outline one factor that might be helpful about having a clear target market. (2)

4 Anna and Lucy are very ambitious and are already considering the best way to continue their growth. Their options include:

♦ Option 1: Grow by developing new products other than muesli.

♦ Option 2: Focus on becoming the number 1 in the market for muesli.

Justify which **one** of these options they should choose. (9)

2 Why new business ideas come about

In 2015, UK sales of Danone's Activia yogurt brand fell back to £170 million. Back in 2011, the brand was the UK's top seller, with sales of £240 million. This decline created space for newcomers. The Greek yoghurt brand Total saw sales jump from £20 million in 2010 to £50 million in 2015, while a brand that was new to the UK in 2013, The Collective, saw sales of £14.5 million in 2015, up by 52 per cent. This is the essence of why new business ideas come about. Consumer tastes change constantly, creating new opportunities for business success. Some are filled by existing big companies with big pockets, but surprisingly many are filled by bright new businesses with new ideas.

New business ideas come about because there are:

◆ changes in what consumers want
◆ products and services becoming obsolete
◆ changes in technology.

> Business opportunities are like buses. There's always another one coming.
>
> *Richard Branson, founder, Virgin Group*

● Changes in what consumers want

We may all *want* a brand-new BMW, but most will not be able to afford one. For changes in consumer taste to matter, they must be backed by the ability to pay. This is known as **demand**.

There are several possible reasons why consumers changed their mind about Activia, leading to a fall in demand:

◆ There may have been a change in customer taste, with people preferring creamier, Greek-style yoghurt.

◆ Social media comments may have weakened consumer confidence in the health story long-promoted by Danone for its Activia brand.
◆ Pressures on household incomes may have pushed customers to buy cheaper brands.

Price is another important factor. The price of a product or service is a key influence on the level of demand. If a company charged too low a price, customers may lose confidence and go elsewhere: a wedding dress for £99.99 might not win hearts and minds.

In the vast majority of cases though, higher prices push demand down. A price increase for Pepsi would cut demand, especially if it made it more expensive than Coca-Cola. Price increases may push products out of people's price range and encourage customers to look for cheaper substitutes.

> An industry begins with customer needs, not with a patent, a raw material or a selling skill.
>
> *Theodore Levitt, economist and business thinker*

● Products and services becoming obsolete

A product or service is **obsolete** if no one wants it any longer. There is no longer great demand for chimney sweeps, as few people have an open fire. Similarly, there's hardly any demand for traditional butcher's shops as people eat less meat and, in any case, buy it in supermarkets. As people change their behaviour, some businesses stop being relevant. Among London's black cab drivers, there's real concern that sat-nav systems and Uber may make them obsolete.

Businesses therefore need to think ahead to how customer habits are changing and try to keep one step ahead. Apple had a fabulously profitable product in the iPod but saw that people would want one hand-held device rather than an iPod and a phone. Apple led consumers towards the iPhone. Today the iPod is obsolete. Long live the iPhone!

Figure 2.1 shows the drift downwards in iPod sales between late 2009 and 2014. The data stops there because Apple decided that iPod sales were no longer high enough to be worth listing in their accounts. In the last quarter shown, iPhone sales outpaced iPod sales by 15:1.

If changing customer tastes keep making products and services obsolete, it is critical to keep coming up with new, bright business ideas. For chocolate companies such as Ferrero, it means keeping up with changing tastes and fashions; for companies such as Dyson and Apple, the key is to keep up with changes in technology.

> Obsolescence never meant the end of anything, it's just the beginning.
>
> *Marshall McLuhan, writer*

Changes in technology

Until mobile phone networks operated at the bandwidth known as 3G, smartphones could hardly function. Vodafone launched 3G in the UK in late 2004, but it was only over the following two years that it became widespread. Apple's iPhone arrived just on cue in early 2007. Without 3G technology, there would be no iPhone as we know it. New technology is a classic cause of new business ideas.

Vodafone was the first network to launch 3G

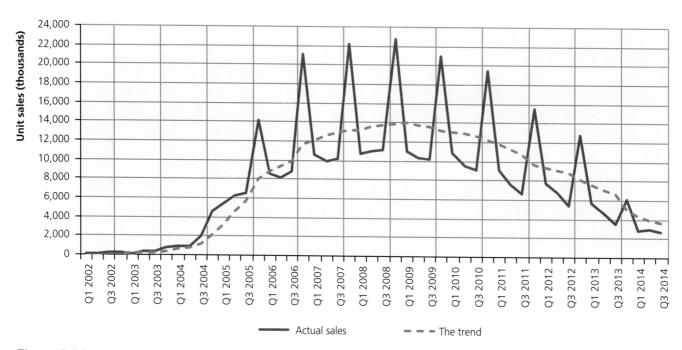

Figure 2.1 Global quarterly sales of the Apple iPod, 2002–14 (Source: Apple Inc. accounts)

Table 2.1 New technologies and their potential uses

New technology	New products/uses
GPS (global positioning system)	Sat nav Pet-monitoring collar Self-driving cars
3D printing	One-off prototypes to test new product ideas Tailor-made artificial limbs Made-to-measure printed shoes
RFID (radio-frequency identification)	Keeping tabs on stock in-store Race timing (how marathon runners are monitored) Libraries (more efficient than barcode scanning)

Changes in technology have two main impacts: they create opportunities for new things, and increase the likelihood that old things will become obsolete. Combined, this means problems for slow-moving companies and exciting opportunities for smaller, newer, speedier ones. The key for new small firms is to keep fully on top of the new technology, and be willing to take risks trying out new ideas.

> Once a new technology rolls over you, if you're not part of the steamroller, you're part of the road.
>
> *Stewart Brand, business author*

◉ Drawing the right conclusions

In 2016, there were more than 600,000 business start-ups in the UK, with more than 200,000 in London. Overwhelmingly, the start-ups occur because individual **entrepreneurs** see new opportunities due to changes in customer taste or the arrival of new technology. The individuals have the initiative and the financial backing to turn their business dream into reality. Their chances of success will depend on:

◆ whether their idea was as original and as relevant as they believed
◆ whether their competitors prove tougher and cleverer than had been expected
◆ whether their customers become customers who stay; customer loyalty is crucial.

Revision essentials

Demand: the number of units that customers want – and can afford – to buy.

Entrepreneurs: business people who see opportunities and are willing to take risks in making them happen.

Obsolete: a product or service with sales that have declined or come to an end as customers find something new.

End of chapter exercises

1 What changes might come about over the next three years in the markets for:

   (a) chocolate

   (b) mobile phones.

2 Outline two factors that might cause sales of the Sony PS4 to decline.

3 Outline two factors that might cause motorbikes to become obsolete.

4 Look at the quote by Marshall McLuhan on page 8. What do you think it means?

5 Read the following extract. Discuss the factors that may have led to the Wii U becoming obsolete by 2016.

The 2017 launch of Nintendo's new games console, the Nintendo Switch, had been predicted for several years. After great success selling 101 million units of the Wii system, the follow-up Wii U achieved a shockingly weak 13 million units. Sales were falling month-on-month. In the first week of June 2016, Sony's PS4 outsold the Wii U by a factor of eight globally. The Wii U wasn't old, but it was becoming obsolete.

6 What factors may prove the most important in ensuring that the Nintendo Switch console will be a success?

Practice questions

In 2012, Rikke Rosenlund was walking her neighbour's dog. She had too many work commitments to own one herself, and she realised that many families have problems with caring for their dogs in holiday times. A keen Facebook user, Rikke started thinking about a social network of dog lovers. It would bring together those with insufficient free time to be a dog-owner and those dog-owners lacking the time to look after their own dogs. But what exactly would a dog website look like and do? The solution was BorrowMyDoggy.com.

BorrowMyDoggy connects dog owners and dog lovers

Rikke took her time developing the site but, by 2014, it was fully open. To become a full member costs dog owners £44.99 and borrowers £9.99 each year. The site quickly attracted more than 50,000 members and today has more than 300,000. Then, with BorrowMyDoggy needing more and more staff to handle the level of demand and develop the website, Rikke opted for crowdfunding as a way to raise extra capital. With such a large community of dog lovers, it was no surprise that £1.5 million was raised in 2015, even though the business had not yet made a profit.

Not many years before, the idea of BorrowMyDoggy would have been laughed at, but changes in lifestyle affect what services people feel they need. For time-poor people, Rikke's idea has been hugely useful.

Total: 20 marks

1 Outline why it may be important for BorrowMyDoggy to keep up with changes in technology. (2)

2 Explain the importance of 'demand' to new businesses. (3)

3 Identify one entrepreneurial characteristic shown by Rikke in this story. (1)

4 Outline one factor that might lead Rikke's business to become obsolete in future. (2)

5 Evaluate whether Rikke's idea will be a success. You should use the information above as well as your knowledge of business. (12)

3 How new business ideas come about

Creative thinking stems from asking questions. Three-year-olds can drive their parents crazy by constantly asking 'why': 'why does granny smell?', 'why are raspberries red?', and so on. In fact, just such a question about raspberries made the producer of Slush Puppie drinks decide to make the raspberry flavour a blue colour. The red (strawberry) and blue (raspberry) made a more eye-catching display.

The ability to ask 'why' is at the root of creativity, innovation and how business ideas come about.

> Disneyland will never be completed, as long as there is imagination left in the world.
>
> *Walt Disney (1901–66)*

● Why not?

It is also vital to ask 'why not?'. The three-year-old is trying to find out the way the world is. Creative thinkers also ask 'why shouldn't the world be different?' In 1933, Percy Shaw became the inventor of one of the world's most widely used ideas. Driving home in dense fog he nearly drove off the road and crashed, but was saved by the flashing eye of a cat sitting on a fence. Two years later he patented the cat's eye, an invention that made him a fortune. Brilliantly, he made a reflector with a rubberised top that would give when cars ran over it; the action of pushing down the rubber top wipes the reflector clean – just like a cat's eye blinking.

Cat's eye reflectors made their inventor a fortune

Many 'why not?' questions are much less significant than Percy Shaw's. For example, why not have a strawberry-flavour Calippo ice lolly? Such an obvious idea might be hugely significant if it proves a commercial success.

● Original ideas

Most of us have lots of creative thoughts. We look in an ice cream cabinet and wish there were a mint choc ice or a mango lolly. The problem is that we may not tell anybody about these thoughts, or – worse – we may try to tell someone but find that nobody listens. It follows that creativity may only have meaning if it is backed up by effective communication. Percy Shaw had his idea and developed it himself. Most of us have neither the money nor the ability to achieve this.

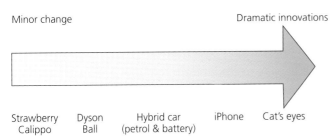

Minor change				Dramatic innovations
Strawberry Calippo	Dyson Ball	Hybrid car (petrol & battery)	iPhone	Cat's eyes

Figure 3.1 A new product will sit at some point along a scale ranging from minor change to dramatic innovation

Well-run businesses encourage the sharing of **original ideas**. Ordering a tailor-made kitchen from German manufacturers used to involve a three-month wait before delivery. Now staff at a leading German kitchen manufacturer have found new ways to use their computer-aided design (CAD) system to cut delivery times to three weeks.

For some businesses, original ideas are the basis of the operation. A good example is Codemasters Ltd, a private company in the UK that produces games software. It has grown from the bedrooms of two teenager brothers in 1984, to employing hundreds of people around the world, but especially in the UK. It is Europe's largest privately owned software business. It built its business on Brian Lara Cricket and LMA Manager, but today its key games are Dirt Rally and FIA Formula One World Championship. Without new ideas a business such as this would inevitably fade away.

> The man who has no imagination has no wings.
>
> *Muhammad Ali, greatest ever boxer*

New ideas and competitive advantage

Competitive advantage is a term given to any factors that help a business to succeed when competing against direct rivals. For airline Ryanair that advantage comes from low-cost operations that allow it to charge low prices. For many other businesses, original ideas are the key. Examples include:

- Swegway hoverboards – the 2015 launch gained a lot of publicity and sales until the government announced that the hoverboards were illegal for use on public roads and pavements. This new idea deserved better.
- The Tesla Model 3 – due to be launched in 2018, this all-electric car promises to deliver a powerful, thrusting engine and be as fun to drive as any petrol car. If it lives up to its promises, the price of around £30,000 should allow it to become the first mass-market electric car.

The hoverboard was declared illegal for road and pavement use

> The creativity that emerges from the company comes from the many ideas of the people who are here.
>
> *John Rollwagen, chief executive*

Adapting existing products and services

The overwhelming majority of new product launches are derived from an existing product success. This is as true for James Bond films as it is for chocolate bars. **Adapting existing products** or services is an attractive business proposition because:

- It usually requires less research and development, and other investment, to develop a new product variation than a completely new product. It is also likely that you have already developed the production machinery and methods that can now be adapted to Product B. Overall, adapting is a much cheaper option, and that makes it possible to enjoy high profit margins.
- It is easy to underestimate how hard it is to find a new product that people love (80 per cent of new products fail). So, if you have a success, it makes sense to milk it. Your chances of making money from a new *Superman* film are greater than from creating a brand new film.

◆ Launching an adapted product can successfully protect your first/main product. If you have created Cadbury Dairy Milk, why leave yourself vulnerable to attack from rivals by leaving open the opportunity to do a bubbly version or one with nuts and raisins.

Here are two examples of successful adapted products:

◆ Monster Energy Ultra, a zero calorie energy drink that tastes more like a soft drink, was launched into the £500 million market for energy drinks. By offering a no-calorie energy drink, brand owners Coca-Cola hope to bring more women into the energy drinks sector.

◆ The 2015 launch of Giant Crumpets pushed Warburton's crumpet sales up 13.3 per cent to £63.3 million, while rival Kingsmill's sales of crumpets fell by 26.3 per cent.

Talking point

Can you come up with a new chocolate bar that can match the advertising slogan once used by Cadbury's Crunchie for 'that Friday feeling'?

●Drawing the right conclusions

For companies such as Heinz, with stable, big sellers like ketchup and baked beans, new ideas are a luxury. If they work, that's wonderful, but if they don't they'll still go on selling more than £500 million in the UK. For other businesses, new ideas are essential. The smartphone market is unforgiving, as shown by the struggles of Nokia, Sony and Siemens. Several companies have done well with one phone but then disappeared from this huge market. The need for new ideas is constant.

The ability to keep coming up with ideas tends to depend on:

◆ Staff who really care and are engaged in the jobs they do: Google, yes; Sports Direct, no.

◆ The amount of cash the company devotes to research and development, market research and investing in new technology. This may require a business to limit its dividend payouts to shareholders to make sure there's enough capital for financing the future.

◆ The diversity of the recruitment approach: if all managers are ageing men, it may be hard to spot the new possibilities in dynamic, younger markets, such as mobile gaming.

Revision essentials

Adapting existing products: finding new products based on the original one, such as Wall's White Chocolate Magnum.

Competitive advantage: a feature of a business that helps it to succeed against rivals.

Original ideas: ideas that have not been done before.

End of chapter exercises

1 Outline two benefits that a business can gain from asking the question 'why'.

2 What might be a correct business response to the following questions:

   (a) Why are organic foods so expensive?

   (b) Why does Aldi keep gaining market share?

3 Suggest two ways in which managers could encourage staff to share their own ideas about new products.

4 Read the following extract. What is the most likely explanation for the high number of suggestions from the Cowley staff? Explain your reasoning.

Encouraging and using ideas 'from the floor' can have dramatic results, as at BMW's Mini factory at Cowley, Oxford. The BMW group announced that suggestions from staff at Cowley have saved the company £10.5 million in two years. Of the 14,333 suggestions staff put forward, three quarters were put into action. They ranged from cutting unnecessary use of paper to more complex engineering solutions.

5 Discuss whether the staff should get a financial reward for the suggestions that are put into action.

Practice questions

In early 2016 Chinese technology brand SpeedX received more than $2.3 million from an American crowdfunding site; 1,500 cyclists were desperate to get their hands on a $1,499 Leopard smart bike. The promotional video for the super-strong bike showed that it could take the weight of a Lamborghini, while offering real-time monitoring, coaching and feedback.

Chief executive Li Gang explained that the idea arose back in 2014, when he had piled on 50 pounds and his partner had developed diabetes. They took up cycling and, while riding, Li thought up ways to make the experience more interesting and more effective. He decided he needed feedback on calories used at different speeds and in different gears, plus data on his heart rate and rate of dehydration.

After a lot of time spent with Chinese bike manufacturers, he knew all he needed about production quality and costs.

Unfortunately for Li, he failed to check on the different rates of import duty and VAT in different countries. Bikes sent to Europe proved impossibly expensive due to high European import taxes placed specifically on bikes from China. Despite this costly learning experience, he still believes the business will be a huge success.

Total: 13 marks

1 If the price is unchanged and sales of the Leopard smart bike hit 12,000 in the coming year, calculate the revenue that will be generated. (2)

2 Outline one possible reason to explain Li Gang's success in launching the Leopard. (2)

3 Li Gang wants to build his business to become the world number 1 in smart bikes. He sees two options:

   ◆ Option 1: Look for original ideas to create different bikes.

   ◆ Option 2: Create new products adapted from his Leopard bike.

Justify which **one** of these options he should choose. (9)

4 Risk and reward

Risk is about chance. What is the chance that a particular outcome will occur? Large firms know that, over the years, only one in five new products is a success. So, the chance of failure is four out of five. Does that mean firms should never launch new products? No. They must either:

◆ make enough profit from existing products to fund five new product launches for every one success

◆ make sure that the one success is big enough to make up for the failures.

> The biggest risk is not taking any risk.
>
> *Mark Zuckerberg, founder of Facebook*

Mark Zuckerberg invented Facebook

● Risks can yield rewards

In 1984, two teenagers, Richard and David Darling, moved on from playing computer games to writing them. They produced the games for fun, but then tried advertising them in a popular computer weekly. A £70 advertisement brought in £7,000 worth of orders. In 1986, they formed a company, Codemasters Ltd. It went on to produce some of the longest-lasting games software brands, such as Colin McRae Rally and LMA Manager. In summer 2015, it held the number two spot in the UK games chart with Dirt Rally. Today the business has sales of over £100 million per year, employs more than 500 people and is worth around £250 million. Risking £70 on an advertisement has resulted in fabulous wealth and an amazing achievement.

Table 4.1 What are the main risks?

At the start	In the early days	When growth is rapid
Identifying a market gap big enough to be profitable	Making sure your initial customers come back for more	'Overtrading' – sales growing faster than you can cope with financially
Raising (more than) enough capital	Running out of cash during the off-season	Struggling to manage rapid rises in staff, especially middle management
Getting the right people working in the right way	Running out of energy and self-belief when times are tough	The entrepreneur owner may struggle to be a good manager
Building a base of initial customers	Coping with competition when it arrives	The boss and staff may become complacent, so the rise leads to the fall

● Risk

Business failure

Half of UK business start-ups fail within five years. That means they have closed their doors. Some others survive but without making enough profit to feel happy. If a teacher hands in his or her notice to start their own business, not only are they giving up a steady salary and a high degree of security, they are also giving up a guaranteed pension in years to come.

Business failure may not only use up all the family's savings, but may also put huge strains on the family itself. Divorce can be a consequence of a business failure. This is why new businesses only tend to be started by people with huge self-confidence and, preferably, deep pockets.

Financial loss

If a limited company gets into financial trouble, the owner is protected personally from business losses. If the company has £200,000 of debts that it cannot repay, the problem stays with those owed the money. The company owner does not have to pay. When companies fail, the people who suffer most are the suppliers and the workers.

But most UK business are sole traders or partnerships, and therefore have unlimited liability (see Figure 4.1). This means that the company founder/boss is liable personally for any and all of the business debts: £100,000 here for an unpaid bill, £150,000 there to an unhappy customer who has successfully sued.

Starting your own business can be a path to huge riches, but it can also be a path to a personal financial disaster.

Figure 4.1 Business organisations in the UK (figures in millions)

Lack of security

Adults often have responsibilities (children, a mortgage, credit card debts) that force them to look

Table 4.2 The way it is: risky business

Business start-up	Business idea	Risks
Top10 Hotels: British business started in 2011; it raised more than £8 million in start-up capital but closed in December 2015.	Website and app giving users a ranking of top ten hotels in more than 100 cities; easier to use than sites such as TripAdvisor, which list thousands of hotels.	Breaking into a competitive market such as hotel listings. The idea was good but not quite strong enough. They ran out of cash before getting established.
Park Bikeworks opened in Derby in 2013, backed by £490,000 of government funding plus £170,000 from the Derby Enterprise Growth Fund. It closed in March 2015.	A city-centre place for bicycle riders to store their bikes, take a shower, have a coffee and then get to work; it also had a wide range of high-end bikes for hire or purchase.	Gaining grants because of its encouragement of environmentally friendly commuting. It didn't reach its monthly break-even point, making it impossible to generate a secure, regular income for the two founders.
Barnsley-based nightclub owner G4 collapsed in February 2016 after two years of falling sales.	G4 mainly provided management services to other nightclub owners, but in a declining market it became impossible to make a satisfactory profit.	The owners of G4 stood to make financial losses personally if the business continued, so they decided to close it down beforehand.

for a secure, stable income. Working for the council or for Marks and Spencer means a regular salary. Even entrepreneurs who have gone on to make fortunes have had periods when they weren't sure of the next pay packet. Starting a business is full of factors that are outside your control, such as an ice cream parlour hit by a cold, wet summer. A regular pay packet may be very difficult to achieve. The **lack of financial security** is a major risk factor when starting a business.

> He who is not courageous enough to take risks will accomplish nothing in life.
>
> *Muhammad Ali, boxer*

Reward

Business success

Excitement comes from taking risks (that is, the risks generate the rewards). It is the difference between riding a bike on the flat and riding it down a steep hill; or watching Brazil play football compared with watching Austria. At every stage in starting and building a business, risks have to be taken and new skills have to be learnt. This provides the buzz that makes it exciting to be an entrepreneur.

Excitement comes from taking risks

Profit and wealth

Starting a small business can generate huge returns. Most working people struggle to save much from their salary. They may be comfortable but can never become rich. Starting a business creates the possibility of selling it once it is established. It could be sold completely, or part of it could be sold to outside shareholders by 'floating' it on the stock market. In 2005, Tim Warrillow and Charles Rolls set out to launch new 'mixer' soft drinks into a super premium-priced sector above long-standing market leader Schweppes. Sales of Fever-Tree sodas went stunningly well, growing to more than £10 million by 2011 and more than £50 million by 2015. The founders were able to sell shares for more than £100 million in 2016, while still holding a dominant stake in the business. Wealth indeed.

Independence

Many people dislike being told what to do, especially if they do not respect their boss. For such people, starting up on their own may be ideal. By becoming **independent**, they can make their own decisions and, if necessary, their own compromises. People with this motivation may struggle if they start to employ others who have different ideas or standards from their own, however.

Risks in business (and in life) are unavoidable. Well-run firms think about the risks that they may face, and then estimate the possible impact. For example, the cost of a football team dropping out of the Premiership is said to be about £100 million. Apart from the top five sides, each of the other clubs will think about the chance of relegation and its cost. If there are three relegation places for 15 teams, there is a 20 per cent chance of relegation *every year*. So, a wise club chairman would have a plan for how the team would cope. Sadly, the experience of teams such as Nottingham Forest and Leeds United suggests that not every club does this.

'With great risk comes great reward.'
Thomas Jefferson, former US president

● Drawing the right conclusions

For a small firm there is more to consider than just **risk and reward**. There are also the consequences. When book publisher Bloomsbury risked a £2,500 advance to JK Rowling, it was not going to break the bank, even if *Harry Potter* proved a flop. Needless to say, that risk brought Bloomsbury a reward measured in hundreds of millions. But if a small firm takes a big risk, failure may drag the business down.

Clearly, it is vital to think not only about the chance of something going wrong, but also the consequences. Apple can risk £500 million on a technology that may or may not work as £500 million is only 0.5 per cent of the money it keeps in its bank account. For a small firm, risking £10,000 may mean risking the whole future of the business.

Clever businesspeople therefore try to weigh up:
◆ the chances of success or failure
◆ the costs or benefits of success or failure
◆ the implications for the business as a whole.

> Educated risks are the key to success.
>
> *William Olsen, chief executive*

The Harry Potter series proved a great success for Bloomsbury after it risked a modest advance on author JK Rowling

Revision essentials

Business failure: the collapse of a business, probably leading to its closure.

Independence: the need by many business owners to make their own decisions and be their own boss.

Lack of financial security: uncertainty for the business owner about day-to-day family income and assets.

Risk and reward: the balance between the worst that can happen and the best that can happen.

End of chapter exercises

1 Outline two significant risks that might be faced by a small sports shop in your local high street over the coming year.

2 Richard Branson started his first business at school, launching *Student* magazine, before going on to found the Virgin group. Outline two rewards Richard Branson may have received from his initiative.

3 Outline the balance between risk and reward in the case of Bloomsbury's £2,500 investment in JK Rowling.

4 Read the following extract. Describe Ted's attitude to risk.

Skye and Ted Barton took over the family fish-and-chip shop when Skye's parents retired. The business kept them going financially but seemed to be going nowhere. Skye looked into buying the shop next door to create the space for a sit-down restaurant section. She was sure that would attract office workers at lunchtime. Her calculations showed that it would cost £18,000 and could generate an extra £9,000 profit a year. Ted rejected the idea, saying: 'You can't be certain. There's a real risk that your figures are wrong.'

5 Explain why it is necessary for all businesspeople to be willing to take risks.

Practice questions

On 1 January 2016, founder Matteo Pantani left Scoop ice cream. Outside investors had always owned the majority of the shares, and they decided to replace him as the company's chief executive. This was a risk Matteo had never expected. The shareholders were his friends. No more. For Matteo, all the struggles to make Scoop a success were wasted.

The business began when a London-based banker friend of Matteo phoned to urge him to come over 'because there's no good ice cream in London'. The banker would organise the finance and Matteo would use his skills to make and market great ice cream.

When Matteo approached estate agents about a central London location for an ice cream parlour, most turned him down. They had all seen ice cream shops enjoy a super first summer then collapse from negative cash flow during the winter. Landlords wanted their properties going to safer businesses that would keep paying the rent.

After a long time looking, Matteo found premises of the right size in Covent Garden, a busy area popular with both tourists and Londoners. By autumn 2008 Matteo's ice cream parlour, Scoop, was a great success. He opened a second, then a third, outlet in central London.

Between 2008 and 2012, Scoop did wonderfully well. Matteo always said that selling high-quality ice cream 'is like selling happiness ... £2 for ten minutes of happiness'. His thrill in running the business came from pride in his product, and in people's reactions to it. He was working 14-hour days, so needed to enjoy it!

➡

The first big problem for Scoop came in 2012, when the London Olympics seemed to suck visitors away from central London. Business was awful. Then rainy weather in 2013 and 2014 kept summer business quite weak. Meanwhile, from 2008 onwards more and more competition had been arriving in London: *gelato* (Italian for ice cream) had been an unusual word in 2008, but was now everywhere.

When 2015 proved another year of struggle to make substantial profits, the shareholders stepped in. Scoop remains, but its founder and inspiration has gone.

Scoop ice cream was a battle between risk and reward

Total: 18 marks

1 Outline how the idea for Scoop came about. (2)

2 Define the term 'competition'. (1)

3 Outline one factor that was important in turning Scoop from a business idea into a business success. (2)

4 State one problem Scoop faced following the start-up period. (1)

5 Evaluate the level of risk for Scoop's future survival from its decision to dismiss Matteo. You should use the information given above as well as your knowledge of business. (12)

5 The role of business enterprise

What is business for? While the individual entrepreneur may want to be the boss and to make money, the only way to do these things is to produce goods or services that people want to buy, or to meet customer needs or wants, in such a way that adds value (see Chapter 6, Adding value, on page 25).

The role of business enterprise and the purpose of business activity are one and the same: to produce goods and services that people want to buy.

> The purpose of business is to create and keep a customer.
>
> *Peter Drucker, management guru*

● Goods or services

Goods are products, so they can be touched and held. Some goods are long lasting, such as furniture, cars and carpets. These can be used over and over again. Households buying such products will care about how long they last and perhaps what image the products create ('my iPhone', 'my BMW', 'my leather sofa'). Products have to be manufactured in some way, probably in a factory.

A selection of electronic goods

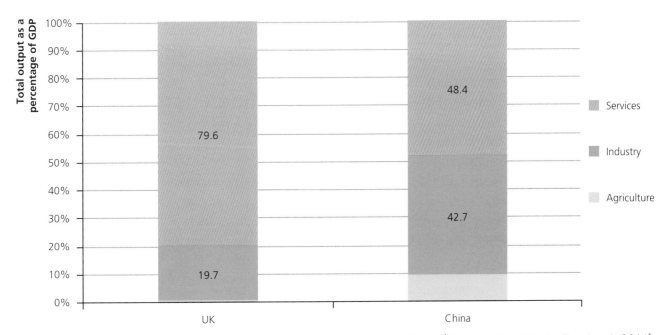

Figure 5.1 A comparison of products and services in the UK and China (Source: CIA World Factbook 2016)

By contrast **services** are usually invisible and certainly can't be touched or held. In the UK, important services include retailing, health and nursing care, sports and leisure. As shown in Figure 5.1 (page 21), services account for nearly 80 per cent of all the business done in this country. The same is true of most developed countries. By contrast, services account for less than half of China's annual output. Producing goods – industry – is currently much more important in China, as is agriculture.

Producing goods requires a huge range of management skills. This is why successful businesses such as Fever-Tree and Cuckoo Foods leave production to others. They buy in the finished soft drinks or muesli breakfasts from an established factory. Even when the products are made elsewhere, there's still a huge amount to do. A producer must:

◆ design the packaging, the brand name and the logos
◆ get the right product range: big enough to be interesting but not so wide as to end up with too many small sellers
◆ persuade shops to stock the product(s)
◆ once orders arrive, make sure deliveries are on time and accurate
◆ design, write and run consumer advertising and promotions, to help make sure that your retailers enjoy big enough sales to keep stocking the product(s)
◆ get the invoicing right, that is, make sure customers pay the right amount, on time.

Services are also a business challenge. Opening a shop or a restaurant may require £50,000 or more in start-up capital, and there are risks aplenty. The most worrying risk is that the business may fail to generate enough day-to-day profit to cover the sometimes huge costs of rent, business taxes and staff salaries. For a small cafe space in London, the rent might be as high as £60,000 a year. If those costs can't be covered, the business will collapse, perhaps leaving sizeable personal debts.

Another possibility is that the business is OK, but not making the level of profit that had been expected. Many businesses keep going for years like this, just ticking over.

Happily, there are also some great success stories:
◆ Helen Raemers started a business in the Alps 15 years ago, to give her regular access to the skiing she loves. The Alpine Club now has an annual turnover of £500,000, and the business is only fully active between December and April.
◆ Hybrid estate agent Purplebricks saw sales revenue jump by more than 400 per cent, from £3.4 million in its start-up year of 2015 to £18.6 million in 2016.

Online and hybrid estate agents can be particularly lucrative

Talking point

Helen Raemers took 15 years to achieve revenue of £0.5 million. Purplebricks managed to reach £18.6 million in less than three years. What might explain the different growth rates?

● Meeting customer needs and wants

Businesses like to say that they meet **customer needs**. Actually, many businesses provide what we don't need but do want. Consider Cadbury for starters. When writing about business it is important to remember that companies present themselves in the best possible light. They prefer to say 'we fulfil needs' than 'we encourage people to buy what they shouldn't'.

An example of a business that fulfils customer needs is a provider of commuter rail services. People need to get to work and there is no other realistic option.

So they go by train. Because few commuter rail services face any competition, train operators are able to provide a poor service with little danger of losing customers.

In many other cases, customer needs are met by businesses that face competition and therefore have to give their best. Someone who wants a pint of milk can probably pick between five and ten places that sell it. To make sure that customers return, they need a well-lit, clean shop, with fast and fairly friendly service.

When it comes to meeting **customer wants**, companies have to do even more. They have to persuade people to buy and then persuade them to keep coming back. This is likely to require powerful advertising, high-quality customer service and terrific distribution.

> Being on par in terms of quality and
> price only gets you into the game.
> Service wins the game.
>
> *Tony Alessandra, US entrepreneur*

● Drawing the right conclusions

In the best companies, meeting customers' wants and needs is a pleasure, not a burden. A happy customer should give pleasure to the workforce, just as a satisfied student makes the teacher's job worthwhile. Some companies are great at keeping everyone focused on the customer. Greggs and Pret a Manger are good examples.

To make sure customers get the products and services they want, companies may:
- hire new staff on the basis of attitude and personality, rather than whether they have great experience, as they'll give friendlier service
- invest heavily in research and development to try to find new products and new technologies
- start a business on the basis of what the founders love doing rather than what they think will make money.

Revision essentials

Customer needs: the products or services people need to make life comfortable.

Customer wants: what people choose to spend their money on, once the weekly bills have been paid.

Goods: products that may be fresh, such as apples, or manufactured, such as Heinz Baked Beans.

Services: providing useful ways to help people live their lives, for example shops, restaurants and hospitals.

End of chapter exercises

1 Why might it be more expensive to start up as a manufacturer of goods than as a service business?

2 (a) From Figure 5.1 on page 21, calculate the amount of the UK's national output that is generated by agriculture; then do the same for China.

   (b) Outline why this information may be important to a producer of tractors.

3 Outline why it might be hard to get a shop to stock a brand-new product for the first time.

4 Read the following extract. Could Mondelez make a case for saying that belVita biscuits are a need, not a want?

The website for belVita tells us that the company is 'passionate about breakfast biscuits'. What? Passionate? It also shows that these biscuits typically contain 400 calories per 100 grams – more calories per gram than Coco Pops! That seems a lot given that belVita promotes itself in ways that imply a healthy start to the day. Owner Mondelez has managed to do a clever job in making customers want belVita. In 2016, UK customers spent £77.3 million on belVita biscuits.

5 Explain why it is important for consumers to think carefully about whether they really need what they want.

Practice questions

In 2014, at the age of 18, Jordan Daykin became the youngest person to get investment in the TV series *Dragons' Den*. Deborah Meaden invested £80,000 in return for a 25 per cent stake. Today the business has been valued at over £13 million. Deborah has done well.

Daykin's pitch was based on a classic consumer need. More and more interior walls are built of plasterboard, but there was no safe way to hang items such as TVs or kitchen cupboards on it. Jordan (and his grandfather) came up with a design that worked. A GripIt fastener can hold a quarter of a ton in weight. Other dragons were worried that the market for wall fastenings would be too small. Happily, the need is the same in America, and Daykin has succeeded in getting distribution in the 2,000-branch US DIY chain Home Depot. The even bigger Wal-Mart seems keen to follow.

What Meaden loved about GripIt is that it is 'a classic invention – one that solves a problem in a practical and affordable way'. And she's happy to see that Daykin has six more product ideas being launched in the next 18 months. A gripping story.

Total: 13 marks

1 Calculate the value of Deborah Meaden's stake 'today'. Then calculate her percentage profit on the investment. (2)

2 Apart from meeting a consumer need, outline one other possible factor that may have persuaded Deborah Meaden to invest in GripIt. (2)

3 If an investor offered to buy GripIt for £15 million, Daykin would have to choose between:
- Option 1: Sell the business and use the capital to start all over again.
- Option 2: Turn the £15 million down and be even more determined to make GripIt a success.

Justify which **one** of these options he should choose. (9)

Deborah Meaden received a big return on her investment

24

6 Adding value

Many shops sell Walkers crisps at 50p per pack. The pack weighs 35 g, which is about 2p of potatoes. Oil, salt and flavouring are also used, but even adding in the cost of the packaging, the total cost per unit is no more than 4p. So, turning potatoes into crisps adds value. It 'creates' value by making the customer willing to pay extra. In the case of crisps, turning 4p into 50p adds 1,150 per cent to the value of the potato (46 / 4 × 100). That's good business.

A sandwich is more than its ingredients – it has added value

Is adding value a rip-off? Not necessarily. A sandwich sold for £2 may contain ingredients costing 40p. So the baker is receiving £1.60 for two slices of bread. Assuming there are 20 slices in a £1 loaf, that's selling a loaf of bread for £16 instead of £1. When people are going out, however, they do not want to take butter, cheese, tomato and a knife with them. They would rather buy a sandwich. They are happy to pay for speed and convenience.

> The real issue is value, not price.
> *Robert Lindgren, Harvard Business Review*

How to add value

Added value is the difference between the cost of materials and the selling price. Value can be added either by pushing the price up or by cutting the costs. Usually it is by adding in a feature that makes the item more valuable to the customer, which enables the price to be increased.

Different ways to make an item more valuable to the customer are:

◆ Convenience and speed: in Britain, most people will pay extra to save their own time, as shown in the table below.

Table 6.1 Adding value by adding convenience

Chicken curry and rice	Price per person
Cook your own	£2.00
Add Sharwood's bottled sauce to chicken	£2.50
Buy supermarket ready meal	£2.75
Buy a takeaway	£4.75
Go to a restaurant	£7.75

◆ Good design: a beautifully designed dress might sell for £200, while one using exactly the same quantity of material might sell for just £20.
◆ High-quality manufacture or service: a Lexus costs £50,000 because it is regarded as one of the best-made cars in the world; it never breaks down and is like sitting in a huge leather armchair.

Innocent is a well-known maker of fresh smoothies

◆ **Brand name:** a Nike swoosh adds tens of pounds to the 'value' of a pair of trainers; a Mercedes badge on the front of a car adds thousands of pounds to the value of a new car. The 1999 start-up Innocent Drinks quickly established its brand name as an indication of quality, freshness and originality.

> A brand is no longer what we tell the consumer it is – it's what the consumers tell each other it is.
>
> *Scott Cook, founder of Intuit*

◆ **Unique selling point (USP):** an original feature that competitors aren't offering; something that makes the product worth paying extra for (for example, a family car with flat-screen TVs and headphones on the back of the front passenger seats).

> In order to be irreplaceable one must always be different.
>
> *Coco Chanel, fashion designer*

Talking point

How could you add value to a white T-shirt?

● The importance of value added

People starting businesses often forget about the everyday costs. There are obvious ones, such as

electricity and phones, but also others, such as the cost of 'wastage' (theft plus damaged goods) or the cost of recruiting and training new staff. All of these costs have to be paid for out of the **value added**. So there needs to be a big enough difference between price and bought-in costs to allow internal costs to be paid for. The fashion clothing company Ted Baker adds £285 million of value to its £185 million of bought-in costs (such as clothes made by outside suppliers). The bar on the right of Figure 6.1 shows how the value added pays for all the company's costs, including the tax on profits.

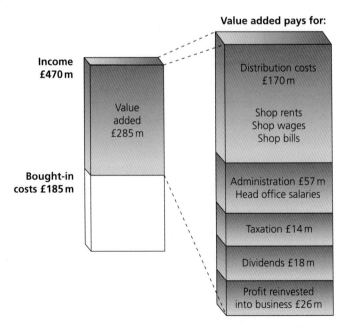

Figure 6.1 What the value added pays for at Ted Baker

As the diagram shows, value added is a necessity in business, not a luxury. Value added pays the wages, pays the bills and generates the profit needed to finance future growth. When starting up, every firm needs to think hard about whether the business idea adds enough value to be profitable.

These are some business ideas that may have a market but do not have enough value added to be worthwhile, for example:

◆ hand-washing cars
◆ babysitting
◆ delivering milk to people's homes.

Delivering milk doesn't have enough value added to create a good enough business

Good businesspeople recognise that high value added comes from clever ideas, presented well and delivered efficiently. That, in turn, makes it possible to run a sustainable, profitable business.

● Drawing the right conclusions

Value added is at the heart of all business activity. Therefore, it can be used to develop answers to lots of different business questions. It will come up regularly as a 9- or 12-mark question in itself, and will be useful when tackling many other exam questions. The key is to remember that value added can be created by psychological factors, such as brand image ('I must have Apple/Nike/Versace'), or by practical factors, such as quality of design or quality of manufacture.

> ### Revision essentials
>
> **Branding**: giving a product or service 'personality', with a name and logo that makes it stand out.
>
> **Unique selling point (USP)**: an original feature of a product that rivals aren't offering.
>
> **Value added**: the difference between the selling price and the cost of bought-in goods and services (the difference that creates the possibility of profit).

End of chapter exercises

1 Why does a company's added value matter to its employees?

2 Briefly explain the sources of the added value in these cases:

   (a) a £5 box of Celebrations chocolates

   (b) a £54 ticket to see Chelsea play Manchester City

   (c) a £3 cup of coffee at Starbucks.

3 Identify the USP that each of these firms is keen to establish:

   (a) Ryanair

   (b) L'Oréal.

4 What might be the consequences of Ted Baker deciding to increase value added by cutting its £185 million spending on the clothes it buys in from suppliers?

The Oban Chocolate Company began in November 2003, backed by £9,500 of funding from a local Scottish Islands enterprise agency. At their shop, cafe and factory premises in Oban, Helen Miller and Stewart MacKechnie make handmade chocolates in the basement for sale upstairs. Good quality chocolate is not cheap, but by making fancy, unusual products such as 'hot chilli truffles',

➡

value is added. Visitors also get a whole experience, including a visit downstairs to see the chocolates being made. In 2015, the cafe was named Best Coffee Shop in North West Scotland. Today the business employs five full-time staff. In the past its problem was that relying on tourists meant little trade during six to eight months of the year. Today, online sales keep things going in the colder months – especially at Christmas, Valentine's Day and Easter.

5 Read the extract on the previous page. Outline two factors that create added value at the Oban Chocolate Company.

6 High value added is great for a business, but only if sales volumes are also high.

(a) Why may the Oban Chocolate Company have a problem?

(b) What might they try to do to increase their sales volumes?

Practice questions

Callum and Jamie were bored with work. Both 21 years old, they had trained as plumbers but working for British Gas was getting dull. Jamie heard that there was a snack wagon for sale – fully equipped with gas, electricity and a fridge – and within three days they had found £3,000 each to buy the van. Their plan was to place the van permanently on a busy road between Wimbledon and Croydon, then employ someone to do the cooking. Callum and Jamie's role would be to keep the van supplied and to make key decisions, such as pricing.

The pricing decisions were largely drawn from their experience of local snack bars: teas and Cokes at around £1, big burgers at about £3 and the occasional item rising above £4. They were able to set down a few details, as shown in the table below.

In addition to these costs, there would be fixed overhead costs such as rent, energy and labour costs. They allowed £500 per week for these.

They served their first burgers in April and by October were making a modest profit. That same month they sold the business for £10,000. They had decided to move to Spain to make a living from plumbing, and later start up their own plumbing business.

Total: 25 marks

1 (a) Calculate how much value is added by making a cup of tea at this snack wagon. (2)

  (b) Outline why it would be wrong to call this value added figure 'profit'. (2)

2 Outline one way in which Callum and Jamie might have added more value to their snack bar. (2)

3 Identify the cost of ingredients for making a burger at Callum and Jamie's snack bar. (1)

4 Analyse how a good location can add value to a business such as Callum and Jamie's. (6)

5 Evaluate whether Callum and Jamie are likely to be able to create more value added with their second business. You should use the information given above as well as your knowledge of business. (12)

Table 6.2 Components and costs

Item	Components	Bought-in costs per unit	Selling price
Cup of tea	Tea bag, milk, sugar, plastic cup, spoon	12p	£1.00
Burger	Frozen hamburger, onions, bun, ketchup, paper napkins	40p	£3.00
Chips	Frozen chips, oil, paper cone, salt, vinegar, ketchup	30p	£1.50

Topic 1.1 Enterprise and entrepreneurship

7 The role of entrepreneurship

An entrepreneur is a **risk taker** who wants to create an organisation that can make a difference. That difference may be for a social reason, such as the bottled water brand One, founded by Duncan Goose to generate profits for a social purpose: funding water charities in Africa. Or it may be because the entrepreneur wants to become very, very rich.

Many people talk about making a difference. The entrepreneur acts on the brilliant Nike slogan 'Just do it'. The phrase sums up the key enterprise skill, which is to make things happen.

A family may be rescued from a mountainside, having gone climbing without proper equipment or training; in this case, 'let's just do it' is reckless

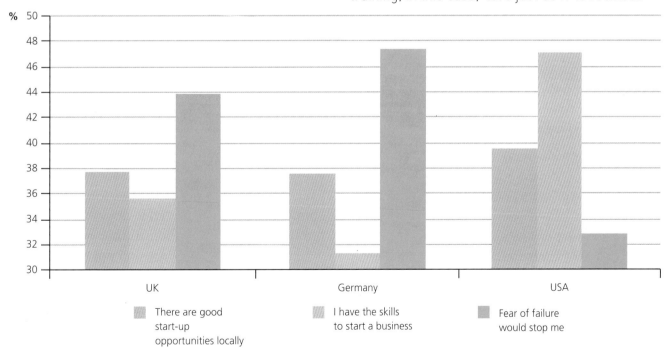

Figure 7.1 Attitudes to entrepreneurship (Source: Global Enterprise Monitor, 2015)

Being enterprising means spotting an opportunity and then having a go. Of course, this could be disastrous. A family may be rescued from a mountainside, having gone climbing without proper equipment or training. In this case 'let's just do it' is reckless. Similarly, businesses are set up by people who have no expertise, no skills and not enough capital. Yet a few examples of stupidity should not put people off. Bold ideas lead to exciting lives and potentially huge rewards – emotionally and financially.

An entrepreneur:
◆ takes risks
◆ makes **business decisions**
◆ organises **resources**.

As shown in Figure 7.1 (page 29), the attitudes and confidence of potential entrepreneurs varies considerably from country to country. The UK is among the most entrepreneurial in Europe, but nowhere close to the USA.

Taking risks

As set out in Chapter 4, risk is about chance. Wealthy dragons in the TV show *Dragons' Den* can use this knowledge in comfort, knowing that if they put £100,000 into ten different businesses, six may fail, three do reasonably well, and one make millions. But each of the ten entrepreneurs involved has only one of those ten chances. Six may use up their family's entire savings on a business venture that fails. Horrible. Three end up wondering whether all the hard work was really worthwhile. And just one ends up on a Caribbean island.

And there are many more risks involved than the start-up one of 'should I do it or not?' Every day the entrepreneur has to make decisions in a state of uncertainty. The reason is simple: when you're starting your first business, you haven't faced these questions before. And sometimes you'll do the wrong thing. And while some individuals would struggle with that failure, a true entrepreneur shrugs their shoulders and gets on with the next decision. Success comes from facing up to decisions and getting the big ones right, most of the time.

Dillons was taken over by Waterstones

> Do you want to be safe and good, or do you want to take a chance and be great?
> *Jimmy Johnson, Dallas Cowboys coach*

Making business decisions

Decision making is crucial, not only in response to opportunities but also in response to difficulties. A hairdresser with three outlets may have one that is losing money. Decisions are required. Perhaps the outlet should close, or perhaps it needs a revamp. When the bankrupt bookstore chain Dillons was taken over by Waterstones, over half the shops were found to have been losing money for years. But no one did anything about it!

To make decisions successfully, the key is to find out as much information as possible, from as many sources as possible. Most important are your staff and your customers. Ask for views and opinions, then decide, and carry the decision through without hesitation. In big organisations decisions are often put back and put back; in new small businesses, there's no time to lose. Even if the decision proves wrong, there's a lot to be said for knowing quickly, so that the decision can be reversed before competitors have had time to respond.

> A ship is always safe at the shore, but that's not what it was built for.
>
> *Albert Einstein*

Talking point

The number of business start-ups in the UK has grown significantly in recent years. Why might that be?

Showing leadership

Leadership has a lot to do with qualities such as decisiveness, initiative and the ability to think ahead. Another important element is the personality and the character to make people believe in you. This might be helped by self-confidence, but some excellent leaders are actually quite shy. Some are great at one-to-one chats, but less comfortable when speaking in public or when chatting in a group of people. Although Richard Branson comes across very well on TV, he is said to be very shy and often tongue-tied.

Good leadership needs to be based on good judgement about the right decision or initiative, plus the determination to see things through. It also requires an ability to make people want to share the leader's path (that is, to help achieve their aims). This requires either charisma or the ability to make people respect and believe in them.

Organising resources

At the start, entrepreneurs are usually on their own. They have to do everything, from making decisions to making the tea. Yet to put a start-up together requires a huge range of skills, contacts and know-how. Even opening a small cafe means organising resources across a wide spectrum of business life:

◆ physical resources, such as choosing the right premises; briefing the builders; designing the kitchen and the interior, and getting it built and decorated; choosing, buying and installing equipment from cookers and tills to chairs and tables

◆ buying daily resources such as crockery, cutlery, containers, ingredients, drinks, till rolls and toilet rolls

◆ hiring the right **human resources**, especially a reliable, competent cook who can help compile a menu and work out prices, plus other waiting and cooking staff.

Table 7.1 Seven main causes of start-up failure

Reason	Brief explanation
Starting the business for the wrong reason	Those starting up to 'make money' or to 'have more time with family' are the most likely to give up. Those with a passion for their business are most likely to succeed.
Poor management	Weak management of resources – physical and human – is a major reason for failure. Simple things like security and fraud must be handled with care.
Insufficient capital	Both the costs of starting up *and* the costs of staying in business must be factored in. Profits rarely come quickly.
Poor location	Critical for a service business such as a restaurant. It is best to go to where the customers are than to expect them to come to you.
Lack of planning	This goes hand in hand with poor management, but focuses more on whether enough time, thought and research was put into the business in the first place.
Overexpansion	A boom in sales is both a thrill and a danger for an entrepreneur. Problems of managing resources escalate when business is booming.
No (or poor quality) website	A good website helps customers to find you, or re-find you. It gives an image of professionalism and allows convenient communication or purchasing. Bad ones don't!

Eventually, managing these resources will become second nature, and perhaps dull. Stelios Haji-Ioannou founded budget airline easyJet in 1995, but stopped running it after five years because it was getting too routine. He hired a top class manager to take over as chief executive instead. Before they become bored though, entrepreneurs have to be masters of a wide range of skills, becoming as good at hiring (and firing) as they are at pricing and planning. Organising human and physical resources is a critical skill. The table below shows why.

● Drawing the right conclusions

The role of the entrepreneur is a remarkable one, requiring business skills and personal qualities that will all be tested fully. The cleverest entrepreneurs are those who learn quickly about their own weaknesses and find someone who can take on that area of responsibility. Julian Dunkerton, founder of Superdry, and Stelios Haji-Ioannou, founder of easyJet, both decided that they needed a new person to take on the day-to-day management of their businesses. More commonly the entrepreneur will take on someone to take care of the financial or the creative side of the business, but remain at the helm.

Revision essentials

Business decisions: choices that have to be made, usually within a short time period.

Human resources: a term used by organisations that simply means employees.

Resources: things or people that can be used to help build and run the business.

Risk taking: making decisions where unknown factors or chances of failure loom large in the decision-maker's mind.

Stelios Haji-Ioannou, the owner of Easyjet, hired a manager to run it

End of chapter exercises

1 What might be attractive to entrepreneurs about taking risks?

2 Look again at Figure 7.1 on page 30 then answer these questions:

   (a) Calculate how much more confident Americans are than those in the UK that they have the skills for start-up success.

   (b) People in which country most fear start-up failure?

3 Why might an entrepreneur find it hard to manage the human resources needed for business success?

4 Read the following extract. Outline one decision made by Paul Harwood that you think should help the business succeed.

After 14 years working for TV chef Rick Stein, Paul Harwood started up The Fish House restaurant in Newquay, Cornwall. He had to organise the finances, the building work and all the resources in order to get the business underway, and then start cooking – he is a chef–proprietor. Prices have been kept low to build up a base of customers rather than relying on August holidaymakers. The location of the restaurant is right on Fistral Beach, boasting beautiful views. The location has a spin-off benefit for Paul too, as he is as passionate about surfing as he is about cooking.

5 Outline two factors that may generate value added for The Fish House.

6 Why may Paul Harwood find the life of a chef–proprietor a bit of a shock?

Practice questions

For most businesses, the early weeks after opening are the most painful financially. Months of big spending to get the business started are followed by loss-making weeks as customers wait to hear from others whether the new place is any good. Not at Waffle Jack's. From 7 a.m. on day one customers kept coming. A crazy morning rush from boys going to the nearby secondary school was followed by locals interested to try this new American-style diner. The menu was certainly accessible – waffles, burgers and shakes – and had a huge array of options (such as six types of burger bun).

For entrepreneurs Adele and Stephan Theron the success was both wonderful and shattering. Waffle Jack's opening hours of 7 a.m. to 11 p.m. seven days a week would be bad enough, but they also owned a cafe about ten minutes' drive away. The pressure was immediate – but luckily both knew enough about start-ups to understand the pressures.

Within a week of starting up, Stephan was already clear about his main problem – staffing. Two staff quit by the end of the week – they found the never-ending queues too stressful. Since then, Waffle Jack's has continued to have

plenty of customers, but staff coming and going is a real strain. Few local British workers have lasted more than a week or so, leaving other EU nationals to keep things going. Stephan is not looking forward to the border controls that may exist once final Brexit arrangements have been made.

Total: 13 marks

1 Outline one possible reason why managing human resources may be the hardest problem for entrepreneurs.   (2)

2 Outline one important decision that Adele and Stephan need to make.   (2)

3 Stephan is thinking ahead to how best to maintain the growth of Waffle Jack's. He sees two options:

◆ Option 1: Build a barbecue cooking and eating area at the back of the premises to generate higher evening revenues.

◆ Option 2: Open waffle-only Waffle Jack's kiosks in busy city sites, such as London's West End.

Justify which **one** of these options they should choose.   (9)

Exam-style questions on Topic 1.1

Don't rush; check your answers carefully.

1 Which **one** of the following explains the term 'venture capital'? (1)

(a) The centre of global enterprise: Silicon Valley, California.

(b) Providing risk capital to a young business.

(c) When a business puts its own capital at risk, for example when buying new machinery.

(d) Obtaining capital for an extreme sports company.

2 You've always wanted to open a cafe and you are sure you have identified a gap in the market. A terrific site has become available near the railway station, and you can (just) afford the £15,000 cost of the lease. Which **two** of the following are good reasons to hold back? (2)

(a) You're not 100 per cent sure that the business will be a success.

(b) You haven't got the capital to cover the cash outflows beyond the cost of the lease.

(c) You've checked on the costs and found that a £2 cup of coffee has a variable cost of 15p.

(d) You cannot see how the personal and financial rewards can ever be that great in this case.

(e) You're not sure you have all the skills needed to run a business perfectly.

3 Which **two** of the following are important in creating a successful manufacturing business. (2)

(a) Using market mapping to find out your customers' likes and dislikes.

(b) Using franchising as a way of stopping others copying your ideas.

(c) Adding value by keeping your costs as low as possible.

(d) Analysing the key features of what your competitors offer.

(e) Making sure you keep your added value low enough to make a good profit.

4 This year looks a tough one to start a house-building firm, but that's exactly what Tamara and Callum plan to do. They have £40,000 in cash savings and can get a mortgage of £180,000 on their three-bedroom house. They think they will need £210,000 to build their first house, which they have the skills to do themselves. They plan to sell it for £250,000.

Which **two** of the following qualities will be the most important for them in the coming year? (2)

(a) Showing leadership.

(b) The ability to persuade.

(c) Willingness to take risks and make decisions.

(d) The ability to analyse competitor strengths and weaknesses.

(e) Determination.

5 Which **one** of the following is a reason why a change in technology might lead to new business ideas. (1)

(a) Because the change cuts the cost of producing existing product lines.

(b) Because the change enables more units to be produced within the working day.

(c) Because the change requires new techniques to be learnt by staff.

(d) Because the change allows production of things that were impossible before.

6 Which of the following businesses produces goods and which produces services? (6)

	Goods	Services
(a) Mars, producers of Galaxy chocolate		
(b) The publishers of *The Sun* newspaper		
(c) John Lewis Partnership, owners of Waitrose		
(d) Aston Villa Football Club		
(e) Coca-Cola Inc. owners of Innocent Drinks		
(f) British Airways		

7 Last week Aliyyah opened her Males' Nails business. The opening party was fantastic and led to full bookings in week one. Now business has slowed right down and Aliyyah is wondering what to do. She has just £10,000 of capital left of the £80,000 she started with. Which **two** of the following actions do you advise her to take? (2)

(a) Hold another party, at a cost of £8,000, leaving her £2,000 for running the business.

(b) Phone last week's customers to check their satisfaction and whether they'll return in future.

(c) Use the £10,000 to run an advertising campaign in the local papers.

(d) Put her prices up, to help cover her costs.

(e) Think of ways to encourage customers to tell their friends about Males' Nails.

Now try this discussion question.

8 Discuss why entrepreneurs are willing to risk starting their own business, even though half of new businesses fail within 5 years. (6)

8 Customer needs

For a business to be successful, it must understand what customers need. There are six main areas to consider.

1 Price: For most people, most of the time, price is a critical factor in purchasing. A family holiday can cost between £1,000 and £5,000, depending on location and accommodation choice (camping versus three-star hotel versus five-star hotel). There are plenty of families who need the price to be towards the lower end, so a company focusing on low-cost holidays may be fulfilling an important customer need. The UK's supermarkets have realised that customers need a range of prices and options across all product lines. During the week we may buy 'value' pasta and sauce; at the weekends we may buy top-of-the-range meals costing five times more. What shoppers need is choice.

Aldi's share of the UK grocery market has grown in recent years

2 **Quality:** When Aldi and Lidl started growing in the UK, their rivals thought that customers were shopping for cheap items. In 2015 and 2016, however, the biggest prize-winners at *The Grocer* magazine's Own Label Quality awards were Aldi and Lidl. Expensive Waitrose and Marks and Spencer came

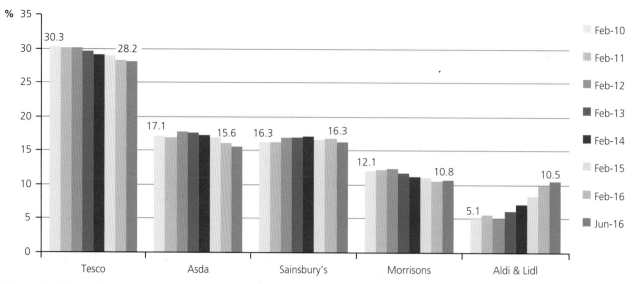

Figure 8.1 UK grocery market share, 2010–16 (Source: Kantar Worldpanel, 12 weeks to date stated)

nowhere. Only after seeing this did Tesco and the others accept that the German discounters were as much about quality as price. Figure 8.1 on the previous page shows how well Aldi and Lidl have done – and at whose expense.

Lidl has enjoyed an increase in popularity in recent years

3 **Choice**: Consumers love choice, even though it can sometimes be hard to make decisions in the face of 'too much' choice. Not only does choice mean that we may be able to find exactly what we want, choice also implies plenty of suppliers, meaning high competition and, hopefully, low prices. The problem for the producer is that choice can be punishing. For Cuckoo Foods, with sales of £400,000 a year, producing five flavours of muesli means inefficiencies of purchasing, production and stock levels. But the customer comes first.

> You expect to be waited on hand and foot, well I'm trying to run a hotel here.
>
> *Basil Fawlty, fictional hotelier in sitcom*
> *Fawlty Towers*

4 **Convenience**: Trade magazine *The Grocer* reports on customer service at the UK's supermarkets. Each week a secret visit is made to all the main stores in a different town, and a winner is announced: the shop of the week. Judging is

Good customer service is one of the keys to success

based on how well each store meets customer convenience. The main factors are:
◆ a full range of stock
◆ short queues at the checkout
◆ a clearly laid-out store.

Different factors will be the key to success in meeting customer needs in other businesses. The table below sets out some of the possibilities.

5 Being efficient and reliable: Customers want their needs met consistently. The trains on the London–Manchester route are smart, new and fast. This meets many customer needs. They also have a highly varied pricing policy, which lets students travel for £30 return while businesspeople may pay up to £320 to be on the same train. No one will be happy, though, if the service is unreliable. Success relies on careful planning and an eye for detail. In the case of a railway or an airline, engineers should make regular checks to prevent things going wrong, rather than waiting to fix things that have broken down.

6 Providing great design: Many customers value design and style above price. They want clothes that make them look great, cosmetics that make them look older – or younger – and cars that make them look successful, or exciting, or smooth. As discussed

Table 8.1 Meeting customer needs

Business situation	Keys to meeting customer needs
Cafe in university student area	Cheap, with generous portions; open until late; internet access; some reference to organic or fair trade items
Dentist	Minimum wait; minimum pain; minimum sense of guilt (at too many sweets or too little flossing)
Buying a new Volvo car	Friendly, efficient service; reliable car that's easy or fun to drive; terrific sound system; petrol usage less punishing than expected
Manufacturing scarves	Great designs to meet different people's needs; different price levels: £6.99 scarves for teenagers, £19.99 scarves for middle-aged customers; making sure stock is available, especially in the autumn
Professional football club	Three points this Saturday, no matter how poor the game, the pies and the programme

below, it boils down to getting close to the customer. Some people will only buy the best; others want £2.99 T-shirts for some days but £24.99 tops for Friday and Saturday nights. Well-run businesses learn what customers want, then recruit people with the right skills to be able to supply them.

> To all our nit-picky, over-demanding, ask-awkward-questions customers: Thank you, and keep up the good work.
>
> *Dell Computers advertisement*

Many customers value design and style above price

● Importance of identifying and understanding customers

Between Thursday 7 July and Friday 15 July 2016, the share price of Nintendo rose by 85 per cent, adding $15 billion to the Japanese company's stock market value. The reason was the amazingly successful launch of Pokémon Go, which instantly became the biggest-ever mobile game download. Nintendo had been remarkably slow to realise the mobile potential of its backlog of classic games

The success of Pokémon Go increased the share price of Nintendo

console characters. But, to the company's credit, it still understood actual and potential customers. Within days analysts were able to forecast that Pokémon Go would make more than $4 billion a year in revenue.

If a business understands who its customers are (age, income and attitudes) and how they behave, it is in a good position to understand them well enough to keep them coming back. Occasional customers become regular, loyal ones, and others start to hear good things and try the product or service for the first time. Sales rise and, so long as costs can be kept from rising too much, profits can be boosted.

In a competitive market, the success of one company can spell trouble for another. Ultimately, all managers want success, whether in the Premier League or in the business world. Understanding customer needs is the starting point – to be followed by adjusting the business to meet those needs better. Many a corner shop is cramped, untidy and unwelcoming; the owner may moan about Tesco and Sainsbury's nearby but they seem unable to make the adjustments necessary to stay in business.

Talking point

'Why do shops die?' (James Marcousé, aged three years, two months)

Revision essentials

Choice: giving customers options and increasing the chance that the product will be perfect for the tastes/habits of one type of customer.

Convenience: making life easier for customers, perhaps by a great location (next to the bus stop) or a product that saves time in preparation or consumption.

Identifying customers: finding out who they are: their age, gender, incomes, where they live and what they want.

Quality: to a customer quality means getting what they want, or perhaps better than expected; some companies use the term 'customer delight'.

Understanding customers: learning why customers do what they do, making it easier to see how to make a product that better suits them.

End of chapter exercises

1 (a) From the data in Figure 8.1 on page 36, calculate which of the supermarkets lost the most market share points between 2010 and 2016.

   (b) Identify one other supermarket chain that performed particularly poorly. Explain why you chose that one.

2 Look at Table 8.1 on page 38 then suggest the keys to meeting customers' needs for a supplier of:

   (a) baby car seats   (b) lipstick.

3 Name two types of customer who might not 'value design and style above price'.

4 Explain the message being communicated by the quote from the Dell Computers advertisement on page 38.

Practice questions

We are based in Bude, North Cornwall, and have been teaching people to surf for over ten years. In that time we have safely and successfully introduced almost 30,000 men, women and children to our wonderful sport. Many return to us year after year.

So, you're thinking of learning to surf? Great! Whether you are looking for a great family day out in the South West or for surfing lessons for your kids, for your school, just for women and girls, or as a group or corporate event, then you've come to the right place. As long as you are over eight years old, are reasonably fit and can swim 50 metres, we can teach you to surf.

We are one of just a few surf schools with top British Surfing Association qualifications and keep a higher coach-to-student ratio than most surf schools – because learning to surf safely is vital.

We have coaches who are specially trained to provide surf tuition for disabled children and children with autism.

We are open all year around, as we now have extra thick wetsuits to keep you all toasty warm in those cooler months!

Big Blue has received very favourable reviews on TripAdviser

Out of 85 TripAdvisor reviews of Big Blue, 83 said 'excellent' and two said 'very good'. One review from June 2016 read: 'I booked a large group lesson as part of my 30th birthday weekend. We were mostly absolute beginners – many of us had never surfed before. The instructors (Cyril and Beth) were really patient and knowledgeable, and by the end most of us could stand on the boards! They were especially kind to my younger cousin (who had never surfed) and by the end she was starting to surf to the shore! Really recommend this company and thanks for a great day.'

Source: www.bigbluesurfschool.co.uk

Total: 18 marks

1 (a) Outline one indication that Big Blue understands its customers. (2)

   (b) Outline one way in which the business may benefit from this understanding. (2)

2 State one reason why the TripAdvisor reviewer recommended Big Blue to others. (1)

3 (a) Calculate the percentage of customers who rated Big Blue 'excellent'. (2)

   (b) Outline one way in which Big Blue might reward Cyril and Beth for their customer recognition. (2)

4 The Big Blue Surf School is considering expanding. The managers see two options:

   ◆ Option 1: Opening a second school in the North East, close to Newcastle.

   ◆ Option 2: Offering cheaper rates to school groups, to attract extra summer business

   Justify which **one** of these options they should choose. (9)

9 Market research

● The purpose of market research

There are four main areas where market research can prove itself value for the money it costs to carry out:

1 to identify and understand customer needs
2 to identify gaps in the market
3 to reduce risk
4 to inform business decisions.

To identify and understand customer needs

The importance of understanding customer needs is covered fully in Chapter 8. While small service businesses are often in touch with customers daily, bigger firms – especially manufacturers – may never deal directly with shoppers, which makes market research essential.

To identify gaps in the market

As will be shown in Chapter 10, market research has an important part to play in 'mapping' the market. It shows which customer requirements are covered, and which are not. When gaps are uncovered it makes sense to act quickly before competitors move in. At the time of writing, gluten-free burgers are seen as a way to fill a market gap. *The Grocer* magazine estimates that the size of this market gap may amount to £40 million a year.

To reduce risk

There are two fundamental risks in launching a new product:

◆ that the market may not want the new product
◆ that demand may exist, but not enough for the new product to be worth all the costs of development and launching.

Quantitative research (see below) should be able to warn against either possibility.

To inform business decisions

In other words, to provide information to help managers make better decisions. Even in quite small businesses a wrong decision may cost a big sum of money. The clothing brand Jack Wills opened a second brand called Aubin & Wills, targeting an older market. After several years of loss making, Aubin & Wills was closed in 2013, pushing the business into a £9 million loss. Well-tailored market research may have asked the right people the right questions and saved the company a small fortune. Good decisions are well-informed decisions. Market research can play a big part in this.

> Advertising people who ignore research are as dangerous as generals who ignore decodes of enemy signals.
>
> *David Ogilvy, advertising executive and author of Ogilvy on Advertising*

⬤ Methods of market research

Secondary research

Many people starting their first business have a clear idea of the opportunity. They may be sure that 'everyone loves takeaway pizza'. This makes it important to check the facts. The starting point is **secondary research**: this means finding out data that already exists, that is, second-hand information. Figure 9.1 shows publicly available data forecasting Easter sales of a variety of goods; for example, £186 million is likely to be spent on Easter eggs. Some of this is data available free, by careful use of the internet or by visiting a public reference library.

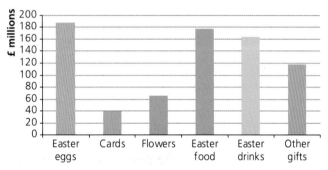

Figure 9.1 Forecast value of Easter sales in the UK (Source: Savvy Marketing, quoted in *Retail Times*, 31 March 2015)

At the time of writing, the internet could provide the following secondary information about pizza takeaway:

◆ An IBISWorld market report about the size of the pizza takeaway and delivery market in 2016 (£2 billion) was available for free, but projections of future sales growth were only available from IBISWorld at a price of £495.

◆ Newspaper reports explained that Domino's Pizza had enjoyed sales increases of 10.5 per cent in its established stores in the 13 weeks to March 2016. Although some of this was down to Domino's successful app, there was no doubt that the market was still growing.

In addition to reports from large market research companies such as Mintel and Key Note, government reports are a useful (and free) source of secondary data. For instance, if you're thinking of opening a milkshake business, it is a great help to find out that the number of 10 to 14-year-olds is forecast to rise from 3.5 million in 2015 to over 4 million by 2020.

Primary research

Having learned about the market background, it is time to consider **primary research**. This is first-hand research in which you find out the precise things you want to know from the people you need to talk to. When starting a business, the people you might want to talk to include:

◆ existing customers (currently buying from companies that will soon be your competitors)

◆ potential customers (those you might be able to persuade to buy for the first time)

◆ potential retailers (the shops that you hope will stock and sell your product).

The value of primary research is that it can tell you exactly what you need to know about your business. The problem, though, is that it is time-consuming and expensive to collect the data. For example, to find out whether your pizza should be priced at £10.99 or £14.99 might require interviewing more than 100 people. That takes time.

In primary market research, customers are asked directly for their opinions

Table 9.1 The main methods of primary market research

	Explanation	Advantage	Disadvantage
Online survey	Online surveys are a cheap, useful way to get a limited amount of feedback	Can be used regularly, e.g. monthly, to check on customer satisfaction	Online surveys will overwhelmingly be answered by those with time on their hands – probably older people
Questionnaire	A business could carry out a questionnaire to assess potential demand for a product/service	A firm can identify its target customers (age, job, etc.) – this can help with promotion and also establish the likely selling price and sales level	Can be very time consuming – taking time to carry out questionnaires is expensive and may not be helpful. Questions can be biased, giving misleading results
Focus group	This allows for more in-depth answers than a questionnaire, as well as more open questions	Interviews give firms an insight into customer perceptions and behaviour; this can help a firm decide on branding and advertising images	Time consuming and expensive. The interviewer can sometimes affect the results, e.g. some interviewees may be too embarrassed to admit how much they really spend on chocolate
Observation	Watching where customers go and how long they spend in different parts of a shop	Can show where people are interested but still don't buy – is the layout too confusing?	Time consuming and expensive

Qualitative and quantitative research

Primary research can be collected in two forms: qualitative and quantitative.

Qualitative research is in-depth research into people's opinions and views, and is usually carried out among a relatively small group of people. It can provide insights that help a business to make decisions. For example, a group of eight people might be asked to discuss their pizza takeaway likes and dislikes. It might become clear that the most common complaint is not knowing exactly when it will arrive – in which case this can become a major part of a new firm's advertising message: 'We'll deliver on time, every time'.

Quantitative research means collecting lots of answers to specific questions. Usually these questions are 'closed', meaning that the answers are limited to ticking a box such as 'yes' or 'no', or 'will definitely buy' or 'will probably buy', and so on. This type of research provides factual information, such as that 20 per cent of people like pineapple on pizza, but 80 per cent do not. Quantitative research is usually gathered by interviewers using questionnaires, either in person or over the phone. Questionnaires can also be completed without an interviewer, for example online or by post.

Social media feedback has become an important alternative to formal market research. Some quantitative evidence is available, for example that 48.9 per cent of 7,000 Center Parcs visitors to the Sherwood Forest site rated the experience as excellent, while only 38.7 per cent of 4,000 visitors to the Woburn Forest site rated it excellent. And, of course, individual comments on social media can be as useful as any qualitative research study.

> The trouble with research is that it tells you what people were thinking about yesterday, not tomorrow. It's like driving using a rear-view mirror.
>
> *Bernard Loomis, US toy developer*

The use of data in market research

Research takes time and money to collect. The key to success, though, is to interpret its findings. With quantitative (yes/no) research, it should be easy. There may be problems, in being sure that the figures mean what they say, however. For instance, 100 people may say they prefer a thin base to their pizza, but can you be sure that the same is true of *all* pizza lovers? You can only be sure of the findings if you are confident that the people who responded are typical of everyone. If a young Bolton businesswoman asked 100 friends to fill in a questionnaire, the results might only be meaningful for young people in Bolton, not the whole market. Needless to say, market research data has to be reliable to be worthwhile.

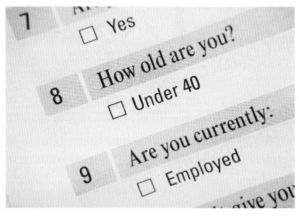

Questionnaires are a useful way to collect information

Qualitative research is even harder to interpret. If three or four people in a group discussion feel strongly about something, so what? For example, a few people may say that they hate herbs on pizza. Should that be taken seriously?

Therefore, market research findings are important and interesting, but need not always be taken seriously. A confident businessperson may be right to ignore some research findings, perhaps choosing to build a business that's a bit different and may not appeal to everyone's tastes.

Talking point

Pizza Hut has gone from being the leading pizza takeaway business to trailing after Domino's. How might Pizza Hut use market research to reboot itself?

Revision essentials

Focus group: a group discussion among people selected from the target market; it draws on psychology to provide qualitative insights into consumer attitudes.

Primary research: research conducted first-hand; it is tailored to a company's specific needs, for example a quantitative sales estimate for a brand new chocolate bar.

Qualitative data: in-depth research into the opinions and views of a small group of potential or actual customers; it can provide insight into why consumers buy what they buy.

Quantitative data: factual research among a large enough sample of people to provide statistically reliable results, for example a survey of 500 people aged 15–24 years.

Secondary research: when a company uses research that has already been carried out for general purposes.

End of chapter exercises

1 How could secondary data about the pizza market be worth £495 of an entrepreneur's money?

2 Outline one aspect of business start-up that Jack Wills might have found out via qualitative research before wasting so much money starting Aubin & Wills.

3 Explain why market research through social media may prove relatively unreliable.

4 Read the following extract. Outline two ways in which Pretty Polly's managers should have been able to keep up with changes in consumers' shopping habits.

On 25 May 2016 tights-manufacturer Pretty Polly went into administration. Of 380 staff based in Belper, Derbyshire, 350 were immediately made redundant. Managers put the blame on the recent collapse of retail chain BHS, but the brand had been struggling for many years. It was making tights in a world of leggings, and supplying BHS in the online world of ASOS and Boohoo.

5 Explain how the use of quantitative research might have helped avoid Pretty Polly's collapse.

6 Do you think it is inevitable that factory workers suffer for the mistakes made by managers?

Practice questions

In 2016, traditional clothes retailer Marks and Spencer (M&S) suffered declining sales; by contrast, online shop ASOS enjoyed yearly growth of 30 per cent. Many people believed the M&S problem was its failure to attract shoppers under the age of 40.

The company announced proudly that it would use its next shareholders' meeting to research the styling and colours for its cardigans; a business newspaper pointed out that this would mean a focus group among its 70-year-old shareholders. Meanwhile, ASOS was using social media both for research and publicity. It organised groups of ASOS customers of different ages to give instant feedback on new clothes designs and encouraged shoppers to upload photos of themselves wearing new items – #AsSeenOnMe – and then monitored comments on the styles and colours.

The value of ASOS' modern approach to market research showed in its share price. In July 2016 its shares were up 15 per cent on 2015; M&S shares were down by 40 per cent.

Total: 18 marks

1 Define 'focus group'. (1)

2 Outline one possible impact on M&S of its focus groups with shareholders. (2)

3 Analyse the impact on ASOS of its approach to market research using social media. (6)

4 M&S must find out how to appeal to clothes-buyers under the age of 40. Financial restrictions mean it must choose between:

   ◆ Option 1: Qualitative research.
   ◆ Option 2: Quantitative research.

Justify which **one** of these options the company should choose. (9)

10 Market segmentation

Market segmentation means dividing customers within a market into smaller groups with common needs or wants, then finding a product or service that fulfils those needs or wants. The boom in Greek yoghurt came when research among 16- to 35-year-old women showed that they wanted an indulgent dessert – but with low fat. Out went Rachel's Organic and in came the Greeks.

No one wants to buy 'a book'. They want a book that fits their taste, their personality and their current mindset (romantic, perhaps). Careful market segmentation allows businesses to target like-minded people. A blockbusting bestseller only has to sell to 1 million people, which is just two per cent of the population. Segmentation helps companies (and authors) to focus on just one type of customer.

There are many ways in which customers within a market can be divided up (segmented), including:

◆ **location** (where people live)
◆ income
◆ **lifestyle**
◆ age
◆ other **demographic** factors.

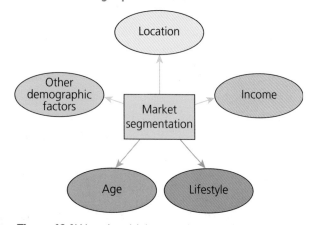

Figure 10.1 Ways in which a market may be segmented

Location

There are some clear, common factors shared by people living in certain areas within the UK; even when people move to a different region or country, they may still feel like a 'scouser' or a 'cockney', for example. This common identification with a specific area can give rise to business opportunities. The British may all like the same milk chocolate, but for some it must be Yorkshire tea, Cornish pasties and Welsh teacakes.

Regional changes in taste make it possible to find gaps in the market that cannot easily be filled by large companies. Nestlé owns Rachel's Organic and would have little interest in a yoghurt targeted just at the Scots (8 per cent of the UK population) or at the Welsh (4.8 per cent). But a small, local business could make a very good living in a market still measured in millions of people.

So, segmentation by location can make good business sense.

> Firms have moved from mass marketing to segmented marketing, in which they target carefully chosen submarkets or even individual consumers.
>
> *Philip Kotler, marketing guru*

Income

Income is one of the most obvious forms of segmentation. As shown in Table 10.1, it is very obvious in the market for hotel rooms. All of the hotel brands listed belong to the French hotel chain Accor; in essence, however much money you've got, the hotel group will be happy to take it.

Table 10.1 Same hotel group, different prices

Hotel brand	Brief description	Price per night (London, room only)
The Savoy	'Quintessentially British'	£469
Sofitel	'Life is Magnifique'	£351
Pullman	'Your business trip at Pullman'	£297.55
Novotel	'Your midscale hotel experience'	£227.50
Ibis, London City	'Comfort at the best price'	£158.30
F1, Porte de Montreuil, Paris (no F1 in London)	'The low-cost brand'	£30.75

In many other markets income is a key form of segmentation. A £300,000 Rolls-Royce and a £10,000 Kia are both in the car market, but are they in competition? Clearly not. Rolls-Royce is in a super-luxury segment defined more by price than anything else – and, therefore, by income.

> Segment or die.
>
> *Philip Kotler, marketing guru*

Lifestyle

Whether rich or poor, young or old, some people are simply different. In the grocery and catering trades, vegetarians matter. The NHS says there are 1.2 million vegetarians in the UK, though other estimates are much higher. Other lifestyle choices include our hobbies and sports. Figure 10.2 shows weekly participation in sport among adults aged over 16. Rugby players represent a small minority, but there are still opportunities for small entrepreneurs.

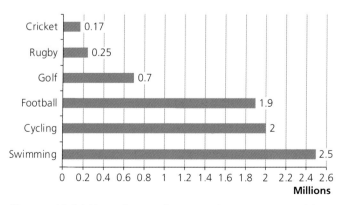

Figure 10.2 Lifestyle markets: swimmers are a big opportunity (Source: Sport England 2016)

Computer games are another lifestyle choice. It may well be that this segment – which is largely male, aged 14–18, playing PS4 and/or Microsoft One – has common characteristics of interest to businesses (perhaps a higher preference for Domino's pizza than the general population).

Age

Age is a huge factor in market segmentation. Not only are there products targeted solely at certain age groups, from soft toys to stairlifts, there are also types of product that can be tailored to a specific age group. In national newspapers, the *Daily Express* targets over-60s; in yoghurt, Munch Bunch and Petits Filous are targeted at the under-10s.

Markets can be segmented by age One of the reasons businesses like to segment markets is because they find they can charge higher prices for carefully tailored products. Homes for the elderly can command a 30 per cent price premium, which might easily mean an extra £100,000 for the developer. These purpose-built estates will have easy access to every home, nursing on site and perhaps a golf course or swimming pool on site. In America, 17 per cent of homes are designed for the elderly. In the UK, the figure is just two per cent but rising sharply.

Markets can be segmented by age

Other demographic factors

Demographics are the characteristics of a population. Age is important, but it can usefully be broken down further: young-adults-with-kids, young single adults; young adults at university, and so on. Each group will have its own patterns of spending. Further potential areas for demographic segmentation include:

- gender (an important factor in markets such as books, toiletries, clothes, magazines and much, much more)
- race (an important factor in markets such as cosmetics, music and eating out)
- religion (an important factor in markets such as food, clothes and toys).

Drawing the right conclusions

Segmentation is the essence of a modern economy. It leads to an extraordinary amount of consumer choice, in which there's usually something that suits or fits. The better a product meets our needs, the more we're willing to pay for it. This enables businesses to make the extra profit needed to pay for all that product development.

To segment means no more than to understand your customers well enough to categorise them – and then develop a products that wows them.

Revision essentials

Demographics: the study of the statistical differences that exist within a population, both now and in the future.

Lifestyle: grouping people by common characteristics in how they live, from their participation in sports and leisure to their views on the environment, taste in music and even nerdier things such as a passion for trains.

Location: the extent to which consumers identify with the place where they were born or grew up.

Market segments: the subsets within a market that have been identified as a result of market segmentation.

End of chapter exercises

1 How might a small, Yorkshire-based bakery use segmentation to help boost profits?

2 Look at Figure 10.2 on page 47. How many weekly rugby players are there for an entrepreneur to target?

3 Look at Table 10.1 on page 47, which shows the prices charged by the Accor hotel chain. Explain how it is possible for customers at Sofitel and Ibis to both consider that their room for the night was value for money.

4 Read the following extract. Outline an age group that might welcome the launch of Scheckter's Organic Energy.

With UK sales of £284 million and £137 million, respectively, energy drink sellers Red Bull and Monster both had a good 2016. However, 62 per cent of UK consumers do not drink energy drinks due to disliking the ingredients and taste. Charles Phillips, founder of Scheckter's Organic Energy, wants to open up a new segment for 'an energy drink that's delicious, free of artificial ingredients, certified organic and provides a natural energy boost'.

5 What business problem might arise if a segment such as the one targeted by Charles Phillips proves to be too small?

6 Calculate Scheckter's sales if it can achieve one per cent of the combined sales of Red Bull and Monster.

Practice questions

A July 2016 report found that the average income for those aged 60 and over is now 11 per cent above its 2007–08 level but, for 22- to 30-year-olds, it is still seven per cent below. The report explained that plenty of young adults have found work but the wage rates have been significantly lower than before. That, in turn, has forced more to stay living at home.

A different source of data showed the effect of this on home ownership among young adults.

For James Turner Ltd, a small Coventry building business focusing on bathrooms, the implications were clear: older people are the target segment, and traditional styles of bathroom are the likely way to appeal to them.

Total: 15 marks

1 (a) Calculate the percentage change in home ownership within the 16–24 age group between 1991 and 2013–14. (2)

   (b) Outline one possible reason why this change occurred. (2)

2 Outline one possible market that may benefit from rising incomes among older people. (2)

3 James Turner Ltd must decide how best to appeal to the over-65s age group. Financial restrictions mean it must choose between:

   ◆ Option 1: Television advertising.
   ◆ Option 2: Advertising in the local Coventry newspaper.

   Justify which **one** of these options the company should choose. (9)

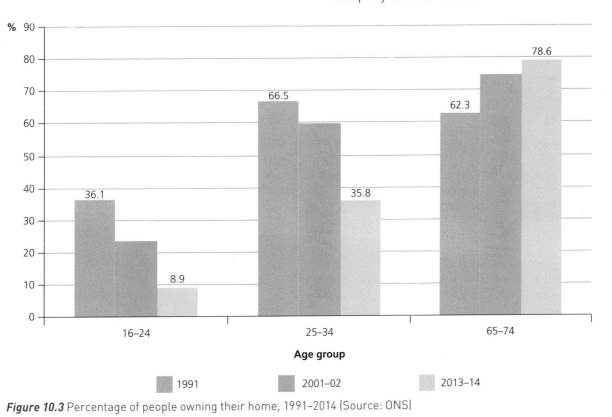

Figure 10.3 Percentage of people owning their home, 1991–2014 (Source: ONS)

11 Market mapping

Years ago, the secret to business success was price **competition**: spot a successful business, copy its idea and offer the same thing, but cheaper. Pepsi did this with Coke; Wrangler did it with Levi's; and supermarkets do it all the time with own-label versions of new products.

To a certain extent it still happens, but within a careful attempt at mapping the market. This means setting out the key features of the market on a diagram, then plotting where each brand fits in. For example, key features of the chocolate market include:

◆ luxury versus everyday eating (for example, Lindor versus Dairy Milk);
◆ filling versus light (for example, Snickers versus Maltesers).

A **market map** based on this idea would look like Figure 11.1.

research evidence to get this market map right. It would usually be based on the opinions of thousands of customers. Armed with this information a decision could be taken, such as to work on a new product that has a luxury feel *as well* as being filling. In other words, to fill the market gap in the top left of the map. In the recent past, Cadbury has tried a praline chocolate bar to fill this **gap in the market**, but no one has launched a successful new brand.

The idea of market mapping is to identify gaps, to show where a sector is overcrowded, and to stop a producer becoming over-reliant on one sector. Mars is very strong in the filling, everyday sector (Twix, Mars and Snickers), but this is a declining sector as people worry more about their health. Fortunately, Mars also owns the Maltesers brand.

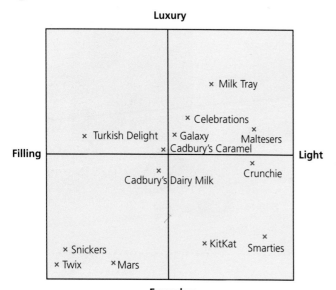

Figure 11.1 Chocolate market map (author's estimate)

A business such as Cadbury would spend a substantial sum each year (perhaps £100,000) gaining the market

The everyday sector of the chocolate market is declining as people worry more about their health

For most businesses, the difficulty is in identifying the key factors to use in the mapping exercise. These might include:

◆ high-priced/low-priced
◆ for the young/for the old
◆ modern/traditional
◆ for men/for women.

Companies decide on the 'right' factors after careful market research. Talking to customers may show that young and old have similar views about chocolate, whereas men and women think differently.

Market mapping is also very useful for a new small business, for example in building services. Internet research may show that there are lots of emergency plumbers but few offering to fit luxury bathroom suites.

Talking point

Where do these fit on the market map?

◆ Pokémon Go (in the games console market)
◆ Jaguar (in the car market

Of course, there remains a potential problem. Perhaps there is a gap because there is no effective demand locally, in which case further market research may need to be carried out. The fact that market mapping is not a magic solution should not stop it being used. All business decisions require thought; no single method provides guaranteed success.

> The aim of marketing is to know and understand the customer so well the product or service fits him and sells itself.
>
> *Peter Drucker, business guru*

● Drawing the right conclusions

In the TV series *Dragons' Den* people often talk about a 'gap in the market'. Market mapping is a perfect way to identify a gap. An entrepreneur can then investigate the product or service that will meet customer needs within that gap. This was how companies found multi-million pound opportunities with products such as gluten-free bread and dairy-free yoghurt.

Revision essentials

(The) competition: companies operating in your market or market sector.

Gap in the market: an area on a market map where few or no existing brands operate, implying a business opportunity to fill an unmet consumer need.

Market map: measuring where existing brands sit on a two-factor grid, for example young/old compared with high price/low price.

End of chapter exercises

1 Suggest two reasons why it may no longer be enough to produce cheaper copies of product ideas.

2 Suggest where Lindor might appear in Figure 11.1 on page 50, the chocolate market map. Explain your reasoning.

3 (a) Look carefully at Figure 11.1. Identify two possible opportunities for a new company entering the market.

(b) For one of those opportunities, outline a product that you think might appeal to consumers. Suggest a price that you think would be appropriate.

4 Read the following extract. Outline one way in which Aliesha might have carried out her market research.

For a recent class project, Aliesha drew up a market map of her local area (Brixton, South London). She identified that there were many takeaways and cafes offering Caribbean food, but nowhere offering a smarter restaurant for special occasions. Her market research showed that 32 per cent of adults locally thought they would go to a smart Caribbean restaurant at least once a year. Aliesha was able to show that this business could be very profitable.

5 Construct a market map for takeaways and fast-food outlets in your local area. Use the following scales:

(i) expensive–cheap

(ii) for young people–for older people.

Practice questions

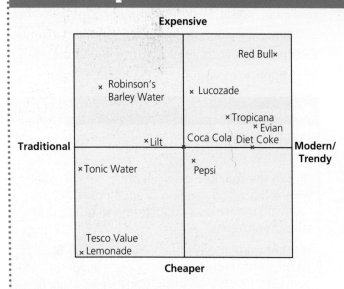

Figure 11.2 Soft drinks market map

In years gone by the soft drinks market was dominated by fizz, with Coca-Cola as the leading brand. With UK sales of over £1 billion a year, Coke is still massive, but in 2015 and 2016 sales fell. In recent years the big winners have been:

- the main water brands, such as Evian
- energy drinks, such as Red Bull and Monster
- adult-focused drinks, such as Fever-Tree and Fentimans
- drinks with a healthy 'vibe', such as Innocent Coconut Water (£2.49 for 500ml).

Oddly, though, in the UK no one has quite managed the trick pulled off by Oasis in America – a big-selling, non-fizzy drink for adults.

Total: 15 marks

1 Outline one possible reason why UK sales of Coca-Cola are declining. (2)

2 (a) Outline where you think coconut water is positioned on the soft drinks market map. (2)

(b) Outline one benefit of that positioning for a business such as Innocent Drinks. (2)

3 Innocent Drinks has ten per cent of the market for coconut water. To build on this, the managers see two options:

- Option 1: Focus on coconut water to build up market share at the expense of rivals.
- Option 2: Launch other plant-based waters, such as cactus juice and maple water.

Justify which **one** of these options the managers should choose. (9)

12 The competitive environment

When you moved into a new house in the 1980s, you did not phone everyone to tell them. You did not have a phone. You applied to British Telecom (BT) to get a line for a phone. It took between one and three months. Within five years, that position was transformed. For the first time, the government allowed competitors to enter the market for phones. BT quickly responded by speeding up their services and increasing choice. The arrival of competition improved things for the customer.

Competition is often the biggest headache for a new, small business. The business may identify a profitable market gap, but what if another firm arrives at the same time as you? Instead of being the only Thai restaurant in the village, there may be two – both half empty. Even if you get there first, your success may simply attract copycats.

This is why starting a business requires self-confidence and a willingness to take risks. Competitors may arrive, making it very difficult, but they may not. In 2006, Trunki was turned down in the *Dragons' Den* because it would be too easy to copy. By 2016, more than 3 million Trunkis had been sold at over £30 each, making £90 million in revenue. Inventor/owner Rob Law says that he has had to spend more than £1 million preventing copycat products coming on to the market. Well worth doing in exchange for £90 million of sales. In 2013, Rob Law's company was valued at £13 million.

Trunki inventor/owner Rob Law has spent more than £1m preventing copycats from coming on to the market

> Competition generates energy, rewards winners and punishes losers. It is therefore the fuel for the economy.
>
> *Charles Handy, Irish business guru*

● Strengths and weaknesses of competitors

To analyse the strengths and weaknesses of your rivals, a good starting point is to talk and, especially, listen. Get focus groups of customers talking about how, when and why they use the rival product or service. What was their experience before and after buying, and would they would buy the same thing again? If not, why not? Before Sammi Garnett started up an Italian restaurant in Northampton, she and her boyfriend simply asked around at pubs in the town for views of the existing places to eat. She learnt that nowhere offered a good deal for office parties of eight or more people, and chose to make that a feature of her restaurant. It proved very successful, providing 25 per cent of all her business.

> Competition brings out the best in products and the worst in people.
>
> *David Sarnoff, former president, RCA*

The features of your competition that you should focus on include:

1 Price: what do they charge and for what? The prices at a sandwich shop may seem quite high but, if there's free delivery to the local area, it may seem good value to busy (or lazy) office workers. In general, people starting a new business focus too much on low prices. If the new business has found a real gap in the market, it shouldn't need to risk looking 'cheap'.

2 Quality: for businesses today, quality is a must rather than a special feature. If the delivered pizza is not hot or looks tired, that's a lost customer. For a new pizza business, nothing could be more worthwhile than ordering pizzas from all the competitors. Those that are slightly second-rate can be targeted, because they are vulnerable to being put out of business.

3 Location: it is a business cliché covering hotels, restaurants and much else, that the three most important factors in success are location, location, location. A rival may have a good business with supportive regulars, yet still be pushed off course by a newcomer with a better location. Of course, the better the location, the higher the rent, so a new business must make sure to balance out the benefits from higher customer numbers against the downside of higher fixed property costs.

> **Talking point**
>
> You're thinking of opening a fashion shoe shop next to a big Asda supermarket. What analysis should you carry out on your big competitor?

4 Product range: when Trunki opened up a new market for suitcases for kids, rival firms soon responded. They copied the idea, but usually with a tweak: Trunki had a dinosaur, but did it have a mammoth? A gap in a product range provides a real chance for a rival to break through. In 2014 and 2015, Apple was losing out quite badly to the Samsung Galaxy. Oddly, the iPhone had a gap in its product range: no phone with a bigger screen. The late 2014 launch of the iPhone 6 Plus filled this gap. In 2015 and 2016, the iPhone's market share rose significantly.

5 Customer service: customers expect efficiency (right pizza, right size), speed (in 20 minutes, as promised) and politeness, even a smile. In many products and services, after-sales service is every bit as important; for example, when an Xbox One player has problems with sound, is it easy to get the problem sorted? If a rival is weak at customer service, it is an open goal for your new business to score in.

Careful analysis of the local competition is a must for a new business. If all the rivals are really strong, you may decide not to start up at all. Unless you know how you can be better, you should not risk your money. Usually, though, businesses are far from perfect. The small grocer may be cramped and unfriendly. The cinema may only have one screen and be uncomfortable. If you can build your strength on your competitor's weakness, the result should be successful.

One pizza delivery firm's 'buy one get one free' offer is quickly matched by rivals

●Impact of competition on the business

Competition forces businesses to be at their best – always. Competition forces firms to:

◆ offer good products and a good service
◆ keep prices down
◆ bring in new, **innovative** products or services to break away from fierce price competition.

These consumer benefits place firms under constant pressure. A bright new idea will soon be copied by rivals. A profitable service may be undermined by price-cutting. This is clearly the case in businesses such as pizza delivery, where one firm's 'buy one get one free' offer is quickly matched by rivals.

Competition can also force businesses to do things that they would prefer to avoid. With high rents,

city-centre bars have to get good trade on Fridays and Saturdays. If your rivals have special deals or 'drink as much as you like for £10' offers, you must join in or close down. Similarly, if other banks have relocated their customer call centres to India, you may feel that you have to cut your own bank's costs by following them.

Fierce competition may force firms to:

◆ cut costs by cutting staff – bad for the staff and perhaps bad for customers
◆ take short-term action, such as price-cutting, which may damage the long-term health of the business
◆ adopt **unethical** practices, such as dumping waste materials or injecting water into meat (bacon often has 15 per cent extra water pumped into it, to plump up the meat and make it easier to charge a price that customers think is good value for money).

> I feel sorry for those who live without competition ... fat, dumb, and unhappy in cradle-to-grave security.
>
> *Donald M Kendall, businessman and political advisor*

Revision essentials

Competitive environment: the strength of competition between companies in the same market.

Innovative: a new, perhaps original, product or process.

Unethical: an action or decision that is wrong from a moral standpoint.

End of chapter exercises

1 From your own experience, analyse the strengths and weaknesses of two local fast-food businesses.

2 (a) Explain the possible effect on UK ice cream businesses if a big American chain chose to open 100 ice cream parlours in the UK.

 (b) Outline two possible drawbacks to staff at existing ice cream shops if a fierce new competitor arrived.

3 (a) Why might it be unethical for a bar to run an offer such as 'drink as much as you like for £10'?

 (b) Why might competition force a bar to run such an offer anyway?

4 Read the following extract. Outline the evidence that Nick Wright understands the role of an entrepreneur.

In March 2016 local boy Nick Wright opened Five Shakes milkshake bar in Exmouth. The nearest competitor is the national chain ShakeAway in Exeter. The local *Express & Echo* newspaper reported: 'I did market research before we opened and the locals seemed to really like it. I've had lots of people wishing me luck and I think people like to see good businesses in the town rather than empty shops, estate agents and charity shops … We're also helping to attract younger people.' He continued: 'I do worry about winter … We'll potentially do a delivery service in Exmouth. I've got a bike!'

5 Nick did some market research, but should he have researched the strengths and weaknesses of ShakeAway?

6 Outline one approach that Nick could take to help Five Shakes survive the winter months.

Practice questions

When the Aston & Magill cafe opened along a busy main road in Merton Park, South London, it had no immediate competitors. The 2015 opening of Waffle Jack's on the other side of the road was the first serious competition, followed shortly by Willow Tea Rooms. It was a difficult period for Aston & Magill but, by mid-2016, the cafe was back 'in the black' (making an operating profit). Then came a real shock: 100 metres down the road, on the same side of the road, a 'Costa Opening Soon' sign appeared over large shop premises. Now the competition would really hot up.

Total: 15 marks

1 (a) Define the term 'competition'. (1)

 (b) Outline one possible reason for Aston & Magill's 'difficult period'. (2)

2 State one benefit to Aston & Magill of its current location. (1)

3 Outline why the arrival of a Costa might be a bigger worry than the arrival of Waffle Jack's and Willow Tea Rooms. (2)

4 The owners of Aston & Magill must decide how best to cope with the arrival of a large Costa coffee shop. They see two main options:

 ◆ Option 1: Keep prices for their food and soft drinks unchanged, but be aggressive on the price of coffee, cutting it from £2.20 to £1.50 – far below the price at a Costa.

 ◆ Option 2: Offer existing customers a powerful loyalty card, giving a 25 per cent discount off all future purchases.

 Justify which **one** of these options the company should choose. (9)

Exam-style questions on Topic 1.2

Don't rush; check your answers carefully.

1 Which **one** is the best reason to use a market map before opening your first cafe? (1)

(a) It is a way of seeing whether there's a gap in the local market.

(b) It encourages deeper thought about how one thing leads to another.

(c) It encourages you to think 100 per cent positively, and therefore avoid the risk of negativity.

(d) It makes you balance rewards against risks.

2 Which **one** of the following is the best definition of market segmentation? (1)

(a) Dividing the market into small enough units to run a group discussion.

(b) Dividing the market into four boxes based on market share and market growth.

(c) Dividing customers up into different types to uncover new niches.

(d) Making sure to check every new idea out on the public, especially those in the target market.

3 Which **one** statement best describes the difference between qualitative and quantitative data? (1)

(a) Qualitative data can be tested for reliability; quantitative cannot.

(b) Qualitative data shows 'how'; quantitative shows 'why'.

(c) Qualitative data is good for sales forecasting; quantitative for finer judgements.

(d) Qualitative looks at the psychology of consumers; quantitative looks at the proportions thinking this or that.

4 Which **one** of the following groups are *all* examples of customer needs? (1)

(a) Quality, choice, convenience, competitiveness.

(b) Price, promotion, product and place.

(c) Choice, convenience, price, quality.

(d) Quality, reliability, durability and creativity.

5 The American Waffle bar in Ipswich has a new competitor: Alabama Waffles. It is only 50 metres away and has a one-month opening offer of free coffee or hot chocolate with every waffle order.

Which **two** factors are most likely to protect the American Waffle bar from this tougher competitive environment? (2)

(a) The American Waffle bar's location.

(b) American Waffle's consistent focus on customer delight.

(c) That an American Waffle is 25p cheaper than an Alabama Waffle.

(d) The American Waffle bar has a special focus on customer demographics.

(e) The American Waffle bar has a special gadget for testing when the waffles are perfectly cooked.

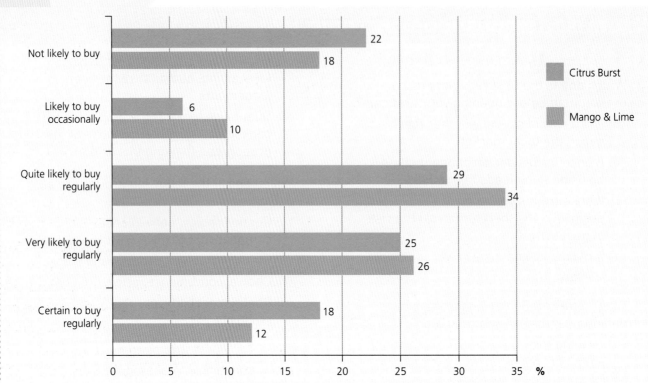

Results from quantitative research into two new real fruit drinks

6 Dave's Drinks must analyse the research above to decide which new product to launch. Experience has shown that strong commitment by interviewees is important.

Which **two** of the following are correct statements? (2)

(a) People are more likely not to buy Mango & Lime than Citrus Burst.

(b) More people considered buying Mango & Lime regularly than they did Citrus Burst.

(c) Citrus Burst looks the better option based on the figures.

(d) 72 per cent of interviewees considered buying Mango & Lime regularly.

(e) Decisions on launching new products would be better made on the basis of qualitative research.

Now try this discussion question.

7 Discuss the importance to a first-time entrepreneur of studying the strengths and weaknesses of competitors. (6)

13 Business aims and objectives

Aims are the broad targets that an entrepreneur has at the back of their mind (for example, 'to get rich'). These may or may not be talked about within the business, but eventually staff will come to understand them. For football manager José Mourinho, the aim is always the same: 'winning'. Another manager might want to build a successful youth academy programme – but José has only one aim.

From aims come **objectives**. Aims are general but objectives are specific. To win the Champions League in the next three years is a precise objective. Businesspeople like to use the term **SMART objectives**. In other words objectives should be:

◆ **S**pecific
◆ **M**easurable
◆ **A**chievable
◆ **R**ealistic
◆ **T**ime-bound (that is, they have a precise timescale).

The value of clear objectives is that they give a clear sense of purpose that all employees can buy into. That, in turn, is motivating as staff try their hardest to achieve the objective. In 2015, Costa Coffee announced a growth objective of going from 344 coffee bars in China to 900 by the end of 2020. Such a clear target helps the managers working on new store openings to ask for – and get – the money and staff needed to make it possible. Objectives provide a focal point for staff activity and decision making.

Another example is Higgidy, started in 2003 by a husband-and-wife team who declared their objective as 'bringing posh pies into the reach of everyone'. As Figure 13.1 shows, this was clearly achieved by 2015.

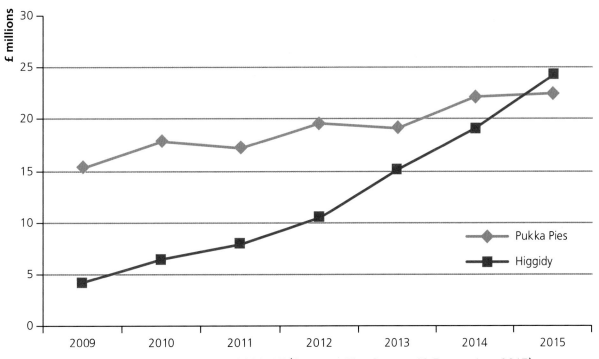

Figure 13.1 Giddy growth for Higgidy, 2009–15 (Source: *The Grocer*, 10 December 2015)

> The greatest danger for most of us isn't that our aim is too high and miss it, but that it is too low and we reach it.
>
> *Michelangelo, artist (1475–1564)*

Talking point

What personal aims do you hope to achieve by the time you're 22? What objectives might you set yourself to make sure you get there?

James Dyson wanted to invent a bagless vacuum cleaner

Why aims and objectives differ between businesses

Aims and objectives differ because business owners differ. Some have their sights set on money; others have a business idea first and see money as a secondary factor. Michael Dubin started Dollar Shave Club in America from disgust at how Gillette's dominance of the market for shaving had allowed the price of razors to reach crazy levels. The *Daily Mail* has claimed that Gillette products in the UK have a 4,750 per cent mark-up – this means that the selling price is 47.5 times more than the cost price, so products that cost £1 to make are sold for £47.50.

Many experts have said that the most successful businesses have an aim other than money. It is business success that leads to money being made. Ask Michael Dubin: Unilever bought Dollar Shave Club for $1 billion in 2016, before it had even made a profit.

People starting a new enterprise usually have one of three objectives:

1 A financial objective, such as to be rich.
2 A business objective, such as James Dyson in setting up his own bag-less vacuum cleaner business – he was determined to prove that his idea would work.
3 A social objective, such as starting a charity aimed at improving water quality in African villages.

Financial objectives

When starting up, most entrepreneurs concentrate on **survival**. In other words, they want to bring in enough cash to pay the bills. This can be hard at the start, with too few regular customers to generate the revenues needed to outweigh the regular weekly operating costs.

Among other financial objectives are:

◆ Profit: at the least to make enough profit to pay the family bills, and at the most to try to make enough to make the family rich. Then there is the important issue of timescale: some entrepreneurs are desperate to prove themselves as quickly as possible. This may lead to corners being cut in pursuit of a quick fortune. Many a company has ended up exposed on *Watchdog* because of doubtful business practices. The best businesses are those with an eye to the long-term, including parents who want to hand their business on to their children.

◆ Sales: some huge fortunes have been made in recent years by entrepreneurs who built sales and customer loyalty, but hadn't figured out how to turn the sales into profit. WhatsApp was bought by Facebook for $19 billion even though it only had sales, no profit; Dollar Shave Club was in the same position when it was bought by Unilever. The pursuit of sales first and profit later has become widespread for new online businesses.

- Market share: while sales are only about scale, market share is about power within a market; this, in turn, can secure a long-term profitable position. In July 2016, Mintel announced that Mars had the number one position in the market for chocolate in China, with 44.4 per cent. Of the top ten in China, nine are Western: Ferrero and Lindt have also been successful, though nowhere close to Mars. With high market share comes high distribution levels – in other words, shops want to stock you. That makes it easy for the leading brand to negotiate hard and charge high prices to the retailers.
- Financial security: having the biggest market share is one way to achieve financial security. Another way is to protect the idea behind your product from being copied by others. In 2010, Nestlé announced that it had taken out 1,700 patents on its Nespresso coffee-making system. Only after some key patents started to expire in 2014 did Nespresso face serious competition.

> Focus on a few key objectives.
>
> *Jack Welch, former chief executive of General Electric*

Non-financial objectives

Some entrepreneurs are motivated by social objectives. The not-for-profit sector is becoming increasingly important. This refers to enterprises that are started with the objective of achieving a social goal, using business methods. A traditional example is a charity such as Oxfam, which is professionally run but has the goal of helping to relieve suffering in developing countries. Today, firms such as One (not-for-profit bottled water) attempt to achieve the same objectives. Between 2007 and 2016, One helped more than 500,000 people in Africa to get access to regular clean water.

Traidcraft is a leading social enterprise that began in 1979. It has built up its turnover to £12 million a year with all profits being ploughed back into the business. Traidcraft began the idea of 'trade not aid' by bringing coffee, tea and household items from developing countries and selling them in the UK. Because Traidcraft wants to encourage trade, even in a year when it made an operating loss (2014–15), it can console itself that its £7.5 million purchase costs represented income to developing country workers who produced the goods.

Other firms with social rather than profit-making motives include:

- the Co-operative Bank, which is owned by its members
- Waitrose and John Lewis, which are owned by their staff
- pressure groups, such as Greenpeace and Friends of the Earth.

Other non-financial objectives for starting a business include:

- Personal satisfaction: for many people it is hard to get satisfaction from being a small cog in a big wheel. They need to break away and show what they can do. This is a particularly strong motive for those who have struggled to show their talents at school. There is a famously high correlation between entrepreneurship and dyslexia and other causes of school struggles. Richard Branson is perhaps the country's best-known dyslexic.
- Challenge: some people are mountain climbers and others prefer a walk in the countryside. Starting your own business is an extraordinary challenge that will test your personal skills, such as leadership, charm and the ability to plan and to prioritise; character traits, such as resilience, energy, dedication and persistence; as well as your intellectual abilities (intelligence). If that all sounds like too much pressure, stick to the country walks.
- Independence: entrepreneurs hate being told what to do; they value their independence greatly. This was especially the case for immigrants who, in the past, found their career progression blocked by discrimination. Independence remains a key attraction of entrepreneurship.
- Control: this is linked to independence. The entrepreneur demands to be in control. This is why many entrepreneurs are reluctant to sell out

for large sums of cash. The control they have within 'their' business is a drug that is hard to give up.

There is a strong correlation between entrepreneurship and dyslexia

Drawing the right conclusions

It is a mistake to think that business is just about making profits. People run businesses because they can be challenging, rewarding and fun. They also provide the scope to achieve social as well as financial progress. Nevertheless, there will always be some firms that are only interested in profit. These may become the cowboy builders who charge high prices for shoddy jobs, or the financial institutions that encourage young people to build up debts they cannot afford. Just as every individual is different, so is every business.

Revision essentials

Aims: a general statement of where you're heading, for example 'to get to university'.

Market share: the percentage of a market held by one company or brand.

Objectives: a clear, measurable goal, so success or failure is clear to see.

SMART objectives: targets that are specific, measurable, achievable, realistic and time-bound.

Survival: keeping the business going, which ultimately depends on determination and cash.

End of chapter exercises

1 Suggest one aim and one objective for a highly promising 15-year-old high-jumper.

2 Suggest one aim and one objective for a 21-year-old about to start her first business (a body-building gym).

3 Explain why Traidcraft can feel happy about its 2014–15 performance, even though it made no profit.

4 Read the following extract. Discuss what financial objectives Johnno should set for the business in its opening year.

Johnno's jams were famous in the family. Everyone loves strawberry jam, but after a jar homemade by Johnno, nothing else seemed the same. So, it was no shock when, one Christmas, he talked to everyone about starting a jam-making business and asked if anyone could invest £10,000. With six relatives and £20,000 of his own, Johnno was ready to start. He went to three courses about food hygiene then set to work turning an empty factory unit into a jam production line.

5 To what extent can Johnno trust that the quality of his jam will pull him through the difficult start-up phase of the business?

Practice questions

In 2012, Michael Dubin became an instant YouTube hit when he uploaded a humorous launch video for his business, Dollar Shave Club. By 1 July 2016 the video (which cost just $4,000 to make) had been seen 22.5 million times. That would be a ho-hum performance by Rihanna, but it is amazing for a business pitch. Much, much better was to come for Mr Dubin. On 20 July 2016, UK giant Unilever bought Dollar Shave Club for $1 billion, cash.

Michael Dubin uploaded his launch video to YouTube

Between 2012 and 2016 the growth in sales of razors was huge, supplemented by other product launches (see Figure 13.2). Today the monthly box of razors may also contain shaving cream, aftershave and hair gel – all ordered online from the company's website. By the time you read this though, Unilever will own the business and Michael Dubin will be getting bored counting his cash pile.

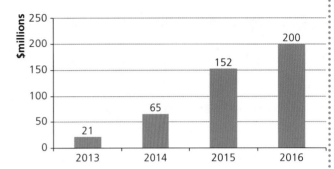

Figure 13.2 Annual sales revenue for the Dollar Shave Club, 2013–16

Total: 20 marks

1 **(a)** Calculate the percentage growth rate in sales between 2013 and 2014. (2)

 (b) Outline one reason why it might be hard to manage a business that is growing so fast. (2)

2 Use Figure 13.2 to identify the year in which Dollar Shave Club sales rose the most in $millions. (1)

3 Analyse the benefits to Dubin of using social media to promote his business. (6)

4 Michael Dubin must now decide on his future plans. He sees two options:

 ◆ Option 1: Stay on as chief executive of Dollar Shave Club, working for new owner Unilever.

 ◆ Option 2: Walk away and work at starting a brand new business.

Justify which **one** of these options he should choose. (9)

14 Business revenue, costs and profit

● Revenue

Sales **revenue** comes from the number of things you sell multiplied by the price you charge. If Yeovil Town FC sells 7,000 tickets at £20 each, its revenue is £140,000. Yeovil decides its own ticket price, so the uncertain factor is the level of demand. Will it sell 7,000 tickets (£140,000) or 5,500 tickets (£110,000)? Even for such a well-run club, the difference of £30,000 is very important.

The formula is:

revenue = quantity × price

● Price

For some businesses, price is out of their control. In Africa, farmers producing cotton were receiving $1.42 per pound (in weight) in July 2011 but, by July 2016, it had fallen to only $0.72. The near 50 per cent fall in their incomes would have hit their already low living standards.

Prices cannot be estimated with confidence when:

- the business operates in a market where prices change in the short term due to variations in supply and demand, for example cotton
- competition is direct and fierce, for example Ryanair competing with easyJet
- you are launching a new product and cannot be sure of the consumer response; for example, the Xbox One launched in the UK in 2013 at £429 but, after weak sales, the price was cut three times by Microsoft during its first year to £329.

Talking point

Richard Branson's Virgin Galactic plans to offer space tourism: five minutes of weightlessness in space. How might he decide on the right price per flight?

● Quantity (demand)

Occasionally, the demand for a product or service can be judged with confidence. Beyoncé concert tours have always sold out so it seems safe to expect them to sell out next time round. Similarly, sales of Heinz baked beans are extremely predictable. A revenue forecast made for six months' time by a Heinz director would prove very accurate; therefore the business can make sure it has the right quantity of machinery, staff and raw ingredients. Managing this type of business is easy.

It is quite different when trying to plan the revenues for an upmarket London restaurant. Customers will usually be a mixture of wealthy Londoners, businesspeople and visitors to London. The restaurant could be full this week, but in six months it might have been emptied by:

- a newspaper review that condemns it as dull and overpriced
- an economic slowdown, leading to cutbacks in luxury spending
- terrorism or another reasons for people to avoid London.

1 A baker sells 120 loaves of bread a day at £2.50 each. What is the baker's daily revenue?

120 × £2.50 = **£300**

2 XYZ Ltd has two main products: A and B. Sales of A are 2,000 units a month; sales of B are 500 units a month. The selling prices for A and B are £4 and £10, respectively. Calculate the revenue.

Revenue = sales volume × selling price
Product A: 2,000 × £4 = £8,000
Product B: 500 × £10 = £5,000
So, total revenue = **£13,000**

Costs

What do you think it would cost to start up a kiosk selling £2 coffees? The shot of real coffee costs 12p, then there's milk and sugar, no more than 3p. Allow 10p for the paper cup and the direct cost of making a cup of coffee is 25p. You can sell it for £2 yet it costs only 25p to make. No wonder Costa Coffee shops have spread like the flu in recent years.

Of course, it is not that simple. There are many other costs: the cost of the kiosk, the cost of machinery, the salaries of the staff and the accountant you need to prevent the taxman from hunting you down.

For someone starting a business, identifying and quantifying all the costs is one of the hardest things to do. The starting point is to realise that there are two types of cost: **variable costs** and **fixed costs**.

Coffee costs barely anything to make but can be sold for a much higher price!

Variable costs

These are costs that vary with the quantity sold and, therefore, the quantity made. They are costs that relate directly to making the sale and, therefore, making the product. If Walkers runs a brilliant new advertising campaign and crisp sales double, they will have to buy in twice as many potatoes, twice as much packaging, and so on. These are variable costs. They rise and fall in relation to sales and, therefore, output.

Examples of variable costs include:
◆ raw materials (for example, potatoes for making crisps, coffee beans for making coffee)
◆ bought-in components (for example, spark plugs for making cars, zips when making jeans)
◆ energy used in the production process (for example, electricity to power the coffee-making machine).

The raw materials involved in making potato crisps

Fixed costs

These costs do not change as output changes. They are fixed in relation to output. Take the rent on a clothes shop, for example – it must be paid regardless of whether sales are terrific or awful. Therefore it is fixed. Note, though, that the landlord can put up your rent, so the fact that it is a fixed cost does not mean that it never changes.

Fixed costs are often related to a time period rather than sales or output. Rent, for instance, might be paid per month, as might staff salaries.

Examples of fixed costs include:
◆ salaries of permanent staff
◆ rent and (council) rates
◆ interest payments on borrowings.

Worked example: interest payments

1 A business took out a three-year loan for £8,000 at an interest rate of eight per cent. The £8,000 is to be repaid at the end of year three. Calculate the business' total interest payments.

Each year it must pay £8,000 × $\frac{8}{100}$ = £640

Over a three-year period, therefore, the payments come to £640 × 3 = **£1,920**

2 A business has an agreed overdraft limit of £20,000 at an interest rate of 12.5 per cent. Over the past year the business has, on average, run an overdraft of £15,000. What are the interest charges?

£15,000 × $\frac{12.5}{100}$ = **£1,875 for the year**

Getting the numbers right

If you plan to open a kebab shop, it may be easy to decide which are the variable costs and which are the fixed costs, but what will the *exact* figures be? The only way to find out is to work at it.

A trip to a local estate agent will tell you what rents are likely at different parts of the high street (they might vary from £2,000 to £8,000 a month, depending on location). The estate agent will also know the level of council tax/rates on different properties. A look at online job advertisements will show the hourly pay rates and salary levels locally. A few phone calls to insurance companies will give an idea of the insurance costs. A builder could give a quote on the cost of turning the shell of an empty shop into a kebab shop, with the electrics, gas and water in the right places. So, most of the fixed costs can be established fairly easily.

It may be harder to estimate the variable costs. An internet search would get you the names of doner kebab meat suppliers. If you were offered enough meat to make 450 kebabs for £135, it would cost just 30p per kebab! Of course, without experience you cannot be sure of the quality of the meat, or that you would really get 450 portions from it, so a sensible businessperson would be very cautious when estimating costs. To be on the safe side you could allow for 60p in meat variable costs (plus the cost of pitta bread, salad, and so on – so perhaps 80p in total).

Getting research done

Having completed your research, you can estimate the following totals:
◆ fixed costs of the kebab shop: £1,200 per week
◆ variable costs per kebab: £0.80.

You can now calculate the **total costs** at different levels of business. If research shows that 600 customers will come per week, your total weekly costs will be:

600 × £0.80 = £480 (variable costs) + £1,200 (fixed costs) = £1,680 (total costs)

As long as the revenues are higher than this figure, there is money to be made.

Worked example: costs

1 A coffee shop has variable costs of 25p per cup and weekly fixed costs of £1,200.

   (a) What are its total costs in a week when it sells 800 cups of coffee?

   Total costs = variable costs + fixed costs
   (£0.25 × 800) + £1,200 = **£1,400**

   (b) What are its total weekly costs if sales double to 1,600 cups of coffee?

   Total costs = variable costs + fixed costs
   (£0.25 × 1,600) + £1,200 = **£1,600**

2 ABC Ltd sells motorbikes. It buys the bikes for £2,000 and sells them for £3,000. It also has weekly fixed costs of £4,000. Calculate total costs if six bikes are sold in a week.

   Total costs = variable costs + fixed costs
   (£2,000 × 6) + £4,000 = **£16,000**

Profit

Profit is the difference between revenue and costs. It is calculated by the formula:

profit = revenue – total costs

If costs are greater than revenue, the result would be a negative number. That means making a loss.

Look at the position of the supermarket Morrisons. It had an awful year in 2015 and made a loss of £800 million. In 2016, its position was much better and it made a profit of £200 million. This turnaround came about through a huge reduction in operating costs. Notice in Figure 14.1 that profit can be a thin margin between revenue and costs.

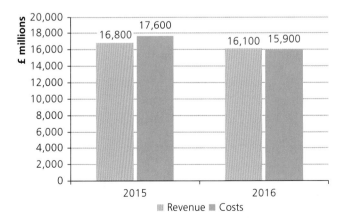

Figure 14.1 Revenue and costs at Morrisons, 2015 and 2016 (Source: Morrisons' accounts)

For new, small firms, profit can be very difficult to achieve in the early days. Costs may be higher than necessary because staff have not yet learned to do things efficiently. Revenues may be low because word has not yet spread about the quality of the service you offer. W.H. Hales, a shop in Croydon supplying and engraving sports trophies, took five years to become profitable – it took that long for the word about the shop to spread among local football teams.

Worked example: profit

1 A coffee shop has variable costs of 25p per cup and weekly fixed costs of £1,200. It sells each cup of coffee for £2.

   (a) What are its profits in a week when it sells 800 cups of coffee?

   Profit = total revenue – total costs
   Total revenue = 800 × £2.00 = £1,600
   Total costs = (£0.25 × 800) + £1,200 = £1,400
   Therefore, weekly profit is £1,600 – £1,400 = **£200**

   (b) What are its weekly profits if sales double to 1,600 cups of coffee?

   Total revenue = 1,600 × £2.00 = £3,200
   Total costs = (£0.25 × 1,600) + £1,200 = £1,600
   Therefore, weekly profit is now £3,200 – £1,600 = **£1,600**

2 ABC Ltd sells motorbikes. It buys the bikes for £2,000 and sells them for £3,000. It also has weekly fixed costs of £4,000. Calculate the profit if six bikes are sold in a week.

   Profit = total revenue – total costs
   Total revenue = 6 × £3,000 = £18,000
   Total costs = (£2,000 × 6) + £4,000 = £16,000
   Therefore, weekly profit is £18,000 – £16,000 = **£2,000**

Talking point

Identify the different ways profit might be used at Liverpool Football Club and the charity Oxfam.

Drawing the right conclusions

To succeed in the long term a business must make profits. The surplus of revenue over costs provides the capital to replace tired machinery and vehicles and to finance growth. Many businesses have an occasional awful year, so having some cash in the bank is important to long-term survival and success.

At the time of writing, easyJet had just announced that Britain's 2016 decision to leave the EU had cost the company £40 million. Keeping profits back 'for a rainy day' makes good business sense.

Revision essentials

Fixed costs: costs that don't vary just because output varies, for example rent.

Interest: the charges made by banks for the cash they have lent to a business, for example six per cent per year.

Profit: the difference between revenue and total costs; if the figure is negative the business is making a loss.

Revenue: the total value of the sales made within a set period of time, such as a month.

Total costs: all the costs for a set period of time, such as a month.

Variable costs: costs that vary as output varies, such as raw materials.

Formulae

Sales revenue = price × quantity sold

Total costs = variable costs + fixed costs

Profit = total revenue − total costs

End of chapter exercises

1 Explain the difference between fixed costs and variable costs.

2 A greengrocer buys punnets of strawberries for 50p and sells them for £1. She must also pay £120 in weekly rent and £180 for other fixed costs.

   (a) What is the total cost of selling 500 punnets per week?

   (b) What is the total cost of selling 1,000 punnets per week?

3 Identify two fixed costs and two variable costs of running:

   (a) a secondary school with 1,200 pupils

   (b) a Tesco supermarket.

4 Use the information in Figure 14.1 on page 67 to explain how the Morrisons turned things around from a £800 million loss to a £200 million profit.

   Toni's ice cream van sells 150 ice creams a day at £2 each. The variable costs are 40p per ice cream; the fixed costs of running the van are £100 a day.

5 Read the extract about Toni's ice cream. What is Toni's profit per day?

Toni's ice cream van sells 150 ice creams a day

6 Toni's daughter wants him to put the price up to £2.40; she thinks that sales will stay at 150 ice creams, but Toni is worried that sales will fall to 125.

   (a) By how much will Toni's profit change if his daughter is right?

   (b) What will the new profit be if Toni is right about the effect of a price rise?

   (c) Outline one reason why Toni might still want to keep the price at £2.

Practice questions

When the Choy Sum Chinese restaurant opened in Wimbledon, it was in a great position to estimate costs accurately. The owners already ran a Chinese restaurant five miles away in Fulham, so they knew how much to allow for the variable and fixed costs of their new outlet. Before opening, their plans showed:

◆ average price per dish = £4.40
◆ average variable cost per dish = £1.80
◆ fixed weekly overheads = £2,000
◆ number of dishes sold per week = 3,000
◆ weekly revenue = £13,200

However, it proved harder than expected. The owners knew how much the ingredients *should* cost in a chicken and black bean sauce dish, but the actual variable costs were 25 per cent higher. The owners checked the figures carefully, trying to see whether staff were stealing food from the kitchens.

The explanation came in two parts. First, the restaurant manager at Wimbledon failed to attract and keep good chefs, so customers sent poor-quality dishes back to the kitchen and the cooking had to be redone. The second problem stemmed from the first: bookings were slow, with only 200 customers buying 1,000 dishes per week. Fresh food went off and had to be thrown away.

Total: 25 marks

1 Based on the owners' plan, calculate the expected weekly total costs. (2)

2 Based on the owner's plan, calculate the expected weekly profit. (2)

3 Analyse why sales proved lower than expected. (6)

4 Actual variable costs were 25 per cent higher than predicted, and the number of dishes sold was only 1,000. Calculate the weekly actual revenues. (2)

5 Based on the data provided in question 4, calculate the weekly actual total costs. (2)

6 When operating a Chinese restaurant such as Choy Sum:

(a) Identify one likely variable cost. (2)

(b) Identify one likely fixed cost.

7 To get the business into profit the owners see two options:

◆ Option 1: Focus all efforts on training and motivating the staff.

◆ Option 2: Focus on building customer numbers by advertising in local papers and on social media.

Justify which **one** of these options they should choose. (9)

15 Break-even

Tushingham Sails Ltd manufactures windsurf sails in Devon. The company has identified a potential market for a new design of windsurfing sail. Everyone who tries the sail reckons it will be a success. Tushingham will sell the sail online through its website, as well as in the 30 sports shops that stock its products.

Before going ahead, the company must make sure it can make some money out of the new sail. One way is to estimate how many sails it can sell then compare them with its **break-even** point. The break-even point is the number of sails the company must sell to cover all the costs of making them. Tushingham will make a profit if it sells more than this number. If it sells less, it will make a loss. Knowing the break-even level is important for any business.

> By failing to prepare, you are preparing to fail.
>
> *Benjamin Franklin, founding father of the USA (1706–90)*

Fixed and variable costs

As explained in the previous chapter, costs in a business can be divided into two types: fixed costs and variable costs. Before a business can calculate its break-even point, it must first collect information about production costs. A business will need to know its fixed and variable costs, and its sales revenue, if it wants to be able to calculate its break-even point.

The monthly fixed costs for the new sail are £18,000. Rental for the premises, managers' salaries and loan repayments are all examples of fixed costs.

The variable costs are £200 per board. The raw materials, packaging costs, and so on, all go up and down in line with the number made and sold.

Tushingham Sails has carried out some market research showing that people are prepared to pay between £400 and £500 for a board, so the managers have decided on a selling price of £450. This makes it possible to calculate sales revenue at different levels of output.

Tom, the finance director at Tushingham Sails, has summarised these costs:
- Fixed costs: £18,000
- Variable costs per windsurf sail: £200
- Selling price per windsurf sail: £450.

Drawing a break-even chart

It can be helpful to draw a diagram that shows the profit or loss at every possible level of output. This diagram is called a **break-even chart**. To draw a break-even chart you need information about the:
- variable costs
- fixed costs
- revenue of the business
- maximum output of the business.

Tom would also need to know the following:
- total costs = fixed costs + variable costs
- variable costs = variable costs per unit × number of windsurf sails
- sales revenue = selling price per unit × number of windsurf sails
- that the maximum monthly production output of the factory is 200 units.

Stage one

Tom can now record the information on a graph with quantity sold across the bottom and costs going upwards. The horizontal scale (across) runs from zero sold to the maximum possible, 200. The vertical (up) scale covers the range from £0 to the maximum revenue possible ($200 \times £450 = £90,000$).

Below you can see the first stage of Tom's chart.

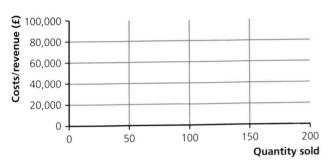

Figure 15.1 Stage one break-even chart

Stage two

Tom needs to draw his £18,000 fixed costs line on his chart. The line is horizontal because the fixed cost figure is the same no matter how many sails are sold.

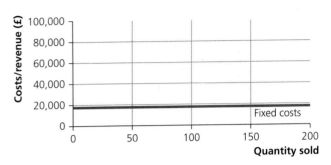

Figure 15.2 Stage two break-even chart

Stage three

Tom needs to show the total costs next. This means adding the variable costs to the fixed costs. If Tushingham sells nothing, its variable costs will be £0 ($£200 \times 0$). If it sells 200 sails, its variable costs will be £40,000 ($£200 \times 200$). These costs must be added to the fixed costs. So, the total costs line starts from where the fixed costs line meets the vertical axis (£18,000). The gap between the total costs and the fixed costs shows the variable costs.

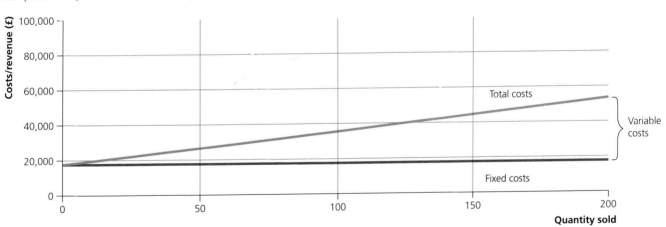

Figure 15.3 Stage three break-even chart

Stage four

The third line drawn shows Tushingham's income from sales – the revenue. If no sails are sold, then no revenue is made ($£450 \times 0$), so the line starts at zero. If customers buy all the sails, the sales revenue would be £90,000 ($£450 \times 200$). So, revenue is a straight line between £0 and £90,000.

Stage five

The point on the chart where the sales revenue line crosses the total costs line is the break-even point. Tom can now draw a vertical line down to the quantity sold and identify the number of sails the firm has to sell in order to ensure that all costs are covered.

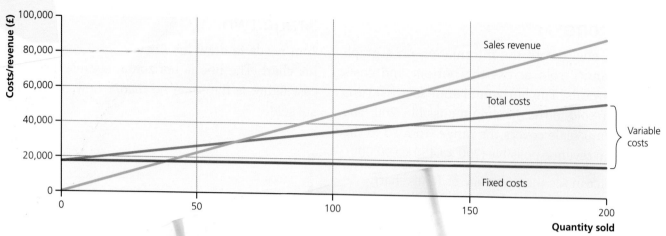

Figure 15.4 Stage four break-even chart

Tom reads the graph and can see that the line meets the horizontal axis at the number 72. This means that Tushingham needs to sell 72 windsurf sails before it starts to make a profit.

The distance between the revenue line and the total costs line shows the profit (or loss) made at that level of sales. After 72 sails have been sold, the difference between the two lines represents profit. From the graph Tom can calculate that Tushingham will lose £18,000 a month if it sells no windsurf sails, yet could make a maximum profit of £32,000 a month.

Talking point

Why is it important to think of future revenue as an estimate, not a fact?

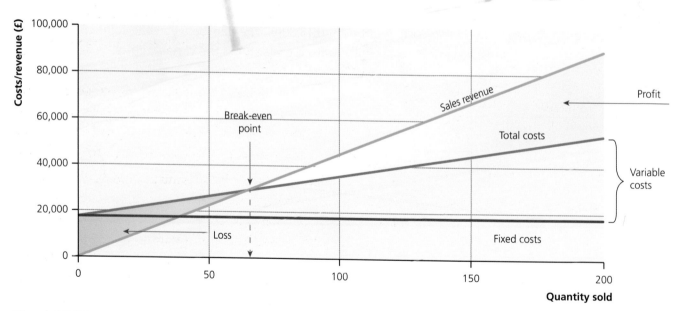

Figure 15.5 Stage five break-even chart

Calculating the break-even level of output

A break-even chart is useful but a bit time-consuming to prepare. If a manager wants to work out the break-even point quickly, there's a formula to do the job:

$$\text{Break-even} = \frac{\text{fixed costs}}{(\text{price} - \text{variable costs per unit})}$$

The answer is in units, not money.

First, work out the bottom bit, the price minus variable costs per unit. In the case of Tushingham Sails, that figure is £450 – £200 = £250.

Then apply the formula:

$$\text{Break-even} = \frac{£18,000}{£250} = \textbf{72 sails per month}$$

Margin of safety

A further use of the break-even chart is to show the **margin of safety**, that is, the firm's safety cushion. If a company's break-even point is 72 units but demand is 100 units, the business can afford sales to slip by 28 units before it starts to make losses. The margin of safety is the gap between sales and the break-even point. The wider that margin, the more comfortable the business can feel.

The formula for calculating this is:

Margin of safety = sales (in units) – the break-even point

> ### Worked example: break-even and margin of safety
>
> 1 A pizza takeaway has 600 customers a week spending an average of £20 each. Variable costs per order are £5 and the weekly fixed costs are £3,000.
>
> (a) Calculate the break-even point.
>
> Price – variable costs per unit = £20 – £5 = £15
>
> $$\frac{£3,000}{£15} = \textbf{200 customers per week}$$
>
> (b) Calculate the margin of safety.
>
> Margin of safety = sales – break-even point
>
> 600 – 200 = **400 customers a week**

Interpretation of break-even diagrams

Business is all about the future – making decisions today for the sake of things happening tomorrow. Therefore managers need methods that help them to make decisions. Break-even diagrams can help show the impact of changes in revenue and costs.

Break-even charts can help a manager answer questions such as:

◆ What if we put our prices up by ten per cent? What would this do to our break-even sales level?
◆ The price of wheat has risen by 25 per cent. What will this do to our profit if we leave our prices unchanged?

Table 15.1 (page 74) shows this in more detail, but the key thing is that these are critical questions for a business. They can all be answered on a calculator, but a break-even chart shows the answer visually. That will often make it easier to use, for example when explaining to staff why the business cannot afford to pay a five per cent pay rise at the moment, or why three staff have to be made redundant.

Table 15.1 How break-even helps answer business questions

Questions break-even can help answer	Impact on the break-even chart
Our landlord has increased our rent by 40 per cent. What will this do to our profitability?	Fixed costs line will rise, pushing the total cost line closer to the revenue line, i.e., cutting profits
The recession has cut demand for our organic eggs by 20 per cent. What will be the impact?	No lines on the chart will change, but the 20 per cent sales fall will reduce the margin of safety, or perhaps wipe it out
Is it right to cut our prices by 10 per cent? Will it increase or cut our profits?	The revenue line will rise less steeply, pushing it down towards total costs; profits can only rise if the sales volume leaps ahead

Critical business decisions can be answered with a calculator but a break-even chart shows the answer visually

Revision essentials

Break-even: the level of sales at which total costs are equal to total revenue. At this point the business is making neither a profit nor a loss.

Break-even chart: a graph showing a company's revenue and total costs at all possible levels of output.

Margin of safety: the amount by which demand can fall before the business starts making losses.

Formulae

$$\text{Break-even output} = \frac{\text{fixed costs}}{\text{price} - \text{variable costs per unit}}$$

Margin of safety = sales − break-even output

End of chapter exercises

John sells hot dogs for a living. He calculates his fixed costs at £20 per day and his variable costs at 10p per hot dog. John sells each hot dog for 75p and is able to cook 50 hot dogs to sell every day.

1 Read the extract above. What are John's fixed costs if he makes and sells 25 hot dogs?

2 What would John's variable costs be if he sold no hot dogs at all?

3 What are John's total costs if he sells 20 hot dogs in an afternoon?

4 What would be the maximum sales revenue that John could take in one day?

5 Explain what is meant by the term 'break-even'.

6 Outline two reasons why a business might want to be able to calculate its break-even point.

7 Explain how to find the break-even point on a break-even chart.

8 Read the following extract. Calculate the total costs and total revenue of the business over the following outputs: 0, 200, 400.

Toys 4 Fun is a manufacturer of children's wooden toys. The company has calculated the monthly costs of producing the average toy as follows:

Rent and rates	£2,000
Electricity	£100
Salary bill for managers	£2,700
Other fixed costs	£200

Average variable costs for producing each toy come to £5. The average price for each toy amounts to £25. The factory's capacity is 400 units.

9 On a large piece of graph paper, draw a horizontal axis from 0 to 400 and a vertical axis from £0 to £10,000. Plot the revenue and total cost figures on to the graph and estimate the break-even output. What is the profit/loss at the following levels of output: 100 and 400?

10 If the company could not sell more than 150 toys in a month, what might the management do?

Practice questions

Birmingham-based online travel agency TurkishHolidays.com enjoyed five good years followed by a sudden 66 per cent downturn in bookings to Turkey. The slump was due to a series of terrorist explosions followed by a violent, but failed, coup. Last-minute holiday bookings were especially hard hit, leaving places unsold.

The business was used to average weekly bookings of at least 240 holidays. Now the figure slumped to 80 holidays. As shown in the break-even chart, things were serious.

Total: 15 marks

1 Using the chart, calculate the profit or loss made by TurkishHolidays.com when bookings are 240 a week. (2)

2 Using the chart, calculate the profit or loss made by TurkishHolidays.com when bookings are 80 a week. (2)

3 Using the chart, calculate the company's safety margin when bookings are 240 a week. (2)

4 To get the business back into profit there are two options:
   ◆ Option 1: Cut costs to lower the break-even point.
   ◆ Option 2: Rebuild revenues, perhaps by offering new destinations such as Portugal.

Justify which **one** of these options they should choose. (9)

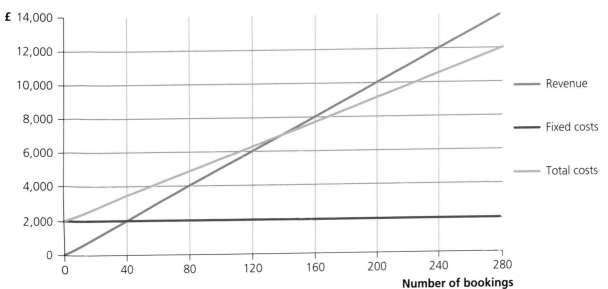

Figure 15.6 Weekly break-even chart for TurkishHoliday.com

16 The importance of cash

Why does cash matter?

Cash matters because, without it, bills go unpaid and a business can be taken to court and perhaps closed down. Staff expect to be paid and will not accept a boss saying: 'Sorry, I can't afford to pay you today. Hopefully we'll be OK next week.' It is hard enough for individuals to *always* have cash available; if you are running a business with 15 staff and 150 customers, the problems are much greater.

There are two times when business cash flow problems are especially difficult:

1 At start-up, when money has to be ploughed into constructing (a restaurant, maybe), hiring, training and paying staff, buying in all the necessary equipment, then perhaps waiting several weeks until the word has spread and the restaurant starts to fill up. Any building delays or cost overruns may turn a cash balance into a worrying deficit.

2 At a time of rapid growth, when there can be serious strains on cash flow again. Your (small) restaurant is full every night and customers are grumbling about slow service, so you find a new, bigger site and get the builders in. Your cash drains away as you are constantly paying out. Many a growing business has collapsed at this point.

> In God we trust. All others pay cash.
> *American saying*

The importance of cash to a business

It is important, here, to realise that 'cash' – from a business point of view – means not only banknotes but also 'cash at bank', that is, money available in the business' bank account. Paying by electronic transfer or by debit card is essentially a 'cash' payment.

The main day-to-day cash payments made by companies are to their:

◆ Suppliers, who usually give an interest-free credit period, such as 60 days to pay. If they're not paid on time, they may stop supplying – leaving your shelves empty. If you are a shopkeeper, it is embarrassing to have empty shelves. If you're a manufacturer, it is even more serious as a missing component can shut down the whole production line.

◆ Employees, such as footballers for Bolton Football Club, who were regularly paid late in the 2015–16 football season. Bolton simply didn't have the cash. Needless to say, the best players will find another employer as soon as possible. And just as a sports team relies on its best players, a company relies on its very best staff.

◆ Paying the overheads, meaning all the bills that must be paid, whether or not the business is doing well. Typical overheads include:
  ◆ salaries for office staff and for directors
  ◆ rent and rates on the company's property
  ◆ 'utility' bills such as gas, electricity and phones
  ◆ If the overhead bills are not paid, the lights could literally go out.

When you have a few large customers, if one of them fails to pay on time your cash position is squeezed badly. It can be even worse when a big customer collapses, as BHS did in 2016. At the time it went under, it owed £52 million to small company suppliers. They will have been expecting to receive money owed by BHS (perhaps £25,000), and suddenly realised that they would be receiving nothing.

> Happiness is a positive cash flow.
>
> *Fred Adler, New York venture capitalist*

Bolton footballers were paid late due to a cash shortage

How should cash be managed?

The key is to forecast the flows of cash into and out of the business. This topic (**cash flow**) is covered in Chapter 17.

In addition to careful forecasting, a business must take care to:

◆ Negotiate a generous **overdraft facility** at the bank. A bank **overdraft** is a flexible way to borrow what you want, when you want and for how long you want. If you have no cash in your bank but expect a fat cheque from a customer on Monday, you can pay your £7,000 salary bill today, Friday, using your overdraft. The cost of borrowing £7,000 for three days would be less than £5 – well worth it to keep staff happy. Overdrafts and other forms of borrowing are explained fully in Chapter 18.

◆ Keep costs under control; cash should never be a serious problem if the business is profitable (that is, costs are lower than revenues). If business is poor, good managers make sure to cut costs – especially inessential ones such as staff mobile phones, expense accounts and renewing company cars.

◆ Keep the cash coming in. Most business in Britain is done on credit, not for cash. In other words, if Versace sells £400,000 worth of dresses to Harrods, the retailer may be given two or three months to pay. A poorly run business may be too soft on customers who fail to pay up on time. Companies allow customers an average of 70 days to pay up, but some allow over 120 days, which is four months! Waiting this long to be paid can strain a company's cash resources and is no way to run a business.

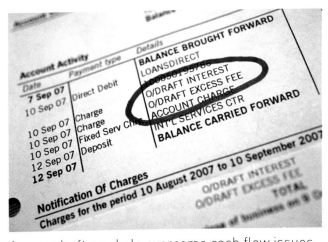

An overdraft can help overcome cash flow issues

Cash flow problems and business failure

Wilson's of Kendal Ltd collapsed in early 2016, making all staff redundant. The accountants brought in to close the business down blamed 'severe cash flow difficulties'. Wilson's had been making Kendal mint cake (effectively a slab of peppermint cream confectionery) since 1913. In 2013, the company responded to rising demand by investing in a brand new, bigger factory. It couldn't cope with the drain on its cash flow, however. It staggered on for a couple of years, shedding jobs, before closing down. More than 120 staff lost their jobs. The business failed because it mishandled its cash flow. Technically, it fell into **insolvency**, meaning it was unable to pay its bills.

The difference between cash and profit

Every Saturday Jen works at her aunt's clothes shop. Last Saturday, for the first time, Jen was asked to 'settle up' at the end of the day. She counted all the cash and deducted the £40 'float' put into the till at the start of the day by her aunt. The net figure came to £422. Then she printed out the day's till receipts (showing the value of sales made in the day). That came to £1,376. Jen was baffled at that point, but her aunt printed out another sheet: the credit and debit card purchases made on the day. Happily that came to £954. Job done.

So, on Saturday £1,376 of revenue was generated, but only £422 of cash flow. The difference shouldn't matter much because the remaining £954 should come in from the card companies within a few days. But the principle is clear, cash inflow and revenue may be different, so cash flow and profit can also be different.

Table 16.1 How different financial actions affect cash flow and profit

Transaction	Effect on cash position	Effect on profit
Borrow £50,000 on a three-year loan	+£50,000	0
Sell £30,000 of goods for £40,000, giving the customer three months' credit	0	+£10,000
Pay a supplier £10,000 for goods bought on credit two months' ago	−£10,000	0
Sell £2,000 of fruit bought for £800 cash this morning	+£1,200	+£1,200

Cash flow shows the immediate impact of a transaction on a company's bank account; profit shows the longer-term impact.

Table 16.1 gives examples of key differences.

> The three most dreaded words in the English language are 'negative cash flow'.
>
> *David Tang, founder of Shanghai Tang*

Drawing the right conclusions

Cash is the lifeblood of every business. Literally, without cash the business dies. Therefore it is vital to plan how much is needed and where to get it from. The best possible source is from your own customers – making sure they pay on time. It is also necessary to allow for the unexpected, which is why a large overdraft facility is helpful. Ideally you would use it rarely, to keep interest charges down. When it is needed, however, its flexibility takes the pressure out of difficult financial situations.

Talking point

What cash problems might be faced by a manufacturer of fireworks?

Revision essentials

Cash: the money the firm holds in notes and coins, and in its bank accounts.

Cash flow: the movement of money into and out of the firm's bank account.

Insolvency: when a business lacks the cash to pay its debts.

Overdraft: the amount of the agreed overdraft facility that the business uses.

Overdraft facility: an agreed maximum level of overdraft.

End of chapter exercises

1 Why do businesses think that money in their bank accounts is part of their cash total?

2 How might a house-building firm suffer if it lacks the cash to buy supplies of bricks in bulk?

3 Outline two cash flow problems that a British seaside hotel business might have.

4 Before her first beauty salon opened, Moira Angell's builders took four months to complete the work – exactly double what they had promised. Outline two ways that this would affect the cash position of the business.

5 Look at Table 16.2, which shows the cash flow for a women's clothes shop. Suggest two ways in which the cash position of the business might be improved.

Table 16.2 Cash flow for a women's clothes shop

Figures in £000s	January	February	March	April
Cash at start of month	90	94	85	83
Cash in	24	16	18	22
Cash out	20	25	20	22
Net monthly cash flow	4	−9	−2	0
Cash at end of month	94	85	83	83

Practice questions

In May 2016, Northampton bakery Oliver Adams Ltd was forced to close nine shops, two of which were 'losing money hand over fist'. More than 20 people were made redundant. The 50-year-old business was first hit by a failed attempt at expansion. It bought two bakery chains in Birmingham that eventually had to be closed down. That, in turn, meant the central Oliver Adams bakery was underused, causing losses. Then, in 2015 and 2016, the supermarket price war saw bread prices fall by 20 per cent. Independent bakeries such as Oliver Adams suffered.

To resolve the company's cash problems, suppliers agreed to accept losses in the sums owed to them by Oliver Adams. The deal allowed Adams to keep going, saving 200 jobs. The company and its workers should feel very grateful towards the suppliers.

Total: 20 marks

1 Outline one possible explanation of why Oliver Adams faced such a cash flow crisis. (2)

2 Outline how the cash problems at Oliver Adams might have been helped if the business had a large enough overdraft facility. (2)

3 Define the term 'losses'. (1)

4 Outline one reason why closing more shops might make the company's problems worse. (2)

5 Define the term 'suppliers'. (1)

6 Evaluate whether clearing this cash flow crisis will enable Oliver Adams to become successful again. You should use the information above as well as your knowledge of business. (12)

17 Cash flow forecasts

Cash flow is the difference between the flows of cash into and out of a business over a period of time. For example, if a company starts up by spending £20,000 of cash on premises and stock in its first month, but receives only £1,000 from sales to customers, its month 1 cash flow is *minus £19,000*.

Cash flow forecasting means predicting the future flows of cash into and out of the business bank account. In effect, it means forecasting what the bank balance will look like at the end of each month. A cash flow forecast will usually be for a 12-month period. Table 17.1 shows the forecast cash flow for the first six months of a brand new nightclub started with £250,000 of capital.

The forecast is based on some key points:
- Building work finished by the end of September, so customers could start coming in October.
- A launch party brings the publicity and customers needed for success.
- Costs prove as expected, but still the business has to dip into the overdraft in September.

> The most important word in the world of money is cash flow.
>
> *Robert Kiyosaki*, author of *Rich Dad Poor Dad*

Successful cash flow forecasts require:
- accurate prediction of monthly sales revenues
- accurate prediction of when customers will pay for the goods they have bought
- careful allowance for operating costs and the timing of payments
- careful allowance for other flows of cash, such as cash outflows when buying land, and inflows from raising additional capital, perhaps from selling shares.

This level of accuracy is very hard to achieve, especially for new, small firms. This is a key reason why the failure rate is so high among new firms. If cash flow proves much worse than the forecast, banks can be unforgiving. If a firm enters a period of **negative cash flow** without having discussed it with the bank, the consequences can be serious. If

Table 17.1 Forecast cash flow for a new nightclub

Figures in £000s	August	September	October	November	December	January
Opening balance	250	65	−10	0	5	35
Cash inflows	0	0	85	65	115	55
Cash outflows	185	75	75	60	85	60
Net cash flow	−185	−75	10	5	30	−5
Closing balance	65	−10	0	5	35	30

a bank loses confidence in a client, it can insist on the overdraft being repaid within 24 hours. This is likely to make it impossible for the business to continue trading.

> The three most important things you need to measure in a business are customer satisfaction, employee satisfaction, and cash flow.
>
> *Jack Welch, former chief executive of General Electric*

The importance of cash flow forecasts

Forecasting cash inflows and outflows is always important, especially for three types of business:

◆ new firms
◆ fast-growing firms
◆ firms with erratic sales (for example, a firework factory that only really brings in cash in October and November – how will it pay its bills from January to August?).

A fireworks factory may only really bring in cash in October and November

Negative cash flow

When cash outflows are greater than inflows, the result is negative cash flow. In other words, the firm is operating in the red. This is sustainable for a few weeks or months, as long as the firm has an overdraft facility or other sources of capital. Ideally, though, the business should act to improve its cash flow.

There are many ways a firm can act to improve its cash position:

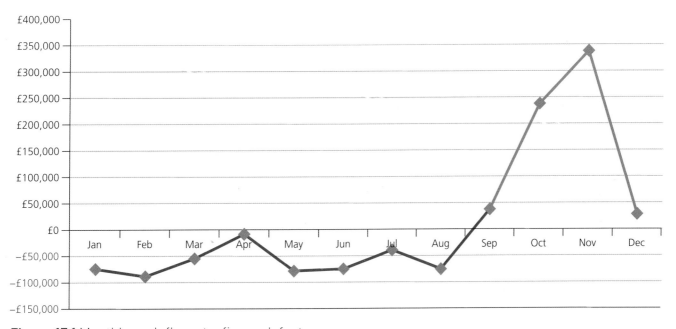

Figure 17.1 Monthly cash flow at a firework factory

1 Cut stock levels: that is, reduce the money the business has tied up in stocks of materials or finished goods. If a firm reduces its orders to suppliers, stocks will steadily fall and so too will the amount of cash tied up. A £40,000 reduction in the levels of stock being held will place £40,000 in the firm's bank account.

2 Increase credit from suppliers: that is, take a longer period before paying the companies that have supplied you with goods. This delays your cash outflows, which will improve the cash flow.

3 Reduce credit to customers: by giving customers less time to pay, you will get your cash more quickly. This may cause some problems if customers decide to go to someone else with longer credit terms. Overall, though, it may be better to deal with a few good payers than with some who take ages to pay.

Talking point

What has been your own worst-ever cash flow difficulty? Did you solve it? If yes, how?

Worked example: cash flow forecasts

1 There are ten gaps in this cash flow forecast, shown by letters A to J. Think about the numbers that should fill each gap, then check against the answer shown below.

Table 17.2 Cash flow forecast (incomplete)

Figures in £000s	January	February	March	April	May	June
Opening balance	50	30	70	E	100	J
Cash inflows	140	B	240	F	210	240
Cash outflows	160	180	D	220	220	220
Net cash flow	–20	40	60	–30	H	20
Closing balance	A	C	130	G	I	110

Answers and brief explanations are given in Table 17.3.

Table 17.3 Cash flow forecast (complete)

Letter	Month	Answer (in £000s)	Explanation
A	January	30	There was 50 in the bank at the start of the month, but the month's –20 net cash flow pulled the bank balance down to 30
B	February	220	Net cash = cash in – cash out 40 = ? – 180 Answer = 220
C	February	70	Closing balance = opening balance + net cash Closing balance = 30 + 40 = 70
D	March	180	Cash in – cash out = net cash 240 – ? = 60 Answer = 180
E	April	130	As March ended with 130, April must start with 130

Letter	Month	Answer (in £000s)	Explanation
F	April	190	Cash in – cash out = net cash ? – 220 = –30 Answer = 190
G	April	100	Closing balance = opening balance + net cash Closing balance = 130 + –30 = 100
H	May	(10)	Cash in –cash out = net cash 210 –220 = –10
I	May	90	Closing balance = opening balance + net cash Closing balance = 100 + –10 = 90
J	June	90	As May ended with 90, April must start with 90

Talking point

Use Table 17.1 on page 80 to consider how worried a business should be if its latest month's cash flow is in the red.

● Drawing the right conclusions

Careful cash flow forecasting is the single most important way to keep a bank manager's confidence. That, in turn, makes it easier and cheaper to borrow extra cash when the business needs it. The word 'careful' implies cautious. In other words, the bank manager will be impressed if a business keeps its forecasts of cash inflow quite low while expecting the worst of cash outflows. If the cash position turns out a little better than expected, who could object?

Revision essentials

Cash flow forecast: estimating the likely flows of cash over the coming months and, therefore, the overall state of one's bank balance.

Closing balance: the amount of cash left in the bank at the end of the month.

Negative cash flow: when cash outflows are greater than cash inflows.

Net cash flow: cash in minus cash out over the course of a month.

Opening balance: the amount of cash in the bank at the start of the month.

End of chapter exercises

1 Give two benefits of cash flow forecasting for a new, small firm.

2 Explain how the cash position of a clothes shop would be affected by having a '50 per cent off today!' sale.

3 A small hairdressing business decides to expand by opening up a second salon on the other side of town. Explain the probable effect of this on the cash flow of the business.

4 Explain in your own words why it is sensible to forecast cash flows cautiously.

Practice questions

In July 2016 upmarket grocery chain Waitrose announced that it would start paying its smallest suppliers within seven days. This would help 600 small suppliers, each of which sells a maximum of £100,000 of goods a year to Waitrose. Waitrose claimed that it was part of its commitment to ethical trading. Sceptics pointed out that Tesco did exactly the same, earlier in the year, and that 600 lots of £100,000 represented no more than one per cent of Waitrose purchases.

Waitrose pays its smallest suppliers within 7 days

Nevertheless, for year-old Oppo (a manufacturer of expensive, sugar-free ice cream) the Waitrose decision was extremely welcome. With sales booming and cash flow under strain, speedier payments from a major customer would be more than welcome.

Total: 15 marks

1 Define the term 'cash flow'. (1)

2 Outline one effect of speedier supplier payments on Waitrose's own cash flow position. (2)

3 Evaluate whether Waitrose was right to make this gesture to 600 of its smallest suppliers. You should use the information above as well as your knowledge of business. (12)

18 Sources of small business finance

When raising finance there are three vital questions to ask:

1 How secure is the source? Capital raised by selling shares is kept within the business permanently, so it is 100 per cent secure. Bank overdrafts, by contrast, can be cancelled at any time, allowing the bank to demand its money back within 24 hours.

2 How expensive is the source? Capital can be expensive to obtain when starting a business because investors want high rewards to balance against the risk of possibly losing the money they have invested.

3 Is enough being raised? Because capital is hard to raise and expensive to manage, many businesses raise just enough to cover their expected needs. Unfortunately, it is hard to anticipate all possible problems in starting up and running a business, so it is wise to obtain at least 25 per cent more finance than seems necessary. This provides a safety net.

● Short- and long-term finance

When raising finance, the first question to ask is about the timing of the cash requirement. Is the finance needed for a few weeks or for several years? If a business wants to buy a ten-year lease on a shop, there is clearly a need for ten years of financing. Therefore, it would be wrong to finance this via an overdraft, which is a useful but expensive way of borrowing money in the short term.

The rule is simple: short-term needs require short-term finance; long-term needs require long-term finance.

Long-term finance can be used to:
◆ provide start-up capital to finance the business for its whole life span
◆ finance the purchase of assets with a long life, such as property and buildings
◆ provide capital for expansion, such as building a new, bigger factory or buying up another business.

Short-term finance can be used to:
◆ get through periods when cash flow is poor for seasonal reasons (for example, a seaside hotel during the winter)
◆ bridge gaps when large customers delay payment, leaving no cash coming in to pay the bills
◆ provide the extra cash needed when a sudden, rush order requires a large sum to buy raw materials and pay overtime wages.

Short-term finance options help overcome situations where extra cash is suddenly needed

Sources of long-term finance

Personal savings

Most new businesses are financed mainly from the personal savings of the owners. This is usually necessary because outside shareholders and **venture capital** houses will only invest if they see that the owners are willing to put their own money at risk. Banks also like to see that the owners have been planning for years, as evidenced by regular saving. No one wants to risk their money on someone else's sudden whim.

Share capital

Ordinary shares give the buyer part-ownership of the business. If you buy 100 shares in a firm that has a total of 1,000 shares, you own ten per cent of the business. This gives you voting rights at the annual general meeting and entitles you to ten per cent of any **dividends** paid from the firm's profits.

For the business, **share capital** has two key benefits:

1 The business has the capital permanently. If shareholders want to cash in their shares, they can only do so by finding someone else to buy them (usually through the stock market); they cannot get their money back from the company.

2 In a bad year no dividends need to be paid. While interest payments to banks must be paid no matter what, shareholders are not promised a dividend payment every year. So, if the firm cannot afford to pay dividends, it need not do so. This makes share capital a safer source of finance than bank loans.

Drawbacks to businesses of share capital are:

◆ If lots of shares are issued, ownership gets spread thinly among many shareholders; this dilutes the power of the founders of the business. The key to retaining control is to keep hold of more than 50 per cent of the shares.

◆ If the business is listed on the stock exchange it becomes vulnerable to takeover bids. This might affect decision making within the firm, for example forcing the whole business to be greedier

for profit than would otherwise be the case (because high profits mean a high share price, making the business expensive to take over).

Loans

Loans are usually obtained from a bank. They may be in the form of a mortgage for as long as 20 years, or a bank loan for five to eight years. The key features of loan capital are:

◆ Interest payments must be paid on time or there is a risk of being taken to court and perhaps being closed down.

◆ Almost all loans are secured against the assets the firm owns; failure to pay means losing an asset, such as buildings, shops or lorries.

If a loan isn't repaid, assets can be repossessed

◆ The interest charges may be fixed or variable. Some firms like fixed rates (for example, seven per cent a year fixed for the five-year life of the loan); others prefer variable rates.

> Neither a borrower nor a lender be; for loan doth oft lose both itself and friend.
>
> *William Shakespeare*

Venture capital

This is a combination of share and loan capital. Providers of venture capital will take risks as long as they can share in the rewards. Therefore, they want a share stake in the business, often in addition to offering a loan. For a young or growing firm, a venture capital company is more likely to provide finance than a large high street bank.

Retained profit

Over 60 per cent of all funds for business expansion come from the profits made by firms. This is the ideal source of capital as it does not require the payment of interest charges or dividends. Well-run businesses fund as much of their capital needs as possible from the profits they make from their regular trading.

Crowdfunding

Crowdfunding means getting investment from a wide range of small investors, each paying for their shares online. This works perfectly for business ideas that are too risky for banks but interesting enough to attract ordinary people who may be investing for the first time. As Figure 18.1 shows, small firms are falling out of love with banks and banking.

Advantages to crowdfunding:

◆ Acts as a mixture of financing and market research: if investors aren't attracted to invest, perhaps the business idea isn't strong or distinctive enough (in which case the failure to finance the start-up may be a blessing in disguise).
◆ Provides an opportunity for penniless but talented people to achieve their dream start-up.

Drawbacks to crowdfunding:

◆ Crowdfunding works best when investors like the idea of the business; it works less well when the business is less interesting, such as street cleaning.
◆ Start-ups using the best-known crowdfunding site (Kickstarter) have only a 33 per cent chance of reaching their target rate of funding – two out of every three are disappointed. In the case of other crowdfunding sites, the success rate for new small companies can be as low as three per cent.

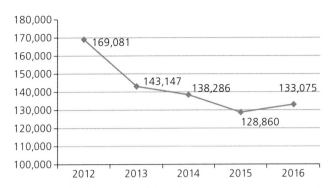

Figure 18.1 New small business accounts opened by UK banks, 2012–16 (Source: BBA, data for Q1 only)

● Sources of short-term finance

Bank overdraft

This is the most common form of finance. It must be understood in two parts. First, the bank grants the business (or individual) an overdraft facility, for example of £5,000. This provides the right to keep spending until the bank account is £5,000 in the red. The actual overdraft level is likely to vary day by day, and even hour by hour, as customers pay up or staff salaries are paid out.

Key features of a bank overdraft are:

◆ Variable interest rate: the cost of borrowing money will change if UK interest rates change, which adds a degree of uncertainty to small business plans.
◆ Flexibility: instead of having a £5,000 bank loan, requiring payments each month based on the whole sum, a £5,000 overdraft facility need only be dipped into occasionally. So, if a firm only needs to borrow money for one day, it will pay 1/365th of the annual interest rate.
◆ The bank can demand full repayment of an overdraft within 24 hours. Many firms that collapse financially were finished off by banks that make this demand.

> When you combine ignorance and debt, you get some pretty interesting results.
> *Warren Buffett, American business magnate and investor*

Trade credit

Small firms rely hugely on good relationships with their suppliers. Big companies can bully their way to get what they want from suppliers; small firms have to be nice or clever. If a supplier knows and trusts a customer, it may be willing to help when the customer is in need. A small clothes shop may be able to persuade Stella McCartney to keep supplying clothes even though earlier bills have not been paid. Getting a longer credit period is an effective way to raise short-term finance.

For small business start-ups, though, it is often impossible to obtain credit at the start. Suppliers demand to be paid cash in advance or on delivery. After all, they do not know whether you will be among the 30 per cent of firms that fail to survive their first year.

● Drawing the right conclusions

When deciding how to raise capital, identify how much you need and how long you need it for. Broadly, there are three options:

1 loan capital

2 share capital

3 internal sources, such as reinvesting the profit the firm is making.

Most experts would then advise balancing out the capital; in other words, not relying too much on share capital and not too much on loans.

Revision essentials

Crowdfunding: raising capital online from many small investors (but not through the stock market).

Dividends: payments made to shareholders from the company's yearly profits. The directors of the company decide how large a dividend payment to make; in a bad year they can decide on zero.

Retained profit: profit kept within the business (not paid out in dividends); this is the best source of finance for expansion.

Share capital: raising finance by selling part-ownership in the business. Shareholders have the right to question the directors and to receive part of the yearly profits.

Trade credit: when a supplier provides goods but is willing to wait to be paid – for perhaps up to three months. This helps with cash flow.

Venture capital: a combination of share capital and loan capital, provided by an investor willing to take a chance on the success of a small to medium-sized business.

End of chapter exercises

1 Explain why the founder of a business is likely to care about keeping 51 per cent of the business' share capital.

2 Identify whether the following situations require short- or long-term finance.

 (a) A toy shop buying extra stock for the Christmas period.

 (b) Buying land nearby in case it is needed for expansion.

 (c) Redecorating your restaurant.

 (d) Buying a new company BMW for the managing director.

3 Why is retained profit the ideal source of capital to finance growth?

4 Outline two possible advantages to an investor of buying shares in a business rather than lending it money.

5 Explain the difference between an overdraft and an overdraft facility.

Practice questions

Three years ago a young mum, Donna Morgan, started up her own business called Baby Suds. She invested £15,000 of her savings. A family member put in a further £30,000, taking 50 per cent ownership. The business idea was a range of affordable, fun children's shampoos that are kind to the skin. They managed to find a manufacturer who could produce the right products. Their eventual product line-up was:

- Baby Suds Pineapple Shampoo and Detangler
- Baby Suds Tangerine Hair and Body Wash
- Baby Suds Banana Shampoo and Conditioner
- Baby Suds 'Kind to Eyes' Baby Bath

After an unsuccessful meeting with Asda, Waitrose proved much more enthusiastic and ordered 200,000 bottles. This required £40,000 of capital to pay the manufacturer before the bottles could be delivered to the supermarket. The business could (just) afford this but, when sales took off, Waitrose placed a further huge order that made extra finance necessary. Morgan tried to sell more shares for £125,000, but eventually borrowed the money needed.

With just 15p of profit per bottle, the business required sales of at least 500,000 to cover its yearly fixed costs. In fact, by the end of its first year Baby Suds had made a profit of £61,000. With many other supermarkets queuing up to buy its children's shampoos, the business appeared to have succeeded.

Total: 20 marks

1 Outline one possible reason why the founders only used share capital to finance the start-up of Baby Suds. (2)

2 The manufacturer who produced the shampoos required to be paid in advance. Outline why it may not have been willing to give Baby Suds any trade credit. (2)

3 Given the information about the manufacturing costs of producing 200,000 bottles, calculate the cost per bottle to Baby Suds. (2)

4 Given the 15p profit per bottle, calculate Baby Suds' selling price to Waitrose. (2)

5 Evaluate whether an overdraft would be the best way to finance any further growth at Baby Suds. You should use your knowledge of the case study above as well as your knowledge of business. (12)

Exam-style questions on Topic 1.3

Don't rush; check your answers carefully.

1 The table below shows the cash flow for a small business. Work out the figures, A and B, missing from the table. (2)

	January (£)	February (£)
Receipts	7,200	8,000
Raw materials	1,400	1,600
Fixed costs	3,000	7,000
Total payments	4,400	8,600
Net cash flow	**A**	−600
Opening balance	400	**B**
Closing balance	3,200	2,600

2 Study this bar chart for XQ Ltd showing the total cost of producing 1,000 units. Calculate XQ Ltd's variable cost per unit. (2)

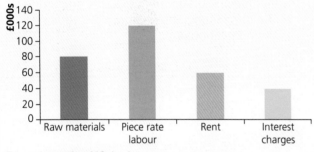

Bar chart for XQ Ltd

3 Which **one** of the following only lists long-term sources of finance?. (1)

(a) Share capital, credit from suppliers and venture capital.

(b) Personal savings, loans and crowdfunding.

(c) Bank loan, retained profit and bank overdraft.

(d) Overdraft, trade credit and crowdfunding.

4 Which **two** of the following would be businesslike objectives for starting a socially minded sports club? (2)

(a) To gain a sense of achievement by creating something to be proud of.

(b) To build a business strong enough to be sold for a lot of money.

(c) To break even within the first two years.

(d) To find a way to franchise the business.

(e) To make the cumulative cash position of the club as high as possible.

Questions 5 and 6 are based on this cash flow forecast for a swimwear producer.

All figures in £000s	April	May	June	July	August	September
Cash at start of month	150	250	360	490	520	520
Cash inflow	400	540	600	**ii.**	620	550
Purchases	120	170	200	290	270	230
Other running costs	180	260	270	360	350	340
Total monthly outflow	300	430	470	650	620	570
Net cash flow	**i.**	110	130	30	0	(20)
Accumulated cash flow	250	360	490	520	520	**iii.**

5 Which **one** of the following gives the correct answer for all three missing numbers (all in £000s)? (3)

(a) i. 100, ii. 600, iii. 540

(b) i. −100, ii. 620, iii. 520

(c) i. 100, ii. 680, iii. 500

(d) i. −100, ii. 620, iii. 500

6 Which **two** of the following might explain why cash outflow is forecast to be so high in July and August? (1)

(a) Because of exceptionally high profit levels expected in those months.

(b) The business may be expecting to buy a lot of stock in those months.

(c) The company may intend to cut back on its advertising in those months.

(d) The managers may intend to pay its suppliers more quickly from August.

(e) The company may be intending to bring in big bank loans in those months.

7 Bejax & Co makes kettles. Monthly sales are 5,000 units. Each one has a variable cost of £8 and they are sold to shops for £12. The fixed costs per month of running Bejax are £8,000. Which **one** of the following gives the monthly profit made by Bejax? (1)

(a) £12,000

(b) £60,000

(c) £20,000

(d) £52,000

8 Calculate the net cash flow achieved by Hobart Ltd in the three months shown in the bar chart below. (2)

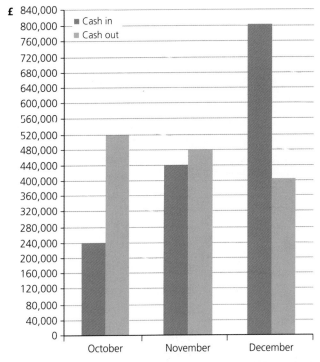

Net cash flow achieved by Hobart Ltd

Now try this discussion question.

9 Discuss the importance of cash flow to a growing young business. (6)

19 Ownership and liability

As many as half of all new businesses close down within three years. All business failures are painful, but there is a big difference between a company going into liquidation and an individual being made **bankrupt**.

When a company goes under, an independent accountant is appointed to try to raise as much cash as possible to repay the firm's debts. If there is a shortfall, the company's owners (the shareholders) do not have to repay the debts. The losses of the shareholders are restricted to the money they invested in the business. This is known as **limited liability**. By investing in shares, they took a risk, but their gamble can only cost them the amount they invested, not a penny more. Their liability is limited.

> Capitalism without bankruptcy is like Christianity without hell.
>
> *Frank Borman, astronaut*

Unpaid business debts could lead to the owner losing his possessions as part of bankruptcy proceedings

By contrast, if the business had **unlimited liability**, financial disaster for the business will become a financial disaster for the owner or owners. Unpaid business debts could lead to the owner(s) losing their house, car and other possessions as part of bankruptcy proceedings. Yet this situation is completely unnecessary, as long as a business is run as a limited company. It is odd, then, that in 2015 there were twice as many sole traders (with unlimited liability) as there were companies (with limited liability), as shown in Figure 19.1.

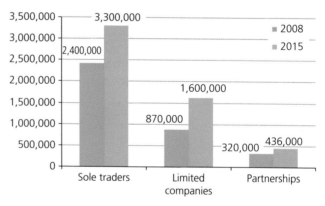

Figure 19.1 Growth in different types of businesses in England and Wales, 2008–15 (Source: ONS)

Limited liability

To achieve limited liability, a business must be started up as a company. This requires an application to Companies House and a payment of around £150. Once the right forms have been filled in, the business becomes a company. Small limited companies must put the letters 'Ltd' at the end of the company name. These businesses have **private limited company** status.

The fee of £150 is a small sum to pay for improved financial security. Other benefits from becoming a limited company include:

♦ A company can have share capital (perhaps 100 £1 shares), which makes it easy to divide up the ownership between different investors. As long as the company's founder keeps hold of 51 per cent of the shares, he or she still has total control.

♦ If the business needs to raise more capital, it is quite easy to issue more shares for sale to other investors.

♦ The business continues to exist even if the founder of the business dies. The company develops a life of its own.

♦ Due to limited liability, the owners/shareholders can be bold about investing in the future of the business. If a bold move goes wrong, the business may suffer but individual shareholders are not liable for the debts.

Given the advantages of limited liability, it is amazing that most businesses in the UK do not bother to turn into limited companies. Presumably the owners believe either that nothing can possibly go wrong, or that they will be able to cope financially even if something does go wrong. The clearest reason to avoid limited liability is that companies need to have their accounts drawn up by a qualified accountant. This means an annual cost of perhaps £1,500 to be paid to an accountant.

> **Talking point**
>
> Can it ever be wise for a business owner to sell a 50.1 per cent share in the business that they founded?

● Unlimited liability

Anybody can start a business in the UK today. All that is required is to tell HMRC (Her Majesty's Revenue and Customs – the tax people). In few countries of the world is it so easy to start up. You would probably need a bank account, but this is unlikely to be a problem unless you are trying to borrow large sums from a bank.

However, unless the entrepreneur forms a limited company, the business and the person are one and the same for tax and legal purposes. This is why failure by the business leaves the entrepreneur liable in full for any debts.

A person running her or his own business without forming a company is called a **sole trader**. It is also possible to join with others in a partnership. Sole traders and partnerships both have unlimited liability.

The only logical reason for ignoring limited liability (forming a company) is if there is no realistic possibility of debts building up. For example, if the business is a market stall, and goods are bought for cash in the morning and sold out by the afternoon, it is hard to see how debts could be built up. So why bother with the cost and paperwork involved in setting up a limited company?

A person running their own business without forming a company is called a sole trader

● Drawing the right conclusions

Everyone starting a business should think seriously about forming a company and, therefore, having limited liability. This is especially important if money is being borrowed to finance the business. Individuals with unlimited liability should not take risks with borrowing or with credit.

Table 19.1 Advantages and disadvantages of the three types of business for start-up

	Advantages	Disadvantages
Sole trader	Can start trading immediately Have 100 per cent control	Unlimited (personal) liability Have 100 per cent responsibility for the business, making holidays a problem
Partnership	Liability is spread between the partners Complementary skills may enhance the business	Unlimited liability, including for business debts caused by partner There may be clashes as one partner seeks overall control
Limited company	Limited liability Can sell shares to outside investors	Risk of losing control Cost of starting up and cost of getting accounts audited every year

Revision essentials

Bankrupt: when an individual is unable to pay their debts, even after all personal assets have been sold for cash.

Limited liability: restricting the losses suffered by owners/shareholders to the sum they invested in the business.

Private limited company: a small family business in which shareholders enjoy limited liability.

Sole trader: a business run by one person; that person has unlimited liability for any business debts.

Unlimited liability: treating the business and the individual owner as inseparable, therefore making the individual responsible for all the debts of a failed business.

End of chapter exercises

1 Why might an entrepreneur be reluctant to sell more than 50 per cent of the shares in their business?

2 Use Figure 19.1 on page 92 to calculate the percentage of businesses in England and Wales that had unlimited liability in 2015.

3 (a) Use Figure 19.1 on page 92 to calculate the percentage growth in limited companies between 2008 and 2015.

(b) Outline one possible reason for this growth in the number of companies in England and Wales.

4 Explain why it is easier to make bold business decisions if your business is a limited company than if you are a sole trader with unlimited liability.

5 K.V. Builders and Sons is an unlimited liability business that builds houses. It employs five people and borrows up to £150,000 to finance each job. Explain two reasons why it should form a company and therefore provide limited liability to its owners.

Practice questions

Jamie Oliver hasn't just done well making TV programmes and selling cookery books, he has also built a business empire. However, in June 2016 the Keystone Group – owner of the Jamie's Italian franchise in Australia – collapsed. That came two years after Jamie had to close down three of his four Union Jacks restaurants in the UK. In the same year (2014), the holding company for his whole restaurant empire (Jamie Oliver Holdings Ltd) made a loss of £12.8 million. Total revenue that year was £39.7 million. This was despite the continued expansion of Jamie's Italian in the UK.

Jamie Oliver's businesses have suffered financially

No one doubts Jamie Oliver's passion for food, but running restaurants is about management as much as cooking. Even Jamie's Italian has problems of consistency, as shown in the customer ratings in Table 19.2.

In 2015, there were stories about Jamie selling his restaurant empire. He probably should.

Table 19.2 TripAdvisor ratings for Jamie's Italian, 23 July 2016

	TripAdvisor rating	Two most recent ratings and comments
Jamie's Italian, Aberdeen	191st out of 488 restaurants in Aberdeen	2/5 'Average food, really poor service' 3/5 'Enjoyable'
Jamie's Italian, City of London	4,230th of 17,073 restaurants in London	3/5 'Lunch' 4/5 'Good service, nice atmosphere, above average food'
Jamie's Italian, Bristol	356th of 1,428 restaurants in Bristol	3/5 'Good Italian, but ...' 3/5 'Vegan pasta option, it's OK'

Total: 20 marks

1 Outline what 'Ltd' means in Jamie Oliver Holdings Ltd. (2)
2 Outline why it makes sense for a business such as Jamie Oliver Holdings Ltd to have limited liability. (2)
3 Calculate total costs for Jamie Oliver Holdings Ltd in 2014. (2)
4 Outline one way in which Jamie Oliver Holdings Ltd might be affected by the collapse of the owner of the Jamie's Italian brand in Australia. (2)
5 Evaluate the importance to a business such as Jamie's Italian of online customer ratings. You should use the information given above as well as your knowledge of business. (12)

20 Franchising

When you have set up a business successfully in one location, the race is on to do the same elsewhere. If you do not 'copy' your idea, others will. Yet how can a small business quickly clone its own idea, many times over? It is hard to start up one business outlet, let alone lots of them.

One answer to this problem is **franchising**. This means selling the rights to use a business idea and methods in a specific location or area. The person or business buying the rights therefore has to do all the work to make it a success. The franchise owner must ensure they select someone who will do a good job – and therefore not damage the image of their business.

There is no better example of this than the Subway chain of sandwich shops. It was started in 1965 in America by 17-year-old Fred deLuca who borrowed $1000 and set up a single outlet. Its success led him to open others, but he saw much bigger prospects, so started selling franchises in 1974. By 2016 there were 45,000 Subway outlets worldwide. The first Subway store came to the UK in 1996 and there are now more than 2,000. The chain is the UK's biggest seller of sandwiches, pushing Tesco into the number two position. In fact, in 2015 and 2016 Subway sales in the USA struggled due to increasing competition, but in the UK they still seem to be growing.

What's in it for the franchise owner?

Expanding a business is expensive and can be difficult. Opening stores requires a large amount of capital. For example, a Burger King store typically costs £500,000. Selling franchises brings money in, instead of paying money out, and eliminates the need to employ huge numbers of managers to check up on every aspect of the store openings. The main benefits of expanding by selling franchises include:

- A firm can expand its sales quickly; this helps fill gaps that other businesses will fill if the firm does not get there first.
- Franchise owners not only sell a franchise, but also receive a share of all future sales. Subway (the franchise owner) receives 8 per cent of the sales revenue of all 45,000 stores; in addition, every store must buy their supplies from Subway, so the central company makes profits there too.
- The franchise owner can concentrate on developing new products and services, and on good marketing and advertising; this was the basis of McDonald's' huge success for many years.

Talking point

What might the advantages and disadvantages be for Tesco if they franchised out their Tesco Express (local) stores?

Starting up a franchise operation

Starting a business from scratch requires a wide range of skills. Anyone can have a bright idea; and many people are good at one particular thing – cooking, for example. Yet simply being a good cook is not enough to run a successful restaurant. You need to:

- identify a menu and an image that customers want
- work out how to run the operation efficiently
- find suitable suppliers
- market the business effectively.

It is not surprising that half of all new restaurants close within three years.

A franchise start-up takes on the brand, products and methods used by other outlets

Benefits of franchising

The key benefits of franchising (buying into a franchise) include:

◆ The franchise operation not only buys its part of an image (for example, McDonald's or BSM – the British School of Motoring), but also a method for doing things (for example, the equipment for making a milkshake, plus the instructions on how to make it, clean the equipment, and so on).

◆ An individual outlet could never afford image-building TV advertising; being part of Subway or McDonald's, for example, enables the franchise operation to benefit from major marketing campaigns.

◆ As the products and methods of working have been pre-tested, the chance of mistakes is lower; therefore the failure rate of franchise start-ups is also lower. This means that banks are much more willing to lend to a franchise start-up than a brand new, independent operation.

> There are a lot of cowboys about.
>
> *Sir Bernard Ingham, former president of the British Franchise Association*

Being part of a franchise may enable you to benefit from major marketing campaigns

Drawbacks of franchising

Franchising is a halfway house towards running your own independent business. When buying into a franchise the buyer is bound by the rules of the franchise owner. This might be very frustrating for an experienced businessperson who wants to be their own boss. The rules may force them to offer products that sell well nationally, but not locally. Among the other possible drawbacks are:

◆ Royalty payments (fees to the franchise owner) of as much as 8 per cent of revenue are common. A typical franchise outlet might have an annual sales figure of about £300,000, so an annual

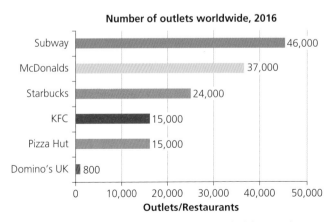

Number of outlets worldwide, 2016

Subway	46,000
McDonalds	37,000
Starbucks	24,000
KFC	15,000
Pizza Hut	15,000
Domino's UK	800

Outlets/Restaurants

Figure 20.1 Number of outlets worldwide: major catering franchises 2016 (Sources: company websites and press releases)

payment of £24,000 is being made. That is no problem when things are going well, but in 2015 and 2016 sales at US Subway outlets fell by 10 per cent. It would be very annoying to pay large **royalties** when sales and profits are falling.

◆ Not all franchises are good ones. In September 2014, six *G-Star* franchise stores were closed, with high rents thought to be the direct cause. Fashion trade magazine *Drapers* was told: 'There just isn't enough of a margin in a franchise store to keep up with the massive rents they are being charged.'

Talking point

If you decided to start a business, would you prefer to be independent or buy into a franchise?

● Drawing the right conclusions

As with any other business opportunity, buying a franchise carries major risks. The buyer needs to check the financial records of the franchise owner and talk to existing franchisees to find out whether they are happy with the service they are getting for their royalty payments. Without doubt, though, buying a good franchise is one of the best ways to start your own business. Having built up business experience running a franchise, an **entrepreneur** could try to start up a completely independent business later on.

Revision essentials

Franchising paying a franchise owner for the right to use an established business name, branding and business methods.

Royalties percentage of the sales revenue to be paid to the overall franchise owner.

Entrepreneur a person who sets up a business and takes on financial risks in the hope of profit.

End of chapter exercises

1 Give two reasons why it is hard to develop a business rapidly.

2 Look at Figure 20.1 on page 97. Domino's UK is growing rapidly, but from a low base. By how many times must it increase its number of outlets to catch up with Subway?

3 Explain one advantage and one disadvantage of running a local Subway franchise compared with running an independent sandwich shop.

4 Explain why a bank might be more willing to lend money to someone opening a franchise outlet than someone opening a fully independent business.

5 Read the following extract. Outline two reasons for and two reasons against Ian deciding to buy a franchise.

Ian Jones had spent ten frustrating years as a journalist, working on a shipping magazine. He had been saving for several years to start his own business. He had £45,000 in the bank and a burning desire to prove to his wife and parents that he could be a financial success. Ian loved eating out, and wanted to start a bar/restaurant. Now he had to decide whether or not to buy into a franchise operation such as Domino's, or start something completely independently. He knew that, if necessary, he could borrow up to £100,000 on the value of the house he owned jointly with his wife.

6 Recommend whether he should buy a franchise or go independent. Explain your answer.

Practice questions

Snap Fitness is a US gym business that has been running since 2003, has 2,000 clubs and offers franchise opportunities in the UK. For a minimum investment of £110,000, you can set up your own gym. Snap Fitness boasts that it 'is dedicated to providing members with more value than any other health club and gives entrepreneurs world class support'. It makes a specific play of saying that the business can be run on a part-time basis and that break-even is achieved within six months.

It isn't hard to find online reports from unhappy franchise customers who say that 12 to 18 months is more realistic for striking break-even and who laugh at the idea of running the business on a part-time basis. There's also this telling phrase from one former franchise customer: 'They really don't do anything to help you succeed, except have their name, which I have found no one is familiar with anyway.' On the other hand, the company website quotes a franchise outlet in Milton Keynes saying: 'From the original build-out to learning how to sell personal training, Snap Fitness has given me the guidance and support to succeed in the fitness industry.'

(20 marks)

1 Outline one way in which an investment of £110,000 might be funded. (2)

2 Discuss the difference to a new franchise business of breaking even in 18 months compared with six months. (6)

3 Evaluate the risks and rewards that might be involved in buying a Snap Fitness franchise. You should use the information given above as well as your knowledge of business. (12)

21 Business location

Once an entrepreneur has decided a profitable opportunity exists, it is time to think about the ideal location. This is much tougher than it seems. If you buy a house, the seller only cares whether you can pay once – that is, pay the asking price. When it is business premises (a shop, say) the owner wants to know whether you'll be able to pay every month for the lifetime of the lease. That might be five to ten years. When Scoop ice cream tried to open its first outlet, it was turned down repeatedly by landlords suspicious about whether an ice cream parlour would last for one London winter – let alone five to ten of them.

It is also important to know that a complex trade-off exists between rental cost and value. Table 21.1 on the following page shows the amazing range of shop rents in London. Effectively, you need to sell 50 times more in Oxford Street than in Bermondsey to pay for the rental cost. That's overwhelmingly likely to be value for money if your shop targets tourists; but not remotely likely if you're selling groceries.

Buildings on Oxford Street in London cost a lot of money to rent

Table 21.1 Shop rental prices in London

London shop locations	Shop size (sq ft)	Annual rent (2016)	Cost per sq ft	Notes
Bermondsey	492	£12,000	£24	Residential area
Shoreditch	1,060	£50,000	£47	Close to trendy Hoxton Square
Knightsbridge	650	£128,000	£197	Nearly half the space is basement
The Strand	290	£78,000	£269	Continuous footfall from Covent Garden
Oxford Street	530	£535,000	£1,010	Basement space not included; location is opposite Selfridges

● Factors influencing business location

Proximity to market

One factor influencing location is nearness (proximity) to the market. For many businesses this is the most important factor. For a physical service such as a shop, restaurant or hotel, customer convenience will be critical to revenue. A hotel in a city centre might be able to charge £175 for a room while an identical hotel chain charges £52 for on the city outskirts. As shown in the Table 21.1, shop rents vary wildly depending on how convenient they are for shop customers.

Proximity to materials

For manufacturing businesses, nearness to materials may be more important than nearness to customers. This is especially true when the manufacturing process effectively shrinks the materials. A good example is steel making. Huge quantities of iron ore and (in many countries) coal are required to make steel. The volume of sheet steel produced is far smaller and, therefore, cheaper to transport. So, steel is made close to where the materials are mined, or close to the harbour where the supply ships arrive. Although much of the steel made in South Wales is used in car factories in the Midlands, it is more cost effective to be near the materials than near to the market.

Proximity to labour

Labour should be quite mobile, in other words able to go where the work is. If there's a job in Bristol and you live in County Durham, however, the difference in house prices (and rents) can halt the move. So, it can be sensible to locate where there are staff willing and able to work, and that have the right experience and skills. This would be particularly true for skilled work such as manufacturing construction vehicles. Locate close to the huge JCB factories in Staffordshire and you'll find people willing and able to switch to you.

Proximity to competitors

Many service businesses want a location far away from competitors – effectively being the only supplier to customers in a local area. For a corner-shop grocer or a dry cleaner, that would be perfect. For others, it is a bit more complicated. Restaurant chains such as Gourmet Burger Kitchen find it best to be on busy high streets with lots of other restaurants, that is, competitors. This is because people meet after work, have a drink and go to places where there are plenty of restaurants to choose from; they walk down the high street and make up their minds. More isolated locations may be busy on Friday and Saturday evening, but grimly empty for the rest of the week.

> Real estate is the key cost of physical retailers. That's why there's the old saw: location, location, location.
>
> *Jeff Bezos, founder of Amazon*

Nature of the business activity

To help identify which of the four factors above matters most, it is important to think about the nature of the business activity. For manufacturers, proximity to materials may be vital, whereas physical service businesses need to be near the market – the customers.

What about businesses that have no physical connection with their customers? Online services such as ASOS and Comparethemarket.com are dealt with later in the chapter, but consider also telephone call centres (which might be in South Wales or Southern India), foreign exchange dealers and the national offices of the AA and RAC. None of these need to be near to customers or materials, and it is irrelevant whether or not they're near to competitors. Nearness to labour is therefore a factor, especially nearness to labour with the right skills and at the right price. Few would doubt that Aviva's switch of call-centre jobs from Norwich and York to India was motivated by cutting wage costs.

Other business activity issues to consider include:

◆ The efficiency, reliability and cost of transport links. For example, Nissan's successful car plant in Sunderland is located close to the Port of Tyne for exporting cars to Europe. For manufacturers, the quality of access to road, rail, sea and air transport are all important.

◆ Proximity (nearness) to where the entrepreneur lived and lives. This may seem a trivial point, but Innocent Drinks was headquartered in West London because that's where the three founders lived. Innocent Drinks' current owners, Coca-Cola, are still based in Atlanta, 150 years after John Pemberton invented the drink there.

The impact of the internet on location

Where is ASOS based? As a customer, who cares? In fact the head office is in an arty part of North London

Primark has a very different approach to location compared to internet business ASOS

Table 21.2 The internet and location decisions

	E-commerce business, such as ASOS	High street retail business, such as Primark
Head office location	Can be anywhere	Can be anywhere
Product display	On a single website, allowing heavy investment in quality photos and customer interaction	In-store, therefore carrying high property and staff costs in multiple locations (and with too few design experts)
Stock range	Can keep every size and colour in stock, so customer disappointments should be rare	Space constraints in many store locations may mean restricted choice of colours and sizes
Customer services location	Can be anywhere; having a single location keeps costs down	In-store, therefore carrying high property and staff costs in multiple locations
Delivery to customer	Critical to have efficient deliveries; may be hard in crowded cities	Not a problem

while the main distribution depot is in Barnsley, Yorkshire. The head office location makes sense for employing fashion-focused staff who can keep the website looking great. The warehouse is close to the M1 motorway and in an old coal-mining area – good for cheap land and people in need of a job. All perfectly sensible, but quite different from the location decisions of a major retail competitor such as Primark.

The impact of the internet on location decisions between e-commerce and **fixed premises** can be seen in more detail in Table 21.2.

> In the future, instead of buying bananas in a grocery store, you could go pick them off a tree in a virtual jungle.
>
> *Yasuhiro Fukushima, Japanese business executive*

Making a location decision

To make a businesslike location decision, likely revenues have to be balanced against likely costs. It may seem wrong to be paying five times the rent to be at one end of the street rather than the other, but if the expensive end has the station and other busy shops, the high rent is probably money well spent.

Take the following example of two shops in the centre of Manchester, both of 950 sq ft. One is in the busy Arndale Centre, the other in relatively quiet Oldham Street. The rent in the Arndale Centre is about three times higher but should bring in double the revenue of the Oldham Street site. In this case, despite the rent being three times higher, the profit is much greater from the busier location. This will not always be the case. What is essential is that every entrepreneur should make careful estimates of revenues and costs before finally deciding on location.

Table 21.3 Revenues and costs at different locations in Manchester

	Arndale Centre, Manchester	Oldham Street, Manchester
Annual sales revenue	£600,000	£300,000
Annual rent on 950 sq ft shop	£102,000	£36,000
Other fixed costs	£56,000	£44,000
Variable costs	£360,000	£180,000
Total costs	£518,000	£260,000
Profit	£82,000	£40,000

Drawing the right conclusions

Location remains an important part of business, but e-commerce and other social factors have changed things. Pizza delivery existed before websites and apps, but e-commerce has boosted this service considerably. A pizza delivery outlet only needs to be somewhere near people – it doesn't need an expensive high street site. But other services will always need great locations, including hotels, snack bars and coffee shops. So, landlords will probably carry on being able to charge high rents.

End of chapter exercises

1 Explain what the text means by the trade-off 'between rental cost and value' on page 100.

2 The text covers four important location factors: proximity to customers, materials, employees and competitors. Explain which **one** you believe to be the most important of the four in the case of locating:

   (a) An ice cream parlour, with all ice cream made on the premises.

   (b) A new waste landfill site.

3 Explain in your own words why it might be worth paying £1,010 per square foot to be located in London's Oxford Street.

4 Table 21.3 on page 103 shows that the high-rent Arndale location yields more profit than Oldham Street. But what if the annual sales revenues at Oldham Street prove to be twice as high as forecast? The effect on profit is shown in Table 21.4.

Table 21.4 Revenues and costs at different locations in Manchester

	Arndale Centre, Manchester	Oldham Street, Manchester
Annual sales revenue	£600,000	£600,000
Annual rent on 950 sq ft shop	£102,000	£36,000
Other fixed costs	£56,000	£44,000
Variable costs	£360,000	£360,000
Total costs	£518,000	£440,000
Profit	£82,000	£160,000

   (a) Copy the figures for the Arndale Centre and work out its profit if sales revenue doubles to £1,200,000.

   (b) Explain why the doubling of sales has such a huge effect on profit at the Arndale location.

Practice questions

Inspired by the growth of craft beer sales, in 2012 Ed Taylor and Robyn Simms started producing and selling handmade soft drinks. Rhubarb soda may not sound tempting to you, but farmers' market shoppers were keen. Seeing a serious business opportunity, in 2013 Robyn gave up her salaried job to see where Square Root sodas could be taken. Premises were found in a railway arch in Dalston – at the heart of trendy East London. Nearby were important farmers' markets plus a series of independent pubs, bars and restaurants: just the places that want to offer their customers something quirky and new.

Ed and Robyn saw their target market as adults who want a natural, tangy alternative to alcohol. Both brought a fanatical approach to sourcing ingredients direct from the farm (such as that rhubarb, brought down from Yorkshire), which helps in generating good publicity. It also helps when everything is done by hand, including hand-squeezing lemons for the lemonade. In 2015, Square Root won the BBC's Food and Farming Award for Best Drinks Producer. A glance at their website (www.squarerootsoda. co.uk) in August 2016 shows several items as out-of-stock – and an advertisement for a new member of the production staff. Good signs that sales are going well.

Total: 15 marks

1 Analyse the probable reasons why Robyn and Ed located production in a railway arch in Dalston. (6)

2 Ed and Robyn are getting concerned about keeping up with demand. They see two options:

 ◆ Option 1: Follow the example of big competitor Fever-Tree and get an established soft drinks producer to manufacture Square Root sodas for them.

 ◆ Option 2: Rent a second railway arch and hire more staff to double the rate of production.

Justify which **one** of these options they should choose. (9)

22 Marketing mix

Marketing means understanding and communicating with customers so effectively that they want to buy from you. For Apple it means designing a must-have product that fits in with modern lifestyles and enhances the customer's personal image. Therefore the customer expects – and is willing to pay – a high price for the product.

The example of Apple effectively explains the marketing mix. This mix is the combination of factors used by a business to persuade customers to buy. Four factors that make up the marketing mix, usually referred to as the 4Ps:

◆ **product**
◆ **price**
◆ **promotion**
◆ **place.**

For Apple's iPhone, the product has to be the best-designed and most technologically advanced; the price has to be at the top-end of the market, confirming the product quality; the promotion is via classy advertising plus a lot of celebrity endorsement; and the place at which iPhones are sold (and serviced) should be as prestigious as possible (Apple shops).

The 4Ps affect all aspects of the iPhone

● Product

After careful market research, a firm should be able to design a product or service that meets a specific market need. This targeting is at the heart of the mix. For example, Lindor chocolates are targeted at special occasions. Having the right luxury product to appeal to the audience is then backed up by:

◆ the right price – it is more expensive than other chocolates, which helps to confirm that it is worth paying for
◆ the right place – distributed in sweetshops and grocers, but also sold at upmarket department stores
◆ the right promotion – spending most of the budget on TV advertising, even in a world dominated by social media. TV shows the uniqueness of the product and creates desire for it.

> The name of the game is new products.
>
> *Michael Shrimi, US chocolate entrepreneur*

● Price

All consumers expect value for money, so price is always important. In many cases, having a low price may be crucial to achieving high sales, for instance when selling packets of sugar or butter. At other times though, being 'cheap' may cause image problems. No one wants cheap baby food or cut-price perfume.

The ideal situation for a business is to have brands so powerful that price is not an important factor for customers. They want Nike, not just trainers; they want a Mercedes, not just a car. Consumers see both of these products as unique, and are therefore willing to pay a higher price.

Other products have to be priced in relation to others in the marketplace. Esso won't do well if it tries to price its petrol above the level of Shell or BP. Drivers buy the cheapest because they regard the different brands of petrol as the same thing.

> Cutting price is usually insanity if the competition can go as low as you can.
>
> *Michael Porter, guru to the gurus*

Promotion

This is the way a business can promote sales of its products. It lumps together methods of promoting the long-term image and sales of the business, using methods such as TV or cinema advertising, and short-term methods, such as sales promotions (for example, buy one get one free).

Most large firms are keen to use every pound spent on advertising to promote the long-term image of the product. TV and cinema advertising are especially effective at achieving this.

Talking point

What might be the key features of the marketing mix for the launch of the first ever self-driving (robotic) car?

Place

This is where (and how) the product is distributed, so that customers can get it when they want it. Mass market products usually seek as much distribution as possible. Coca-Cola uses the phrase 'an arm's length from desire'; in other words, they want such good distribution that customers should only need to stretch out an arm to get a Coke. Coca-Cola wants this (which is why there are so many vending machines) because they know that the more people see Coke, the more they buy.

For other products, the same does not apply. Chanel won't allow cut-price retailers such as Superdrug to sell its perfumes; its managers worry that cutting prices may damage the image of the brand.

Vending machines are a way to achieve large-scale distribution

Successful marketing mix

For success, a firm must make sure that its mix is co-ordinated and coherent. A stylish product aimed at a stylish market should have a high price, be promoted in stylish magazines and stocked in the most stylish shops. Similarly, a product aimed at the environmentally conscious buyer should have little advertising support, a moderate price premium and aim to be sold through a limited number of local outlets. The marketing mix puts the public face on a product or service. That face must make sense.

How the elements of the mix work together

Balancing the marketing mix based on the competitive environment

The competitive environment means the degree and closeness of competitive pressure placed on a business. For Rolls-Royce, the competitive environment is always quite calm as no other car maker in the world tries to offer a car quite like a 'roller'. For easyJet on the other hand, the competitive environment is always tough; it is squeezed by Ryanair on price and by airlines such as Lufthansa on comfort.

Between April and June 2016, Apple saw a fall in its share of global smartphone sales. It sold 7 million fewer iPhones as Samsung and China's Huawei ate into its market share. This forced Apple to think hard about its marketing mix, notably its pricing policy. Quietly it did deals with networks such as Vodafone to make it cheaper to sign up for an iPhone. So, the competitive environment matters, even for a brand as powerful as the iPhone.

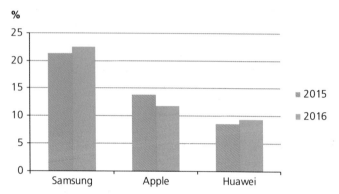

Figure 22.1 Global market share of smartphones, April to June 2015 and 2016 (Source: IDC Worldwide, 28 July 2016)

Sometimes companies need to rebalance their marketing mix because of increasing competitive pressures. While Apple did so by quietly reducing prices, cosmetics companies such as Rimmel have been switching their promotion spending towards social media. Reports from America suggest that Instagram is now the most powerful medium affecting cosmetics purchasing (all those 'selfies').

The impact of changing consumer needs on the marketing mix

A long-standing consumer trend is the need for greater convenience. Once, cooked breakfasts gave way to bowls of cereal; now the bowls of cereal have given way to breakfast bars and other on-the-go food. As consumer habits change, so must the marketing mix. Packets of cereal were bought from supermarkets, so Kellogg's developed terrific distribution links to get their brand into *place*. When demand switched from Rice Krispies to Rice Krispies cereal bars, distribution changed – with sweetshops and corner shops becoming much more important.

Other important changes in consumer needs (or wants) are outlined in Table 22.1.

Table 22.1 Changes in consumer needs and wants

Change	Effect on marketing mix
Cycling switching from a leisure activity to getting to work/daily commuting	Distribution (place) switches from bike shops in the suburbs to bike shops in city centres
The boom in UK holidaymakers going to Thailand and the South East Asia	Product development, such as Branston launching its Sweet Chilli Pickle in early 2016
Increasing consumer demand for 'free-from' foods, such as lactose-free and gluten-free	Despite food prices falling generally in 2015, 'free-from' food prices increased as suppliers took advantage of the surrounding hype

The impact of technology on the marketing mix

In July 2016, a global social phenomenon arose when Pokémon Go was launched by Nintendo. For small businesses in particular, buying Pokémon 'lures' boosted customer numbers – often significantly. So, the marketing mix was tweaked to allow for higher spending on lures. This might cut spending on traditional media, such as advertising in the local paper, or might lead to a boost in the overall budget for marketing as companies seized the short-term opportunity created by the Pokémon craze.

Table 22.2 Other impacts of technology on the marketing mix

Changing technology	Effect on marketing mix
The rise of m-commerce (mobile commerce): e-commerce on-the-go via apps rather than websites	Promotional offers have to be simpler and clearer so that they can be understood quickly
Hi-tech but lighter materials have made airplanes much more fuel-efficient and less polluting than in the past	There's an opportunity for flight prices to be cut, especially on long-haul flights

Revision essentials

Place: how and where the supplier is going to get the product or service to the consumer; it includes selling products to retailers and getting the products displayed in prominent positions.

Price: setting the price that retailers must pay, which in turn affects the consumer price.

Product: targeting customers with a product that has the right blend of functional and aesthetic benefits without being too expensive to produce.

Promotion: within the 4Ps promotion means all the methods that a business uses to persuade customers to buy, for example branding, packaging, advertising to boost the long-term image of the product and short-term offers.

End of chapter exercises

1 Why is it important for a business to target a specific customer need?

2 Outline the marketing mix used by one of the following:

(a) Cadbury's Creme Eggs

(b) Tesco stores

(c) Ryanair.

3 Why might 'buy one get one free' be a poor way to boost the long-term image and sales of a brand?

4 Explain one argument for, and one against, Chanel's attempt to stop Superdrug from stocking its Chanel No. 5 perfume.

Practice questions

In early 2005, Twinings launched an 'Everyday Tea'. Before then Twinings had only focused on special teas, such as Earl Grey. Now it was going head-to-head with the big beasts: Tetley and PG Tips.

Twinings' marketing idea was to launch a tea with a comparable taste to Tetley and PG, but with a superior image backed by the 300-year-old Twinings brand. TV commercials featured the actor Stephen Fry, known for his good taste and his typical 'Englishness'. Twinings Everyday Tea sold at a 20 per cent price premium to Tetley and PG. The new product was promoted by £4.5 million spent on TV and radio advertising. The distribution was through supermarkets and grocers, plus restaurants and hotels.

The effectiveness of Twinings' marketing mix can be seen in Figure 22.2.

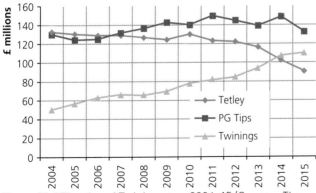

Figure 22.2 The rise of Twinings tea, 2004–15 (Source: *The Grocer*, UK market annual sales)

In August 2016, Twinings was still selling its Everyday Tea at a significant price premium to PG and Tetley, and Twinings has overtaken Tetley to become Britain's second-favourite tea brand.

Table 22.3 Comparison of tea sales (prices as at 1 August 2016)

	Tesco	Sainsbury's
Twinings Everyday Tea (100 bags)	£4.99	£3.50
Tetley tea bags (80 bags)	£2.29	£2.30
PG Tips Pyramid tea bags (80 bags)	£2.49	£2.50

Total: 20 marks

1 Define the term 'marketing mix'. (1)

2 Calculate Sainsbury's price per tea bag for Twinings and Tetley. (2)

3 Calculate the percentage extra that Twinings charges per bag compared with Tetley. (2)

4 Outline one way in which a business such as Twinings benefits from charging a price premium. (2)

5 Use Figure 22.2 to identify the year in which sales of Twinings Tea overtook sales of Tetley. (1)

6 From the data provided, evaluate the effectiveness of the marketing mix used for the launch of Twinings Everyday Tea. You should use the information given above as well as your knowledge of business. (12)

23 Business plans

A **business plan** is a document setting out the business idea and showing how it is to be financed, marketed and put into practice. It is likely to be a crucial part of an attempt to raise finance from outside sources such as a bank.

Starting a business requires a lot of different tasks to come together in a co-ordinated way at the right time. If you are opening your first restaurant, all these tasks must be completed before your opening night: building work; decoration; kitchen equipment bought and fitted; staff hired and trained; menu chosen and printed; wines chosen, delivered and wine list printed; food supplies bought; tills and credit card-reading equipment in place. For this to work without a clear plan is asking for the impossible. A business plan is therefore essential for start-up success. Yet most entrepreneurs treat a business plan as something that banks ask for; that is, something for others, not for themselves.

> Every moment spent planning saves three or four in execution.
>
> *Crawford Greenewalt, former president of Du Pont*

The role and importance of a business plan

A good plan should be persuasive to an outside investor and useful to the entrepreneur. It should explain what makes the business special and help the entrepreneur to never lose sight of what she or he is trying to achieve. Despite this, it is clear that a business that needs capital will concentrate mainly on the outside investor. This might be a bank or a venture capital investor who buys an ownership stake in the business.

The heart of the business plan should be based around competitive advantage; this means identifying the features of your own product or service that will make it succeed against competitors. This may be based on a unique idea, a better product or service, or the power of a great brand. On the other hand, a business may decide to strip a product or service down to make it possible to be the cheapest in the market. Ryanair's competitive advantage is based on being Europe's lowest-cost airline; this allows it to charge the lowest prices, yet still make a profit.

Every business plan should contain the following sections:

1 The business idea: explain it from the customer's point of view; for example, when describing smoothies, do not say 'we'll crush fruit and put it in bottles', but 'it'll provide busy people with two portions of fruit in an enjoyable, messy-free way'. If others already offer the service, you must explain what is different about your idea.

2 Business aims and objectives: is the aim to provide something of value to society (a robot that irons clothes perhaps?) or is it just to cash in on a money-making opportunity? Some investors want their money put to good use, as well as to profitable use. The company objectives should turn the broad idea into specific, measurable goals.

3 Target market: focus on market trends rather than market size, such as whether the market is growing and, if so, how rapidly. Identify the key customers within this growing market. The more narrowly they can be defined (20–25-year-old men, perhaps)

the easier it is to target them through advertising and marketing. Hugely helpful would be good quality, independent market research with a large enough sample size for the findings to be reliable.

4 Marketing plan: how do you plan to communicate with the customers you are targeting? How expensive will this be? Within this section, there should be an explanation and justification for the prices you plan to set, plus a forecast of likely sales per month for the first two years.

5 Forecast revenue, costs and profit: together these will provide an effective way to work out the break-even point and margin of safety. The revenue forecast requires research to be used to estimate likely sales. The forecast of possible costs relies on the ability to break costs down into fixed and variable. Typically a business would be looking to reach break-even within 12–18 months.

6 Cash flow forecast: even businesses that go on to make spectacular profits may start with awful cash flow problems. This is a particular problem for businesses where customer loyalty needs to be built over time, such as seaside hotels. In the first trading year or two, a seaside hotel may struggle to bring in enough cash to cover the outgoings. So, cash needs to be forecast, planned and managed with great care. One approach that will delight a bank manager is to plan cash inflows as cautiously as possible (on the low side) while forecasting cash outflows on the high side. Then surprises should be pleasant rather than shocking.

7 Sources of finance: having forecast the cash flow on the start-up, capital needs can be thought through. The entrepreneur should want to invest as much as possible personally, in order to have maximum possible control of decision making. Beyond that, plans must be made for a balanced approach between short-term and long-term capital raising, and a mixture between share and loan capital.

8 Location: as discussed in Chapter 21, the ideal location depends on a mixture of factors, such as whether the business needs to be close to its market. A further factor is simple affordability. All the evidence may say that an expensive location

will work best, but that may be unaffordable. It may be necessary to start the business in a relatively cheap location and then move when there's enough cash to do so.

9 Marketing mix. the business plan will set out the overall marketing objectives and the mix that can achieve those goals. If launching a new, classy cosmetic it may be necessary to produce a stunningly over-the-top product and box, priced relatively high, stocked in upmarket stores (no thanks, Debenhams) and advertised in the classier end of fashion magazines.

A business plan needs to be detailed

The business plan: benefits and problems

Table 23.1 (page 112) summarises the benefits and problems an entrepreneur may encounter when writing a business plan.

The key thing to remember is that the business plan is only as good as the information it is based on. As much of this will have to be estimated or guessed, it is clear that no one should treat a business plan as a factual document. It may help steer the business in the right general direction, but it may be an exaggeration to see it as a 'sat nav'.

The following table is advice from The Prince's Trust on how to write a good business plan. The trust is a charity set up by Prince Charles to support young people in various ways, including becoming successful entrepreneurs.

Table 23.1 The benefits and problems of writing a business plan

Benefits	Problems
Forces the entrepreneur to think carefully about every aspect of the start-up, which should increase the chances of success	Making a forecast (e.g. of sales) doesn't make it happen; entrepreneurs sometimes confuse the plan with reality; poor sales can come as a terrible shock
May make the entrepreneur realise that she or he lacks the skills needed for part of the plan, and therefore try harder to employ an expert or buy in advice	Problems arise if the plan is too rigid; it is better to make it flexible, so that you are prepared for what to do if sales are poor (or unexpectedly high)
If the plan is well received by investors, they may compete to offer attractive terms for obtaining capital	Plans based on high sales will include lots of staff to meet the demand; risks are lower if the business starts with a low-cost/low-sales expectation
Many entrepreneurs have the whole plan in their head, not on paper; if illness or accident strikes, others will only be able to keep things going with a paper plan	Business success is often about people, not paper. An over-focus on a perfect plan may mean too little time is spent visiting suppliers or talking to shoppers

Talking point

What do you think Dwight Eisenhower, war hero and US president, meant when he said: 'Plans are nothing; planning is everything'?

The purpose of planning business activity

Research suggests that business plans make little difference to the success rate of new business start-ups, but do make a difference to later growth rates. In other words, business planning helps in achieving higher rates of growth once the start-up phase is passed.

So, it may be that constructing a business plan makes little difference to the risks involved in the start-up phase. Of course, a really good plan would identify possible threats to the new business and may identify ways of overcoming them.

Many business plans are done quite cynically – their task is to persuade a bank or an investor to put their money in, so risks are played down. The entrepreneur may then be acting on a plan that is overly optimistic, which is no help at all. Of course, without capital there can be no start-up, so getting loan capital from a bank and/or share investment from a venture capital-provider is a vital step in an overall plan. The key, then, is for the entrepreneur to treat this capital-raising as

Table 23.2 Top tips for writing a business plan from The Prince's Trust

Top tips	Detail
Be concise	It is really important that potential investors can understand what your business is all about from a quick glance at your plan. Make sure you include a summary of your business, and how it will make money right from the start, and use simple language throughout.
Be specific	Being specific is just as important as being concise. The details will help you drill down into how you will actually deliver your plan.
Know your market	A big part of knowing whether your business will be successful is understanding your audience. Make sure your plan is clear about your target market – who will you be selling to and how many other companies are already selling similar products?
Know your finances	The other essential part of a business plan is the finance section. If your business isn't going to make any money, it won't be successful, so you need to be very clear on how you will make a profit. Use it to your advantage – your plan will be incredibly useful when it comes to securing loans and investment, but that's not its only use: it is also a personal tool to help you understand your objectives.

simply a step forward rather than an achievement in itself. Good business requires a profit, not simply the cash that has come in from investors.

Drawing the right conclusions

In order to start a great new business an entrepreneur needs to have a good idea based on a strong understanding of the customer and the competition. Then the entrepreneur needs to have the personal qualities to build effective relationships with suppliers, retail buyers and staff. If drawing up a business plan helps in that process, that's fine. The worry is that if entrepreneurs bury their heads in paper plans, it may divert them from the important tasks associated with starting a new business. A business plan can help to get investment from outsiders and may help a disorganised entrepreneur to make fewer mistakes, but it is no substitute for having strong enterprise skills.

> **Revision essentials**
>
> **Business plan**: a detailed document setting out the marketing and financial thinking behind a proposed new business.

End of chapter exercises

1 Explain in your own words the meaning of the term 'business plan'.

2 Why may young entrepreneurs need a business plan more than middle-aged ones? Briefly explain your answer.

3 Some people think that a business plan aimed at investors should be different from one aimed at bankers. Outline two ways in which a plan aimed at investors may be different from one aimed at a banker.

4 Why may an entrepreneur find it easier to write a business plan for a second business start-up than for their first?

5 If you were to open your own business after leaving school, do you think you would complete a business plan? Explain your answer with reference to your own strengths and weaknesses.

Practice questions

In 2009, Kirsty Henshaw realised that her four-year-old son Toby had some serious food allergies. She bought a £30 foodmixer and devised a recipe for dairy-, sugar- and gluten-free ice cream. Friends and neighbours loved it as much as Toby. Using £2,500 saved from a student loan she launched Coconice, a range of allergen-free, healthy desserts. The following year, she gained a £65,000 investment from Peter Jones and Duncan Bannatyne on *Dragons' Den*. They took 30 per cent of the shares in her private limited company but helped her get supermarket distribution in Waitrose, Ocado and Sainsbury's.

Taking the advice of her dragons, Kirsty renamed the business Kirsty's and branched out into allergen-free ready meals. In 2015, sales of £3.6 million yielded a profit of £72,000. In 2016, sales should exceed £4 million. Although she didn't have a business plan in the early days, she now keeps one up to date, finding it a helpful way to co-ordinate the company's growth.

Total: 18 marks

1 Outline one benefit to Kirsty of having her business set up as a private limited company. (2)

2 (a) Calculate Kirsty's 2015 profit as a percentage of her sales revenue. (2)

   (b) Outline one way in which she might be able to boost that profit percentage in the future. (2)

3 From the data provided, evaluate the possible reasons why Kirsty was able to start her business successfully despite having no business plan. You should use the information given above as well as your knowledge of business. (12)

Exam-style questions on Topic 1.4

Don't rush; check your answers carefully.

1 Which **one** of the following is a disadvantage of buying into a retail franchise operation? (1)

  (a) The brand name will already be known to many customers.

  (b) There will be training available on how to use the electronic tills.

  (c) You won't be able to form a private limited company.

  (d) A fee of perhaps five per cent of revenue can strip away most of the profit.

2 Tim and Nattasja are setting up an extreme sports travel agency in London. They're aiming at young adults wealthy enough to spend £1,500–3,000 on a holiday based on skydiving, mountaineering or jungle trekking. They need to recruit three staff to work in the front office, selling directly to customers.

Which **two** of the following factors would be the most important when choosing who to recruit for these jobs? (2)

  (a) A warm, outgoing personality.

  (b) A very well presented CV.

  (c) Enthusiasm for unusual, tailor-made holidays such as these.

  (d) Some understanding of travel industry computer-booking systems.

  (e) Their GCSE and A level results.

3 Which **one** of the following is the best definition of unlimited liability? (1)

  (a) Provides the entrepreneur with a limitless opportunity to make high profits.

  (b) Ensures that, if things go wrong, the owners can only lose the money they invested.

  (c) It is the method used by the majority of businesses in Britain.

  (d) The business owners can be held responsible personally for any debts of the business.

Questions 4 and 5 are based on the following chart, which shows sales data for Dave's Drinks Ltd.

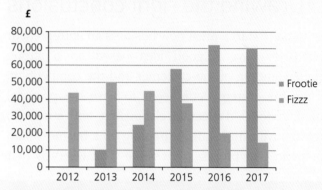

Sales data for Dave's Drinks Ltd, 2012–17

4 Which **two** of the following are correct statements about sales at Dave's Drinks? (2)

  (a) Total sales in 2014 were £10,000 higher than in 2013.

  (b) Frootie outsold Fizzz by £70,000 in 2017.

  (c) Fizzz sales in 2016 were £20,000 down on the 2014 figure.

  (d) Total sales in 2017 were £85,000.

  (e) Frootie sales in 2017 were £35,000 higher than in 2014.

5 The boss of Dave's Drinks wants to put £50,000 behind advertising either Frootie or Fizzz in 2018. Which **one** of the following provides the strongest business argument? (1)

  (a) It should be Fizzz because without advertising the product will die.

  (b) It should be Frootie because its sales are higher.

  (c) It should be Frootie because it makes a higher profit per pound of sales than Fizzz.

  (d) It should be Frootie because the brand was Dave's own idea.

6 Jackson's has a policy of pricing low to attract sales. This forces it to cut a few corners, but owner Tess Jackson is proud that her business has the second highest sales volume in the industry. The industry number one is GFH Ltd. Tess has just hired a new manager who used

to work for GFH Ltd. This has allowed her to find out about her rival's customer service figures.

	Jackson's	GFH Ltd
On-time deliveries	88.4%	93.6%
Damaged deliveries	2.4%	0.65%
Customer returns	3.1%	1.05%
Customer satisfaction	78.4%	91.7%

Which **two** of the following conclusions can be made from these figures? (2)

(a) The low-price policy at Jackson's is definitely working.

(b) Tess can feel proud that only 3.1 per cent of customers send their goods back.

(c) Tess urgently needs to look into why 21.6 per cent of her customers are unsatisfied.

(d) There is a serious risk that repeat purchase levels at GFH Ltd will fall in future.

(e) Tess should discuss these figures with all her staff, inviting ideas for improvement.

Now try this discussion question.

7 Discuss the value to a first-time entrepreneur of buying into a franchise instead of starting up independently. (6)

24 Stakeholders

Stakeholders are the people or groups with an interest in the success or failure of an organisation. Some work inside the business and some outside, and all are likely to have slightly different objectives. Shareholders and staff, for example, may want very different things from the business.

Among the main stakeholders in business are:

◆ the owners/shareholders
◆ the staff/managers
◆ the customers
◆ local residents, who may be affected by traffic noise from deliveries or by pollution from a smelly or smoky factory or farm
◆ local government, which is the organisation that will give a yes or no to future planning permission, for example on whether the business is allowed to build a larger warehouse
◆ **pressure groups**, for example Greenpeace, who may organise protests if they feel that an organisation's activities damage the environment.

Pressure groups may be regarded as stakeholders in a business

Stakeholders and their objectives

Greggs plc (Britain's biggest chain of bakeries) has always been proud to say that its two key stakeholders are its customers and staff. It places its shareholders in third place, on the grounds that as long as staff and customers are happy, the business will be a financial success. Other companies take a different view. Britain's high street banks, in particular, have shown a consistent tendency to exploit rather than serve their customers.

Greggs two stakeholders are customers and staff

Staff, customers and shareholders are by no means the only stakeholders a business may have to consider. The owner of a good restaurant will consider suppliers to be massively important. He or she may buy steak from a local farmer who produces tender, organic meat. The restaurant's reputation depends on the quality of the farmer's deliveries. Therefore the supplier becomes a key stakeholder.

Table 24.1 sets out the different objectives of the different stakeholder groups.

Table 24.1 Different stakeholders and their objectives

Stakeholder	Different objectives of each stakeholder group
Shareholders (owners)	Shareholders in family-run, private limited companies usually focus on long-term organic growth. Shareholders in public limited companies (plcs) are more likely to care mainly about the short-term share price – they may be delighted to sell at a big profit if the company is bought by a rival, or to see sharp cost-cutting to boost profits
Employees	Security of employment; opportunities for career development (so organic growth is a key objective); fair pay and good 'fringe benefits' such as pensions, holidays and perhaps a company car
Customers	Consistently high-quality products and service; honest and fair dealing from the company; bright, innovative new products that make life better (or more fun)
Managers	Security of employment; opportunities for career development (so organic growth is a key objective); fair pay and good 'fringe benefits' such as pensions, holidays and perhaps a company car
Suppliers	Honest and fair dealing from the company, especially on prices and credit terms; good communication about future plans; strong organic growth meaning rising demand for supplies
Local community	Honest and fair dealing from the company, especially on plans that affect local employment and the environment; some locals may want to see the business grow, others may not
Pressure groups	Honest and fair dealing from the company, especially on plans that affect customers and the environment; often pressure groups seem to be against growth, perhaps focusing overly on the downside of business activity
The government	Honest and fair dealing from the company, especially on tax arrangements, employment plans and location plans (HSBC threatened to leave the UK to try to water down legislation controlling banking practices; it succeeded)

> **Talking point**
>
> Consider which Samsung stakeholders might have agreed with each other when the company launched the (unintentionally!) exploding Note 7 smartphone.

Small business stakeholders

For most small firms, the keys to success are customers, staff and suppliers. Treating them well is essential, partly because you never know when you may need them to help you. A really committed restaurant supplier would drop everything and rush to a client that had run out of chicken half way through the evening. A really committed customer may help out when needed (for example, paying in cash to help a supplier with cash flow problems). Most important of all are the staff, because if they are well motivated, their enthusiasm will rub off on to customers and suppliers.

Are shareholders number one?

The directors of most public limited companies have little choice but to treat shareholders as the most important stakeholder. This is because the shareholders have the right to vote the directors out of office if they believe that the business is being run badly. Companies such as Dixons are open about the priority given to profit and, therefore, shareholder returns. Others prefer to suggest that they treat all stakeholders equally. The record of companies such as Volkswagen (cheating on exhaust emissions), GlaxoSmithKline (bribing doctors) and those involved with the collapse of BHS suggest that shareholder profits remain the priority for most.

> A lost job can put the smile on any shareholder's face.
>
> *Eric Reguly, Canadian journalist*

How stakeholders are affected by business activity

In the UK, manufacturing generates just under ten per cent of all economic activity. Our economy is dominated by services, from retailing through music to banking. So the main effects of business on stakeholders relate to the service sector; in other words, few people are affected by industrial pollution. Far more serious is the pollution of the body (and the mind) caused by over-processed foods, by the casual prejudice based on race or gender shown by certain newspapers and their online sites, and by the treatment of staff trapped in low-wage, insecure, zero-hour jobs in businesses such as Sports Direct and Amazon.

Zero hours contracts

Key points:

- Zero hours contracts normally mean there is no obligation f workers to accept it.
- Most zero hours contracts will give staff 'worker' employme
- Zero hours workers have the same employment rights as r have breaks in their contracts, which affect rights that acc
- Zero hours workers are entitled to **annual leave**, the Natior and pay for work-related travel in the same w

Zero hour contracts affect business activity

It is important to also recognise the fantastic good done by many businesses, such as:

- activities for small children and their parents, which bring people together
- specialist restaurants that give people a taste of home or the chance to eat out in a way that suits their diet/lifestyle
- shops that focus on organic meat and other produce, giving an outlet to suppliers who might otherwise struggle to run their own businesses.

In other words, the impact of business on stakeholders can be beneficial as well as damaging.

How stakeholders impact business activity

The effect of stakeholders on businesses has become a major concern for all companies that operate in the public eye. Big companies have whole departments devoted to the management of their image and their relationships with outside groups. This process covers social media management (or even manipulation) and careful management of contacts with the press. In 2016, Philip Green received awful publicity about the collapse of the BHS store chain, but for ten years before that he'd had praise heaped upon him by the press.

Occasionally, though, stakeholders have an impact on business activity. After the ghastly Rana Plaza disaster killed more than 1,100 clothing workers in Bangladesh in 2013, media and pressure group activity forced clothing retailers to be more careful about where they bought supplies from. Look at the End of chapter exercises box for an account of the impressive work done by pressure group Human Rights Watch.

Possible conflicts between stakeholder groups

Some conflicts between stakeholder groups are inevitable. When Japan's giant SoftBank company bought Britain's ARM computer business for £24 billion in 2016, ARM's shareholders enjoyed a 43 per cent profit overnight. For ARM's staff and UK suppliers, however, the takeover may be disappointing, even worrying. But the shareholders accepted the bid and took their profit.

Examples of other potential conflicts between stakeholder groups include:

◆ A supermarket's shareholders, managers and employees are happy to launch a new range of luxury sandwiches; a pressure group later reveals that each sandwich contains more fat and calories than a Big Mac and chips. Customers are shocked (but perhaps keep eating).

◆ Managers keep their regular salaries, fringe benefits and secure jobs, but push various 'worker' jobs on to contractors that employ staff on short-dated contracts at low wages and with no sick pay or pensions. Shareholders may feel happy with this arrangement until, years later, they find how poorly these jobs are done.

> The way you treat your employees is the way they will treat your customers.
>
> *Richard Branson, founder, Virgin Group*

◉ Drawing the right conclusions

Companies need to think about their public image. It is, therefore, important for managers to think about their wider responsibilities. If they fail to do so, the result might be bad press or a social media storm, with local residents or national pressure groups making complaints. Nike has suffered bad press in the past from the use of low-cost (even child) labour in making its (very expensive) trainers. Pressure groups (and customers) blamed Nike for ignoring its responsibility to its suppliers.

The issue of stakeholders simply urges firms to think more widely about the effects of their business activities. Well-managed firms have always done this. The risk today is that every firm claims to care about its stakeholders, whereas day-to-day business decisions continue to make profit the top priority.

Revision essentials

Pressure groups: organisations formed to put forward a particular viewpoint, such as promoting organic farming.

Stakeholders: all those groups with an interest in the success or failure of a business.

End of chapter exercises

1 What is the difference between a shareholder and a stakeholder?

2 Which three stakeholder groups do you think are the most important for:

(a) your school/college

(b) your nearest sweetshop or grocers.

3 Outline two possible disadvantages for staff who work for a business that only focuses on the needs of shareholders, not stakeholders.

4 Read the extract and answer the following questions.

(a) Examine how the work of HRW might affect the activities of a business such as Marks and Spencer.

(b) Based on this evidence from Cambodia, what conflicts might there be between a company's responsibilities towards its shareholders compared with its responsibilities to society.

Cambodian factories supplying high street names – including Marks and Spencer, Gap, H&M and Adidas – are mistreating their workers, a rights group said, quoting employee complaints about abuse including forced overtime, firing of pregnant women and underage labour.

Many of the 73 factories investigated by pressure group Human Rights Watch (HRW) were subcontractors in murky supply chains. That makes it much harder to hold the brands selling final products to account, the group said, calling for greater accountability.

The group singled out Marks and Spencer for particular criticism because of its secrecy about suppliers and because the firm 'did not respond to the substantive concerns HRW raised with them around subcontracting,' the group said. 'By contrast H&M, Gap and Adidas responded to our concerns.'

In interviews with 270 workers and dozens of other union and government officials and monitoring groups, HRW compiled a list of intimidation and ill treatment. Interviewees alleged that pregnant women in some factories were pushed out of work, and other factory workers were denied toilet or meal breaks, punished for taking sick leave or trying to organise unions, sexually harassed and kept on illegal short-term contracts.

Source: *The Guardian*, 12 March 2015

Practice questions

Giant multinational Reckitt Benckiser had an interesting start to 2016. In April the company was fined nearly A\$1.7 million after an Australian court criticised its misleading way of marketing Nurofen. The packaging suggests that 'Nurofen Back Pain' offers 'fast targeted relief' specifically for back pain, but in fact it is just the same as any other Nurofen.

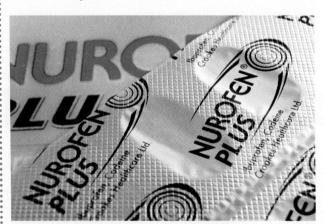

The makers of Nurofen were fined by an Australian court for misleading marketing

More importantly, in May the head of Reckitt Benckiser Korea was forced to apologise for the deaths of 92 customers whose lung injuries were caused by a product sold only in South Korea. He also apologised for the company's repeated denials of wrongdoing as they kept selling the product for years after the problem came to light: 'We were late. Five years have passed.' On 29 July 2016, Reckitt announced a £300 million charge on their profits to cover possible fines and compensation to be paid in South Korea.

The news was happier for Reckitt's chief executive, Rakesh Kapoor, who received a £23 million pay package. Shareholders objected noisily to such a huge pay award (roughly double the 2015 figure), but the pay package was approved.

Total: 15 marks

1 Analyse which stakeholder groups Reckitt Benckiser seems to have been prioritising in recent years. (6)

2 Rakesh Kapoor is thinking about how best to rebuild Reckitt Benckiser's reputation in South Korea. He sees two options:

   ◆ Option 1: Turn Reckitt Benckiser Korea into an employee co-operative along the lines of John Lewis/Waitrose.

   ◆ Option 2: Sack the existing senior management team in Korea and replace them with UK managers who had nothing to do with the lung injury scandal.

Justify which **one** of these options he should choose. (9)

25 Technology and business

Technology affects business through products and process. Products are what the customer buys, from smartphones to streaming services such as Netflix. Process is the technology used by the business to make itself more efficient and effective, such as GPS to map the best route to deliver five items to different parts of the city.

Modern developments in digital technology can be attributed to what has become known as 'Moore's Law'. Gordon Moore, former boss of chipmaker Intel, suggested in 1965 that technical development enabled the computing power of a microchip to double every two years. Remarkably, that 'law' proved good for the next 50 years, allowing computing power to grow at a staggering rate.

Despite the amazing progress in digital technology, western economies have seen productivity (efficiency) slow down rather than speed up. That, in turn, has slowed the pace of economic growth. As shown in Figure 25.1, only the UK managed to keep its economic growth constant (pre-Brexit). Even America, the home to so many digital innovations, saw its growth rate slip.

> When consumers adopt new technologies, they do old things in new ways. When they internalize technology, they begin to do new things.
>
> *James McQuivey, business author*

Types of technology used in business

E-commerce

E-commerce means selling online rather than in a physical one-to-one transaction. This might be done through a PC/laptop via a website or, more commonly, through a smartphone via an app. This mobile form of e-commerce can be called m-commerce. Figure 25.2 shows that by the first half of 2016 Domino's UK was

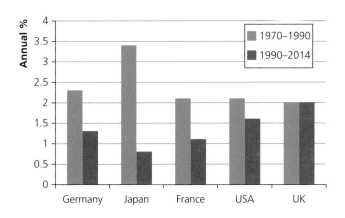

Figure 25.1 Average annual growth in GDP per capita (Source: Unicef statistics, 2016)

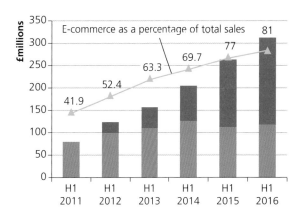

Figure 25.2 Growth of e-commerce at Domino's Pizza (Source: Domino's interim accounts 2011–16)

receiving 81 per cent of all sales via e-commerce. Within that total an increasing part of the sales mix was via the Domino's app (the red bars). With 81 per cent of sales coming electronically, the switch to e-commerce is almost complete for this business.

For other businesses though, e-commerce may be a relatively minor issue (for instance less than five per cent of UK food sales are online), or even an irrelevant one. In July 2016, US airline JetBlue ordered 30 A321 aircraft from Europe's Airbus Group. Each has a list price of $125million, so this order was potentially worth $3,750million. Inevitably, no one is going to make such a purchase through e-commerce. There will be fierce negotiations on price and detailed discussions will be needed on how the interior of the aircraft will be fitted out. E-commerce will never have a significant part to play in this kind of big business activity.

> In e-commerce your prices have to be better because the consumer has to take a leap of faith in your product.
>
> *Ashton Kutcher, actor and investor*

Social media

Social media such as Facebook and Instagram are used by businesses for two-way communication with customers. In its 2016 half-year report to shareholders, Domino's Pizza boasted that its 'digital engagement' efforts included:

◆ collaboration with vloggers/Twitter users to 'engage in a natural way' with customers
◆ The launch of a Domino's GIPHY channel, achieving 54 million views including 18.6 million views of a 'heart-hugging pizza' GIF
◆ direct expenditure on a Snapchat area for users to record and share pizza videos.

Some businesses believe that consumers are relatively unaware that many bloggers are in effect paid to advertise and promote certain products. In traditional media, advertisements were clearly separated from editorial; in social media the lines are more blurred. It could be said that this is against the consumer's best interests as it overly favours businesses.

Digital communication

Digital communication may seem to revolve around social media, but it is important to remember email as an outstanding and cheap means of achieving one-to-one conversation. A customer sends in a query, which can be answered specifically and personally – as long as the company is set up to do this. The risk is that the query gets directed to an outsourced call centre where a generalised answer is given by a non-expert. Many companies have even outsourced 'customer service'

Table 25.1 Advantages and disadvantages of e-commerce

Advantages of e-commerce	Disadvantages of e-commerce
Enables a small business to start up from a back bedroom, testing the market before spending a lot on offices and staff.	In many sectors, winner takes all (e.g. Amazon in book sales). Dominant (monopoly) businesses rarely serve customers well in the long term.
Enables a small business to sell to the world without needing an expensive overseas sales and distribution set-up.	Dubious environmentally as there are large numbers of van deliveries and returns ('wrong size, not sure I like it'); this is surely a carbon-loaded way of trading.
Provides scalability – that is, you can finance faster growth than is true of old-style retail or service businesses (see the growth of ASOS, pages 192–3).	For first-movers, websites and apps work well, but it is very difficult for late-arrival competitors to make themselves seen and heard by the market – and creates issues regarding monopoly.
Use of social media makes it possible to build a relationship with customers even though you do not meet them physically.	Some customers effectively blackmail businesses (e.g. 'give me a free bottle of wine or I'll give you a bad write-up on Twitter/TripAdvisor').

to low-wage countries overseas. In this way, they are using technology to cut costs instead of raising the speed and quality of the service. Many companies have found, however, that the loss in customer confidence outweighs any benefit from lower costs.

Payment systems

Payment systems such as PayPal are at the heart of all e-commerce. Before PayPal was established, people were concerned about the security of their money when using e-commerce. With PayPal the level of security improved dramatically, giving people the confidence to spend more freely online. Other electronic payment systems include:
◆ Electronic Funds Transfer – this is a method by which payments can be settled and bills paid online.
◆ M-Pesa – this mobile banking system (which was launched in Kenya in 2007) was the innovator in offering a full banking service over the phone ('M' stands for mobile and 'Pesa' is Swahili for money).

How technology influences business activity

Technology affects every aspect of business management, but there are three areas of special focus: sales, costs and the marketing mix.

Sales

Sales are affected by product and by process. In certain sectors, technology is the driving force behind customer behaviour. Figure 25.3 shows worldwide sales of Sony's PS4 games console versus Xbox One since their launch in November 2013. The graph also shows the initial sales of Sony's previous console PS3, to give a comparison. The impressive new technology of the PS4 has allowed Sony to far outstrip sales of the PS3 and, of course, rival Microsoft's Xbox One.

Technology can also affect the sales of items such as kebabs. The UK firm Just Eat has enabled small, independent fast-food outlets such as kebab shops to make sales online. Without this possibility, Domino's Pizza would have gained an even larger share of the fast-food delivery market. In this case, technology has improved the process rather than the product.

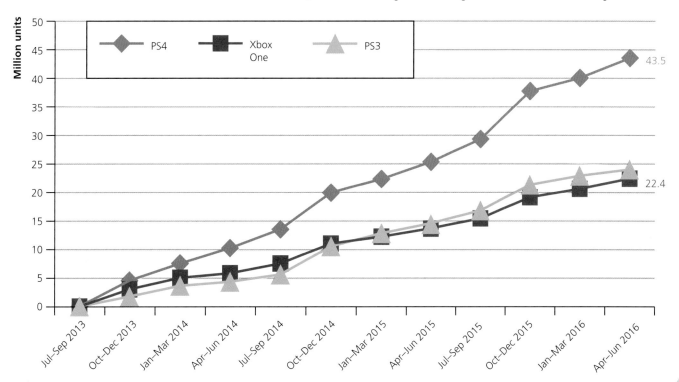

Figure 25.3 Global sales of games console hardware (Sources: various, including Sony accounts)

Costs

Costs need to be split into fixed and variable. Technology has an impact on each of these. An important fixed cost is advertising. Traditional media advertising using TV, for example, had the disadvantage of being ill-focused. Saga Holidays will use TV in the afternoon to target retired people, but there will still be some younger people watching. So to achieve a £2 million advertising hit on older people, they might need to spend £4 million. Digital technology changes that by targeting individuals. The advertisers gather data on your choices and habits which means that a teenager doing a Google search will never be targeted with a Saga Holiday. Less of the advertiser's money is wasted, allowing a cutback in advertising spending and therefore cutting fixed costs.

With variable costs such as raw materials, the huge benefit from technology is to make it easier to quickly find out the prices charged by different suppliers. This makes it easier to find the lowest costs, thus cutting variable costs.

Marketing mix

Technology affects the 4Ps in different ways for different businesses. As mentioned above, there is a tendency for price competition to become greater because people know all the available product prices. It took five minutes to find out the following price comparison of a TV set.

Table 25.2 Price comparison of a TV set (August 2016)

	Currys	Argos	Tesco
Samsung 50 inch LED TV	£699	£629	£626.95

This means that companies have to treat their pricing decision as more important than they might have done previously.

Other mix factors are also affected by technology:

◆ Product – improved technology can enable a product to gain market share.
◆ Promotion – digital marketing can improve the effectiveness of marketing spending, allowing the cost to fall.
◆ Place – in many cases today, 'place' changes from being a physical location such as a shop, and becomes a digital exercise conducted online.

● Drawing the right conclusions

Technology changes constantly, but not always significantly. Baked beans are mass-produced today in much the same way as 30 years ago. What is certain, though, is that being one technological step ahead of competitors is always a great place to be. A business can potentially charge customers more while facing lower production costs. This enables the business to be much more profitable.

Revision essentials

E-commerce selling online rather than in a physical one-to-one transaction. An important part of e-commerce is m-commerce, meaning commerce using apps/smartphones rather than websites/PCs.

Social media interactive channels of communication, via words, photos or videos, such as blogs, Facebook and Instagram.

Digital communication messages or conversations conducted via email, text or social media.

Payment systems ways of paying electronically such as PayPal.

End of chapter exercises

1 Moore's Law still seems to work 50 years on. Why might that be important to a business such as Sainsbury's?

2 As of the second half of 2016, Primark still had no plans to move towards e-commerce. Is the clothing retailer making a mistake?

3 (a) Look back at Figure 25.2 on page 121. In the first half of 2014, Domino's Pizza's total sales revenue was £292.68 million. What were its total e-commerce sales?

(b) In the first half of 2016, the company's e-commerce sales were £311.5 million. What might explain the huge increase since 2014?

4 (a) Look back at Figure 25.3 on page 123. By what percentage did accumulated sales of PS4s outstrip those of Xbox Ones in April to June 2016?

(b) Explain two possible reasons why PS4 achieved this position.

Practice questions

In 2012, Will Shu was transferred from New York to the London offices of Morgan Stanley. He quickly noticed that although it was easy to get ordinary takeaway food delivered, London lacked New York's delivery options from better restaurants. After six months' research, in 2013 he founded Deliveroo. Whereas Just Eat simply links the customer to a fast-food restaurant, Deliveroo actually carries out the deliveries. Also, Deliveroo's links are to restaurants rather than pizza takeaways and kebab shops. Such was the success of Just Eat that Will had no problems in raising $100 million of capital to start his business. A further $100 million was raised in November 2015 to fund Deliveroo's expansion. By then Deliveroo employed 300 cycle delivery riders.

In practical terms, the heart of the business is technology. The Deliveroo app is slick and effective and the company has found favour with Twitter users such as the comedian Jack Whitehall. Its London presence is clear from the number of Deliveroo bikes flying around, but the business is also building up a presence in 30 other British cities and 20 more across Europe.

Total: 15 marks

1 Analyse the necessary qualities of an app to make an online delivery business stand out from the competition. (6)

2 Deliveroo wants to create a far stronger social media presence than Just Eat. Will Shu sees two options:

◆ Option 1: make a series of links with celebrities providing free food and other incentives linked to tweets and other favourable mentions of Deliveroo online.

◆ Option 2: hire a social media advertising agency to create fun viral video clips of Deliveroo, its customers and its delivery riders.

Justify which one of these options he should choose. (9)

26 Legislation and business

In December 2015, the owners of the Real China restaurant in Eastleigh, Hampshire, were fined £70,000. This was because 100 diners had been hospitalised from salmonella food poisoning. Food Inspectors found 'rotting meat in a sink' and other 'totally unacceptable' practices. The owners were prosecuted under EU laws relating to food safety and hygiene. Such things happen but, happily, very rarely in the UK. The **legislation** protecting consumers in the UK is among the tightest in the world.

● The purpose of legislation

Principles of consumer law

Consumer law is passed by parliament to try to protect consumers from:

◆ harm caused when the supplier knows more than the consumer, for example in the decades when the tobacco industry knew more about the harm done by cigarettes than their customers

◆ harm caused when the consumer is lied to or misled, for example in the days before the 1968 Trade Descriptions Act, when Guinness beer claimed to be 'good for you', or the dog food PAL claimed to 'Prolong Active Life'

◆ exposure to unsafe or unhealthy foods or other products, as in the case of Real China.

● Consumer protection legislation

There are two especially important pieces of consumer protection legislation: the Consumer Rights Act 2015 and the Trade Descriptions Act 1968.

Before the Trade Descriptions Act, Guinness claimed: 'Guinness is good for you'

> Good people do need laws to tell them to act responsibly, while bad people will find a way around the laws.
>
> *Plato (428–348*BC*)*

Consumer Rights Act 2015

This law was passed in 1893 and was one of the world's earliest examples of legislation to protect consumers. It has been updated many times since then, including in 2015 when it was updated to incorporate digital products and services. This act gives you the right to take back a faulty item and get your money back, for example, when the zip on a dress gets stuck the second time it is worn, or a vacuum cleaner that breaks down after only six months.

◆ The key features of the **Consumer Rights** Act are:
◆ goods must be fit for the purpose for which they are sold; relevant aspects of 'fit for purpose' include freedom from defects and the appearance, finish, safety and long-lasting nature of the product
◆ the buyer has a right to get their money back, or could choose to have it repaired at the seller's expense
◆ the person responsible for correcting any problem is the seller (the shop), not the manufacturer.

Talking point

An angry householder wrote on the Cowboy Builders website: 'Our loft conversion was completed using the wrong materials, the insulation was incomplete and our new deck has too few supports.' How might the householder make use of the Consumer Rights Act 2015?

Trade Descriptions Act 1968

This act (passed in 1968) put an end to 100 years of misleading advertisements. One example was the cigarette brand Heartsease, which claimed to be good for your heart. The Trade Descriptions Act insists that all advertising, packaging and public statements made by firms about their products must be 'demonstrably true'. In other words, there must be evidence for them. Key features include:

◆ It is an offence for a trader to use false or misleading statements.
◆ It is an offence to misleadingly label goods and services.
◆ The act carries criminal penalties and can therefore lead to a jail sentence.

Although specific statements must be proven, for example that Yakult helps digestion, advertisers can still get around the act in clever ways. Few of the claims about 'superfoods' have any scientific support, but a yoghurt manufacturer could add acai berries to their yoghurt and then make reference to the belief that acai is a superfood.

Despite the tricks some companies use, there is no doubt that the Trade Descriptions Act has reduced substantially the number of customers being deceived by suppliers.

⬤ Other key acts

Among many other acts passed to protect consumers are:

◆ the Consumer Credit Act 1974 (updated in 2006): every item sold on credit must have a clear indication of the APR – the annualised percentage interest rate – being charged
◆ the Weights and Measures Act 1985 (updated in 2006): if the bag says 500g, that is what it must contain
◆ the Food Safety Act 1990: to prevent illness from eating food sold to the public, by insisting that sales staff have hygiene training and that premises are inspected regularly.

It is not important to remember these other acts, but it is important to know that there are more than just the two main acts. This is because firms often complain that they are overwhelmed by the amount of legislation they must cope with.

⬤ Why have employment legislation?

Parliament also passes laws that try to protect employees from being exploited at work. There are three main areas for employment legislation: recruitment, pay and discrimination.

Recruitment

The main law involved in recruiting new staff is the Equality Act 2010. This brought together many other acts of parliament largely concerned with preventing discrimination. Years ago companies complained about interference in their right to make decisions, but today few would doubt that the law points towards good business logic: companies benefit when they recruit from as wide a pool as possible, and hire as diverse a workforce as possible. It is hard to imagine that Marks and Spencer would have made such a hash of winning younger clothes shoppers if it had a younger, more diverse board of directors.

Pay

With the Equal Pay Act dating back to 1970, it is amazing that there are still such huge pay differences in the workplace. In 2015, the average full-time working man earned nearly 20 per cent more than a woman. For black graduates the position is even worse, as they can expect to be paid 25 per cent less than white counterparts. These inequalities have been reduced since legislation such as the Equal Pay Act, but clearly remain significant.

Discrimination

Although the above evidence on pay smacks of discrimination, there are other important issues in relation to discrimination. Recruitment is a concern, but the biggest issue may be promotion. Figure 26.1 shows that 57 per cent of women in shop-floor roles at John Lewis achieve only 29 per cent of the jobs in the boardroom. The problem is probably much, much worse in terms of race. John Lewis avoids giving comparable data for white and non-white staff, but it does publish data showing that in 2016 just 8.9 per cent of all manager and director posts went to non-white people. Legislation alone may be insufficient; individual and social attitudes also need to change.

The percentage of women who achieve roles in the board room is much lower than the percentage of men

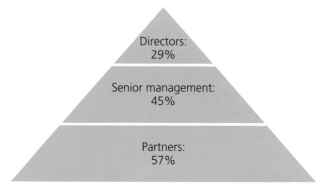

Figure 26.1 Percentage of John Lewis staff who are women, 2016 (Source: John Lewis annual report 2016)

●The impact of legislation on businesses

The Federation of Small Businesses has carried out research among the owners of small firms. The results showed that 50 per cent thought that excessive regulation would hinder their growth in the next few years. But are firms right to feel this way? After all, just as football managers always have 'reasons' (excuses?) for their latest defeat, is it possible that business owners like to blame government for their own failings?

Many businesses say:
◆ too many rules mean too much paperwork, which costs time and money, and that can damage our ability to compete with foreign companies
◆ rules can restrict our creativity and initiative
◆ we don't mind rules that apply directly to us, but we object to **red tape** that we have to complete but isn't designed for 'firms like mine'.

Others argue that:
◆ it helps firms to know what is acceptable and what is not, for example that every cafe must have separate fridges for cooked food and uncooked food; it lets managers concentrate on doing things better
◆ rules do take time and money, but not enough to damage a firm's drive for success
◆ consumer protection law is too valuable to dismiss just because firms find it time consuming; people can die from faulty drugs, unsafe cars or a dodgy kebab.

During the 'credit crunch' of 2007–09, several major banks collapsed. They were guilty of reckless lending at a time when the government had relaxed the rules on banking. The managers, customers and shareholders of the banks would have benefited from more, not less, red tape. So too would ordinary taxpayers. The National Audit Office says that, at its height, UK government backing of the financial sector amounted to more than £1,000 billion (a trillion pounds).

> If there were no bad people there would be no good lawyers.
>
> *Charles Dickens, author*

Drawing the right conclusions

Some politicians talk as if our small businesses are weighed down by legislative red tape. In fact, international surveys such as Ease of Doing Business Index suggest that the UK is in the world's top ten countries. Furthermore, living in the UK in the twenty-first century is amazingly less polluted, safer and more pleasant than the days of the British Empire in the mid-nineteenth century. Many of the improvements are down to legislation.

Revision essentials

Consumer law: acts of parliament that are intended to protect customers from misleading or dangerous practices by companies.

Consumer rights: laws that empower the consumer to demand certain minimum standards from every business supplier.

Legislation: laws passed by acts of parliament; breaking these laws may result in a fine or even a prison sentence.

Red tape: the term given to laws that (some people say) tie the hands of businesspeople, making it hard to act entrepreneurially.

End of chapter exercises

1 Real China was sold off by the owners before the court gave its verdict on the restaurant.

   (a) Outline two possible reasons why the owners ran the business so carelessly.

   (b) Explain one reason why it may be possible to rebuild the reputation of Real China in future.

2 State whether the following incidents are covered by the Consumer Rights Act, the Trade Descriptions Act, or neither:

   (a) A shop puts up a 'sale' sign but doubles the prices before 'slashing them by 50 per cent'.

   (b) A pair of running shoes splits open when the wearer is running fast, eight weeks after buying them.

   (c) An advertisement promises that 'L'Oréal For Men will cure baldness in a week'.

   (d) A 'Kate Moss' dress, bought last month, is condemned by *The Sun* as being 'more like last year's cast-offs than this year's fashion'.

3 Explain why a well-run business would want to avoid employment discrimination of any kind.

Practice questions

Over half of smaller business owners (55 per cent) say that their company's growth is being held back by the amount of time they have to dedicate to business administration, according to new research from the Federation of Small Businesses (FSB).

The findings show that a small business owner spends over 33 hours every month on internal business administration, which represents almost a quarter of an individual's working hours. In addition, the average small business sees around 70 hours of employee time tied up in business admin alone.

Smaller businesses struggle to focus on their primary purposes because of the amount of administration

Two-thirds of smaller businesses (67 per cent) say the administrative burden is preventing them from focusing on their business' primary purpose. The study reveals that three-quarters of business owners (76 per cent) spend more time than they would like on business compliance, tackling issues ranging from tax, employment law issues and insurance to dealing with workplace pensions, accounting tasks or health and safety issues.

Source: Federation of Small Businesses, 19 May 2016

Total: 18 marks

1 Outline one example of a possible 'employment law' issue. (2)

2 Outline one example from the article of an administrative task created by legislation. (2)

3 From the article, outline one example of a business administration task that isn't really to do with legal 'red tape'. (2)

4 Evaluate whether the FSB has made a strong enough case to justify the headline about 'battling red tape'. You should use the information given above as well as your knowledge of business. (12)

27 Introduction to the economy

Even if you make good decisions at every key point, starting up a new business is difficult. Making it harder still are factors outside any manager's control. Many stem from changes to the economy. For instance, a slowdown in the economy may lead to rising unemployment. If people are out of work they cut back their spending, especially on luxuries. This may lead to a sharp decline in takings at restaurants, jewellers and more expensive shops.

Many businesses start up when times are good and it seems easy to make money from free-spending customers. It is important to remember, though, that hard times can be around the corner. This should be OK as long as you have thought about how to respond to an economic downturn. In 2008–09, Britain suffered a sharp economic downturn that became the worst **recession** for more than 50 years. At times like this, well-run businesses find new ways to appeal to customers.

> Recession is opportunity in wolf's clothing.
>
> *Robin Sharma, business writer*

What is the economy?

The British economy is the collection of business transactions that takes place throughout the country, throughout the year. If you add up the value of all the goods and services produced in Britain in a year, the total figure comes to over £1.5 trillion (£1,500,000,000,000). The 'economy' is made up of lots of companies buying and selling with each other, lots of firms selling directly to customers (some here and some overseas) and lots of money raised and spent by the government.

The key to understanding the economy is to see it as a series of connected loops. If I buy a new Mini Cooper in London, I pay £20,000 to the dealer. That triggers a series of payments to:

- Oxford, where the car was made
- Swindon, where the steel body panels were made
- Hams Hall, Warwickshire, where the engine was made
- Port Talbot, South Wales, where the steel was made, and so on.

Higher demand for Minis injects money and jobs into the national economy

In fact, over 2,000 suppliers are involved in producing every Mini Cooper, and they come from Scotland and the North East as well as the areas immediately around Oxford. The higher the demand for Minis, the greater the injection of money and jobs into the veins of the national economy. As workers become more confident of their future prospects (secure job, good income, and so on), they become more willing to spend – perhaps on a new Mini. Greater prosperity feeds on itself, creating an upward spiral.

Needless to say, if things start to go wrong, the reverse happens. During an economic downturn there is a downward spiral of falling confidence and lower spending. Cutbacks by customers in London can have knock-on effects in Oxford, Swindon, Scotland, and so on.

Figure 27.1 The economy is a series of interconnected loops

Figure 27.2 Recession creates a downward spiral

What makes the economy go up and down?

It is important to remember that Britain is one of the world's most open economies. Trade with other countries accounts for more than 30 per cent of the value of all goods and services produced in Britain per year. Therefore, if America gets flu, we also catch a cold. Cutbacks by American consumers would hurt our large companies in banking, insurance and car production, all of which rely on **exports**. Poor economic conditions in Europe hit us even harder, as 50 per cent of all British exports are to EU countries such as France and Germany.

Problems can also hit the economy from within the country. In 2008, falling house prices led to a series of banking failures. This led to dramatic falls in consumer confidence. Solid businesses such as John Lewis saw falls in sales as high as 20 per cent. Weaker firms such as Woolworths collapsed. Job losses led to rising unemployment and the start of a major recession.

> **Talking point**
>
> From your general knowledge, how well or badly is the British economy doing at the moment?

What do businesspeople need to know about the economy?

The way interest rates can change

The interest rate is the amount a lender charges per year to someone who has borrowed money. It is measured as a percentage, for example eight per cent – in other words, the borrower has to pay the lender £8 per year for every £100 borrowed. In addition, the lender must pay the £100 back, perhaps on a monthly basis.

In mid-2016 banks were charging between six and nine per cent for money borrowed to finance a business start-up. There have been times before when the rate has risen as high as 15 or even 20 per cent, making it very hard to afford the repayments. Whenever possible it is wise to get the bank to agree to a fixed interest rate, so there are no nasty surprises.

The way exchange rates can change

The exchange rate is the value of the pound measured by how much foreign currency can be bought per pound. For instance, in April 2016, £1 could be exchanged for $1.55 when travelling to America. By August the pound had fallen to being worth just $1.30. For a British tourist, the lower exchange rate would dampen the shopping thrills of New York. For Rolls-Royce, selling a £50 million engine to an American airline, the stakes are higher. A falling pound makes UK exports more profitable.

The firms who would be most concerned about changes to the pound's exchange rate are:

◆ big importers, such as electrical goods companies or car showrooms
◆ big exporters, such as Rolls-Royce, who export more than 90 per cent of the products they make; for Rolls-Royce, a higher pound squeezes the profitability of their exports
◆ UK producers competing in the UK against foreign companies, for example JCB, which has to compete directly against the Japanese Komatsu and US firm Caterpillar.

The threat of recession

During a sharp economic downturn, thousands of people are likely to be put out of work. Some businesses cut back on staffing levels; others may collapse altogether. A few firms may flourish despite the difficulties, however, such as Poundland, Lidl and Aldi. For most, though, it is a nightmare.

A recession is a severe downturn in the economy, often described as when economic activity falls for two successive quarters of the year. Firms can usually expect that **consumer spending** will grow a little each year, perhaps about 2.5 per cent. When spending actually falls, companies struggle to cope with falling revenues and shrinking cash inflows.

Well-run companies look ahead, both to check that no recession is looming and to make sure that they can cope if one arrives. For instance, if a recession hit Europe, falls in sales of expensive VW Audis might be compensated for by rising sales of more economical VW Skodas.

Poundland flourished during the recent economic downturn

Revision essentials

Consumer spending: the total spent by all shoppers throughout the country.

Exports: goods produced in one country but sold overseas, for example a British-made Mini sold in France.

Recession: a downturn in sales and output throughout the economy, often leading to rising unemployment.

End of chapter exercises

1 Give two examples of transactions where one business would sell to another business.

2 Explain what the text means by an 'upward spiral'.

3 If a small British firm wanted to start exporting for the first time, would it prefer the pound to be high and rising, or weak and falling? Briefly explain your answer.

4 Read the following extract. Outline two possible benefits to small firms of finding export markets for their goods.

Students often ask: 'what does Britain export?' A surprising answer is food. In 2016, British exports of food and drink exceeded £18,000 million. Many of the success stories were small firms such as Walkers Shortbread and The Ice Company (yes, exporting ice!). The ten per cent fall in the pound following the 2016 vote to leave the EU should help these exporters. It makes it easier for British firms to sell goods abroad. Britain exports a lot of food and drink to Ireland, France and Germany.

5 Small firms usually charge higher prices in export markets than in Britain. Explain why that might be necessary in order to make exporting profitable.

Practice questions

The number of new restaurant openings in London has hit a record level of 179 over the last year, according to the London Restaurant Guide.

The figure passes the pre-recession peak of 158 and outstrips the number of restaurant closures by three to one, with twice as many openings in East London as West London.

The increased rate of openings is a sign that London can still compete on the global dining scene after the slump following the recession. Peter Harden, co-founder of Harden's London Restaurant Guide, commented: 'The growth of London's restaurant scene is jaw-dropping in comparison to its recent past, never mind the "Dark Ages" in which we founded our guide 25 years ago. It is wonderful to be celebrating the guide's silver anniversary in what is a golden age for restaurant goers.'

Source: www.startups.co.uk, 10 November 2015

Total: 18 marks

1 Define the term 'recession'. (1)

2 Outline one challenge for entrepreneurs in opening a successful restaurant. (2)

3 Given the boom outlined in the article, analyse why there are still restaurant closures. (6)

4 Shortly after opening, a new restaurant finds that a rise in interest rates is pushing up its costs. The boss sees two options:

◆ Option 1: Push up menu prices to make up for the rising costs.

◆ Option 2: Accept lower profits and therefore wait longer to recover the £200,000 spent on opening the restaurant.

Justify which **one** of these options they should choose. (9)

28 The economy and business

Changes in the wider economy add to the uncertainties involved in starting and running a business. In this chapter, six economic factors are looked at to give an idea of the impact of the **economic climate** on businesses. They are:

1 unemployment
2 changing levels of consumer income
3 inflation
4 changes in interest rates
5 government taxation
6 changes in exchange rates.

⊙ Unemployment

Unemployment is when someone of working age wants a job but cannot get one. As shown in Figure 28.1, unemployment is heavily associated with the overall state of the economy. During the recessions of the early 1990s and 2009–10, unemployment became a serious problem, especially for younger people. More than 20 per cent of 18- to 24-year-olds were unemployed in the UK in 2012 and 2013.

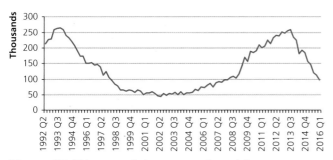

Figure 28.1 Young adults unemployed for more than 12 months, 1992–2016 (Source: ONS)

The impact of unemployment on companies varies considerably. Producers of essentials such as toilet paper and soap will find little effect from economic highs or lows, but those producing luxury goods may find a huge effect from economic change, perhaps forcing them to make staff redundant during a recession. This can have a horrible long-term effect on trust between management and staff. A broad explanation of the effects of unemployment on companies is given in Table 28.1.

Table 28.1 The effects of unemployment

	Favourable for companies	**Unfavourable for companies**
Unemployment is low	Demand for most goods will be high, especially luxuries such as overseas holidays	May be labour shortages, especially in skilled work, which will make people press for higher pay
Unemployment is high	Large numbers seeking work keeps pay demands down, and stops staff leaving for better-paid jobs elsewhere	Demand for luxury goods falls, and manufacturers may worry about retail customers collapsing, as BHS did in 2016

Talking point

Look at the graph of unemployment among 18- to 24-year-olds in Figure 28.1. Describe the main changes that take place over time.

Changing levels of consumer income

Changes in the rate of economic growth can have big effects on small businesses, especially if their products are those that customers love in good times. At the start of the last recession, jewellery chain Signet reported a fall of 15 per cent in UK sales. Small, independent jewellers may have suffered even more from consumer cutbacks. Just two years before, sales of gold and platinum rings and bracelets had been booming.

But not all products have the same pattern of sales. In November 2008, with car sales down by 33 per cent, sales of e-bikes (bicycles boosted by a battery that can be recharged at night) were booming. They allow you to ride around town at a cost equivalent of 1,000 miles per gallon of petrol. Sales of e-bikes rose by 50 per cent in 2009, so retailers who specialise in them were finding that tough times equal boom times!

Well-run small firms remember that when business is booming, cash must be put aside. The old cliché 'put money away for a rainy day' is true for businesses and families alike. The graph in Figure 28.2 shows how consumer spending struggled in the period 2008–13 because of the weakness in **consumer incomes**. The big recovery in retail spending in 2014 and 2015 was partly due to rising incomes, and partly due to an increased willingness by consumers to take on debt. 2015 was a record year for sales of new cars in the UK; 80 per cent of those sales were on some kind of credit package. That's OK in the short term, but if households take on too much debt, they may struggle to keep up with the repayments.

Talking point

Can you think of any businesses that should do well during a recession?

Inflation

Inflation is the rate of rise in the average price level. In other words, it measures how much prices are rising. It does this in percentage terms. The 'rate of inflation' means the percentage change in prices compared with a year ago. The graph in Figure 28.3 shows that inflation varied between 0 per cent and 8.4 per cent between the first quarter of 1989 and the second quarter of 2016. That represents a very significant variation from a company's point of view.

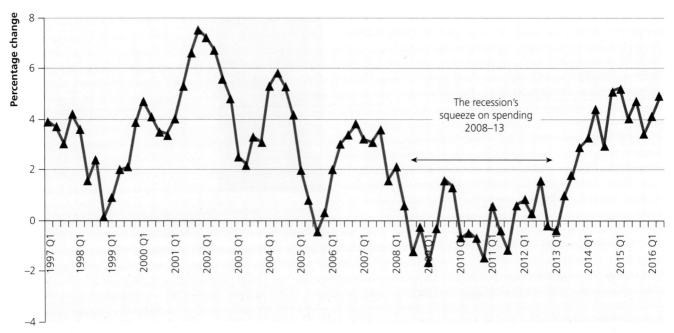

Figure 28.2 Annual percentage change in UK retail spending, 1997–2016 (Source: ONS)

When inflation is low (less than two per cent) businesses can easily cope with changes to input costs such as materials. But if prices are rising more sharply (above four per cent) not only are costs a problem but also prices. Every company feels pressed to increase prices, but then they may worry about the reaction of consumers.

For many years the government has asked the Bank of England to try to keep inflation at or around two per cent a year. As Figure 28.3 shows, they have often failed in this task.

● Changes in interest rates

Seven million households in the UK have a mortgage. So, they own their home, but with the help of a building society or bank. If **interest rates** rise, their payments may rise, possibly forcing them to cut back on other types of spending. Even those with no mortgage may have big debts on credit cards or other forms of borrowing, and also need to cut back. An important concern about rising interest rates is the general effect on consumer spending and, therefore, business revenue. A travel agent may have no debts yet be hit hard by rising interest rates because of the debt position of its customers.

What are the effects of lower interest rates on businesses?

A cut in interest rates has two main effects on firms:
◆ Lower interest rates mean more spending, especially on luxuries such as leisure, holidays and entertainment. Higher spending means more revenue for businesses and, therefore, higher profits (and more jobs).
◆ Lower interest rates mean lower interest charges on firms' borrowings. As most small firms are financed largely through overdrafts, lower interest rates provide an important reduction in fixed overhead costs.

There is, therefore, a double benefit from lower interest rates: revenues go up and costs go down.

What are the effects of higher interest rates on businesses?

Simply, the opposite:
◆ Households with mortgages need to cut back on spending because they are paying more to the bank/building society.
◆ Firms have higher fixed overhead costs, which squeezes their profits.

Both factors may force firms to cut back on investment spending and, perhaps, on staffing.

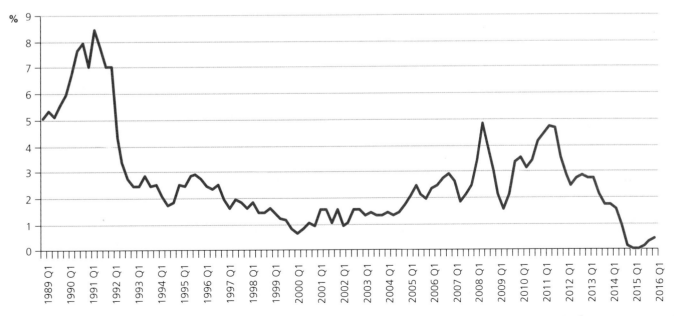

Figure 28.3 Inflation in the UK, 1989–2016 (Source: ONS Consumer Prices Index, August 2016)

Government taxation

Taxes affect businesses directly and indirectly. The direct effect is from corporation tax, which is a tax on company profits. In 2016, the rate of tax was 20 per cent. So, after companies have deducted all their costs from their revenues, the remaining profit is taxed at 20 per cent, the same rate that the average householder pays in income tax. If corporation tax is increased to, say, 25 per cent, companies would argue that they will be less able to afford to invest in their future. So, companies are always pushing government to reduce the corporation tax rate.

The other impacts on business come from the way that government taxes people and goods. With the UK leaving the EU, it is possible that there will be import taxes charged on goods brought into the country from the EU in future. If there was a ten per cent tax on imports from Germany, for example, gearboxes and other components will cost more to manufacturers such as Jaguar Land Rover. So the level of import taxes matters.

Another key factor is **taxation** on households, including VAT and income tax. Broadly, the higher the rate of tax, the harder it is for households to spend and, therefore, the worse it is for businesses. The big compensation is that if government is trying to raise more income in the form of taxation, it perhaps wants to spend more on goods and services. Overwhelmingly governments spend their income on products supplied by the private sector, for example textbooks bought from publishers or new schools or roads bought from private sector construction companies.

Changes in exchange rates

The rate of exchange shows the value of one currency measured by how much it will buy of other currencies. If £1 buys $1.40 in March and $1.45 in April, the pound has risen in value because it buys more dollars. If the pound buys more dollars, it makes it cheaper for us to buy American goods.

Over the past 15 years the value of the pound has varied from $1.20 to $2. If £1 buys $2, then every price you see in an American shop can be halved to work out the British equivalent. For example, a $1 bottle of Coke costs 50p (with $2 to the pound, you can buy two Cokes for £1).

CURRENCIES	WE BUY	WE SELL
EXCHANGE RATES		
AUSTRALIA	5.76	6.70
CANADA	6.82	7.79
CHINA	1.06	1.19
EURO	10.01	11.39
JAPAN	0.06	0.07
KOREA	0.06	0.07
PHILIPPINES	0.14	0.19

The exchange rate is the value of one currency measured by how much it will buy of another currency

Why does a strong pound matter?

It matters because a strong pound (lots of dollars to the pound) makes it cheaper to import goods from America. This is great for us as consumers because American goods will seem great value. However, it is tough on British firms that are trying to compete with cheap imports from America. A British shopper is happy if the price of an American tablet has fallen from £350 to £290; a British computer company with production costs of £320 can make a profit at £350, but will make a loss at £290.

So, a strong pound is good for British shoppers but bad for British producers.

The knock-on effects could be even greater. A British producer that cannot compete with

American imports may find it has to cut its staffing levels. A strong pound could lead to jobs being lost in Britain.

What if the pound is weak?

If the value of the pound is falling against foreign currencies, it is said to be weak. That means the pound buys less of any foreign currency (for example £1 used to equal $1.50, but now only buys $1.20). When the pound is weak it costs a British buyer more to buy from overseas. So, imports become more expensive, which means that people will buy fewer of them. A computer game that sells for $54 in America and used to sell in Britain for £36 ($54 ÷ $1.50), is now priced in Britain at £45 ($54 ÷ $1.20).

This increase in the price of imports is great for UK producers, however. Suddenly they find it easier to compete with the higher-priced imported goods. They will also find it far easier to sell overseas, because a weak pound makes our exports better value for foreign buyers.

So, a weak pound is bad for British shoppers, but good for British producers.

Exchange rate calculations

Here are the rules to follow when making an exchange rate calculation.

1 Rule 1: when exchanging from pounds to a foreign currency, multiply.

2 Rule 2: when exchanging from a foreign currency to pounds, divide.

For example, when £1 = $1.40, a £200 Burberry jacket should sell in New York for £200 × $1.40 = $280. At the same time, a $840 Calvin Klein suit should sell in Britain for $840 ÷ $1.40 = £600.

If £1 = €1.40, what price should be charged in Britain for a €21,000 Audi?

● Drawing the right conclusions

Companies can be affected greatly by changes in the economic climate. Following the 'Brexit' vote, hotels are enjoying a boom as more tourists come to Britain because the pound is weak. But house-builders are worried that fewer foreigners will buy houses in the UK – perhaps causing a downturn in demand for construction workers. It is rare for the UK economy to be so stable that businesses can simply forget about it.

Revision essentials

Consumer incomes: the amount households have available to spend after income taxes have been deducted.

Economic climate: like the weather, the economy can run cold or hot; the economic climate is a measurement of the current economic outlook, which might be promising or worrying.

Exchange rate: the value of one currency measured by how much it will buy of other currencies.

Inflation: the rate of increase in the average price level.

Interest rate: the annual cost of a loan to the borrower.

Taxation: charges placed by government on goods, imported goods and the incomes of individuals and companies.

Unemployment: when someone of working age wants a job but cannot get one.

End of chapter exercises

1 Outline how a general fall in UK consumer spending might affect:

  (a) Rococo, a small business making and selling luxury chocolates.

  (b) T. Hughes, a small bakery with loyal, local customers.

2 Explain why a strong pound is bad for manufacturers based in the UK.

3 Briefly explain the likely impact of a sharp rise in interest rates on:

  (a) Tesco plc.

  (b) A car sales business specialising in new Porsche cars.

  (c) A house-building firm specialising in starter homes for young families.

4 What price could be charged in London for $175 Nike trainers when the exchange rate is £1 equals $1.25?

5 (a) If £1 equalled €1.30 last month but €1.20 this month, has the pound risen in value or fallen in value?

  (b) What would be the effect of this change on the export price to Europe of a £200 UK-made coat?

6 Suggest one approach that could be taken by British Airways to ensure that it does not suffer too severely when the next recession arrives.

Practice questions

JCB is based in Rocester, Staffordshire, and exports more than 60 per cent of its more than £2 billion annual sales. It thrives when the world's construction businesses are thriving. The impact of the global recession in 2009 is clear to see on Figure 28.4. In 2015, the company's owner, John Bamford, campaigned strongly for Britain to leave the EU. After the Brexit vote in June 2016, the value of the pound slumped by around ten per cent. It remains to be seen whether JCB exports to EU countries will suffer when the full exit arrangements are completed. Around 6,000 jobs in the UK are at stake.

Total: 13 marks

1 (a) Calculate the percentage decline in sales between 2007 and 2009. (2)

(b) Outline one way in which JCB may have responded to this decline in sales. (2)

2 After the ten per cent fall in the pound in 2016, JCB has two options:

◆ Option 1: Cut the overseas prices of its excavators by ten per cent.

◆ Option 2: Keep the overseas prices of the excavators the same.

Justify which **one** of these options it should choose. (9)

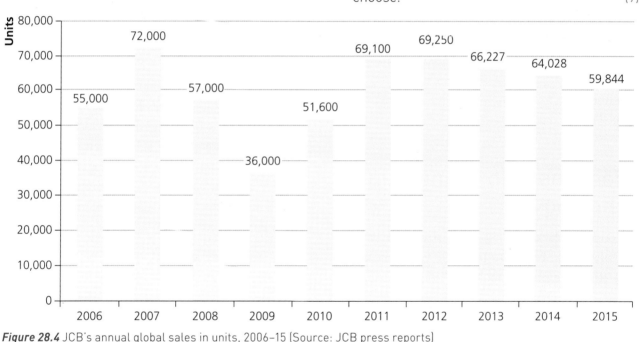

Figure 28.4 JCB's annual global sales in units, 2006–15 (Source: JCB press reports)

29 External influences on business

Although entrepreneurs want to control the future of their businesses, the reality is more complex. Individual companies find that external changes get in the way of their plans. The bigger and older the business, the more likely it is to devote time and money into an attempt to control these external influences. But when external change cannot be controlled, the company must respond effectively to the new challenge. This decision making has to cover changes in:

◆ technology
◆ legislation
◆ the **economic climate**.

◉ Responses to changes in technology

For London's black cab taxis, the arrival of Uber was a ghastly shock. For more than 100 years black cabs had a strong semi-monopoly position, but suddenly it was swept away. It meant the two years spent passing 'The Knowledge' test was wasted. Cabbies saw their weekly earnings halved in the two years to early 2016. Then they decided to fight back. Black cab campaigners pressed for all black cabs should have free, ultra-fast wi-fi, contactless card readers and new zero-emissions cabs to take to the streets by 2018. The taxi business was responding to technological change – to the customers' benefit.

In other parts of the world the response has been different. In the German city Frankfurt local cab drivers have been successful in pressing the local and national government to keep Uber at bay: their response to the technological change was to use legislation to resist it. After all, you can reasonably complain that Uber drivers are unregulated, causing potential dangers to passengers and to fellow road users.

Other examples of responses by businesses to changes in technology are outlined in Table 29.1.

The arrival of Uber changed the market for black cabs

Table 29.1 Business responses to changes in technology

	The action	The logic
Sainsbury's	In early 2016, Sainsbury's bought Argos for £1.3 billion	Sainsbury's believes that Argos has better systems for 'click and collect' and, therefore, it is part of its e-commerce battle against Ocado and Waitrose
Airbus	In May 2016, UK aircraft factories installed their first robots	Cheaper, faster and more flexible robots, plus the challenge of increasing the output of its A320 plane by 50 per cent, have made the robots a worthwhile investment
The Independent newspaper	Scrapped its print edition in February 2016	With sales slumping, the Russian owner decided to close the daily and Sunday print editions; the paper is now only available online

> The internet, like the steam engine, is a technological breakthrough that changed the world.
>
> *Peter Singer, philosopher*

Responses to changes in legislation

New laws can represent opportunities or threats to businesses. Businesspeople tend to focus more on the perceived threats, calling the new legislation 'red tape'. But it is useful to think about the business opportunities provided by new laws, and how companies have responded to those opportunities. Here are two examples:

1 Legislation introduced the Landfill Tax in 1996; it is a charge on rubbish taken to landfill waste sites. It was first charged at £7 a ton, rising to £84.40 a ton in 2016. Construction companies moaned that it would be a disaster but its main effect has been to encourage recycling. In 1999, 30 per cent of construction and demolition waste was recycled. By 2015, the figure had risen to 86.5 per cent. Companies responded to the ever-rising charges on landfill by becoming better at recycling, and new companies started up to handle the recycling for busy building firms. (Unfortunately a few rogue businesses responded to the new landfill tax by illegally 'fly-tipping', dumping their rubbish anywhere but the official, taxed sites.)

2 Revisions to the Food Safety Act in 2013 forced businesses to take further measures to protect consumers. These included keeping records about who supplied each batch of food (known as traceability). Various new small businesses set up to provide simple software programs for recording food origins, and suppliers started to help restaurants and cafes by texting the source of the food.

On the other hand, many businesses bemoan the efforts they have to make to keep up with legislation. This was a factor in the 'leave' campaign for Brexit. The suggestion was that EU membership led to a big increase in laws that wasted the time and money of businesses, and that this, in turn, led British businesses to be less competitive compared with businesses in, say, Singapore, China or the USA.

Among the possible responses by businesses to changing legislation are:

◆ Hire new staff to cope with the paperwork. This *was* necessary for banks and insurance companies after the Bank of England imposed tougher rules following the credit crunch of 2007–09. This would have added to their costs and hit their profits. More normally, though, legislative changes are planned to create as little administrative burden on businesses as possible.

◆ Cut back or even scrap a whole area of business. In early 2015 new regulations came in to restrict 'payday lenders' such as Wonga from charging interest of more than 100 per cent of the sum borrowed. Several small payday lenders decided to stop lending (before, they had been charging 1,500 per cent or more).

Responses to changes in the economic climate

As the economy is changing constantly, all established businesses become used to the need to respond to economic ups and downs. In good times companies want to hire more staff, invest in equipment and spend more on developing and launching new products. The very best companies anticipate the situation by hiring and training new staff regularly, so that the right skills are available to meet rising demands. Unfortunately, many companies operate with very short-term thinking. Rising demand for skilled labour can be met with panic, and perhaps hiring skilled staff from overseas.

In the longer term, bigger companies respond to the ever-changing economic climate by spreading their risks. Jaguar Land Rover used to produce only in England, but that left the business vulnerable if a rising pound hit export profitability. Today there are JLR factories in China, Brazil, Austria and Slovakia. The value of the pound is therefore much less of an issue.

For the British multinational Unilever, long-term thinking has had an even more dramatic effect. In 2001, it amazed the business world by announcing a target of having 50 per cent of its sales in developing

JLR spread its production facilities across the world

countries. In fact, it has beaten that figure: today nearly 60 per cent of Unilever sales come from faster-growing developing countries such as China and India.

Drawing the right conclusions

Entrepreneurs soon learn that change is a regular fact of life. Responding to changes in the fierceness of competition or strength of the pound are a regular part of daily decision making. The businesspeople with real talent are those who don't just react to today's changes but – like Jaguar Land Rover or Unilever – look ahead to protect the business from future uncertainties.

Revision essentials

Economic climate: like the weather, the economy can run cold or hot; the economic climate is a measurement of the current economic outlook, which might be promising or worrying.

End of chapter exercises

1 Outline how a dramatic improvement in technology might affect:

  (a) the market for games consoles, currently dominated by the Sony PS4

  (b) the market for takeaway pizza, currently dominated by Domino's.

2 Explain how a UK manufacturer and exporter of cars might respond to a strong pound.

3 The government brings in a new law that all babysitters must pass a test of competence. Outline the possible effect on:

  (a) businesses

  (b) parents.

4 Suggest one approach that could be taken by discount grocer Lidl to ensure that it does well even when the economy is booming.

Practice questions

The Bank of England needs to act fast to combat a severe economic downturn caused by the vote to leave the EU, warns one of Britain's most respected independent economic forecasters. In a grim assessment of the UK's economy after the vote for Brexit (Britain exiting from the EU), the National Institute of Economic and Social Research (NIESR) said 320,000 jobs would be lost by the third quarter of next year and warned that the economy had a 50 per cent chance of slipping into recession in the next 18 months.

Inflation would increase to more than three per cent for the first time in five years in late 2017 as the weak pound pushes up the price of imports, and the government would be forced to borrow an extra £47 billion in the next four years, NIESR said on Wednesday.

According to NIESR, economic growth would slow to 0.2 per cent in the current quarter from 0.6 per cent in the previous three months, and stagnate for the rest of the year. Growth is forecast at one per cent for all of next year but conditions could worsen, it said. Its report followed a series of dire business surveys, including one showing the economy shrinking at its fastest pace since the 2009 recession.

NIESR said the slowdown was caused by reduced business investment after Brexit, which threatened to disrupt companies' most important trading relationships. Rising unemployment, muted wage growth and uncertainty would also hit consumer spending, it added.

Source: *The Guardian*, 3 August 2016

Total: 15 marks

1 Outline one reason why inflation of 'more than three per cent' might be a worry for UK businesses. (2)

2 Outline one way in which a UK-based food manufacturer such as Cadbury might respond to a weak pound. (2)

3 Outline one way in which a business such as Costa Coffee might respond to rising unemployment. (2)

4 If the UK economy falls into recession, a construction company such as Costain has two options:

   ◆ Option 1: Cut its workforce, perhaps by making ten per cent of staff redundant.
   ◆ Option 2: Risk making a loss by keeping all staff employed.

Justify which **one** of these options they should choose. (9)

Exam-style questions on Topic 1.5

Don't rush; check your answers carefully.

1 Which **two** of the following are probable effects of a cut in interest rates by the Bank of England? (2)

 (a) The value of the pound may start to rise against other currencies.

 (b) Furniture shops may find it easier to sell goods on credit.

 (c) It may help the price of oil to fall.

 (d) New, small firms with big overdrafts will enjoy falling interest charges.

 (e) New, small firms will have less tax taken from the company profits.

2 Which **one** term means a sustained rise in the price level within an economy? (1)

 (a) Higher interest rates

 (b) Reflation

 (c) Inflation

 (d) Deflation

3 The government forecasts that consumer incomes will rise significantly in the coming year. Which **one** of these businesses would be the happiest if that forecast proves true? (1)

 (a) A business that imports low-cost clothes from Sri Lanka and sells them on to street markets.

 (b) A new sweetshop located in the soon-to-be-renovated Birmingham New Street station.

 (c) A funeral service that has operated in Preston for the past 52 years.

 (d) A newly opened clothes shop focused on expensive designer brands.

4 A banking analyst has forecast the following trend in exchange rates in the coming year:
January next year: $1.30 to the pound
April next year: $1.38 to the pound
June next year: $1.43 to the pound
Which **two** of the following are probable effects on British firms if the forecast proves accurate? (2)

 (a) UK importers of US computers would find that the cost of imports would rise.

 (b) Importers of US computers would find that the cost of imports would fall.

 (c) Exporters to America, such as Jaguar Land Rover, would be better off.

 (d) All British firms would suffer as a result of this rise in the dollar.

 (e) Exporters to America, such as Jaguar Land Rover, would be worse off.

5 Qatar Airways has just cancelled an order for the Airbus A320 plane because of delivery delays. Airbus, in turn, blames the US engine-maker Pratt & Whitney, who have had delivery hold-ups. The cancellation threatens jobs at Airbus' French and British production centres.

 Which **three** stakeholders in Airbus have been identified in this passage of text? (3)

 (a) Local residents

 (b) Shareholders

 (c) The government

 (d) Staff

 (e) Customers

 (f) Suppliers

6 Which **one** of the following is a reason why UK businesses grumble about the high standards imposed by health and safety legislation in the UK? (1)

 (a) They say it makes it hard to compete with overseas-based producers.

 (b) They worry that they're forced to make goods to too high a standard.

 (c) They think consumers should be free to make their own decisions about what they buy.

 (d) They think the NHS will be able to deal with unhealthy staff perfectly well.

Now try this discussion question.

7 Discuss what an entrepreneur could consider when deciding whether to open a new business when unemployment is high. (6)

Theme 2

Building a business

30 Methods of growth

When a market is growing, it is especially important for businesses to grow. If you get left behind you become less and less significant as your market share declines. That, in turn, threatens your existence. Retailers may stop selling your products.

There are two main ways to grow:

1 **internal (organic) growth**, which can come from selling more of your existing products, opening new stores/outlets, or developing and launching new products

2 **external (inorganic) growth**, which comes from buying other companies or merging with another business.

> It's very easy to be different but very difficult to be better.
>
> *Jonathan Ive, chief design officer at Apple*

In 2005, two experienced food marketing executives started Fever-Tree. The brand's proposition is all-natural soft drinks, such as tonic water. The premium positioning and pricing helped Fever-Tree to quickly gain acceptance by 75 per cent of the world's top restaurants. Entirely by organic growth, sales fizzed up from £2.3 million in 2008 to £59.3 million in 2015. The expectation is that sales will continue to rise, at perhaps 50 per cent a year for the next few years. The company's growth has come from launching new, successful products, finding more retail distribution and launching into more than 50 countries. Fever-Tree exports more than half its sales.

⬤ How to grow organically

New products

Most companies begin with one product idea. If it is successful then it is natural to look for related products that might also be successful. Fever-Tree started with tonic water; when that was well-received by restaurants and bars, the company developed a ginger ale, then a bitter lemon, then a Sicilian lemon, and so on. When a product range expands in this way, it becomes possible to interest more customers. A bar might not be interested in stocking Fever-Tree tonic alone, but if it can buy all of its mixers from one company, it may throw out its previous mixers and go with Fever-Tree exclusively. In this way, the company can enjoy sustained, substantial growth.

For most companies, the only way to persuade retailers to stock a new product is if it is distinctive and innovative. **Innovation** means bringing something new to the market. The Swiss chocolate-maker Lindt did this successfully with its Lindor brand – different in taste and mouthfeel, and more luxurious than traditional, beloved Cadbury. With UK sales of £99 million in 2016, Lindor now outsells all the traditional chocolate boxes (Nestlé's Quality Street, Mars' Celebrations and Cadbury's Roses).

Lindt brought something different to the chocolate market

To be innovative, companies need to spend consistently on **research and development (R&D)**. This means scientific research into, perhaps, melt-free chocolate (crucial for building sales in hot countries such as India) or into strong but light materials to enable cars and airplanes to become more fuel efficient. This must be followed-up by careful technical development to make sure that the idea can be turned into a business reality, through careful engineering and production testing and planning.

Table 30.1 The benefits of good R&D

Examples of science-led innovations	Examples of technical developments
The development of lithium batteries in the 1980s has been crucial for developing electric cars, notably the Tesla supercar.	After ten years' work, Toyota launched its hybrid Prius car in 2001; it is still the world's biggest-selling eco-friendly car.
In 2015, Nestlé patented a method for making chocolate that is heat-resistant up to 40°C; it claims the mouthfeel is unchanged.	Years ago, every chocolate bar was wrapped individually, creating high labour costs; today most are flow-wrapped by a continuously moving wrapping machine – cutting costs sharply.
Contactless payment cards were first issued in the US in 1997 and introduced to the UK in 2007 by Barclaycard. They work on radio-frequency recognition.	The newest aircraft, such as the Airbus A350, are 25 per cent more fuel efficient and much quieter than in the past, due to the use of newer, lighter materials.

New markets

For most businesses, finding and developing new markets is difficult and expensive. Although it said things were going well, in 2016 SuperGroup plc (owners of Superdry) warned investors that its development plans for America and China were eating into profits. It was confident of the long-term future, but counting the cost in the short term.

To grow by moving into new markets overseas means a series of (often expensive) challenges:

◆ promoting an unknown brand into a market that you don't yet know and understand

◆ learning about the local distribution system, so that you can master the 'place' aspect of the marketing mix

◆ building a new management team and structure in a new country, and all the recruitment and training mistakes that this can entail.

Table 30.2 UK successes and failures in looking for new markets overseas

Successes	Failures
Despite entering the Chinese market ten years after Starbucks, Britain's Costa Coffee now has a 25 per cent market share in China and plans to double its number of stores to 900 by 2020.	Tesco wasted £2 billion in failing to establish a grocery chain in America, and paying a Chinese company to take Tesco China off its hands.
Despite struggling for many years, in 2015 Innocent Drinks had success in Europe at last, with sales of more than £100 million across France, Germany and – newly – Russia.	In November 2014, fashion retailer New Look announced that it was withdrawing from Russia, closing 20 stores. It blamed the political situation, but also closed stores in Thailand and Morocco.
Ella's Kitchen, a company producing organic baby food, started in 2006. By 2016 had sales of more than $100 million, including exports to more than 40 countries.	*The Guardian* newspaper invested heavily in newsrooms in America and Australia; although it is one of the world's most-visited online news sites, its operations have plunged into big losses.

The great strength of the UK's membership of the single European market was that it gave UK companies free access to a market of more than 500 million consumers.

New markets don't have to be overseas, however. Companies with technological expertise can use it to develop different opportunities. At the core of Google is a mastery of computer logic; this is what makes its search engine so effective. The company thinks that this expertise can be used to make self-driving cars safe, effective and desirable. On the face of it, a move from computer search engines to making cars is an extraordinary one, but welcome to the world of Google. Companies with a strong base in technology have every chance of growing by developing new, interesting market opportunities.

A final way to move into new markets is to rethink your marketing mix. Few have done this as brilliantly as Lucozade. For decades this had been marketed as a drink to provide energy for the elderly – a present for gran. It was in a big glass bottle. In the 1980s Lucozade Sport was brought out, with completely different packaging and a bright new image. The whole marketing mix was re-thought – and the results were spectacular. Sales went from less than £20 million a year to today's £400 million plus.

How to grow inorganically

Takeovers

In 2008, the world's biggest chocolate business, Mars, bought the global leader in chewing gum, Wrigley, for $23 billion. This gave Mars a growth boost because, while global chocolate sales were grinding to a halt, the chewing gum market was growing. It also gave huge scope for financial benefits in two ways:

◆ It made the combined business an even more powerful negotiator when talking prices with supermarket chains, therefore helping to push prices up.

◆ It enabled costs to be cut, for example merging the Mars and Wrigley salesforces and delivery systems into one (at the cost of many jobs).

Buying Wrigley helped Mars diversify its business

When one private limited company wants to take over another, phone calls are made and – if the price is right – a deal is done. It can only happen if the owners of more than 50 per cent of the share capital wish to sell up. As many private limited companies are family owned, there is some scope for big rows and falling outs but eventually a decision is made.

> [When making a takeover] go for a business that any idiot can run – because sooner or later any idiot is probably going to run it.
>
> *Peter Lynch, businessman and investor*

With public limited companies (plcs) things can be more complicated. To persuade the shareholders of another company to sell up, the bidder must offer a reasonably generous price premium. This is usually 25–40 per cent. So, the shareholders stand to make a profit of 25–40 per cent instantly. But they may realise that a rival bidder may appear, potentially pushing the share price still higher – and so may refuse to sell. In 2016, a bidding war between Microsoft and Salesforce.com meant that LinkedIn was eventually bought by Microsoft at a 50 per cent premium to the pre-bid share price.

The **takeover** becomes a reality when more than 50 per cent of shareholders have sold to the bidder. The other 49.9 per cent might as well accept the bidder's terms, because the battle has been lost.

Once the bid has gone through, a number of things tend to happen:

◆ The winner takes full control, and many of the losing company's senior staff leave.

◆ Over the following months a series of decisions will be made about who stays and who goes, and who will be appointed to the new, bigger management jobs.

◆ Later, there may be important decisions about cutting back on products, brands or services that overlap. After Poundland bought 99p Stores in 2015, a number of 99p Store branches were closed down because they were too close to existing Poundland stores. Staff lost jobs as a result.

So, who are the winners and losers? The only guaranteed winners are the shareholders who sold out at a profit. Shareholders in the winning company often do much less well, as research shows that most takeovers prove a disappointment. Among other winners are the City advisors, who may receive hundreds of millions of pounds for their advice.

The losers include the managers and staff who lose their jobs, and the customers who find there's a little less competition in the high street, or that their favourite beer or chocolate bar is no longer made.

Merger

A **merger** happens when the shareholders of two similarly sized businesses agree to share ownership and control. The two separate businesses become one, of approximately double the size, and therein lies the problem. If your school was to suddenly double in size, it would put great strains on the school leadership and management, and that's what happens when mergers occur. The change is often too much and too fast.

The Dixons and Carphone Warehouse merger has been successful

One of the biggest merger disasters was when Daimler-Benz (Mercedes) of Germany merged with Chrysler of America. Despite both being in the car business, there were constant disagreements. By the time they agreed to part, Mercedes had lost more than $50 billion, while Chrysler lasted only a year before needing to be bailed out by the US taxpayer.

By contrast, the merger of Dixons and Carphone Warehouse to form Dixons Carphone seems to be a success. There is a core management team representing both sides of the business and there are clear – but favourable – overlaps between Currys PC World selling electronic items and hardware while Carphone sells mobile phone services and software.

> Every single time you make a merger, somebody is losing his identity. And saying something different is just rubbish.
>
> *Carlos Ghosn, boss of Nissan and Renault*

● Drawing the right conclusions

Many businesses have tried to succeed simply by external growth; it has very rarely worked. World-leading companies – such as Google, Facebook, Toyota and Airbus – have organic growth at their heart, even if they have used a few takeovers along the way. Organic growth ensures that staff have a sense of what the business is really about: be it knowledge (Google) or social connection (Facebook).

While organic growth is preferable, there are times when a takeover is necessary, such as when Coca-Cola bought Innocent Drinks to provide access to a faster-growing sector of the soft drinks business, or when Unilever (owners of Wall's ice cream) bought Russia's leading ice cream-maker to access to the huge Russian market.

As with every aspect of business, there is no single answer to the question of growth.

Revision essentials

Innovation: bringing a new idea to the market, such as Warburtons' clever idea of an extra-large crumpet.

Inorganic (external) growth: growing by buying up other businesses or by merging with a business of roughly equal size.

Merger: when two businesses of roughly equal size agree to come together to form one big business.

Organic (internal) growth: growth from within the business, such as creating and launching successful new products.

Research and development (R&D): the scientific research and technical development needed to come up with successful new products.

Takeover: obtaining control of another business by buying more than 50 per cent of its share capital.

End of chapter exercises

1 Outline two significant risks that might be faced if Sainsbury's decided to expand by opening a chain of stores in France.

2 Outline two things that might go wrong for Poundland after its successful purchase of 250 99p Stores in 2015.

3 What is the difference between research and development and market research?

4 Read the following extract. Why did Tricia decide on inorganic growth?

   Glory Shakes was started in Leeds in 2013. Its over-the-top, enormous shakes made it a huge hit, enabling the business to finance a second shop in 2014. Founder Tricia Burton was then too busy managing the two shops to find time to open a third. She decided to buy a retail business with a food and drink licence, with up to ten stores. One was soon found, with eight stores, mainly in Yorkshire – and therefore fairly near Leeds. Tricia made a slightly cheeky offer of £150,000 for the business and was surprised to see the bid accepted instantly.

5 Explain why Tricia might struggle to manage her new purchase of eight stores.

Practice questions

Genius Foods was founded by chef Lucinda Bruce-Gardyne, who wanted better-tasting gluten-free bread for her son, who had been diagnosed as gluten intolerant. After failing to find any decent products for sale, she decided to create something herself. Genius bread hit the supermarket shelves in 2009.

The growth of the business was sensational. Bruce-Gardyne had stumbled upon a rapidly growing sector of the grocery business, so-called 'free-from' foods. Genius sales hit £40 million by 2014, and market experts suggested that sales would rise a further 50 per cent by 2016. Much of the growth came from the launch of innovative new breads and other baked goods such as gluten-free crumpets, pizza bases and pitta bread.

In addition to this organic growth, Genius made two important takeovers. In 2013, it paid £21 million for two free-from bakeries from the Finsbury Food Group. This allowed the business to bake its own products for the first time. And, in October 2015, it paid £3.5 million for Chapel Foods – a producer of gluten-free filled pastry.

In 2016, Genius announced the launch of a range of frozen, gluten-free pastry products, from steak pies and sausage rolls to apple pie. Supermarkets such as Waitrose and Sainsbury's were quick to announce that they would be stockists. Genius wanted its slice of this market and also announced plans to launch in Germany, France and Holland. Its growth ambitions were made clear when Bruce-Gardyne told *British Baker* magazine in April 2016 that her aim is for Genius to become the world's leading free-from bakery business.

Total: 15 marks

1 Define the term 'organic growth'. (1)

2 Outline one reason why innovation can be important when growing organically. (2)

3 Calculate Genius sales in 2016 if the 'market experts' were right. (2)

4 Define the term 'aim'. (1)

5 To keep growing, Genius may have to choose between:
   ◆ Option 1: Organic growth.
   ◆ Option 2: Inorganic (external) growth.

   Justify which **one** of these options Genius should choose. (9)

31 Finance for growth

On a snowy night in Paris in 2008, Americans Travis Kalanick and Garrett Camp had trouble getting a taxi. They came up with a simple idea: tap a button, get a ride. Uber was born. In October 2010, it got its first venture capital investment of $1.25 million. By late 2015 the business was valued at an astonishing $50 billion.

How does any business finance expansion? There are broadly two options: from within the company's own resources (internal finance) and from outside (external finance).

Internal sources for financing expansion

Retained profit

Richard Branson began his empire at the age of 17 when he launched the magazine *Student*. His early venture was so successful that he used his profits to set up Virgin, a mail-order record company. Today, most small businesses think the same way. They try to finance growth from retained profit. Unfortunately, that tends to mean quite slow growth. To make a leap forward (perhaps by buying a rival) it is often necessary to go outside, that is, to look for external finance.

Selling assets

In 2016, Richard Branson made over £500 million from the sale of Virgin America (a discount airline) to Alaska Airways. Over many years Virgin has done this: develop a new business idea then sell it off – using the cash to invest in something new. This keeps Richard Branson in control (as compared with selling shares in the Virgin Group) and avoids building up big debts.

Smaller firms might sell off their buildings and then rent premises, or may sell off computer equipment and choose to lease equipment instead. The main drawback is that while this can be an effective way of raising large sums of capital, it can work out more expensive in the long term.

One of the best-ever examples of selling assets was when Whitbread plc sold off David Lloyd Leisure and invested the money in a small chain of coffee shops. When they bought Costa there were just five outlets. Today there are more than 3,250, and it is hugely profitable.

External sources for financing expansion

Loan capital

Debt is never desirable, but it may be necessary sometimes. A bank loan is the most common source of external finance for expansion plans. Research done in 2015 showed that 70 per cent of external finance for expansion came from bank loans. The same research, though, said that more than 50 per cent of loan applications from young businesses (under five years' old) are turned down. Banks only lend if they can charge substantial interest rates, and only if they can get the loan secured against a specific asset (usually property).

> A bank is a place where they lend you an umbrella in fair weather and ask for it back when it begins to rain.
>
> *Robert Frost, poet*

Share capital

A limited company can sell more shares to finance its growth. A private limited company is not allowed to advertise the sale of shares, so they are only sold to family or friends. It is nice to keep control within the family, but few families are wealthy enough to provide a really big injection of cash. In this case the business may need to apply to become a **public limited company (plc)** and perhaps list the shares on the stock market. The process of getting a stock market listing is called **flotation**.

● Public limited companies

The basics

A plc is likely to be listed on the stock market. Therefore, its shareholders may be numbered in the hundreds of thousands (as with Tesco and Marks and Spencer). All these small shareholders are likely to be interested mainly in whether the business is making big profits. They are hoping for big annual dividend payouts to shareholders plus a booming share price. Although all shareholders have the right to attend the annual general meeting (to grill the company directors), few bother.

The benefits

Plcs have access to the massive financial power of the stock market. In June 2016, a company called Sepura plc raised £65 million in share investment on one day. Its reason for the capital raising was to use the cash to pay off loan capital (its debts). This is, quite simply, a marvellous opportunity for a business

A further benefit of the plc structure is that the known value of the shares makes it easy for a business like Sepura to make a bid to take over another company. So, the organisational structure of a plc makes it easier to make external growth happen.

The downsides

Plcs not only find it easier to buy other businesses, but are also more vulnerable to being bought by others.

In early 2016 Argos was bought by Sainsbury's. There is no reason to suppose that Argos' management wanted to sell; it was just that Sainsbury's offered such a good deal that Argos' shareholders sold out.

Argos was bought by Sainsbury's in 2016

In the long term it may hurt our economy that we accept so many takeover bids from foreign firms for our companies. Examples include:

◆ Jaguar Land Rover was bought by Tata Motors (India) in 2008
◆ Cadbury was bought by Kraft (America) in 2010
◆ Weetabix was bought by Bright Food (China) in 2012
◆ Lucozade and Ribena were bought by Suntory (Japan) in 2013
◆ McVitie's was bought by Yildiz (Turkey) in 2014.

● Stock market flotation

In May 2016, the fashion retailer Joules was floated on the London stock market, raising £140 million. Founder Tom Joule started the business when he was 21 and was now enjoying a £48 million payday, though his shareholding was cut from 80 per cent to 32.3 per cent. The rest of the capital raised was used to pay off bank loans and to provide capital for expansion. Table 31.1 shows the advantages and disadvantages of stock market floatation.

Table 31.1 Advantages and disadvantages of stock market flotation

Advantages	Disadvantages
Provides a sudden, possibly huge, injection of share capital into the business.	A sudden injection of a lot of money can tempt managers to be too ambitious, e.g. SuperGroup plc, which grew too fast after its 2010 flotation.
An excellent source of capital for a rapidly expanding business (safer than big bank borrowings).	Suddenly selling so many shares means the founder's holding may fall below 50 per cent, therefore losing control.
'Going public' raises the profile of the business (perhaps making to easier to win big contracts from big companies).	The higher profile means shareholders and the media critique each quarter's results – perhaps encouraging short-term decision making.

Talking point

Richard Branson's Virgin Group was once on the stock market but he chose to buy it back to keep it as a private company. Why may he have chosen to do this?

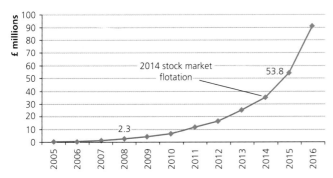

Figure 31.1 Fever-Tree's annual sales turnover, 2005–16

Figure 31.1 shows how the growth of Fever-Tree was helped by its 2014 stock market flotation.

Risk and business expansion

One of the riskiest times for businesses is when they are growing fast. It is easy for the cash outflows to rise faster than the cash inflows. So, it is important to get enough finance and to make sure it is the right type.

The worst type of finance is an overdraft. This is because, if something goes wrong, the bank can demand to be repaid within 24 hours. The best type of finance for growth is share capital, because this never has to be repaid. The business has the shareholders' investment forever. If shareholders want to get their money back, they must sell their shares to another buyer (which is what the stock market is all about).

A good way to look at financing risks is to look at the difference between debt and shares. There are two main reasons why shares are less risky than debt:

◆ Borrowing money forces a company to pay interest even in a tough year, whereas share capital involves dividend payments that can be cancelled if necessary. Debt (such as a bank loan) has interest that must be paid. If it isn't paid, the company can be closed down.
◆ Borrowed money has to be repaid, therefore a three-year bank loan of £200,000 not only involves a lot of interest, but the £200,000 also has to be paid back. Money raised by selling shares *never* has to be repaid. So £200,000 raised by selling shares is much safer than £200,000 borrowed.

Drawing the right conclusions

Business growth requires careful financing. Entrepreneurs should forecast their cash flows then look to find internal sources of finance to cover any shortfalls. Only if that looks insufficient is there a need for external finance. A careful balance then needs to be struck between the desire for control (therefore *not* selling shares) and the desire for financial safety (therefore *not* getting into too much debt). No one said business is easy.

Revision essentials

Flotation: listing company shares on the stock market, allowing anyone to buy the shares. This means the price can float freely (up and down).

Public limited company (plc): a company with at least £50,000 of share capital that can advertise its shares to outsiders and is, therefore, allowed to float its shares on the stock market.

End of chapter exercises

1 A 20-year-old wants to start an aerobics gym. It will cost £60,000 to set up, but she only has £16,000. Outline two suitable ways of raising the rest of the capital.

2 A local double-glazing company is considering expanding its product range to include conservatories – it needs £300,000 to do this. Discuss the external options available to the company to raise this amount of cash and make a recommendation about what it should do.

3 A local hairdresser has the opportunity to buy a second shop. Her family has offered to buy a 60 per cent share in her business – this will give her the money she needs for expansion. Alternatively, she could take out a loan. What should she do?

4 Outline one reason for and one against moving from private to public limited liability status.

5 A rapidly growing computer games business is planning to finance expansion using three large bank loans. It is a private limited company 75 per cent-owned by the founder/boss. Explain why the business should consider floating as a plc.

Practice questions

In 2015, Yee Kwan appeared on the BBC's *Dragons' Den* looking for finance for her range of 23 oriental ice creams and sorbets. Although some flavours (such as Matcha Tea) are very unusual, others, such as mango sorbet, could appeal to most people. Once the dragons had tasted some of the flavours Deborah Meaden and Kelly Hoppen fought hard to invest. Deborah Meaden won, paying £50,000 for a 30 per cent share stake in the business. The money was used to increase production capacity and to train a new ice cream-maker, freeing Yee to spend more time selling and managing the business.

Yee started her business in 2009 and, by 2014, had a sales turnover of £100,000 a year, selling to some upmarket shops such as Harvey Nichols and some Japanese and Chinese restaurants. In 2013, she opened an ice cream stall in Moor Market in her home town of Sheffield, but she had to close within six months because of lack of interest.

Following the *Dragons' Den* appearance – and with the help of Deborah Meaden – Yee Kwan's business has flourished. Stockists now include Whole Foods Market, Ocado and a string of well-known restaurants in London and around the country.

Total: 20 marks

1 Outline one reason why Deborah Meaden might have been willing to invest £50,000 in Yee Kwan ice creams. (2)

2 Analyse why Yee may have chosen to appear on *Dragons' Den* rather than take a loan from the bank. (6)

3 Evaluate whether this form of venture capital investment was the right way to finance Yee Kwan ice creams. You should use the information given above as well as your knowledge of business. (12)

Aims and objectives were introduced in Chapter 13. But why might a company's aims and objectives change over time?

> Arriving at one goal is the starting point to another.
>
> *John Dewey, nineteenth-century philosopher*

◉ Why aims and objectives change as businesses evolve

Businesses evolve over time as they adapt to changing circumstances; those that fail to evolve may die out like dinosaurs. As part of the process of evolving, aims and objectives often change. When Associated British Foods (ABF) opened the first Primark shop in Derby in 1973, it expected little from this new initiative. Back then, ABF was a highly profitable producer of sugar, wheat and bread. In the years that followed the strengthening of the supermarket chains made it harder to make profits from basic foods like sugar and bread. So, ABF steadily put more and more investment behind Primark, seeing it as a path to future security and prosperity for the business. In 2015, more than half of ABF's profit came from Primark – the evolution was complete.

Aims and objectives change in response to:

◆ Changing market conditions: In the ABF example, the increasing dominance of supermarkets such as Tesco was an important factor. For Cadbury, the market share gains made in the UK by Ferrero and Lindt (Lindor) were the first thing to dent its success in years. In response Cadbury is setting new objectives in relation to the luxury/higher priced segment of the UK chocolate market. If competition strengthens, you must respond.

◆ Changing technology: For many years Ted Baker plc chose to grow slowly and steadily. It carefully made sure that it had mastered the market in Germany before tackling America. Then came e-commerce. Suddenly Ted Baker could generate accelerated global sales growth from its UK website. It could be more ambitious in its aims and, especially, its sales targets/objectives. In its 2016 financial year, Ted Baker's 45.8 per cent increase in e-commerce sales helped the whole business grow by 17.7 per cent.

◆ Changing performance: If a company's costs start to slide upwards, its profits will inevitably be squeezed. This happens most commonly when things are going well, perhaps thanks to a fashion-based boost to sales. So, sales are up and revenues are up, but management allows costs to go up as well (pay rises for staff, new job titles and salaries for managers, bigger expense accounts, and so on). Then, when the fashion tide turns, revenues slip back but those new, higher costs stay high. Either the existing boss has got to do an amazing job of getting costs back down or (more probably) a new boss will be appointed. The new one will set new objectives in relation to costs and profits, and make the necessary, perhaps severe, cutbacks.

◆ Changing legislation: In the period after the 2016 vote to leave the EU, there was huge uncertainty about what changes would be made to EU laws by the British parliament. Some changes might benefit particular companies; others might be damaging. But uncertainty is the worst thing of all for businesses. Uncertainty makes it impossible to set new objectives and start planning for how to achieve them.

In its 2016 financial year, Ted Baker's 45.8 per cent increase in e-commerce sales helped the whole business grow by 17.7 per cent.

◆ Internal reasons for change: The aims and objectives of a business can be affected hugely by a change at the top. If a boss is pushed out and a new one appointed, it is common for there to be some change to the aims and objectives. Even if there's no change to the written aims and objectives, the new person's priorities will soon get through to senior managers.

After a visit to the Hawksmoor steakhouse, customers are sent a questionnaire from the office of Will Beckett, one of the founders. A complaint about the steak gets a quick response from Will and the offer of a free steak by way of apology. When Will follows up with the kitchen, it is clear to all that quality is the top priority, and that no aim is more important than preserving Hawksmoor's excellent reputation. If someone like Will is brought in as the boss of an averagely run restaurant, the importance of the change will soon be clear to all the staff (and then the customers).

> Pursue one great decisive aim with force and determination.
>
> *Carl von Clausewitz, German general and strategist (1780–1831)*

How aims and objectives change as businesses evolve

Aims and objectives can change in the following ways.

Focus on survival or growth

When David Potts took over Morrisons supermarkets in 2015, he was clear from the start that survival was an issue. In other words, unless Morrisons made significant changes quickly, it might go out of business. He cut back sharply on the number of senior managers, sold off loss-making small 'convenience' stores and did an e-commerce deal with Ocado. He also found the finance to hire more shop-floor staff to reduce the queue length in-store. As we saw in Figure 8.1 (page 36), Morrisons had been suffering as much as Asda and Tesco from the Aldi/Lidl onslaught. David Potts' changes seem to have stabilised the position of Morrisons. Its percentage share of UK grocery sales has stopped falling.

In other cases the change will be to seize growth opportunities, in just the way that Aldi and Lidl did in the aftermath of the 2009 recession. With British families struggling financially, these German discount grocers hired top-quality staff to rethink the discount stores for the British market. The managements were set ambitious targets for sales and market share growth. The remarkable result is shown in the leap from 5.1 per cent to 10.5 per cent market share between them.

Entering or exiting markets

Sales of cosmetics in China in 2015 were more than 200 billion RMB (£20 billion), up dramatically since 2010. More than a tenth of the Chinese market was made up of imports. So, for a business such as UK-manufactured Rimmel, entering the Chinese market would be a bold but logical objective. Entering a new market is bound to be expensive as it is likely to involve heavy spending on advertising.

Exiting markets is also sometimes necessary. Morrisons needed to exit the convenience store segment of the UK grocery market because it didn't have the time or the money to take on Tesco and Sainsbury's in that sector. It wisely exited the market by selling up.

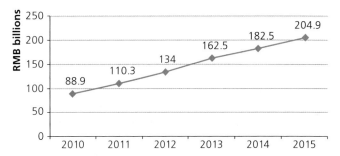

Figure 32.1 Sales of cosmetics in China, 2010–15 (Source: National Bureau of Statistics, China)

Growing or reducing the workforce

In late July 2016, Lloyds Banking Group axed 3,000 jobs and closed 200 branches. This was expected to save the business £400 million a year at a time of a sharp switch away from the use of bank branches. Online banking plus automated cash machines are steadily making bank branches less relevant. The decision to reduce its workforce came at a time when interest rates were expected to fall, making it harder for Lloyds to make good profits from ordinary banking.

In different circumstances, increasing the size of the workforce may be an important part of how to achieve a growth objective. On a random day in August 2016, games software business Codemasters had 20 job vacancies available on its website under the heading: 'Search for your perfect job'. Having enjoyed a couple of excellent years of sales growth, the company wanted to expand its new games development programme and needed new people to help.

Talking point

How might the appointment of Tesco's first woman chief executive affect the aims and objectives of the business?

Increasing or decreasing the product range

There are only two ways to grow organically: get customers to buy more of your existing products or hook them into buying new ones. When beards became trendy in 2013–16, a host of new products followed, from 'beard oil' to 'face and stubble wash'. By increasing their product range, companies hope to attract new customers, who may then start to use their other products. In 2001–14, Apple was delighted to see its sales of Mac computers rise as iPhone sales boomed.

It is also important to see the possible benefits from reducing the product range. If you're offering customers 15 models of bicycle, they're not only expensive to produce but it is also likely that customers struggle to decide which one they want. For decades Coca-Cola was proud to say that it offered one bottle of one product at one price (the original glass bottle of Coke). It came to choice later and more reluctantly. A tight product range has every chance of being highly profitable.

> Times and conditions change so rapidly that we must keep our aim constantly focused on the future.
>
> *Walt Disney (1901–66)*

Revision essentials

Entering markets: when a company decides to open up in a market it hasn't been in before, for example Walkers launching cereal bars.

Exiting markets: choosing to leave a market, probably because it was loss-making and looked set to continue.

End of chapter exercises

1 Why might a business change its objectives in response to a boom in demand for its products?

2 Why might the managers of a British retail chain such as Topshop decide to enter the clothing market in China?

3 (a) Using Figure 32.1 on page 159, calculate the percentage increase in sales of cosmetics in China between 2010 and 2015.

   (b) Between 2010 and 2015 prices rose in China by 20 per cent. Explain how that is relevant when thinking about sales figures.

4 Read the following extract. Explain how leadership changes might affect the aims and objectives of a business such as AG Foods.

   After its chief executive left suddenly, AG Foods plc appointed a new boss. She believes that the company must focus on healthier foods and drops two product lines that are exceptionally high in fat and calories. Following that approach will result in 120 job losses but ensures that the company is seen as being serious about good nutrition. Her main focus is: 'to create certainty by focusing on brands we can be proud of, not on products that might embarrass the company'.

5 Discuss how AG Foods' stakeholders might feel about the change in the aims and objectives proposed by the new boss.

Practice questions

A catering business has invested £40,000 in moving to premises three times the size of its existing site in Leeds. Salt's Catering launched in 2012 and has now moved to a 4,200 sq ft unit at Wellington Road Industrial Estate. It delivers to a corporate base across Leeds and Bradford, and also provides catering for weddings, conferences and private functions.

Bruce Salt, a director at Salt's Catering, said: 'One of the main causes of our growth has been the way we have moved into new markets. While corporate catering is still the lifeblood of the business, in the last couple of years we have teamed up with venues across Yorkshire to provide catering for weddings and conferences, while also securing a large proportion of our work through private functions too.'

He added: 'The new unit gives us the scope to grow by another 500 per cent. We are looking to invest an additional £50,000 in new equipment and building improvements so we really feel we are in our strongest position yet to take on bigger orders, more ambitious events and larger catering contracts.'

Source: www.thebusinessdesk.com, 28 January 2015

Total: 20 marks

1 Outline one way in which the £50,000 of extra investment could have been financed. (2)

2 Outline one reason why Salt's Catering has had to evolve so quickly. (2)

3 State the sum of money Salt's Catering plans to spend on new equipment and building improvement. (1)

4 Analyse how Bruce Salt's aims and objectives have changed over time. (6)

5 Bruce Salt's next big question is whether to expand into new markets in EU countries. He sees two options:
   ◆ Option 1: Open new sales outlets in France and Germany, relying on the good English spoken widely by French and German businesspeople.
   ◆ Option 2: Hire a new team of French- and German-speaking sales staff.

Justify which **one** of these options he should choose. (9)

33 Business and globalisation

Globalisation is the tendency for economies to trade increasingly with each other, creating opportunities for international and multinational companies. Exports (and **imports**) represent a much higher percentage of national income than was true 50 years ago. Years ago, one company (British Leyland) had more than 50 per cent of all the car sales in the UK; today it is difficult to get a ten per cent share of the market because there is so much tough competition from round the world. Today, car buyers enjoy terrific product quality, reliability and value for money, but far fewer Brits are employed in car manufacturing.

In the 1960s, The Beatles were a global music phenomenon; but also they recorded versions of their hit songs in German and French to meet local needs. Adele's best-selling album *25* was only recorded in English but sold worldwide. Markets have become far more globalised (and English is a global language). Globalisation worries those who fear immigration and fear competition, but it is great for those who feel that they have the skills and the ideas to succeed anywhere.

> Globalisation has enriched the planet beyond belief, leading to ever-greater demands of perfection. And, thanks to 24/7 communications, we all instantaneously know when these expectations aren't met.
>
> *Victor Hanson, US commentator*

● The impact of globalisation on business

Imports

Imports are goods or services bought from overseas companies. There are broadly three types of imports:

1 Goods that have to be bought from abroad because we don't grow or make them, such as olive oil (made from olives, which only grow in hot climates).

2 Goods that require a lot of labour time, and are therefore much cheaper to make in a country such as Bangladesh, where wages may be only 25p per hour. Clothes are a good example.

Clothes are imported as production abroad is cheaper

3 Goods that are made in the UK and elsewhere, largely using high technology and high skills, meaning Britain is competing with equally developed countries such as Germany, France, Italy and America. In January to June 2016, 86 per cent of cars sold in Britain were imported. Fortunately car producers such as Nissan and Jaguar Land Rover also export many cars from the UK.

Competition from overseas

In the British car market, the toughest competition comes from Germany. VW Audi, BMW and Mercedes are powerhouses of our car market. Their success is nothing to do with wage rates, as German wage costs are higher than in the UK. The success of their competitive push has been down to heavy investment in new product development and product design. Many British families aspire to have an Audi or a Mercedes. The same applies in markets such as games consoles and washing machines – we import because consumers have chosen foreign producers over ours.

Buying from overseas

In addition to consumer goods bought from overseas, many British producers buy supplies from abroad. Cars contain thousands of components; in the case of British-made cars, more than 50 per cent of the components are imported. So, even a British-built car is not really a British car. Jaguar Land Rover has said that it would love to buy more components from Britain, but there are just not enough component manufacturers here – so they have to import.

> It is clear our nation is reliant upon big foreign oil. More and more of our imports come from overseas.
>
> *George W Bush, former president of the USA*

Exports

Exports are UK-produced goods or services bought by an overseas customer. Every export sale represents income flowing into the UK, which helps to pay for the country's import bill. Although only ten per cent of the UK economy is generated by manufactured goods, about 50 per cent of exports are manufactured. Services generate the other 50 per cent of exports, such as banking, tourism, insurance and the creative arts, from music to computer games software.

To sell to overseas markets successfully, our exporters need to:
- keep their costs down in order to keep prices down
- produce original, well-designed and well-made items (or well thought through services)
- deliver on time and provide excellent service and after-sales service.

Changing business locations

In 2014, Jaguar Land Rover produced all its cars in British factories. As sales flourished overseas, the company opened factories in China, Brazil, Austria and Slovakia. This is partly to benefit from lower wage rates and partly to do with overcoming tariffs (see below) charged on imported goods. To stay competitive, Jaguar Land Rover has found it necessary to change some of its locations.

Talking point

The former head of the World Trade Organization Pascal Lamy has said that 'Globalisation is incredibly efficient but also incredibly unjust.' What do you think he means by that?

●Barriers to international trade

Tariffs

Tariffs are taxes imposed on imported goods. China places tariffs on imported luxury cars of at least 25 per cent, so when Jaguar was sending £40,000 Evoques to China, tax of no less than £10,000 was charged. If the country also has a system of sales tax or VAT, that would get added on top. No wonder Jaguar built a factory in China that opened in 2015.

Table 33.1 Trading blocs and their features

Name of the trading bloc	Trading bloc members	Main features of the bloc
EU (European Union)	27 members (after Britain's withdrawal) led by Germany and France	Free movement of goods and labour with a single market backed by common, EU-wide legislation
ASEAN (Association of South East Asian Nations)	Ten members including Thailand and Vietnam, but excluding China	Free movement of goods; started in 1965 with five members; members have enjoyed high economic growth
NAFTA (North American Free Trade Association)	America, Canada and Mexico	Free movement of goods; just three members: two rich and one much less so (Mexico)

The effect of tariffs is to:
- 'protect' home producers by making imports artificially expensive, which is likely to make the imported goods less attractive to the customer. If a Jaguar was £40,000 and a Mercedes £45,000 I might buy Mercedes but, if the Mercedes was £60,000, I'd definitely buy British
- increase the cost of living for consumers, effectively reducing a household's living standards. If import prices go up, everyone's pay packet buys a bit less, making people worse off
- get in the way of globalisation: wide use of import tariffs would encourage people to buy home-produced goods and therefore stop the growth of global trade.

Trade blocs

A **trade bloc** is an agreement between countries to trade freely with each other behind a tariff wall that discourages outsiders. For 40 years Britain was a member of the world's biggest trading bloc, the EU. The decision to leave in 2016 threatens to make the UK one of the outsiders. This might damage our exports, and therefore our economy in general, but is especially worrying for our manufacturing companies. Some believe there will be new opportunities for Britain outside the EU, however.

The world's largest trading blocs are described in Table 33.1.

How businesses compete internationally

Use of the internet and e-commerce

For small businesses, e-commerce provides the opportunity to sell globally without the cost of setting up operating divisions worldwide. This makes it possible for a new business to sweep to global success on the back of one trend or even a short-term fad. This might be a clothing fashion or perhaps a new celebrity-endorsed diet.

For larger businesses, the use of the internet/e-commerce may provide a dynamic business opportunity, or simply become a minimum requirement for business success.

> The Chinese government clearly sees the internet and mobile innovation as a major driver of its global economic competitiveness going forward.
>
> *Rebecca MacKinnon, CNN journalist*

Changing the marketing mix to compete internationally

If a business changes from operating only in Britain to operating internationally, it would need to rethink its use of each of the 4Ps.
- Product: for a car such as BMW's British-produced Mini, **competing internationally** means that the

car has to be offered with left-hand drive and with the flexibility to provide the safety systems and exhaust/pollution systems to fit local laws in a variety of different countries. This adds to the total costs per unit and, therefore, needs to be recovered by charging a slightly higher average price.

◆ Price: the Mini has a reputation for being cool and classy, but that reputation may be stronger in some countries than others. If it is especially strong in America, for instance, the Mini should perhaps be priced higher there than in other countries. Doing so will make it possible to charge a lower price where local competition is especially fierce.

◆ Promotion: few companies manage to run just one advertisement globally. The advertising image often needs to be different in different countries because of cultural differences. So, this aspect of the mix may have to be changed to reflect cultural differences.

◆ Place: while Britain is highly advanced in e-commerce, others are less so. Figure 33.1 shows the data for different regions of the world. In 2015, about 15 per cent of Britain's retail sales came from e-commerce. For a British company, a move into South America or Africa would require a different attitude to distribution/place.

> German export successes are not the result of some sort of currency manipulation, but of the increased competitiveness of its companies.
>
> *Wolfgang Schäuble, German finance minister*

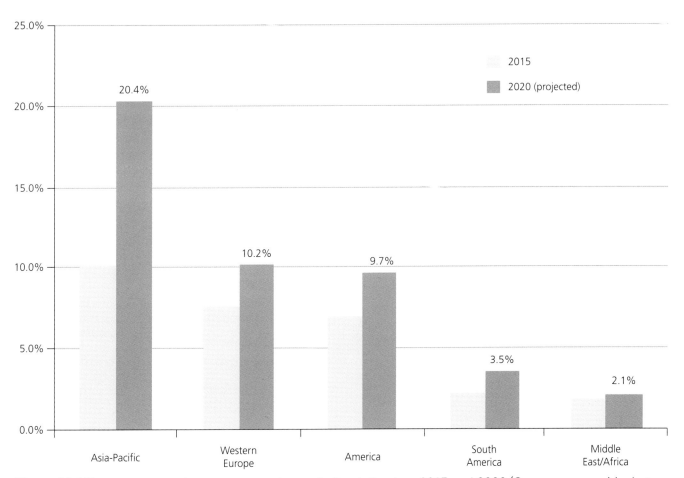

Figure 33.1 E-commerce sales as a percentage of all retail sales, 2015 and 2020 (Source: www.eMarketer.com, December 2015)

● Drawing the right conclusions

Globalisation is often regarded as a bad thing, especially by those who seem to be losing out, but most companies love the opportunity to take a successful product or service and offer it to the world. Costa has done this brilliantly in China – developing the second-biggest coffee chain (behind Starbucks). Years ago that would have been impossible. Globalisation also implies more opportunities for bright people to be able to work anywhere they choose – perhaps Tokyo for a few years, followed by New York, before returning to Britain. But with attitudes changing in America and Brexit in Britain, perhaps the steady growth of globalisation is coming to an end.

Revision essentials

Competing internationally: finding a way to succeed against rivals from overseas.

Free trade: trade between countries with no barriers, for example no tariffs.

Globalisation: the increasing tendency for countries to trade with each other and to buy global goods, such as Coca-Cola, or services, such as Costa Coffee.

Imports: goods or services bought from overseas.

Tariffs: taxes charged only on imports.

Trade blocs: a group of countries that have agreed to have free trade within external tariff walls.

End of chapter exercises

1 What point is being made in the text on page 162 about The Beatles and Adele?

2 The EU is unusual for making free movement of labour a key part of the trade bloc. Explain why businesses may favour the free movement of labour.

3 Look at the Figure 33.1 on page 165. Compare the figures for Asia-Pacific with those for Western Europe.

4 Read the following extract. Explain how Cadbury has changed its marketing mix to compete internationally.

With Halloween becoming a more popular event in countries in Europe and Asia, Cadbury is thinking of launching its Screme Eggs (Creme Eggs with a green filling) globally. Managers see no reason to change the packaging, labelling or advertising approach, because English text will make the products seem more American and, therefore, Halloweeny. Pricing will be higher, however, partly because of the costs of getting the new brand established, and also because a high price gives credibility to a brand in a country such as Japan. So, instead of a price of around 60p in Britain, a Screme Egg will be the equivalent of £1 overseas.

5 Discuss whether the globalisation of Halloween/Screme Eggs is a good or bad thing for chocolate producers such as Cadbury.

Practice questions

'Jean genie Lidl magics up £5.99 denims,' shouted the headline in a newspaper last weekend as it extolled the brilliance of the cut-price supermarket chain in once again undercutting its rivals. The German retailer, it explained, was continuing its assault on the traditional supermarket giants by targeting the high street fashion-conscious with jeans selling for an astonishing £12 less than a similar pair in Tesco.

How could these retail wizards do it? The unchallenged line from Lidl was that its huge buying power was the answer. It was just good at doing deals. But let us be clear. This is not magic. It is not Harry Potter making these jeans, it is a young woman in a factory in Bangladesh and one of the main reasons they are so cheap is that workers like her are paid as little as 2p for every pair they make.

Still, £5.99 is quite an achievement when even Primark – no slouches in the cost-cutting field – have only managed to get their lowest price down to £8. So how do they do it? 'Lidl surprises' is the slogan the supermarket currently uses to punningly flog its wares, but it is no surprise to discover that the firm, like many of the British high street retailers, does much of its clothes shopping in Bangladesh, where the minimum legal wage for a garment worker is 23p an hour.

What goes into the cost of a pair of jeans?

- Material: £2.40; zip 10p; buttons 4p; rivets 1p; label 7p; thread 19p
- Washing and checking: 47p
- Labour: 2–9p per pair (23p an hour and output of ten pairs of jeans per hour = 2.3p per pair)
- Shipping: 80p

Source: *The Observer*, 13 March 2016

Total: 20 marks

1 Outline one reason why a government might set a minimum legal wage. (2)

2 State the minimum hourly wage for a garment worker in Bangladesh. (1)

3 Outline one reason why Lidl might want to offer jeans at £5.99 a pair. (2)

4 Analyse how the case of Lidl's £5.99 jeans could be used to criticise globalisation. (6)

5 Lidl enjoyed huge sales of its £5.99 jeans, but is wondering what to do now that sales have slipped back. Management sees two options:

- Option 1: Push to get a new supplier in Bangladesh to make jeans that can be sold for £4.99.
- Option 2: Make slightly better jeans and charge the Primark price of £8.

Justify which **one** of these options the management should choose. (9)

Lidl sells jeans for £5.99

34 Ethics and business

All businesses have to follow legislation and failure to do so will result in their being prosecuted, but this is not the same as unethical behaviour. Being legal means operating within the law; being ethical means doing what is right.

Ethical behaviour covers every aspect of business, including who a business buys supplies from, how it treats its employees, how it acts towards its competitors, the impact it has on the environment and the impact it has on its local community.

And what does it mean to be unethical? Here are examples of unethical business activity:

◆ Cost-cutting measures at oil company BP led to 15 deaths in an explosion at an oil refinery in Texas, USA, in 2005. Then, in 2010, the *Deepwater Horizon* oil rig explosion and oil spill – the largest environmental disaster in US history – killed 11 and cost shareholders nearly £50 billion.

◆ British Aerospace admitted to (and was fined for) corrupt payments to win deals including a £30 million air control system in Tanzania.

◆ In 2016, top London model agencies were accused of price fixing; this would artificially add to the costs of manufacturers and retailers, thereby increasing price tags paid by customers.

> Ethics is nothing else than reverence for life.
>
> *Albert Schweitzer, philosopher*

● What about profit?

A business may have to accept lower profits when behaving in a socially responsible way. In January 2014, Lidl became the first UK grocer to remove sweets from all its checkouts. It means less chocolate slipped casually into the basket, and earned them the thanks of many parents. The decision may lower profits in the short term, but it was based on what was right for the customer and the long-term reputation of the business.

Companies have to make a large enough profit to pay off loans, pay dividends to shareholders and finance new growth initiatives. But as long as those needs are covered, a business should want to make decisions that are morally right.

How ethical considerations influence business activity

One view is that ethical considerations are becoming a stronger part of business decision making. People with that view might point to the efforts made by Mars to reduce the calorie and fat level in a Mars bar or a Snickers. They might also be impressed by the array of organic, recyclable and 'natural' products on supermarket shelves. The same optimism could be used to praise companies that are operating more apprenticeship schemes and are appointing more women and ethnic minority candidates to senior management posts.

Unfortunately, pessimists can make a strong case too. In 2016, it was announced that **fair trade** sales had fallen for the first time in 20 years. People were switching to cheaper alternatives. And as for companies such as Mars making chocolate bars ever-smaller, it can be argued that they're just encouraging people to buy more 'Duo' bars and more multipacks. Recent years have seen a series of awful business scandals, including companies such as Volkswagen of Germany and GlaxoSmithKline of Great Britain.

This doesn't seem to be a time to be complacent about improvements in ethical standards.

What's not in doubt, though, is that modern businesses are finely tuned towards the latest consumer concerns. If people want foods free from gluten, fat or dairy, companies will respond quickly. Does that make them ethical? Not at all – it simply means that they want to gain sales wherever they can. Whether, like Warburtons, they are selling crumpets with or without gluten doesn't matter to the company. Businesses just want to be responsive to changes in customer tastes (that is, give the customer what they want) regardless of whether it is right or wrong.

Possible trade-offs between ethics and profit

Businesses suggest that they are naturally ethical because high standards mean high consumer reputation. This generates the profits to keep standards high, as Figure 34.1 shows.

Unfortunately, that often proves not to be the case. A **trade-off** occurs when a business chooses one course of action instead of another. It is an either/or moment. A business might happily follow green policies when they save the company money, but what if an ethical approach would hurt profit? What would a business do at that point? Go ethical or go profitable?

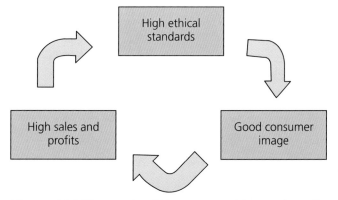

Figure 34.1 The trade off between ethics and profit

> A business that makes nothing but money is a poor kind of business.
>
> *Henry Ford, father of all modern manufacturing*

Go ethical

Not that many years ago, cigarette companies were among the country's biggest advertisers. Many advertising agencies made a good living working on these multi-million pound campaigns. One agency refused to deal with tobacco companies, however. One of the founders of Allen, Brady & Marsh had seen a loved-one die of cancer, so the decision was taken to never deal with cigarettes. This ethical stance impressed no one in the industry at the time, so the decision was entirely for **ethics** at the expense of profit.

> Being good is good business.
>
> *Anita Roddick, founder of The Body Shop*

Pressure groups

A pressure group is an organised group of people that seeks to influence government policy, legislation and business behaviour. Pressure groups include Greenpeace and Friends of the Earth (environmental), Amnesty International (which campaigns for human rights) and Searchlight (which aims to combat racism and prejudice).

If a business behaves in a way that a pressure group disagrees with, the media may turn against the company. Nike suffered serious sales declines when its expensive trainers were revealed to be produced by low-wage Asian factories. Pressure groups can embarrass companies and damage the company's image. This could lead consumers to boycott the business, damaging the profits and therefore upsetting the shareholders.

Pressure groups and the marketing mix

If a pressure group targets a particular business, the business has little alternative but to respond. This may involve product changes. In response to a sustained attack by pressure group Lynx to the use of real animal fur, many clothes manufacturers switched to 'faux fur' products. This should enable the manufacturers to cut the selling price, as the cost of fake fur is much lower than real fur. It might also lead to a switch in retail distribution: many shops refuse to sell real fur, but fake fur can be sold by anyone. Other important business-related pressure groups include:

◆ Greenpeace, an international pressure group focused on the environment

◆ Campaign Against Arms Trade

◆ Corporate Watch, which tries to hold businesses to account for unethical behaviour.

⬤ Drawing the right conclusions

In business it is easy to confuse ethics with '**ethical considerations**'. Ethics is the real thing – doing what seems right morally. 'Ethical considerations' may mean no more than thinking about how to make money out of the appearance of being ethical. Proof that a decision is ethical comes when the business accepts a hit to its profit. It is tough for a business to do that, but sometimes it will find long-term benefits in terms of customer image and when trying to recruit bright young people.

Revision essentials

Ethical considerations: thinking about ethics, which may lead to morally valid decisions or may lead to the manipulation of customer attitudes (that is, pretending to be ethical).

Ethics: weighing up decisions or actions on the basis of morality, not personal gain.

Fair trade: a social movement whose goal is to help producers in developing countries achieve better trading conditions and to promote sustainability. It ensures that the price paid is high enough to allow fair wages to be paid to the workers who produced it. Fair trade certification can be found on many products, including KitKats.

Trade-offs: how having more of one thing may force you to have less of another; for example, higher ethical standards may mean less profit.

End of chapter exercises

1 Explain in your own words what is meant by a business being 'ethical'.

2 Briefly explain the possible impact on its profit if:

  (a) SuperGroup put all its prices up by 10 per cent 'to ensure that workers making Superdry clothes are better paid.'

  (b) a car manufacturer stopped producing 4×4 (petrol-hungry) cars.

3 Use the internet to research one of the three pressure groups listed above. Outline one activity it has been involved in recently.

4 Explain two potential benefits to a retailer of selling fair trade items.

5 Read the following extract. Give two possible reasons for the Co-op making the decision to sell such a large range of fair trade products.

The Co-op Food supermarkets are built on a foundation of social responsibility, having developed from the co-operative movement started by the Rochdale Pioneers. In 1999, it made the decision to stock fair trade tea and coffee in all its stores; by 2010, it stocked over 120 fair trade products. Since then the Co-op has won prizes for corporate social responsibility due to its promotion of fair trade products. In 2016, the Co-op's 'fair trade fortnight' featured 250 fair trade products.

6 How might receiving awards for corporate social responsibility help the Co-op achieve its aims and objectives?

7 Should Tesco follow the Co-op's example? Explain your reasoning.

Practice questions

In August 2016 the Byron hamburger chain faced customer protests which included releasing thousands of bugs in busy restaurants. People were protesting at what seemed like a management conspiracy to trap its own staff in a raid by immigration officers. As staff meetings were held, in came immigration enforcement officers who hauled away about 35 illegal migrant workers. Some were deported within days. The company protested against the unfairness of a system in which UK law means companies can be fined £20,000 per worker if the business has failed to check the legal status of the worker. In other words, they had to co-operate. Protesters complained that deliberate entrapment was going too far.

Byron faced some problems in 2016

Then it emerged that Byron's owners, who paid £100 million for the business in 2013, were engaged in an effective tax avoidance wheeze. By pretending that the business was owned overseas, and by loading Byron with debt, UK corporation tax bills were eliminated. This approach – also adopted by many other UK businesses – effectively ensured that buoyant Byron was paying no tax on its profits. The company howled that it was 'a considerable contributor to the UK exchequer' – presumably from paying national insurance contributions and council rates.

Total: 20 marks

1 Outline one reason why a business such as Byron should look after the interests of its staff. (2)

2 Analyse why the owners of a business might feel justified in paying no tax on their profits. (6)

3 Evaluate whether Byron will be able to recover from these knocks to its reputation. You should use the information provided as well as your knowledge of business. (12)

35 Environment and business

In 2015, more than 16,000 houses were flooded during the wettest December in a century. Rivers in Lancashire and Cumbria were at their highest recorded levels. Many small businesses were flooded out, in some cases for the third time in two years. Meanwhile, Australia's 2015–16 bush fire season was the worst for years, with nine people dead and the loss of 500 business-related buildings, such as shops. Whether or not these incidents were the result of global warming, there is no doubt that the environment matters to business.

● How do environmental considerations affect business?

Environmental considerations can have both short- and long-term effects on a firm.

In the short term, the environment can be an important stakeholder issue. In the developed world, few staff are willing to work in unpleasant or dangerous conditions. This problem has been relieved, in the past, by bringing in workers from Eastern Europe. When Britain leaves the EU, this may no longer be possible. The environment also affects us all as residents and shoppers. *The Guardian* reported in early 2016 that 9,000 Londoners die each year due to breathing problems made worse by air pollution. Many of the problems can be traced back to over-purchasing of diesel cars, and to then-mayor Boris Johnson's preference for flashy diesel 'Boris Buses' instead of the available zero-emissions alternative.

In the longer term, firms need to help to overcome the challenge of global warming. The threat of global warming is changing many businesses. The 2015 Paris Agreement was signed by 195 countries, pledging to reduce their CO_2 emissions. This can only happen if industry can reduce its emissions, but this could damage the economy.

Some British companies are taking steps to cut their carbon emissions. This is partly to help the government meet its international target of CO_2 reduction, but also because companies need to be seen to be responsible. This can be important to a company's public image and can help when recruiting young, bright staff.

Natural energy sources such as coal and gas are being used up and energy companies have to look at alternative fuels for the future. Electricity companies are anticipating growing markets for wind power and for more energy-efficient appliances. Figure 35.1 shows the big increase in 'alternative energy' supply in Britain between 2012 and 2015. Unfortunately, even in 2015, these natural, renewable sources of clean energy were tiny compared with oil and gas.

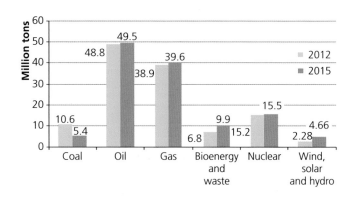

Figure 35.1 UK production of energy, 2012 and 2015 (Source: Department of Energy, July 2016)

Global warming could change other industries, too. Many environmental scientists believe that, even if we do reduce emissions, the earth will still warm by several more degrees in the next few decades. That could cut agricultural harvests, raise sea levels and bring more extreme weather.

For businesses, this presents both threats and opportunities. Insurers may face more floods, storms and other disasters. Farmers must adjust crops to changing climates. In the south of England, wine producers are having more success since their crop is now rarely affected by frost.

> I think the environment should be put in the category of our national security. Otherwise what is there to defend?
>
> *Robert Redford, actor*

● Sustainability

All manufacturing requires resources. Plastics, paints and detergents are made from oil, steel requires iron ore and coal, and paper is made from wood. Note the difference, however. Wood is sustainable: as you chop down one tree you can plant another.

The world need never run out of trees → wood → paper.

Every gallon of petrol used today is irreplaceable

Oil, iron ore and coal are very different. The oil used today has been formed underground over the last 10–160 million years. So, every gallon of petrol used today is, in effect, irreplaceable. Oil is a youngster compared with coal, which was formed 300 million years ago! Minerals such as iron ore (or copper or lead) are even more irreplaceable, as the earth cannot remake them.

The point is, then, that using certain resources is a once-only exercise. They are not sustainable. For businesses that depend on these items, careful use is essential. A plumber should never want old copper pipe to end up in landfill, because it could and should be recycled.

Sustainability can be improved by careful business decision making. Making something from plastic means using up unsustainable oil; make the same thing from wood and the item becomes sustainable, because trees can be replanted.

> **Talking point**
>
> Are businesses to blame for global warming?

● Trade-offs between the environment, sustainability and profit

It should be natural for a business to see sustainability and profit going hand-in-hand. To keep making profits year after year, Nissan UK needs raw materials and components to keep flowing into its factories. If something 'runs out' then the business cannot function.

Unfortunately, it doesn't always work like that. In 2006, an American documentary film was released called *Who killed the electric car?* US car giant General Motors had invested hugely in an electric car codenamed the EV1, but cancelled the programme in late 2003. This was at a time when the oil price was just $20 a barrel. So, although electric cars could be powered in a sustainable way (electricity could be generated from wind or sun) General Motors couldn't see a way to make the programme profitable in the short term. Profit trumped sustainability.

Some businesses are based entirely on the **environment**, such as the makers of wind turbines or the operators of solar power 'farms'. Others find ways of doing their best to operate ethically in relation to the environment. A third batch operate 'greenwash'. This means operating as normal, but dressing up their actions as if they care about green issues. This type of business finds one part of their normal activities to dress up as a huge environmental commitment. For example, a maker of aluminium cans proudly boasts 'zero waste'. In fact the company has no waste because aluminium is expensive and it makes business sense to reuse any waste materials. It has nothing to do with the environment. Greenwash should be an embarrassment to all in business, but is rarely singled out as being a hypocritical action.

> Regulatory failings mean that the cost of breaking the law is far below that of obeying it – businesses are happier to pay fines than to control pollution.
>
> *Ma Jun, Chinese environmentalist*

Pressure groups, the environment and the marketing mix

Companies have learned to be clever about **environmental considerations**. Many shops, charities and brands offer a 'bag for life', priced anywhere from 99p to £19.99, and almost every modern brand makes some environmental claim. For pressure groups such as Greenpeace, it can be difficult to find a chink in the armour of many companies. Only occasionally does a huge slip occur, for example when Volkswagen was caught cheating on exhaust emissions on its diesel cars. In early 2016, Greenpeace arranged for 17 statues across London to be fitted with face masks as part of a protest about air pollution. That protest is mainly about the over-promotion of diesel cars in the UK and elsewhere across Europe.

Many modern companies think carefully about their environmental image and adjust their marketing mix accordingly. This might lead a toilet roll producer to plan a marketing mix that covered:

◆ product: made from recycled sources; for every tree cut down we plant another two
◆ promotion: 'kind to your skin; kind to the planet'
◆ price: a small price premium to reflect the presumed extra costs
◆ place: 'we produce in the UK, cutting delivery miles and cutting our carbon footprint'

Drawing the right conclusions

As with ethics, the key requirement with the environment should be to 'do the right thing'. In fact, all Western countries have found it necessary to introduce tough environmental legislation to get firms to behave. The incentive to achieve profit has often outweighed the desire to do good. Does that mean that all firms are bad? Not at all. Marks and Spencer has run its 'Plan A' programme of environmental improvement for nearly ten years – even though it is not widely known. But when companies shout loudly about doing the right thing, it is sensible to wonder whether this is greenwash rather than actual green ethics.

Revision essentials

Environment: the condition of the natural world that surrounds us, which is damaged when there's pollution.

Environmental considerations: factors relating to 'green' issues, such as sustainability and pollution.

Sustainability: whether or not a resource will inevitably run out in the future; a sustainable resource will not.

End of chapter exercises

1 **(a)** Use Figure 35.1 on page 172 to calculate the percentage increase in energy produced from wind, solar and hydro sources between 2012 and 2015.

(b) Explain the environmental benefit that should result from this increase.

2 Explain why 'sustainability' is important to businesses and society.

3 Outline how two different UK businesses might benefit from warmer temperatures in Britain.

4 Explain how your school can change to become more environmentally friendly.

5 Read the following extract. Explain two possible reasons why Marks & Spencer is pursuing its Plan A.

In 2007, Marks & Spencer introduced its 'Plan A' strategy for improving its environmental performance. Now it has set new green targets for 2020. One small example of its actions is provided on its website:

'We've now installed the UK's largest single roof-mounted solar panel array on Castle Donington, our distribution centre in the East Midlands. The array will span the 900,000 square foot roof and will generate over 5,000 MWh of electricity a year – enough energy to power 1,190 houses! The 24,272 panels (which would cover 25 miles if they were laid end to end), will lower our carbon footprint by 48,000 tonnes over 20 years. Castle Donington, which is big enough to hold 11 football pitches, is fully automated – the roof will generate nearly 25 per cent of the energy that the site needs.'

Source: http://corporate.marksandspencer.com

6 How might consumers respond to information about Marks & Spencer's sense of environmental responsibility?

7 Marks & Spencer is closing stores at a likely cost of hundreds of jobs in the UK. Should it re-think its focus on Plan A?

Practice questions

In April 2016, one of the biggest waste-management companies in the South East was given a record fine over illegal treatment of hazardous material including asbestos at its huge Willesden depot. Powerday, run by London Irish rugby club co-owner Mick Crossan, disposes of waste for major clients including Barratt Homes, Berkeley Homes and Carillion.

The firm was ordered to pay more than £1.2 million at Harrow Crown Court for offences related to two separate cases which, combined, saw more than 17,000 tons of waste deposited and stored illegally. The materials came from across London and from a power station in Nottinghamshire. The record fine came under tough new sentencing guidelines for environmental crimes. The case was brought by the government-financed Environment Agency, which checks that businesses stick to environmental laws.

Source: *Evening Standard*, 14 April 2016

Total: 20 marks

1 Outline one reason why the court decided on such a high fine for Powerday. (2)

2 Analyse why the government pays for an agency to check that businesses stick to environmental laws. (6)

3 Evaluate the possible trade-offs within Powerday between the environment and profit. You should use the information provided as well as your knowledge of business. (12)

Exam-style questions on Topic 2.1

Don't rush; check your answers carefully.

1 Which **one** of these factors is a long-term environmental concern? (1)

(a) Sustainability

(b) Noise pollution

(c) Traffic congestion

(d) Air pollution

2 Which **one** of the statements below is a reason why the Co-op Bank may have decided not to deal with companies such as manufacturers of cigarettes and weapons? (1)

(a) To concentrate on other types of customer.

(b) To please the shareholders of the business.

(c) Because of ethical concerns.

(d) Because the Co-op Bank sees other customers as more profitable.

3 Which **one** of these factors might lead to an increase in imports to the UK? (1)

(a) A fall in the value of the pound against the euro.

(b) A rise in the competitiveness of UK companies.

(c) A rise in consumer spending in the UK.

(d) Strong growth in the economies of China and America.

4 Which **one** of the following is the best explanation of the phrase 'business ethics'? (1)

(a) Focusing new product development on customers' new interest in organic foods.

(b) Making sure to think about the concerns of all the business stakeholders.

(c) Basing strategies on one principle: doing what's right for shareholders.

(d) When decisions and actions are underpinned by moral principles.

5 A UK public company has bid £40 million to buy a direct rival. The boss of the bidding company says that this will help to bring costs down and help the business compete internationally. Given this information, which **two** of the following statements are true? (2)

(a) The business seems to be focusing on existing markets.

(b) The objective of the bidder seems to be growth.

(c) The bidder may struggle to finance this, as it has no access to the stock market.

(d) The bidder is choosing to grow inorganically.

(e) Organic growth such as this gives great prospects for international success.

6 Which **one** of the following is the best explanation of a 'tariff'? (1)

(a) A way for a government to raise taxes from its successful exporters.

(b) A way for a government to give an unfair advantage to its importers.

(c) A way for a business to encourage foreign firms to buy its products.

(d) A way for a government to prevent imported goods from being too competitive.

Now try this discussion question.

7 Discuss whether a growing business could benefit from spending on environmental considerations. (6)

36 Product

At the heart of the marketing mix is the product. The key is to design a product (or service) that matches the needs or wants of your chosen target market. It doesn't matter if over-50s hate the new, red Nike Air Max 90 as long as under-25s love it. Having identified the target market, companies have to work out customer priorities. A classic way to do that is through the design mix.

● Design and the design mix

The design mix uses a pyramid diagram to encourage managers to decide on the main design priorities for a new product. Every product needs the right balance between:

◆ **Economic manufacture**: making sure that the design allows the product to be made cost effectively; a complex design might add 50 per cent to the manufacturing cost, making the product too expensive for some customers.

◆ **Function**: the design must make sure that the product works well and works every time. A stunning new car may have its sales undermined if there are doubts about its safety, or about its acceleration. 'Function' means: how well does it work?

◆ **Aesthetics**: how well does the product appeal to the senses? It may work well and be inexpensive to make but look or feel cheap. No one buys an iPhone just because it is reliable and has good battery length – they buy it because it looks beautiful and feels good in the hand.

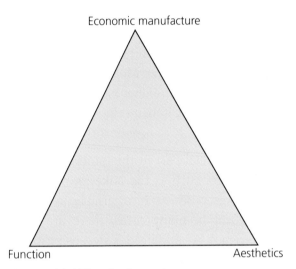

Figure 36.1 The design mix

> Design is not just what it looks like and feels like. Design is how it works.
>
> *Steve Jobs, founder of Apple*

● The importance to a business of differentiating the product/service

Product differentiation means making your product stand out from the competition, making people see it as really different and distinctive. This may help the product become a market leader, as *The Sun* is within the British newspaper market; or, like BMW, the distinctiveness may allow high prices to be charged. Table 36.1 on the next page gives some more examples.

Table 36.1 Examples of differentiated products/services

Market	Differentiated product or service
Chocolate	Lindor
Smartphones	Samsung Galaxy Edge
Lipstick	MAC
Cars	Porsche

High differentiation is important because customers can become loyal to something that they see as being different, even unique. Most *Sun* readers buy that paper and that paper alone; most iPhone users would buy a new iPhone if their original one was lost or stolen.

Design plays a crucial part in this process. It starts with a brand logo, such as the Nike 'Swoosh' (the tick). This makes products recognisable in a shop and when worn. In many cases, there are other key characteristics. As a Mercedes sweeps past, it is usually recognisable without seeing the badge on the bonnet. Its designers try to keep all Mercedes looking as if they are from the same family of cars.

A well-designed product will stand out from the crowd and will make the user take pride in using it/wearing it. That will help in achieving product differentiation which, in turn, will make it easier for the producer to set its own price, not really worrying about the prices charged by rivals.

> Strategy is about deliberately choosing to be different.
>
> *Michael Porter, business guru*

Product life cycle

When deciding on marketing approaches, such as pricing or advertising, businesses have to examine sales trends: are sales getting better or worse? One technique a firm can use to do this is the **product life cycle**.

A product's life cycle is the amount of time a business expects the product to sustain profitable sales.

Cadbury's Dairy Milk was launched in 1905 and still has many years of profitable life. By contrast, games consoles have a much shorter life cycle: in the week ending 16 July 2016, the PS4 outsold Xbox One by 20,579 to 73 in Japan. Xbox One's life cycle in Japan will soon be at an end.

There are four stages in the product life cycle. These give an idea of where the product is in its lifetime – a bit like a human life.

1 Introduction: First the company spends a lot of time and money researching the product and the market for the product. The product will be tested and market research carried out before it is launched. There will be no sales at this time. The business will be preparing an advertising campaign. At this stage costs are high and there are no sales. The product is then launched and placed on the market. There will be low product sales and small-scale distribution initially. Any advertising will be informative to make people aware that the product exists. The product might be the only one of its kind at this stage, so the selling price will probably be high. At this stage sales are low and costs are high.

2 Growth: At this stage the product becomes known in the market and there will be a wider distribution network. The business will continue with advertising but it will be less frequent than at the product's launch. At this stage customer awareness increases, the price will still be high, and sales and profits start to rise.

3 Maturity: The market may become saturated as 'me-too' or copycat products are launched on to the market. Sales growth flattens out and cash flow improves. Advertising is persuasive and is used to remind the market that the product exists. The business may try to increase promotion in an attempt to maintain market share – money spent on reinforcing the brand image or packaging. Profits are still good. The product is in a highly competitive market and weak brands often disappear at this stage, as they cannot compete.

4 Decline: The product's sales and profits start to fall. The product is no longer offering what customers

want or new technology used by other products has made it out of date. Some businesses will stop their marketing to cut costs but will still make some profits between now and when the product is finally withdrawn. Eventually the product is taken out of production. The last products are often sold at a reduced price, meaning a further reduction in profits. The product is eventually withdrawn from the market.

In reality the length of each stage can vary a lot. Businesses can take actions to prolong a stage, such as heavy brand advertising to try to stop maturity turning into decline. Not all products go through each stage – some go straight from introduction to decline (they are flops).

It is important for businesses to know what stage of the life cycle their products are at so that they can plan the correct marketing mix for the product. Just because a product has reached the maturity stage or even started to decline does not necessarily mean it is the end. Some products will have **extension strategies** launched for them to start to increase sales again, for example by changing the product's design or use.

> **Talking point**
>
> Marketing guru Phillip Kotler has said: 'Watch the product life cycle; but more important, watch the market life cycle.' What do you think he means by that?

● Extension strategies

Firms may try to prevent sales going into decline by using extension strategies. There are various techniques they can use:

1 Find new uses for the product: Johnson's Baby Powder was originally marketed only for babies; realising its sales potential among adults was a major breakthrough for the company.

2 Change the appearance, format or packaging: Coke cans, bottles, etc.

3 Encourage use of the product on more occasions: for example, cereals not just for breakfast, ice cream in the winter.

4 Adapt the product: make it 'new and improved'.

● Drawing the right conclusions

If a business has the right product, loved by loyal customers, marketing becomes an easy and cost-effective task. Girls who love MAC make-up don't need much prompting to go and buy more. And, thanks to e-commerce, they don't even need a MAC shop in place nearby. Services can have the same loyalty, such as people who love their local football team, or holidaymakers who go back to the same hotel every year. This has led many to conclude that 'product' is the most important aspect of the marketing mix (the 4Ps).

> **Revision essentials**
>
> **Aesthetics**: how things appeal to the senses; do they look great, smell good, feel nice, sound solid (the 'ker-lunk' of a BMW door shutting) and taste great?
>
> **Economic manufacture**: making the product cheaply enough to make it profitable.
>
> **Extension strategy**: an attempt to prolong sales of a product for the medium to long term, to prevent it from entering its decline stage.
>
> **Function**: how well the product or service works for the customer; for example, are the beds comfortable at a hotel; does the smartphone take sharp photos?
>
> **Product differentiation**: the extent to which consumers see your product as being distinct from its rivals.
>
> **Product life cycle**: the theory that every product goes through the same four stages of introduction, growth, maturity and decline.

End of chapter exercises

1 Describe what happens during the introduction stage of a product's life.

2 Outline what could happen to profits for a product that is at its maturity stage.

3 Explain one possible reason why some products have much longer life cycles than others. Use examples to illustrate your answer.

4 Look at the examples below and match up the statement to the life cycle shown in Figure 36.2.

(a) A product that is very popular but which, after a time, loses its popularity.

(b) A new product that flops.

(c) A product that becomes popular very quickly and continues to have good sales.

(d) A product for which sales vary, season by season.

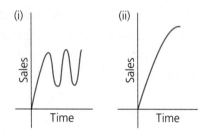

Figure 36.2 Sales/time graphs

Practice questions

The first Apple iPad was launched in April 2010, quickly becoming a must-have item. The launch of the much-improved iPad2 a year later saw sales zoom ahead. iPad2's most important feature was a backwards camera, unlocking Facetime software. As the product started to mature, Q4 (Christmas) sales became steadily more important. The product had gone from must-have to must-give. The launch of the iPad Air (2013) and iPadPro (2015) helped to keep the iPad's product life cycle reasonably long.

Total: 20 marks

1 Define the term 'product life cycle'. (1)

2 (a) Use Figure 36.3 to estimate the average sales boost achieved by the iPad in its fourth (Christmas) quarter. (2)

(b) Outline one disadvantage to Apple of having such high seasonal variations in sales. (2)

3 Identify the time period when actual iPad sales were at their peak. (1)

4 Outline why a business might like it best when its product is a must-have item. (2)

5 From the data provided, evaluate the effectiveness of the extension strategies used by Apple for its iPad. You should use the information given above as well as your knowledge of business. (12)

Figure 36.3 Global sales of Apple iPad, 2010–16 (Source: Apple Inc. accounts)

37 Price

The key is to ensure that the price is 'right'. In some cases this may be very expensive. A Lexus RX 450 costs £47,000; it will never outsell the Ford Focus, but Lexus customers wouldn't want everyone to have one! At £47,000, though, Lexus customers are still able to convince themselves that they are getting value for money.

Broadly, there are two different types of pricing:
◆ pricing low for high volume but low **profit margins**
◆ pricing high for low volume but high profit margins.

In its luxury segment of the market, Lexus has a strong enough brand name and product that it can price high. Weaker brands have to price low, such as the *Daily Express* newspaper, which sets its price below that of its stronger rival, the *Daily Mail*. At the time of writing the *Daily Mail* is 65p; the *Daily Express* is 55p.

Strong brands can set their own prices; weaker ones have to follow the lead set by others.

Table 37.1 Prices set for strong and weak brands

Strong brands set their own prices	Weaker brands follow the lead set by others
Manchester United season tickets	Kingsmill bread
Heinz Ketchup	Double Decker chocolate bar
Wrigley's Extra gum	Kia motor cars

In Figure 37.1, all five products contain exactly the same dose of ibuprofen (a painkiller often used to treat headaches). Although they contain the same active ingredient, two of the products are branded

items (Nurofen). There are also wide variations in the own-label products: the Waitrose own-label product costs 14 times more than the Asda one.

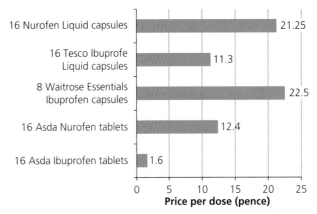

Figure 37.1 Pricing differences on ibuprofen (painkiller)

> **Talking point**
>
> What might explain why Waitrose can sell ibuprofen at 14 times the price charged by Asda?

● Pricing strategy for different market segments

Mass market

In the mass market price is likely to be kept low in order to fight off the competition. That will lead to high sales volumes but at low profit margins. If you make just £1 of profit per sale but sell 500 items per day, you will make £500 profit a day. Not bad. The problem comes if further competition pushes price and sales volumes down even more. A 50p profit on 400 items means just £200 of profit.

Businesses such as New Look, Primark, Lidl and Aldi have shown that a successful, profitable business is possible at low prices in the mass market. But it is important to remember the nature of the mass market that these four retailers operate in. A fully mass market needs:

◆ Little effect from seasonality: if sales are high at Christmas but thin for the rest of the year, it is not a really mass market – therefore low pricing is unlikely to generate enough revenue to cover the costs.

◆ Little effect from regionality: if sales are high in one region but weak elsewhere, low pricing is unlikely to cover the fixed costs.

◆ High levels of consumption: while few households would buy more than one fridge every five years, they might be buying ten packs of yoghurts every week; when households buy lots of one item, price become far more important.

> Price is what you pay. Value is what you get.
>
> *Warren Buffett, American business magnate and investor*

Niche market

A niche market is based on a particular type of customer who needs or wants something different from the majority. Sports cars are a niche market; so too are electric cars. In January to July 2016, Jaguar sold 14,000 cars in America while Ford sold 1,400,000. So, Jaguar's sales were one per cent of Ford's sales. It is understandable, then, that Jaguar needed to charge significantly higher prices in the US than Ford. Jaguar was working on the basis of high price–low sales volume, but high profit margin. That's a good way to ensure that profit is made even though sales volumes may be quite small.

How technology influences pricing strategies

The big change to pricing decisions in recent years has been due to the increased use of information

researched on the internet, as well as the increase in e-commerce. Table 37.2 gives an example of the value of 'Googled' information. A ten-minute search for 'Toyota Avensis Estate 1.8 Active' revealed the following:

Table 37.2 How technology has affected pricing

	High street dealer	Three online retailers of new cars		
	Currie Motors, Kingston	UK Car Discount	Orange Wheels	Cars2buy
List price	£19,265	£19,265	£19,265	£19,265
Quoted price	£19,010	£15,691	£16,062	£15,176
Saving	£255	£3,574	£3,203	£4,089

As a high street dealer, Currie Motors know perfectly well that no one will come to them via this sales channel. Businesses like this must try extra hard to gain favour from existing customers to keep them coming back.

Another way to look at pricing is in relation to e-commerce. In the past a specialist record shop may have had little prospect of selling vinyl album *1928 sessions* by Mississippi John Hurt. It would probably put it in a bargain basket at perhaps £3. Actually, the album is a Blues classic, and a modern e-commerce business could price it higher because it is easy for people round the world to access the website. So, potential demand is higher, which allows the supplier to charge a more realistic price, perhaps £12. Needless to say, the difference between a price of £3 and £12 is hugely significant in terms of profitability.

Pricing strategies at different stages of the product life cycle

Introduction

Many businesses change their pricing approaches as a product goes through its life cycle. Restaurants usually start off with moderately priced menus, enabling reviewers to say 'good value for money' and for staff to enjoy a buzzy atmosphere and busy services (more tips). If the place gets busy, menu prices will steadily move upwards. By starting with a low price–high volume approach, the restaurant gains a large number of regular customers who may be willing to accept future price rises.

But not all restaurants use the same pricing method at their introductory stage. Just after the Russian-owned Novikov restaurant opened in London, *The Guardian* reviewed it by saying: 'It's massive, expensive and the food is shocking. But what's truly surprising about Novikov is that it's always full.' Here, the owners' pricing policy was different to most. They wanted Novikov to be the place of choice for celebrities and rich Russians. The high prices guaranteed that only the wealthy would go there, which was exactly what those customers wanted.

> **Talking point**
>
> If a new pizza delivery place opened locally, what problems might it face later if its opening launch price was £2.99?

Growth

In the early stages of growth many companies are thrilled to see revenues and profits rising – and they keep prices relatively low. Once the growth is more established, price rises are irresistible. If prices can rise, the business can finance growth without having to worry about finding an external source of capital. Once growth is established then, most businesses charge higher prices, even if this tends to hold down sales volumes.

Maturity

When growth is at an end, new pricing decisions may be needed. For the growth period the business may have thought, 'let's keep prices down in order to keep this growth going'. If managers accept that growth is over, they may want to squeeze prices up – even though sales may decline slightly. Managers may want to get more profit from the brand before decline sets in – especially if they've decided that new investment is needed to develop a new product.

Decline

When sales have made a decisive step downwards, further thoughts are needed on pricing. For many years Fry's Turkish Delight suffered falling sales. Brand owner Cadbury reasoned that sales were falling because few new customers were coming to the brand. Old ones were staying loyal but there were too few new customers to keep sales up. So, thought managers, let's push the price up and enjoy good profits: they did. Nowadays, though, the brand has become too minor to keep its own pricing; Tesco, for example, just bundles it in with a general 'buy any three chocolate bars for £1.20' offer.

> The sole purpose of marketing is to sell more to more people, more often and at higher prices. There is no other reason to do it.
>
> *Sergio Zyman, former marketing executive at Coca-Cola*

● Drawing the right conclusions

Pricing is an area of business that is more art than science. In other words, pricing is usually a matter of judgement. MAC lipsticks sell for £17 while Superdrug ones are £1 and Rimmel is £5.49. The price of the MAC one perhaps does two jobs: it places the MAC product far out of reach of the majority, and confirms in the consumer's mind that the MAC one is stylish/high quality.

> **Revision essentials**
>
> **Profit margins**: profit as a percentage of the selling price (one unit) or as a percentage of total sales revenue (for the business as a whole).

End of chapter exercises

1 Explain the importance to a business such as the *Daily Mail* of charging 10p more per paper than the *Daily Express*.

2 Explain one possible reason why Apple might change the price of its latest iPhone when sales move from growth to maturity.

3 (a) Use Table 37.2 on page 182 to calculate the saving a Currie's customer can make by going to Cars2Buy.

(b) Explain one possible reason why the online car dealers were able to offer lower prices for the Toyota than the high street dealer.

Practice questions

In 2015–16 the UK market for crisps proved exceptionally tough. With supermarkets trying to cut prices to compete with Aldi and Lidl, suppliers such as Kettle Chips were put under real pressure. The business managed to hold on to its sales revenue by cutting prices by 10.7 per cent over the year. McCoy's was the only brand whose management refused to join in with the price cutting. By running fewer price promotions (six packs for £1), the average price of McCoy's rose by 6.8 per cent in the year. But this led to a dramatic 19.9 per cent fall in sales. McCoy's managers were shocked to find that the brand name was weaker than they had believed. Even the mighty Walkers lost a lot of sales value – the 5.7 per cent fall meant sales were down by nearly £40 million on the previous year.

Table 37.3 The UK market for potato crisps, 2015–16

	Value		Volume		Price	
	£ million	% change over 12 months	Kg (million)	% change over 12 months	£/Kg	% change over 12 months
Walkers	660.2	–5.7	82.6	3.4	7.99	–8.7
McCoy's	102.8	–14.4	11.5	–19.9	8.93	6.8
Own label	100.7	–2.3	16.4	2.1	6.16	–4.3
Kettle Chips	96.9	–0.3	10.9	11.7	8.91	–10.7
Tyrrells	56.8	+19.9	5.5	26.4	10.25	–5.2

Source: *The Grocer*, 30 April 2016

Total: 15 marks

1 Use the data to outline how Tyrrells achieved its 19.9 per cent increase in sales revenue in 2015–16. (2)

2 Define what is meant by the term 'brand'. (1)

3 Calculate what McCoy's sales value will be in 2016–17 if it suffers the same percentage decline as in 2015–16. (2)

4 Identify the highest priced crisps. (1)

5 The boss of McCoy's crisps is considering two options for rebuilding sales revenue:
  ◆ Option 1: Cutting prices.
  ◆ Option 2: Increasing the sales team to work at improving distribution.
Justify which **one** of these two options the McCoy's boss should choose. (9)

38 Promotion

A strategy is a medium- to long-term plan for meeting your objectives. Objectives are what you want to achieve; strategy is how to achieve it. **Promotional strategy**, therefore, is the plan for how to communicate so effectively with customers that the business achieves its sales revenue target.

● Promotional strategy for different market segments

Advertising

In the mass market the role of advertising is often to achieve name recognition, and little more. Home-delivery customers have heard of Just Eat, therefore they feel more comfortable using it than an unknown business that might run off with their credit card details. Of course, over time the business would love to develop the strong brand image of Chanel No. 5 or Audi, for example, but that takes a huge, long-term investment in advertising. Audi first used the slogan 'Vorsprung Durch Technik' in 1982 when the brand was a mass-market competitor to Ford. More than 30 years with the same slogan has helped the business be a huge seller, but at premium prices – the manufacturer's ideal.

Of course, in a smaller market segment the advertising approach might be quite different. G-Star RAW is a modern, international clothing business that remains focused on the under-25s. It has avoided television advertising, not only because it is hugely expensive but also to help with its street credibility. Its 'urban' image requires digital advertising, plus price promotions through coupons that are little known about. The customer must 'find' them.

Years ago people believed that all you needed to do was to 'build a better mousetrap'

> Sell the problem you solve, not the product.
>
> *Anon*

Sponsorship

Sponsorship means paying to have your brand or company name attached to an activity that has credibility with your customers. The activity is often focused on sport, but might also be based on music, art or other cultural events.

Sponsorship has been used brilliantly by Red Bull to help enhance the credibility of the brand. Sponsoring extreme sports and Formula 1 has given the brand global coverage as well as an edgy, 'risk-taker' image.

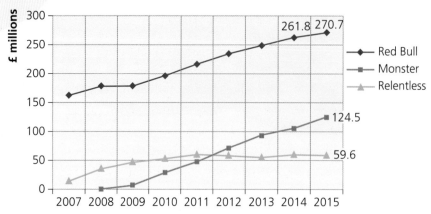

Figure 38.1 UK market for energy drinks, 2007–15 (Source: *The Grocer*)

Originally Red Bull needed a strong image simply to build the energy drink category in the UK and elsewhere. Since 2007, it has also needed to fight off two Coca-Cola-backed brands, Monster and Relentless. As can be seen in Figure 38.1, Red Bull keeps growing.

But what is the cost of using sponsorship as a form of promotion? An article in *Forbes* magazine in 2014 suggested that Red Bull had spent $1.2 billion over the previous ten years on its Formula 1 sponsorship. The precise benefits of this spending are hard to identify.

Further examples of the high costs of sponsorship include the following:

◆ In 2015, Adidas did a £750 million, ten-year deal to sponsor Manchester United's shirts.

◆ Barclays Bank was paying £40 million a year to sponsor the Premier League, but decided to end this in 2015. Clearly they decided the name recognition was not worth £40 million a year.

◆ In 2013, golfer Rory McIlroy signed a £150 million sponsorship deal with Nike. Incredibly, in 2016, Nike announced it was withdrawing from making golf equipment, but still had seven years to go on its McIlroy contract. It remains unclear whether that contract can now be cancelled.

> If you look at the sponsors who were in the sport 15 years ago compared to now, there are a lot fewer. Why? Because those runners who took drugs tainted the sport. They tainted all of us in it.
>
> *Maurice Greene, former 100 m world record holder*

Branding

When done well, nothing in marketing is quite as effective as **branding**. In the market for baked beans, truly 'Beanz Meanz Heinz' (an advertising slogan dreamed up in 1967, and still going strong 50 years later). The trick with branding is to give the brand an identity, even a personality. Richard Branson's Virgin brand is seen as being bold and independent; Innocent Drinks is seen as quirky, and Red Bull as edgy. Successful branding can mean that an image stays with people years, even decades, after the reality has changed. Innocent Drinks, after all, is now a small unit within Coca-Cola; and Virgin is a corporate empire owned by a guy soon to turn 70. So, successful branding can represent great value for money for a company. A special offer can boost sales for a short time but branding can boost sales for decades.

'Beanz Meanz Heinz' is still a successful slogan

Product trials

A product trial means giving potential customers a free taste – or longer trial – of your new product. This approach is used when there is known to be a hurdle that is likely to prevent customers from making a purchase of their own. For example, a new brand of luxury ice cream might be priced at £4.99, making it a lot to pay for something that you might not like. A free sample, handed out in a mini cone, might convince a customer that it is just what they want for a birthday treat.

It is important to remember that activities such as this are very expensive to run – not because of the free product but because of the labour time involved. Hiring people is always an expensive thing to do, so most companies could only afford to use product trials in a very targeted way. It might be best to use some form of social media to boost the impact of the trial, for example by recording and uploading videos.

Special offers

Special offers should be regarded as the last resort. No company wants to 'give away' product, as with a 'buy one get one free' (BOGOF) offer. Can you imagine Apple running a BOGOF on the latest iPhone? It would undermine the image of the brand. For every business, the short-term benefits that can result from special offers should be set against the long-term damage to the brand. That said, there are times when special offers may work well:

◆ Your sales are always weak after Christmas, so you run a special offer in January and February: 'free: 40 per cent bigger pack'.
◆ A new competitor has just launched a product like yours, but cheaper; you run an on-pack competition with fabulous prizes to help lock your customers in.
◆ You are launching a new chocolate bar, so you bundle a 'free trial size' to every pack of your best-selling brand.

The use of technology in promotion

Targeted advertising online

In 2015, UK spending on digital advertising (£8.6 billion) far outstripped television advertising (£5.3 billion). By 2017, more than half of all promotional spending in the UK will be on digital advertising. The reason for the growth in spend on digital advertising is partly that that's where the people are, especially children and young adults. Advertisers also love the targeting that is possible with digital advertising.

Through the use of 'cookies' and other ways of capturing information about individuals, advertisers today know who supports Scunthorpe Football Club, who loves Drake, and who's a fan of M&Ms. All the data is then used to target those individuals, so June–July advertising of Scunthorpe season tickets goes only to those who are known fans; those living in Scunthorpe who support Leeds receive advertising for season tickets for Elland Road.

For advertisers of mass market brands, such as M&Ms and Coca-Cola, television advertising can still be cost effective. When promoting products that only appeal to a smaller segment of the population however, targeted advertising online can be much better value for money.

> Focus on how to be social, not how to do social.
>
> *Jay Baer, business author*

Viral advertising via social media

In the three years after Evian launched its one-minute 'Evian baby and me' video online, it has received over 130 million views. A one-minute national advertisement in the final of X Factor, to be seen by 10 million viewers, can cost £400,000. The Evian campaign was a bargain by comparison, and the advertising agency that created the video has said that Evian sales in the UK have risen by 30 per cent.

Of course, it is easy to see why great video advertisements can 'go viral', in other words get passed on from person to person via Tweets and other social media. But every company asks for great advertising, and rarely gets it. **Viral advertising** via social media is a wonderful success when it is done well but all too often will fall flat. A Heinz 'viral advertisement' launched at the same time as the Evian one received 300,000 views in three years – a trivial number for such a big brand. Creative genius is always a wonderful thing – but not something to rely on.

> Marketing is no longer about the stuff you make, but about the stories you tell.
>
> *Seth Godin, entrepreneur*

E-newsletters

If you buy a cinema ticket online, you are likely to end up receiving the cinema's weekly newsletter. It will tell you about major new films, and maybe offer discounted tickets for Monday or Tuesday evenings. From the company's point of view, the direct cost of sending out the newsletter is virtually zero. The costs involved are to do with setting up the IT system (perhaps no more than buying in a software platform) and then getting someone to write and design the content. Compared with the cost of advertising in the local paper (the traditional method), this is cheap.

E-newsletters can be a cost effective way of spreading information

Of course, many businesses want to do something more exciting or at least more interactive with their newsletters. This is perfectly possible but likely to cost a lot more. The wonderful thing about digital promotion is that the initial costs can be quite small, and it is possible to become more ambitious when you can afford it; a new, small business can perhaps spend £1,000, while an established but ambitious business can spend £15,000.

> It no longer makes economic sense to send an advertising message to the many in the hope of persuading the few.
>
> *Lawrence Light, former chief marketing officer at McDonald's*

Drawing the right conclusions

Promotion seems like the easiest part of the 4Ps. In fact, there are plenty of ways things can go wrong. For many years the Tesco slogan 'Every little helps' was a positive message, but when customers came to question the company's profit focus, people said that 'Every little helps Tesco'. This shows how the key to promotional success is to take customers seriously – by listening every bit as much as talking. Then promotion gets a whole lot easier.

Revision essentials

Branding: giving your product or service a name that helps recall and recognition, and gives a sense of personality.

E-newsletters: regular updates on the activities of a business sent electronically to actual or potential customers.

Promotional strategy: a medium- to long-term plan for communicating with your target customers.

Sponsorship: when companies pay to have a brand associated with an iconic individual or event (usually connected with sports or the arts).

Viral advertising: when people start to spread your message for you through social means, be it word of mouth or via social media.

End of chapter exercises

1 Would clothing company G-Star RAW be better off promoting their product through online media or traditional media such as TV or cinema? Explain your thinking.

G - Star RAW outlet

2 Explain why promotions such as 'buy one get one free' may be a mistake for some brands.

3 Look at Figure 38.1 on page 186. Outline two possible reasons why sales growth of Red Bull slipped in 2009.

4 Explain one reason why it makes more sense to use television advertising for big, mass-market brands than for brands that appeal to a small segment of the market.

5 Look at the pie chart in Figure 38.2, then answer the questions.

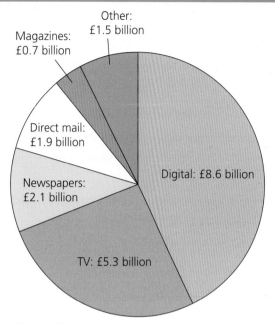

Figure 38.2 Money spent on advertising in the UK, 2015

(a) What percentage of all advertising spending was digital in 2015?

(b) The total spent on digital rose by 17.3 per cent in 2015, whereas for newspapers it fell by 11 per cent. Explain why this change might have happened.

(c) Total UK advertising spending rose by 7.3 per cent in 2015. What might lead the amount spent on advertising to fall in a future year?

Practice questions

Children in the UK are spending more time on the internet than in front of the TV for the first time, according to new research into the media habits of under-16s. Research firm Childwise found that on average 5- to 15-year-olds were spending three hours a day using the internet, compared to 2.1 hours watching TV.

The amount of time children spend in front of a television screen has been declining steadily from a high of three hours in 2000–01, and was at 2.3 hours last year. However, time online has seen a huge surge according to the research, up 50 per cent from two hours last year.

The research, which is based on an online survey of more than 2,000 children, did not distinguish between TV-like services on the internet, such as Netflix and iPlayer, and other forms of browsing such as Facebook, meaning it is unclear whether children are merely watching shows in different ways. However, the report says that YouTube has taken 'centre stage in children's lives', with half accessing it every day and almost all using it at least occasionally.

Source: *The Guardian*, 26 January 2016

Total: 15 marks

1 Define what is meant by the term 'online survey'. (1)

2 Outline why there may have been a surge in time spent online by 5- to 15-year-olds. (2)

3 Evaluate whether Cadbury should change from its traditional focus on TV advertising to the use of digital advertising media. You should use the information provided as well as your knowledge of business. (12)

39 Place

This element of the marketing mix is about how to get the product from the producer to the customer. There are three main **distribution** channels – traditional, modern and direct – but, today, the easiest way is to sell directly, via the internet. Many people love to go shopping, though, so retail sales remain important.

In addition to choosing the most appropriate channel, firms must decide on the type of store they wish to be distributed in. When it first launched, posh crisp maker Tyrrells decided it would rather not have its products on sale in Tesco. The directors believed the image of the brand would be built more successfully by being seen in small shops, plus the more upmarket **retailers** such as Waitrose and Booths. After ten years establishing its image, Tyrrells approached Tesco and a deal was done.

Methods of retail distribution

As shown in Figure 39.1, there are three main ways to get products from the producer to the consumer. The first (the 'traditional' channel) means that producers sell in bulk to wholesalers, who sell in smaller quantities to small and independent retailers. So, a big truck goes from Mars to a wholesaler, such as Palmer and Harvey, full up with the full Mars product range. The one full delivery means that the delivery cost per item is small, allowing the wholesaler to sell quite cheaply to the local grocer.

Without wholesalers, small shops couldn't exist, as it would be too expensive for the producer to deliver to all the different outlets.

The second method is the most important by far in the grocery sector: the producer delivers huge quantities directly to a supermarket's distribution depot. Trucks deliver to the Waitrose depot in Bracknell from all over Europe; Waitrose trucks are then loaded up with the right supplies to be taken to individual stores. Then we do our shopping.

The third method is buying directly from the producer. This has always been possible from companies that

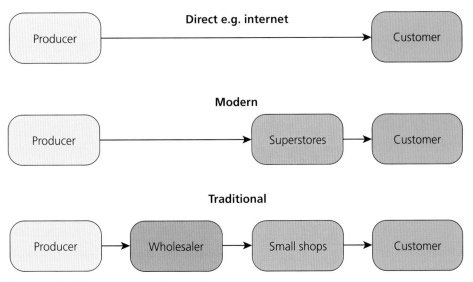

Figure 39.1 Distribution channels

Table 39.1 Physical retail distribution and the consumer

Advantages	Disadvantages
Customers can touch, hold, feel, smell and wear products before buying; makes it easy to compare with rival products	'Going shopping' is time consuming, especially when it seems important to make full comparisons (e.g., visiting lots of shops)
You can choose a lean piece of meat or a nearly-ripe piece of fruit; e-commerce can't match that	Choice can be overwhelming, leading to too much time being spent
You can take it away instantly; not even same-day delivery can match that	You have to carry everything; especially hard for those without a car (30 per cent of households)

offered a mail-order service (such as the original Next Directory). Today it is a booming segment of the market because of the convenience of shopping online, via e-commerce or m-commerce.

> A product with superior distribution will always win over a superior product with poor distribution or customer access. It's not fair. It's not right. But it's reality.
>
> *Stephen Davis, managing director*

Gaining retail distribution

First-time entrepreneurs are often surprised to find that getting retail distribution is hard – and keeping it still harder. Tesco would be delighted to stock own-label products plus some top brand names, but they are wary of small brands that may sell slowly and perhaps go out of date. To gain distribution a company needs to:

◆ show that its brand(s) offer something really different to the customer

◆ show the strength of marketing support to be put behind the brand

◆ provide an acceptably high level of profit to the retailer.

To keep in stock over a period of years the company will have to:

◆ provide regular promotional support to keep sales moving, such as half-price offers, financed entirely by the manufacturer

◆ make sure that sales flow through even when there's no special offer, for example by advertising that persuades new customers to try it out.

Talking point

Would you rather work in an e-commerce distribution depot or work face to face in a shop?

E-tail distribution or e-commerce

There are two main types of e-commerce:

◆ direct sales from producer to consumer, such as buying a MacBook computer direct online from Apple

◆ sales through an **e-tailer**: in other words, an electronic shop, such as ASOS.

Direct sales from producer to consumer are great for the producer, who receives the full retail price instead of having to make do with the wholesale price. E-tailers are more important today, however. Their shops display products online and have sufficiently slick, efficient systems to make it easy to purchase, deliver and even collect (when a disappointed customer wants to return the item). Because the e-tailer is saving the cost of running all those shops in local high streets, it can live with customers returning a higher percentage of their purchases than would ever happen in physical retailing.

The graph of ASOS' sales growth in Figure 39.2 shows the huge attractions of starting – or investing

Table 39.2 Online retail (e-tail) distribution and the consumer

Advantages	Disadvantages
The convenience of being able to order from home or when on the move is almost essential for carers looking after kids or the elderly	Familiarity with a single app might make shoppers lazy – ordering online when going out might actually be better (the elderly need exercise)
You don't have to waste time driving, parking and shopping	Eventually, delivery charges will have to reflect costs
You can easily make price comparisons, allowing grocery shopping to be far better value	For staff, working on zero-hours contracts at the minimum wage in a giant warehouse can be far more soul destroying than working in a shop

in – an online retail start-up. The company's growth has been staggering.

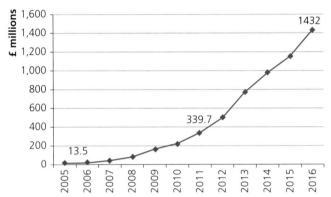

Figure 39.2 ASOS sales: from millions to billions, 2005–16 (Source: ASOS accounts)

● Drawing the right conclusions

Will online retailing inevitably keep growing at the expense of high street shops and shopping? Certainly it has a lot of momentum behind it, which probably means that more shop closures are to come. In early 2016, the British Retail Consortium (of employers) predicted that 900,000 retail jobs would disappear by 2025. That's 30 per cent of the total. But it may be that new, independent shops will open up in place of chain stores. As baseball coach Yogi Berra once said: 'It's tough to make predictions – especially about the future.'

Revision essentials

Distribution: how ownership changes as a product goes from producer to consumer.

E-tailer: an electronic retailer; in other words purchasing electronically, either by e-commerce or, more likely these days, mobile commerce (m-commerce).

Retailer: a shop or chain of shops, usually selling from a building in a high street or shopping centre.

End of chapter exercises

1 Which type of product are you most likely to buy online? Explain why.

2 Which type of product or service are you most likely to buy offline, in other words, from a shop?

3 Look at Figure 39.2 above and answer the following.

  (a) Calculate the percentage sales increase between 2005 and 2011.

  (b) Calculate the percentage sales increase between 2011 and 2016.

  (c) Outline why sales may have followed this growth path?

4 Read the following extract. Outline two possible reasons why customers may increase their grocery e-tail purchases in future.

In 2015, the chief executive of Aldi said the discounter wouldn't move into online selling because 'no one is making money online'. A 2016 report called grocery e-tailing 'a hardly profitable operating model'. Another report calculated that 'picking' (the shopping) and delivery swallow up £15 per order, but customers are reluctant to pay any meaningful delivery charge. So, grocers that charge £6 for delivery risk making a loss every time a customer places an order. In 2016, less than 5 per cent of Britain's food was bought online; as this figure rises the problem of its profitability will have to be solved.

5 Discuss how a supermarket such as Sainsbury's might solve its e-tail profitability in future.

Practice questions

A record £1 billion of items were returned after last year's Black Friday as online customers adopted a 'buy now and decide later' attitude. Some stores – mainly women's fashion outlets – saw more than 60 per cent of online sales returned within 30 days. Business consultants *Clear Returns* suggests that returned parcels may be costing UK retailers £60 billion a year.

Many store chains have invested heavily in online distribution channels – only to find that stock management is made doubly difficult and expensive due to customer returns. George Mensah, a retail expert at consumer analyst Shore Capital, says the volume of online returns was a major concern for some retailers. 'Last year the disruption caused by having to deal with a high level of returned items in late December meant retailers struggled around Christmas time, and this year it could be even worse.'

'It can cost double the amount for a product to be returned into the supply chain as it does to deliver it,' says Iain Prince, supply chain director at KPMG. He points to the online purchase of a coat, for instance: 'To pick and deliver an order costs between £3 and £10 — it could cost double or treble that to be processed on the way back.' The risk is thats 'All your (profit) margin is consumed in the process of handling and repackaging,' as a *Clear Returns* executive suggests.

According to some experts, around 20 per cent of fashion purchases on the web are for multiple items of a similar size, shape or colour. Customers deliberately over-order – intending to send back some items given that returns are free or cheap. Of course, from a customer point of view it makes sense. In a shop, you try things on and decide what fits and what looks good. When buying online it seems fair to pick and choose – forgetting the cost to the retailers.

Despite the problems, retailers cannot walk away from online. In December 2016 24.3 percent of non-food sales were online – up by 7.5 per cent

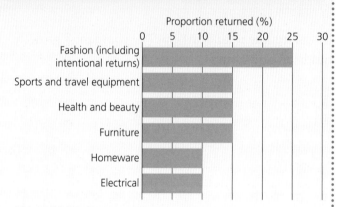

Figure 39.3 Online returns

compared with 2015. 'We want our customers to be happy and if they want to return items, we want to make that process as simple as possible,' says John Lewis. 'As such we will continue to focus on customer convenience.' Figure 39.3 shows how costly that might prove.

Total: 18 marks

1 (a) From Figure 39.3, identify which product category has the highest rate of customer returns. (1)

(b) Outline one possible problem for retailers about encouraging customers to buy online. (2)

2 Use the text to help analyse whether customer returns are mainly an online, e-retailing problem. (6)

3 Companies such as John Lewis worry about the increasing cost of customer returns. They see two main options:

◆ Option 1: Charge customers the actual cost of delivery, as would happen if items were posted.

◆ Option 2: Continue with free delivery, forcing shop customers to subsidise online ones.

Justify which **one** of these two options a business such as John Lewis should choose. (9)

40 Marketing mix and business decisions

Business decisions are always about the future. So, when the marketing mix is being used to inform and carry out business decisions, it is also about the future. Because no one can know what the future holds, however, it involves uncertainty: a decision that seems right today may prove wrong tomorrow – through no one's fault.

Today I decide to switch my declining brand's image away from luxury towards being more of an everyday consumer choice. Tomorrow a luxury rival pushes its price up sharply. This would have boosted sales and profits for my brand, but I've effectively switched the brand out of that position in the market. My brand gains nothing when it could have gained a great deal. Bad timing. Unlucky.

Table 40.1 shows some real examples of good and bad marketing decisions.

> **Talking point**
>
> Which bad marketing decisions can you think of in recent times? Explain why you think they were bad.

How each element of the marketing mix can influence other elements

The key to the marketing mix is that it should all fit together in a way that works for the target market. Health-focused parents may want toddler snacks that have no added sugar and fit in the pocket. Success comes from a complete, credible marketing package:

- Product: 20g packs of BEAR's Yoyo 'fruit nibbles', made from whole fresh fruit, giving one of your five-a-day 'with no added nonsense'.
- Promotion: a cute, quirky, slightly amateur website (www.bearnibbles.co.uk) to make the customer feel that the products are made by nice people, not by a company.
- Place: originally launched into Waitrose and Ocado (good for middle-class credibility) but now in Tesco, Sainsbury's and Caffè Nero.
- Price: 49p for a 20g pack. That's £24.50 a kilo – an extraordinarily high price for stewed fruit – but

Table 40.1 Examples of good and bad marketing decisions

Good marketing decisions	Bad marketing decisions
In 2012, recent start-up BEAR launched an advertising campaign to increase awareness of its Yoyo pure fruit rolls (for kids). In the year that followed, sales rose by 72 per cent and kept rising to £22.5 million by 2015.	In May 2012, owners Nestlé launched a TV and digital advertising campaign for Rachel's Organic yoghurts. Sales fell over the years 2013–15, following this campaign, leading to Tesco dropping the brand in 2015.
In late 2015 the Pot Noodle brand distribution strategy was changed. The new emphasis was to be on smaller, convenience stores rather than supermarkets. Rethinking 'place' encouraged a 6.7 per cent rise in sales to £112.1 million, at a time when all its rivals suffered sales declines.	In March 2015 The Ice Co. launched three frozen cocktails, including a pina colada, but it launched into a sector (ready-to-drink) that had seen a sales decline of 29 per cent in the previous year. In the year to July 2016, total sales of all three products were less than £1 million.

YoYo started in Waitrose and Ocado and branched out into other supermarkets

it hasn't caused any problems. It is reassuringly expensive for a baby treat but, of course, at just 49p a time it is easily affordable.

In the case of Yoyo, a price that's too low may damage credibility. So too might the news that the business is no longer owned by founder Hayley Gait-Golding but by Belgian biscuit-maker Lotus Bakeries. But there's definitely no sign of that news on the BEAR's website.

> We won't be different for different's sake. Different is easy ... make it pink, make it fluffy! Better is harder.
>
> *Jonathan Ive, chief design officer at Apple*

How the marketing mix informs business decisions

A successful business understands its customers, and therefore knows what products or services they want and how best to communicate with them. A critical business decision can come after a successful launch phase, when the business needs to expand. Customer demand is higher than the factory can cope with, so a new factory is needed. But how big?

Entrepreneurs use their understanding of the four marketing mix factors (the 4Ps) to get a sense of just how big demand might become. After all, the business may have spent little so far on advertising,

in which case sales could be pushed up significantly simply by telling more potential customers about the product. In these circumstances it looks safe to build a factory much larger than the first one. If sales aren't strong enough to use up all the production potential, a strong advertising campaign should solve the problem. So the entrepreneur's understanding of the marketing mix has provided key information for making the right business decision.

Other ways in which the marketing mix could **inform** a business decision include:

◆ Having a firm understanding of the impact of price changes on sales could help in deciding whether to increase prices in future. A six per cent price rise will increase revenue and profits if the number sold falls by only four per cent.

◆ Market research evidence that a brand image is strong – and backed by a consistent marketing mix – might encourage a business to launch a new product based on the same brand name.

◆ If a company knows it is losing distribution in supermarkets but gaining in small convenience stores, it may be sensible to develop and launch smaller pack sizes, such as a box of four eggs.

> Marketing is a contest for people's attention.
>
> *Seth Godin, author and entrepreneur*

How the marketing mix can be used to implement business decisions

Once a decision has been made, it is time to put it into practice. That's where decisions on the marketing mix come into play. For example:

◆ A head teacher decides to go ahead with an expansion plan: as the extra classrooms are being built, a marketing plan is needed to recruit 50 extra pupils for next September. The marketing mix comes into play (except for 'price', unless it is a private school).

◆ The boss of Tyrrells crisps decides to launch the brand in America, aiming for $20 million of sales within two years; the marketing manager must find the right marketing mix to achieve this objective.

What is needed is a three-part process:

1 Identify the decision objectives (50 extra pupils, or $20 million sales).

2 Agree how the 4Ps are to be used to achieve those objectives. Often this will require more money; in other words, the business may have to provide a bigger **budget** for marketing. If you're launching a brand in America, extra spending will be needed, for example, on advertising.

3 Carry out the plan; in other words, make the required changes to the product, price, promotion and place.

Once the plan is in action, well-run companies analyse their sales figures to check whether it is working well. Sometimes adjustments are needed. For example Tyrrells launching in America may find it tougher than expected to get good retail distribution. US supermarket chains may keep saying no. They may need to switch away from supermarkets to target small shops, or perhaps focus distribution on bars and cafes instead of the grocery sector.

Drawing the right conclusions

Good business decisions can take several years to show their merits. That's fine as long as the business has long-term objectives. If Primark's boss decided to make the business a big player in the clothing market in China, it might be four or five years before it was clear whether it was the right thing to do. But whether the decision making is long term or short term, it is only likely to come good if the business truly understands its customers. That's where marketing comes in – especially market research and the marketing mix.

Revision essentials

Budget: a ceiling on the amount of money that can be spent; a marketing budget of £1 million means the marketing manager can spend up to that figure, but no more.

'Inform' decisions: evidence that can be used to make a better decision; a company can gain a better understanding of its customers through the 4Ps, which helps in decision making.

End of chapter exercises

1 Explain briefly why all business decision making is rooted in uncertainty.

2 Take one of the two 'good' marketing decisions from Table 40.1 on page 195. Explain in your own words why the decision was a good one.

3 Take one of the two 'bad' marketing decisions from Table 40.1 on page 195. Explain in your own words what went wrong.

4 Use the 'three-part process' to imagine how one of the following plans might be put into action:

(a) Lidl decides to start up a chain of better-value pizza delivery outlets across the UK.

(b) Primark decides to start up a chain of better value cinemas across the UK.

Practice questions

The chocolate market in India is quite small in international terms, but one of the world's fastest-growing. Despite the heat of India, the market is worth more than £1 billion a year. The biggest name is Cadbury, which has a market share of over 55 per cent; Cadbury's Dairy Milk holds more than a 30 per cent share on its own.

India is a developing nation and, while there are many affluent people there, the average Indian is relatively poor, so chocolate makers produce small bars at remarkably low prices, typically around 7p. Perhaps that's why Cadbury, Nestlé and Ferrero have been trying to boost the luxury end of the market (currently 12 per cent of the market). Cadbury has focused on boxed assortments for gifts at birthdays or festivals such as Diwali. These can sell for around £2. Nestlé has introduced KitKat Senses for an everyday luxury at 10p, while Ferrero has launched Kinder Joy for a 12p kids' treat.

Although the market is dominated by multinational companies, local milk producer Amul has managed to stay neck-and-neck with Mars by producing international-looking brands at Indian prices. Amul focuses its promotional spending purely on packaging design. It doesn't see the need to advertise; its low prices ensure good shop distribution.

The big market share winner in recent years is Italy's Ferrero, which uses TV advertising to attract children to its Kinder range.

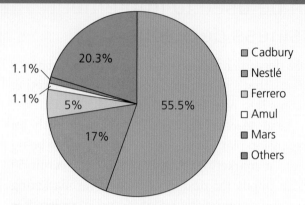

Figure 40.1 Chocolate market share in India

Total: 20 marks

1 Define the term 'multinational company'. (1)

2 **(a)** Calculate Cadbury's sales (in pounds) in India. (2)

   (b) Outline one way in which they may have achieved such high sales. (2)

3 Analyse how Ferrero is using the marketing mix to boost its sales in India. (6)

4 Mars is considering two options for boosting its market share in India:

   ◆ Option 1: Focus solely on the market for adult chocolate gifts.

   ◆ Option 2: Attack Cadbury's Dairy Milk by launching Galaxy.

   Justify which **one** of these two options Mars should choose. (9)

Exam-style questions on Topic 2.2

Don't rush; check your answers carefully.

1 Which **one** of the following best describes an 'extension strategy'? (1)

(a) A boost to the sales of a product in its maturity phase.

(b) A medium-term plan for extending a product's life cycle.

(c) Developing a new product to replace the existing one.

(d) A plan for getting a product back below its break-even point.

Questions 2, 3 and 4 are based on this information.

Mars launched the MaltEaster Bunny as a rival to Cadbury's Creme Egg. It was priced higher than the Creme Egg but Mars felt confident that it would achieve a high level of distribution.

2 Which **two** elements of the MaltEaster Bunny's marketing mix are not mentioned in the above text? (2)

3 Within the marketing mix, distribution is known as which **one** of the following? (1)

(a) Position

(b) Place

(c) Packaging

(d) Prominence

4 Which **one** of the following statements explains why Mars may be wrong to price the MaltEaster Bunny higher than Cadbury's Creme Egg. (1)

(a) Creme Egg is the market leader with £50 million of sales in each of the past 20 years.

(b) The MaltEaster Bunny has higher production costs than the Creme Egg.

(c) The MaltEaster Bunny is highly differentiated.

(d) Eating Creme Eggs is an annual ritual for many people in Britain.

5 Which **two** of the following are benefits to a business of having a strong brand name? (2)

(a) Customers will be more willing to try new products with that branding.

(b) The name ensures that sales are protected from competitors' actions.

(c) A strong brand name makes it unnecessary to spend on advertising.

(d) A good name makes it easy to cut product quality without losing sales.

(e) Greater customer loyalty should make future sales a bit more certain.

Questions 6 and 7 are based on this information.

Before Pepsi launched 'Raw' cola into Britain, it carried out qualitative and quantitative research among those who already bought cola drinks – and those who didn't.

6 Which **one** of the following is an example of qualitative research? (1)

(a) Group discussion

(b) Sampling and selling

(c) Questionnaires

(d) Population statistics

7 Which **two** of the following items of information might Pepsi discover through quantitative research? (2)

(a) The sales growth achieved by Pepsi Max.

(b) The estimated sales for a proposed new product.

(c) The reasons behind consumers' likes and dislikes of brands.

(d) The cost of producing the number of goods people want to buy.

(e) The percentage of the target market that want a blue pack instead of a red one.

Questions 8 and 9 are based on this pyramid diagram.

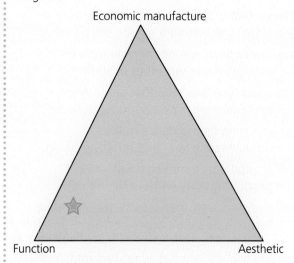

8 Which **one** of the following is the name given to this diagram? (1)

(a) Market mapping

(b) The design mix

(c) The product life cycle

(d) The marketing model

9 Which **one** of the following products might be represented by the star on the diagram? (1)

(a) A new luxury perfume from Chanel.

(b) A new smartphone to be sold only through Aldi stores.

(c) A new robotic mini-excavator for construction sites.

(d) A new ice cream flavour from Ben & Jerry's.

Now try this discussion question.

10 Discuss whether a growing e-commerce business could benefit from opening its own shops. (6)

41 Business operations

In late 2015, Renault announced that it would cut hundreds of jobs at its factory at Chennai, India. The market was growing more slowly than expected, and Renault's main product line in India was the low-cost Dacia range. Production costs needed to be low enough to compete on price with local manufacturers such as Maruti Suzuki and Tata.

Even companies as massive as Renault have to make sure that they keep costs low enough to be competitive. If Tata is offering a fuel-efficient family car in India for £5,000, Renault has to make sure that its production costs are low enough to do the same. If it costs Renault £6,000 to make each car, everything it sells will be at a loss.

The same is true for a local builder. If they have to charge £1,000 for building a wall but a rival can do it for £700, there is only one possible result: the more expensive builder must either give up or find a way to operate at a lower cost.

Every business has to be aware of its costs and how much its competitors charge

The purpose of business operations

'Operations' is the name given to the section of the business that provides the customer with the goods or services he or she has ordered. While the marketing department tries to get people to buy, business operations makes sure customers get what they want. When the product is produced in a factory, every part of the factory is part of 'operations', so too is the delivery process. Services such as window cleaning also require operations – that is, a process from website or app ordering through to appointments being made and kept, and perhaps a quality control system to make sure that customers are happy.

To sum up, business operations ensures that the right goods or services are supplied to customers at the right time and to the right quality standards.

> Manufacturing is more than just putting parts together. It's coming up with ideas, testing principles and perfecting the engineering, as well as final assembly.
>
> *James Dyson, British industrialist*

Production processes

There are three types of 'production' process – job, batch and flow – and they apply to the supply of services as well as goods.

Job production

Job production is one-off production for a one-off order. It is tailor-made to the specific requirements of a single customer, and therefore requires a high input of labour rather than machinery. For example, a tailor-made wedding dress requires careful measuring, fitting and refitting, plus hand-cut fabric. It might require 50 hours' work. That's no problem in a low-cost country such as Bangladesh where labour might be 25p an hour, but if the labour cost is £9 an hour, that's £450 just for the labour.

Examples of job production include:
- a loft conversion in an unusually-shaped 80-year-old house
- a tailor-made suit for Prince Harry
- a babysitter for Mrs Jenkins between 7.30 and 11.15 p.m. on Friday night.

Table 41.1 on the next page outlines the advantages and disadvantages of job production.

Batch production

Batch production means producing a limited number of the same item. It might be a huge batch of 10,000, or a small batch of four – either way it is batch production. With a small batch of four identical cakes, there are labour and energy-cost savings in mixing the ingredients, making the cakes and baking them all together. With a huge batch, a production line could be used for a day or two to produce 10,000 XL Manchester United shorts, followed by 8,000 XXLs. Batch production is often quite cost efficient because a degree of automation can be used, making it less dependent on labour time than job production.

Examples of batch production include:
- the production of 1 million Cadbury's Screme Eggs for Halloween
- ten open-top, double-decker buses for the New York tourist authority
- a meals-on-wheels lunch service for 20 elderly people in West Leeds.

Table 41.1 on the next page outlines the advantages and disadvantages of batch production.

Flow production

Flow production is continuous output of identical products. The world's biggest baked bean factory is in Wigan; it produces 3 million tins of Heinz Beans a day, working 24/7 for the past 70 years. Flow production allows a factory such as this to be highly automated: the labour cost per tin of beans is below 0.1p – effectively nothing. For a product with a long product life cycle, such as Heinz Beans, flow production is a sensational way to achieve high profits while making something that seems good value to customers.

Examples of flow production include:
- Cadbury's Dairy Milk
- Cadbury's Creme Eggs – surprisingly, they are produced all year round even though they're only on sale between Christmas and Easter
- Nissan Jukes (in Sunderland) and BMW Minis (in Oxford).

Table 41.1 on the next page outlines the advantages and disadvantages of flow production.

●Can there be a mixture? Part-batch, part-flow?

Yes, and there often is. When a birthday cake is ordered from a baker, a batch of ten cakes may be baked; the job production element is just the iced decoration, whether it is 'Happy 6th birthday Rosie' or a couple of poodles for a dog-loving granny. Modern car manufacture is a mixture of flow, batch and job production. The flow of saloon cars may be interrupted for two days' production of a batch of estate cars, and each car is tailored to the customer's specifications – one is blue with a sunroof and alloy wheels, the next is red with black leather seats, and so on.

Table 41.1 Advantages and limitations of job, batch and flow production

	Advantages	Disadvantages/Limitations
Job production	Highly flexible; gives the customer exactly what they want Satisfying work for the individual as it requires skills and flexibility	It will always be expensive in a developed (high-wage) economy The skills may be in short supply, making it hard for the business to grow
Batch production	Gain some cost advantages from producing several items at once … yet still able to offer customers the colour/size they want	May be limited scope for automation, making production costs far higher than with flow production Not as flexible as job production
Flow production	Can automate production fully, making it highly cost effective (which should be good for customers as well as suppliers) Many customers value consistency, and flow will provide an identical product each time	Likely to be expensive to set up and inflexible to use; could be a disaster if a product life cycle proves much shorter than expected Modern customers like to see products tailored to their specific needs

> In the end, all business operations can be reduced to three words: people, product, profits. Unless you've got a good team, you can't do much with the other two.
>
> *Lee Iacocca, US businessman*

Keeping costs down

Consider the costs involved in building a brick wall:

◆ Materials: bricks and cement; these must be ordered in the right quantity and at the lowest prices available from suppliers.

◆ Other direct costs: hiring a cement mixer for a day or two, hiring a skip for the building waste.

◆ Labour: this is a function of the amount of work involved, the hourly wage of the workers and the productivity of those workers.

◆ Fixed costs: the fixed costs of the management time taken to win the order, supervise the work and deal with office administration.

To keep costs to the minimum, careful ordering of materials and other supplies is very important. Every business, though, will be trying to buy at the lowest price and making sure not to buy more than is needed to complete a job. Therefore cost savings through purchasing are rarely crucial.

Labour costs per unit depend on productivity

Far more important is good management of labour costs. Pay rates vary significantly in different parts of the world (see Table 41.2 on the next page), though China is catching up fast.

Table 41.2 Income in China is growing fast

Average annual income (US$)	2008	2015
UK	43,552	41,384
Germany	41,367	44,925
Japan	35,352	35,780
Hungary	21,214	19,999
Mexico	16,005	14,867
China	7,375	17,400

For companies to keep employing workers in Britain, they must find a way to get value out of the high wages being paid. This could come about if workers in Britain have skills that cannot be found elsewhere, for example the ability to write computer games or deal in foreign exchange. People can also be worth the money they are paid if they are highly productive (they produce a lot of work in the time they are employed). This means having high productivity.

● Measuring productivity

Gavin is a bricklayer. He can lay 800 bricks in a day and is paid £120 per day. His friend John is a builder who is skilled at many different tasks (plastering, flooring, carpentry) but he can only lay 400 bricks a day. So, if both are paid £120 for a day's work:

Table 41.3

	Pay	Output	Labour cost per brick
Gavin	£120	800	15p (£120/800 = £0.15)
John	£120	400	30p

Productivity is efficiency, usually measured as output per person. In this case, Gavin is twice as productive as John, which means that John is twice as expensive to use. High productivity enables the labour cost to be spread across lots of output. Low productivity (John) means higher labour costs per unit.

Productivity differences can be much bigger than this. In 1999, Renault bought the Romanian car business Dacia. It employed 27,000 people and made 110,000 cars a year. In the same year the Nissan factory in Sunderland, UK, was producing 270,000 cars with just 2,750 people. Therefore the productivity difference was:

Table 41.4

	Staff	Output (cars)	Productivity (cars per worker per year)
Dacia	27,000	110,000	4 cars per year
Nissan	2,750	270,000	98 cars per year

Even at the much lower wage rates in Romania, it was far better value to manufacture cars in Britain. Since 1999, Renault has turned this situation around. In 2015, 17,000 Dacia workers produced 551,000 cars, pushing productivity per worker from four in 1999 to 32 in 2015.

In general, higher productivity is one of the keys to success when up against competition. Ways of increasing productivity include:

◆ investing in up-to-date machinery to help workers work faster, or to replace them with automated equipment or robots
◆ encouraging staff to work more enthusiastically, and therefore harder and faster; this can be achieved through improved morale and motivation
◆ encouraging staff to work smarter – to come up with new ways to do things more effectively. Toyota says it receives more than 100,000 employee suggestions per year.

> The three most important things right now are costs, costs and costs. And costs can be summed up in one word: productivity.
>
> *Financial analyst quoted in the New York Times*

● Competitive costs mean competitive prices

If high **productivity** keeps costs per unit down, a firm can compete. As shown in Table 41.5, if Ryanair cuts its prices, IAG (the airline group that includes British Airways) will struggle. Ryanair and IAG carry a similar number of passengers, but Ryanair's staff costs per passenger are about one tenth of those of British Airways.

Table 41.5 The impact of productivity on labour costs per unit (staff cost per passenger)

January to June 2016	IAG (British Airways)	Ryanair
Number of passengers flown	46,676,000	62,400,000
Staff costs	£2,467,000,000	£331,600,000
Staff cost per passenger	£52.85	£5.31

● Drawing the right conclusions

If marketing is about generating revenue, business operations are about delivering to the customer while keeping the costs down. Only then can a profit be made, and without profit no business will last long. Successful operations are as important to services as they are to manufacturing businesses. All customers want good service and reliable delivery. That's equally important whether it is a new Mercedes or a margherita pizza.

Revision essentials

Batch production: producing a limited number of identical products.

Flow production: continuous production of identical products, which gives scope for high levels of automation.

Job production: one-off production of a one-off item for a single customer.

Productivity: a measure of efficiency, usually output per person per time period (for example, Nissan UK's 98 cars per worker per year).

End of chapter exercises

1 Tata can sell a car in India for £5,000 that costs Renault £6,000 to make. In this situation, how might productivity improvements help Renault?

2 (a) Bartex Ltd, a small lighting factory, employs 150 staff and has a monthly output of 180,000 lamps. Calculate the factory's monthly productivity.

   (b) A rival based in Hull pays similar wages and has monthly productivity of 1,500 lamps. Outline two ways this might affect Bartex.

3 In the section on measuring productivity on page 204, Gavin is twice as productive as John. Give three possible reasons why this may be the case.

4 Outline two ways that Renault could have improved productivity at Dacia.

Practice questions

A Cambridge start-up is attempting to go head to head with drugs giant Pfizer with a new vaccine aimed at eradicating the potentially fatal lung disease caused by *Streptococcus pneumoniae*. ImmBio's new vaccine is about to go into human trials for the first time and could come to market within the next five years. It will rival the Pfizer vaccine Prevenar, the global market leader; 6.4 billion courses of the vaccine are sold each year at a price of at around £100 per course.

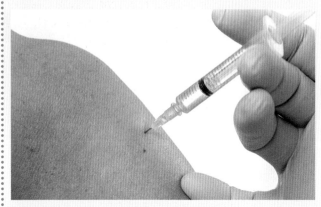

ImmBio is hoping to rival Pfizer's vaccine

ImmBio chief executive Graham Clarke said that it was only worth going up against the pharmaceutical giants with 'game-changer' products, claiming: 'We are making a product that works, works better than the current product, and is cheaper.' The company claims that their product can guard against multiple current strains and even future mutations.

Streptococcus pneumoniae bacteria are the most common cause of pneumonia, septicaemia and meningitis, and these pathogens kill more infants than malaria, tuberculosis and HIV combined.

ImmBio, which has been working on the vaccine since 2010, has now raised a total of £20 million from a consortium of early-stage investors, including biotech specialist Oxford Technology, to develop its vaccine, which it claims is a completely new approach to bolstering the human immune system.

'People think that big always wins,' said Mr Clarke, who worked at GlaxoSmithKline before joining Immbio. '[Big pharma] has huge sales forces, big marketing, efficient manufacturing and can industrialise their research and development, but it is still true that smaller, more flexible, agile companies have a competitive advantage.'

Source: *The Telegraph*, 1 May 2016

Total: 20 marks

1 Define the term 'competitive advantage'. (1)
2 Outline whether it would be best to produce a vaccine by job, batch or flow production. (2)
3 Outline one way in which a big producer such as Pfizer might benefit from efficient manufacturing. (2)
4 Analyse whether ImmBio should set up a factory for producing its vaccine in the UK or somewhere where labour costs are lower. (6)
5 ImmBio is considering two options for taking on Pfizer:

   ◆ Option 1: Raise finance from venture capital providers.
   ◆ Option 2: Float the business as a plc on the London Stock Exchange.

   Justify which **one** of these two options ImmBio should choose. (9)

42 Technology, productivity and production

New technology is a constant force propelling businesses forward. It creates opportunities for new products that people want even though their older versions are still working well ('I must have that new iPhone'). This boosts production, the volume of output. It also creates new ways to manufacture, such as robots, which boost efficiency. This in turn boosts productivity, as measured by output per worker (per unit of time, perhaps per year).

Every generation thinks that its era has seen the most dramatic ever changes to technology, especially this one. Dramatic changes to computing power seem to have transformed everything. The graph in Figure 42.1 is, therefore, surprising: it shows that a long-standing productivity growth trend (of about two per cent a year) pretty much stopped dead in 2007.

By the first half of 2016, productivity returned to its 2007 level, but in any other ten-year period it would have grown by around 20 per cent. In this time of dramatic technological change, productivity growth has weakened significantly. These figures are for the UK, which has a particular productivity problem, but a similar slowdown has happened worldwide.

The benefits of technology

Successful production involves three main things:
◆ producing the right quantity at the right time
◆ producing to high standards of consistency and quality
◆ producing cost efficiently.

High-tech equipment can help with all three. **Automation** (producing by machine) is especially

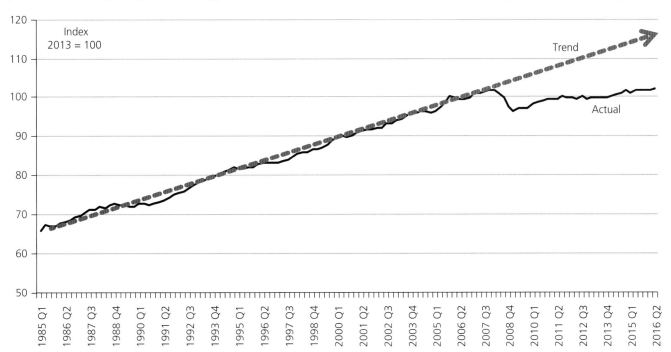

Figure 42.1 UK productivity growth (output per worker), 1985–2016 (Source: ONS)

effective at ensuring consistent quality and low labour costs per unit, and the availability of more recent technology, such as **robots**, can make it easier to produce more when needed. Robots don't mind working at the weekend.

Talking point

What do you think are the jobs that are *least* likely to be done by robots in the future?

On the other hand ...

Traditionally factory design in the West was a top-down process designed by engineers and managers. It focused on labour productivity and, therefore, automation. The job of shop-floor factory staff was to do what they were told.

Japanese companies, such as Nissan and Toyota, brought a broader view of efficiency to the UK. Instead of focusing on labour costs, the Japanese considered every aspect of waste: materials waste/scrap; energy waste; and the waste of time, labour and materials that comes from quality rejects (which have to be done again).

In 2016, sandwich-maker Greencore undertook an efficiency project with Sainsbury's – one of its biggest customers. Focusing on the production lines for two of its biggest-selling sandwiches, a careful assessment plus long discussions with staff identified the potential to:

◆ save 200 tonnes of lettuce wastage per year
◆ save 200 tonnes of other food waste per year
◆ save 500 tonnes of packaging waste per year.

The savings on food required changes to the way staff worked; the savings on packaging required a redesign of the sandwich box based on the views of the production line workers.

Sometimes efficiency requires new technology – perhaps a machine designed by staff and engineers together – but surprisingly often improvements come from reorganising the workplace based on staff ideas, which are based on logic and a bit of a rethink.

There is nothing so useless as doing efficiently that which should not be done at all.

Peter F. Drucker, business guru

Impact of technology on production

Customers want products that fit their needs and wants at a price they can afford. If technology can help to achieve this, it is valuable. There's always a risk, though, that technology will end up distorting this process. Buy a peach at the roadside in Italy in July and it is completely different to the tasteless fruit sold in the UK in the spring. Technology has allowed the fruit to be stored safely through the winter and transported to the UK. Unfortunately it is no longer worth eating. Like everything else, technology has downsides as well as ups.

A well-run business aims to use technology in a balanced way to match the needs of the customer and the needs of the business. There are four main elements to balance:

◆ Production costs, which in turn affect the price set for customers. Technology affects production costs through its impact on staff health and safety as much as through improved productivity. The earliest robots in British car factories were paint sprayers, which meant staff were no longer exposed to the danger of breathing in paint particles. Today, the first one into a dangerous demolition site will be a robot not a human. With risks reduced, companies no longer need to pay 'danger money', so costs are reduced and employee health improves. Win–win.

◆ Productivity can be boosted by mechanising some parts of a production process and automating others. If labour costs per unit fall, that's not only useful this year, it will keep paying the business for the lifetime of the machinery (perhaps five to ten years). High productivity means lower labour costs per unit and, therefore, lower overall costs per unit. That allows the business to either cut prices or enjoy higher profits, which can be invested in even better technology.

♦ Quality means different things to different people but an important starting point is that customers should get what they want. This means that **flexibility** is important. There is a risk that technology may get in the way of that, as it encourages mass production of the same thing. In a cleverly run business, the benefits of technology are matched with the advantages of human flexibility – giving customers consistent quality tailored to their own requirements.

♦ Flexibility relates to quality, but also to overall delivery. A menu offers pie and chips, but a request for pie and mash could be met with a smile and a good plate of food. Some large businesses combine an automated till system with a rigid approach to staff decision making, in which scenario the request for pie and mash is turned down because the computer/till says 'no'. This makes no sense to the customer and – in truth – no sense for the business either. But if staff are used to doing only what the rules and the menu allow, their inflexibility is inevitable.

● Drawing the right conclusions

From a consumer point of view, better technology is fantastic. Cars that park themselves, Facetime and virtual reality are all examples of things that people want to buy and want to use. But technology can also be a huge distraction within businesses. Inefficiencies in workplaces are usually down to poor communication and poor organisation/management – and jumping at new technology solutions can be a mistake. In the ten years to 2016, hugely increased computing power provided the opportunity for greatly improved productivity. In fact, as Figure 42.1 (page 207) shows, productivity in the UK didn't improve at all. So, there's a lot more to improved productivity then technology.

Revision essentials

Automation: using machines that can operate without people.

Flexibility: the ability to switch quickly and easily from one task to another.

Robots: machines that can be programmed to do tasks that can be done by humans, such as welding, spray painting and packing.

End of chapter exercises

1 Look at Figure 42.1 on page 207 and explain the difference between 'trend' and 'actual' data.

2 Why may 'consistency' in production be a useful benefit of automation?

3 Explain the ups and downs for staff if managers decide to talk to them more about how production could be improved.

4 In the future, technology may allow buses to be self-driven, with no human involvement. Outline one benefit and one drawback to passengers and to bus companies.

Practice questions

Morrisons stores are struggling to get to grips with the new 'sales-based' online ordering system. Contributors to a staff intranet have expressed concern about the new software. The new cloud-based system generates orders automatically based on which products are going through the tills. One poster said: 'We are a few weeks in and already have tripled our backstock [stock held on-site in a storeroom]. We have no idea how big our deliveries are going to be day by day and we have gaps everywhere on the shelves.' Another said: 'My store is five weeks into the new system. The backstock has doubled but we've more gaps than ever.'

Morrisons admits that it is trialling a new system and claims that everything is going well. It agreed, though, that some staff might need more training on how to adapt from the traditional order pad system.

Total: 15 marks

1 Outline the problem for a business such as Morrisons when 'backstock has doubled but we've more gaps than ever'. (2)

2 Outline one reason why implementing new technology in the workplace can be disappointing. (2)

3 Outline one reason why Morrisons might have benefited from more flexibility from its staff. (2)

4 Morrisons is considering what to do next about the ordering problem. It is considering two options:

◆ Option 1: Scrap the new system and return to order pads operated by individuals at work.

◆ Option 2: Keep going with the new system, but spend more on staff training.

Justify which **one** of these two options Morrisons should choose. (9)

Online shopping has become important for supermarkets

43 Managing stock

In early December 2015, parents of three-year-olds were facing a crisis. The must-give toy of the year was the Paw Patroller – £59.99 if you could find it in the UK, but certainly not at Argos or The Entertainer. Both had sold out and were told there could be no new supplies until after Christmas. Without **stock**, sales cannot happen. Manufacturers and retailers need to make sure they supply the right amount of goods to keep the shelves full.

Simply ordering lots of stock carries other risks, however. In August 2015, French Connection announced that it had to extend its summer sales to sell off 'excess stock'. Weak sales in the first half of 2015 left the retailer with too much stock, so it had to be sold off cheaply.

As consumers, we are hugely demanding and quite intolerant. We expect to find every product we are looking for in stock, whenever we want it. Retailers, on the other hand, have to find a balance between too little stock and too much. If all they do is keep masses of stock of every item, their costs will be too high to stay in business.

● Bar gate stock graphs

Successful stock management requires the right balance between reliability and cost. Too little stock and customers can be let down. Too much stock and high costs will force high prices (or losses and potential closure).

The traditional approach is shown in Figure 43.1 on the next page. It illustrates how stock levels should ideally be maintained and is based on three things:

1 Level of demand for the product: stock levels of a popular item will need to be kept high, and orders for fresh supplies may have to be sent regularly.

2 Decision on the right level of **buffer stock**: this is the minimum amount of stock the manager thinks should be held at all times. For example, a busy sweetshop might like to keep a minimum of one box of Cadbury's Dairy Milk in stock (48 bars) as customers expect to always find it on the counter.

3 Decision on how often to order from the supplier: a monthly order is likely to be four times the size of a weekly order and might therefore provide bulk-buying benefits.

A busy sweetshop might like to keep a minimum of one box of Cadbury's Dairy Milk in stock (48 bars)

Take, for example, the management of stocks of Heinz Beans at Bob's Grocery. He has steady sales of 20 cans a week and likes to buy four boxes of beans at a time, each containing 20 cans, as his supplier gives him an extra ten per cent discount when buying in bulk. He chooses to keep a minimum of ten cans in stock at all times (his buffer stock).

The **bar gate stock graph** in Figure 43.1 shows how the delivery of 80 cans pushes his stock up from 10 to 90. Then, as shoppers steadily buy the cans, stock slips down from 90 to 70, then down to 50, then 30, then 10. At this point he needs a new batch of 80 cans, which pushes the stock back up to 90. As long as customers keep buying 20 cans a week, and the supplier delivers on time, this process will go on working smoothly.

Graphs such as this one are built into the scanning software used by many shops. When the barcode scanner shows that stocks of Heinz Beans have fallen to ten tins, it can either flash a warning to the shopkeeper or reorder from the supplier automatically.

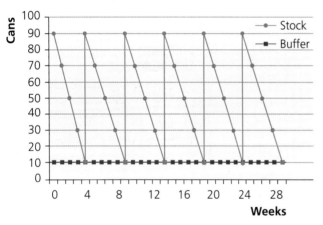

Figure 43.1 Bar gate stock graph for Heinz Beans at Bob's Grocery

Just In Time

Buffer stocks help ensure that customers always find what they want on the shelf; however, cost money and they also take up space. Fifteen years ago, a supermarket might have used up 20 per cent of its floor space in stockrooms. These rooms were closed off from the public, just holding stocks. Tesco was one of the first stores to recognise that this was a terrible waste. Why not turn the stockroom into an extra sales floor, perhaps to stock non-food items such as clothes?

Tesco started insisting that suppliers should deliver more frequently, but in smaller quantities, creating less need for a big storage room. It also started using **Just In Time (JIT)**. This means ordering extra supplies 'just in time', before the old supplies run out. In other words, it does away with buffer stock. Tesco believes it is so efficient that it does not need a buffer; it will order the right quantities at the right time. In truth, it will sometimes make a mistake, leaving a shelf empty. Clearly its managers find that the benefits of Just In Time outweigh the costs of lower customer satisfaction.

> Use of JIT [means] every component has to fit perfectly first time because there are no alternatives available.
>
> *Toyota website*

Table 43.1 Advantages and disadvantages of Just In Time

Advantages	Disadvantages
Eliminating buffer stock cuts storage space, allowing more sales space	A greater risk of running out of stock and therefore disappointing customers
Low stock and more frequent supplier deliveries mean fresher produce	Buying smaller quantities more often means losing out on bulk-buying discounts
Less of the business' capital is tied up in stock	Any mistake or misjudgement could cause out-of-stock and poorer customer service

Drawing the right conclusions

Managing stock is difficult to get right. All it takes is for Mary Berry to mention 'muscovado sugar' one night on TV and the shelves of Britain will be empty by 10 a.m. the next day. If a business sets its sights on providing fantastic customer service, it may need to set high buffer stocks to ensure that no shelf is ever empty. If, however, the business is focused on low prices and low stocks (like Primark, Aldi or Lidl), a JIT system may be needed to keep costs down. Different firms have different needs and, therefore, different policies.

All it takes is for Mary Berry to mention muscovado sugar one night on TV and the shelves of Britain will be empty the next morning

Revision essentials

Bar gate stock graph: a diagram to show changes in the level of stock over time.

Buffer (stock): the minimum stock level held at all times to avoid running out.

Just In Time (JIT): running the business with so little stock that new supplies have to arrive 'just in time' before they run out.

Stock(s): items held by a firm for use or sale, for example components for manufacturing or sellable products for a retailer.

End of chapter exercises

1 Explain the meaning of the term 'stock levels'.

2 Outline one reason why a small grocer's shop might set:

   (a) a low buffer stock for fresh grapes

   (b) a high buffer stock for Cadbury's Creme Eggs.

3 Look at the bar gate stock graph in Figure 43.1 on page 212 and answer these questions:

   (a) In what way does the graph show that Bob wants to keep ten cans in stock at all times?

   (b) What is the maximum number of cans of beans held in stock?

   (c) Explain what the graph would show if Bob's supplier forgot to deliver the 80 tins of beans.

4 Give two reasons why a factory owner might be worried about ordering raw materials on a JIT basis.

5 Take one of the disadvantages of JIT shown in Table 43.1 on page 212. Explain how it might affect sales at:

   (a) a shoe shop in a busy shopping centre

   (b) the Manchester United Club Shop, Old Trafford.

6 Read the following extract.

(a) Draw the firm's buffer stock level on the graph below

(b) Plot the shop's stocks of Samsung phones. The shop starts with 400 units at the start of the month.

(c) Label the graph carefully.

Each week, the mobile phone shop at Meadowhall, Sheffield, sells 90 Samsung phones. It receives its supplies from Samsung at the end of each four-week period. Samsung requires two weeks' notice for delivery (that is, the order must be placed two weeks before the delivery is required). The phone shop likes to have a minimum stock level of 40 Samsung phones.

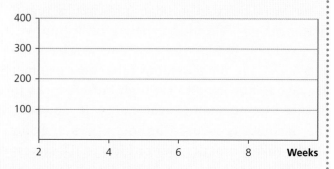

Practice questions

Many businesses face highly erratic sales. With Sony's PS4, sales in one month can be six times higher than in another month. That would be quite difficult to manage even if the figures were predictable, but some Decembers go better than others. The previous December was a bit disappointing – largely because arch-rival Microsoft offered exceptionally good deals on its Xbox One. Those offers 'stole' market share from the PS4.

So, how should Sony manage its stock control for the PS4? Build up production in September and October to have plenty of stock for the Christmas period, or try to keep stocks low at all times, to keep in with the Japanese idea of JIT?

Total: 13 marks

1 Calculate the percentage increase in PS4 sales between August and October 2015. (2)

2 Outline one reason why big variations in sales make it hard to manage stocks. (2)

3 Sony is considering what to do about the huge increase in sales before Christmas. It is considering two options:

♦ Option 1: Take a JIT approach, producing 705,000 units in August and 4,445,000 in December.

♦ Option 2: Produce more in September and October to build up a PS4 stockpile.

Justify which **one** of these two options Sony should choose. (9)

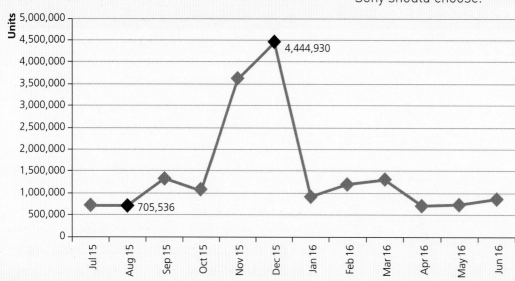

Figure 43.2 Monthly global sales of the PS4 console, 2015–16

44 Procurement: working with suppliers

Very few businesses produce 100 per cent of a product or service. Almost all use suppliers. In some cases suppliers may do most of the operational work. Companies that 'bottle' Coca-Cola buy in: the aluminium cans, already printed with the can design; the water; the carbon dioxide used to create the fizz; and the secret Coke syrup (sent from the Coca-Cola factory in America). They may also get a distribution company to make all the deliveries to wholesale and retail customers. So what does the Coca-Cola bottler actually do? Well, it is responsible for **procurement** – finding the right suppliers, ordering the right quantities and checking that everything is done on time and to the right standards. If Waitrose orders a container load of Diet Coke to reach its Bracknell depot at 10 a.m. on a Tuesday morning, does it turn up on time? If not, why not?

For many companies, procurement is a key to success. A homemade ice cream parlour may do all the production operations on-site but still relies on suppliers of: fresh fruit, fresh milk and cream, sugar, wafer biscuits and cones, paper cups and plastic spoons, and so on. To run the parlour successfully, all the operations have to be carried out successfully. If you run out of cones and cups, the best ice creams will remain unsold.

A company must therefore select suppliers that deliver the right goods reliably, and must negotiate low enough supply prices to make it possible to run the business economically.

> When consumers purchase a Toyota, they are not simply purchasing a car, truck or van. They are placing their trust in our company.
>
> *Akio Toyoda, president of Toyota*

Building relationships with suppliers

There are five main factors at the heart of the relationship between a company and its suppliers: quality, delivery, **availability**, cost and **trust**. If one had to be picked out of the five, it would be trust.

Quality

If you're making a Bentley, it is obvious that top-quality leather is needed for the car seats. Less obvious is that the quality of supplies may be even more important if you're making a Dacia Logan (one of the cheapest cars on the market). That's because Logans are mass-produced on a conveyor belt, where every component has to be identical or else the car won't fit together. And if there's a faulty gearbox, no one will know until the customer has a breakdown and demands their money back. The point is that high quality is essential to be able to produce low-priced items. And your supplier must know that. Your need for quality is fundamental to your business; it is not a minor add-on.

Delivery

Supplies at the right price and of a high quality may be of little use if they arrive late. Failure to deliver supplies on time can bring a manufacturing process to a halt or leave shops with empty shelves. Suppliers' reliability will be easy to assess once a business has started working with them. However, a new business or a business procuring new supplies may need to rely on word-of-mouth reputation to inform its choice. Larger firms will impose financial penalties on suppliers who prove unreliable, but small businesses will be in a weaker position if they try to threaten a supplier.

A further important aspect of delivery is speed and, therefore, a short lead time (the length of time between placing an order and receiving a delivery). This is why suppliers try to locate their factories right alongside their customers. If a spark plug-manufacturer is located right next to Nissan's Sunderland factory, it might be able to get the lead time down to 30 minutes.

Availability

In a similar way to ensuring the right frequency of supplies, many firms will need to find a supplier with the capacity to cope with widely varying orders. Businesses selling products with erratic demand patterns, caused by changes in the weather or fashion, will need to find suppliers that can meet their ever-changing needs. Probably the most common scenario is to ensure that suppliers have the spare capacity available to cope with sudden rush orders. In addition, some firms will need to find suppliers that can supply at the right time (night-time deliveries may be banned in residential area, for example).

Cost

Cheaper supplies mean lower variable costs and higher profit margins. Therefore, the price charged by a supplier will be a key factor in the relationship between a firm and its suppliers. Large businesses may be able to almost dictate prices to their suppliers; because the quantities they purchase may account for most of the supplier's output, it gives a huge amount of power to the buyer.

For small businesses with limited purchasing power, the supplier may have the upper hand. As a result of this, small businesses may be tempted to shop around, looking for the cheapest supplier they can find. This may not always be the most sensible course of action, however; building a long-term relationship based on trust may be more important than short-term cost-cutting.

Trust

Most business transactions are on credit, not for cash. If Tesco wants to order 2,000 cases of Heinz Beans, the bill is unlikely to be paid until 60 or more days after the goods have been delivered. This gives Tesco time to sell the beans, providing the cash to pay the supplier. Small business start-ups will struggle to get the same terms. A newly opened corner shop will not be given credit by Heinz. The supplier will want to be paid in cash until the new business can be trusted to pay its bills. So, a new small firm has to pay up front, placing extra strain on its cash flow.

Trust is crucial in lots of other ways. An aircraft manufacturer such as Airbus wants to keep its ideas for a new plane secret, but it may have to share them with a trusted supplier who is needed to develop a new, lightweight landing gear mechanism. Without trust in the supplier's ability to keep a secret from a rival, like Boeing, no business can take place.

> I faced a number of challenges whilst I built Biocon. Initially, I had credibility challenges where I couldn't get banks to fund me ... Even in the businesses where I had to procure raw materials, they didn't want to deal with women.
>
> *Kiran Mazumdar-Shaw, billionaire Indian entrepreneur*

Talking point

Why do may women entrepreneurs still face a credibility problem with some businessmen?

● The impact of logistics and supply decisions

Logistics is the science behind efficient movement of materials. In wartime it is about getting the right guns and ammunition to the right troops in the right place at the right time. Your training counts for nothing if you've run out of ammo.

For businesses, it is the same thing. In early 2016, Airbus was embarrassed to have more than 20 planes 'parked' outside its French assembly factory. A320s were waiting for aero engines to be brought from Pratt & Whitney in USA, while its A350s were waiting for cabin equipment that had not arrived from a French supplier. Financial experts estimated that Airbus would face delayed cash inflows worth more than €1 billion – just because the physical process of getting parts from A to B was being delayed. Better management of logistics would have helped hugely.

Delays in supply can affect other parts of the production process, as Airbus learned

Well-managed logistics and supply decisions help to achieve:

◆ a better reputation based on reliability and high-quality service
◆ lower costs if production can be completed more quickly, and better cash flow if the bills can be presented more quickly
◆ high customer satisfaction if the right product, with the right quality, is delivered to the right place at the right time, and at the right price; not much to ask!

> Leaders win through logistics. Vision, sure. Strategy, yes. But when you go to war, you need to have both toilet paper and bullets at the right place at the right time. In other words, you must win through superior logistics.
>
> *Tom Peters, business writer*

Drawing the right conclusions

Procurement sounds easy – a bit like going shopping. But for a business to be super-efficient it must get its procurement spot on. It must buy from the right supplier, at the right price, and make sure that it gets supplies of consistently high quality, which are delivered on time. But procurement is about more than just the mechanics of getting things delivered. It is also about trust and business relationships. In the 2014 loom band craze, any shop that could get fresh supplies was guaranteed to sell out in minutes; but which buyers had the procurement skills to get the supplies? Poundworld proved to be a loom band winner.

Revision essentials

Availability: knowing how to get the right supplies quickly – just when you need them.

Logistics: ensuring that the right supplies will be ordered and delivered on time.

Procurement: obtaining the right supplies from the right supplier.

Trust: building a business relationship in which both sides know that the other won't let them down.

End of chapter exercises

1 Explain why the cheapest supplier may not always be the best choice.

2 Identify two businesses for which daily deliveries may be absolutely crucial.

3 Briefly explain two problems that may arise when a firm uses a supplier with poor levels of quality.

4 Describe how a car manufacturer such as Volkswagen may benefit from including its component suppliers in the development process when designing a new car.

Practice questions

BJK Ltd is a small manufacturer of toys for pets. Having developed a brand new doll for dogs, it is considering which supplier to use for the plastic used in moulding (see Table 44.1). Having started up only 12 months ago, the business has done well and is eagerly anticipating the Christmas rush that will begin soon. The management hopes that the new doll will be a best-seller this Christmas.

Table 44.1 Potential suppliers for BJK Ltd

Supplier	A	B	C
Price per unit (£)	4.20	4.80	4.99
Reject rate (per 1,000 products delivered)	28	18	5
Lead time (days)	7	1	4

Total: 20 marks

1 Identify which supplier offers the best:
   (a) quality
   (b) speed of response. (2)

2 Analyse why lead time would be important to a business such as BJK. (6)

3 Evaluate which supplier BJK should choose, and why. You should use your knowledge of the case study above as well as your knowledge of business. . (12)

45 Managing quality

Quality is the ultimate test of a business organisation. Do customers who arrive or phone or email have a positive experience? Do bloggers and social media comments give positive feedback? For producers of goods, quality is about practical matters such as reliability. For service businesses, quality is often about personal things such as politeness and a genuine smile.

With restaurants, quality is partly to do with the product (is it well cooked and served hot?) but also to do with the service: are staff friendly, well trained and on the customer's side? A customer who leaves feeling angry will never return; even a weakly positive response may not be enough. To return, we have to be thrilled. Customers should be delighted, not just satisfied.

> Quality means doing it right when no one is looking.
>
> *Henry Ford, father of all modern manufacturing*

Quality control

Quality control is a system of inspection to try to make sure that customers don't experience a poor-quality product or service.

Many businesses regard quality as a management issue, to be controlled by careful systems. Managers may put in place practices such as:

- factory inspectors at the end of a production line, who check every fifth car or carpet before it is sent to the customer; if several cars fail to start, they might decide to check the whole day's output; any faults found are corrected

- a 100 per cent inspection system, just as Gordon Ramsay does in his restaurants: the head chef checks every plate before it is sent to the high-paying customers; if the steak is slightly burnt, Ramsay throws the whole plate of food away and demands that his chefs start again

- a feedback system, such as a customer feedback questionnaire, which you might find in a hotel room or be given at an airport; this is a check on the final experience enjoyed or suffered by the customer.

The problem that these systems share is that they rarely feel part of the life of the worker. A car worker who is putting left front doors on to Minis all day long cannot even see the end of the line where the inspectors are checking the quality. Similarly, the hotel cleaning staff do not see the feedback questionnaire responses – indeed they may rarely see a hotel guest. Only in the Ramsay kitchen does the chef see his cooking thrown away in disgust by an angry head chef.

Most systems of quality control, therefore, are flawed. They try to put a lid on a problem rather than solve it. They work on the basis of 'acceptable' quality. In effect, they accept that staff will not think much about quality, therefore the managers have to 'sort it out'.

Quality assurance

Although the best businesses create a high-quality culture, this cannot be achieved overnight. If staff treat customers as an inconvenience, the short-term solution may be to use quality assurance. While quality control is a system of checking at the end, quality assurance attempts to build quality into the system. In other words, every member of staff has quality responsibilities. These are set out on paper, often in detail. In this way, everyone knows exactly what they must contribute towards quality.

The hope is that, over time, making individuals responsible for quality will ensure better results. Once staff see quality as their personal responsibility, they may see ways to do things even better. In this was a system of quality assurance can be built into a quality culture.

> Manufacturing is more than just putting parts together. It's coming up with ideas, testing principles and perfecting the engineering, as well as final assembly.
>
> *James Dyson, British industrialist*

Talking point

Discuss whether the quality of your homework would be improved by a thorough system of quality assurance, checking what you do at every stage.

Quality culture

In the ideal business, quality is fundamental to everyone's attitude to work. If you're going to an ice cream parlour, what you want is someone behind the counter who delights in offering you free samples of 'two terrific new flavours' – and enjoys building up the ice cream on the cone to make it look great. When you go to Next, you want the staff to really help you find something that fits well, rather than look frustrated when you don't buy the first couple of things you try on. Ideally, everyone would be enjoying their job of serving you.

Business **culture** means the general attitudes and behaviours among staff within a workplace. Years ago, the Manchester United dressing room was famous for a hard-drinking, hard-gambling culture. Then came Alex Ferguson, who steadily transformed the culture to a passion for sporting excellence, rather than excess. Successful businesses ensure that a quality culture develops among staff. This comes from pride in the business and what it does for its customers.

> Quality is remembered long after the price is forgotten.
>
> *A Gucci saying that was first coined by Sir Henry Royce of Rolls-Royce*

Table 45.1 looks at what quality means in the production of services as well as products.

A customer feedback questionnaire is one system of quality control

Table 45.1 Quality and its importance for the production of goods and services

	Production of goods	Production of services
Quality of initial impact	Well packaged and well presented (posh cars even need to smell new and posh)	Restaurant: food looks and smells great Hotel: room looks clean and smells fresh
Quality in usage	Few or no niggles at the start; reliable and hard wearing	Everything works well/tastes good/proves comfortable (in hotels, a great night's sleep)
Quality of after-sales service	Friendly follow-up call four weeks after purchase; any problems dealt with quickly and cheaply (preferably free)	When calling back for that lost iPhone, staff really care/look/find!

A hospital nurse's quality assurance task may be to record the medication that patients have been given

Quality, cost control and competitive advantage

High-quality production means things are right first time: this means that a job has to done once and once only. As a result, high quality means:

◆ less wastage, for example of materials, ingredients or components having to be scrapped

◆ lower wage bills: staff only use their labour time once per task – if quality is poor, everything has to be done twice; it is the same as when a teacher demands that poorly done homework be redone: it takes twice as much of your time

◆ fewer managers – each needing a high wage – focused on quality: if staff become excellent at producing high-quality output, fewer quality control staff are needed.

Faced with higher quality and lower costs, a business can start looking at overseas competition. Under British ownership, Jaguar was famous in America for the unreliability of its stylish-looking cars. Since 2008 and the takeover by Tata of India, Jaguar quality has improved significantly. In the first half of 2016, Jaguar's US sales rose by 40.3 per cent on 2015.

In Jaguar's case, the important thing was sufficient production quality to make its cars competitive with others on US forecourts. In many other cases, quality becomes the heart of the product or service's competitive advantage. Examples include Hermès of Paris (bags); Fever-Tree UK (posh tonic water) and Dyson Appliances UK (vacuum cleaners and stunningly expensive hair dryers). If customers want your product for quality reasons, you no longer have to worry about pricing. Broadly, you can charge what you want. That's the secret behind Bentley cars, Burberry coats and Waitrose grocers.

> Almost all quality improvement comes via simplification of design, manufacturing and layout.
>
> *Tom Peters, business writer*

Drawing the right conclusions

High quality is achieved by providing an efficient service: the right product of the right quality at the right time – with a human face. This is hard to attain 100 per cent of the time, because mistakes do happen. The best way to achieve it is to establish a culture of quality based on motivated staff who care about the customers and about the company's reputation.

Once the culture is established, further quality controls may not be necessary. For example, if a fully qualified surgeon is carrying out an operation, no one else will peer over their shoulder to check on the quality. He or she is trusted. However, at Gordon Ramsay restaurants and Toyota car factories, further inspections are carried out to make 100 per cent sure that the quality is spot on. So, a combination of quality culture and quality control is probably the best of all worlds.

Revision essentials

Culture: 'the way we do things round here'; in other words, the accepted attitudes and practices of staff at a workplace.

Quality control: putting measures in place to check that the customer receives an acceptable level of quality.

Warranty: the guarantee by the producer that it will repair any faults in a product for a specific period of time – often one year.

End of chapter exercises

1 Explain how 'customer delight' might affect a firm's sales.

2 Outline one possible weakness in a quality-control system based on factory inspectors checking a sample of the finished product before it is sent to customers.

3 BHS went out of business in 2016, after years of a worsening reputation for the quality of its goods and service. How might that reputation have affected the business?

4 At school, you and your parents are 'customers'. Outline one example of good and one example of poor quality service that you or your parents experience from the school.

5 Explain why highly motivated staff are more likely to deliver high-quality service.

6 Would a system of quality control or quality assurance be better for:

(a) Boeing, which manufactures passenger aeroplanes

(b) Mars, which produces chocolate bars.

Practice questions

The cornerstone of Toyota's quality-control system is the role of the team members in the production process. The principles on which Toyota was founded are employed at the Georgetown plant in the USA. Toyota involves its team members by:

♦ encouraging an active role in quality control

♦ utilising employee ideas and opinions in production processes

♦ striving for continuous improvement (known as *kaizen* in Japan).

New-product planning emphasises a product that is as defect-free as possible. In other words, Toyota designs quality into the automobile. Quality control during production ensures that the correct materials and parts are used, and that they are fitted with precision and accuracy. This effort is combined with thousands of careful inspections performed by team members during the production process.

Team members on the line are responsible for the parts they use. They are inspectors of their own work and that of co-workers. When a problem on any vehicle is spotted, any team member can pull a rope – called an andon cord – strung along the assembly line to halt production. Only when the problem is resolved is the line restarted. This process involves every team member in monitoring and checking the quality of every car produced.

In 2015, Toyota announced a multi-million dollar expansion of the Georgetown plant and 750 new jobs producing their upmarket Lexus models alongside the Toyotas. The company said this was a tribute to the high quality standards at Georgetown.

Total: 20 marks

1 Define the term 'quality control'. (1)

2 State one way in which Toyota is ensuring high-quality output. (1)

3 Analyse how Toyota may benefit from the high quality standards it achieves. (6)

4 Evaluate whether Toyota's quality management at Georgetown is based on quality control or a quality culture. You should use the information provided as well as your knowledge of business. (12)

46 The sales process

As she walked into the Italian bakery, she was greeted with: 'Hello, I remember you … Mrs Draper?' She smiled and said: 'It's great to be back … I moved two years ago and I miss your Nutella croissants.' The baker grabbed a croissant, disappeared, then returned with a coffee plus croissant. He said: 'Please have the coffee on me. Nice to see you again.' She paid £1.20 for the croissant, sighed and left with a wave.

To be effective, customer service must be:

◆ rooted in a clear understanding of what customers really care about

◆ practical and cost-effective enough to ensure that it can be kept going regularly

◆ based on a genuine wish to help, rather than an attempt to seem helpful

◆ offered at the right time in the right way at the right place.

Great customer service is a wonderful thing, but there is far more than that to the sales process. To succeed with sales, a business must make sure it provides:

◆ strong **product knowledge** and, therefore, helpful advice

◆ speedy and efficient service

◆ **customer engagement**

◆ responses to **customer feedback**

◆ excellent **post-sales service** (or after-sales)

> In the world of internet customer service, it's important to remember your competitor is only one mouse click away.
>
> *Doug Warner, vice president at Hewlett Packard*

Product knowledge

Customers expect that staff will be sufficiently well trained and well motivated to have good knowledge of the products and services being offered. No one would be impressed if – at a cocktail bar – the barman had to look up the ingredients for a Mojito or a Martini. Similarly, supermarket customers want staff to be able to show them where the Marmite is shelved. In certain businesses, product knowledge goes from being desirable to essential. A travel agent knows you can get from Zurich to Milan by plane, but that it is cheaper and more convenient by train.

To get staff to have strong product knowledge, certain things are essential:

◆ Good training: at the famous River Café restaurant in London, waiters help chefs to prepare ('prep') the food in the morning, and are flown out to meet different suppliers in Italy each year; their product knowledge is – naturally – amazing.

◆ Loyal staff that stay for years: if staff only stay for three to six months, they can never get a rich understanding of the product and services; well-managed businesses that pay fairly and treat staff well can get the loyalty that's needed.

◆ Staff who are committed to customers: this is affected by good recruitment, good training and by the degree of commitment staff feel towards the business as a whole. Some staff in a health food shop may care hugely about healthier eating and living – making them care about being knowledgeable.

Good service can be a higher priority than cost

Speed and efficiency of service

Good customer service is designed for the customer, not the company. It is efficient because it works well, works quickly and gives the customer the sense of being cared for. With good service a call to a company is answered by the receptionist who knows that the managing director is out today. With bad service, a call puts you into a voicemail loop and you wait several minutes listening to tinny 1990s music; only then do you get through to someone at a call centre 25 – or 10,000 – miles away. That person tries to put you through to the managing director – and keeps failing.

Efficient service:

◆ gets products to you exactly when you want them …

◆ in good condition …

◆ and if there is something wrong, it will be sorted out as soon as possible and in the right spirit (if you leave a jacket in a shop, it would be great for them to contact you, instead of you having to figure out which shop you left it in).

Good service may cost the customer extra, but that is fine as long as it represents value for money. It must relate to what customers want and what they are willing to pay for. A discounted 'Upper Class' flight on Virgin Atlantic to New York is priced at £2,800 return. This is about six times the price of a standard class ticket. For that you get a seat that doubles as a bed, an on-board massage and better food. It is hard to see that this *can* be value for money – yet Upper Class seats are usually full. Some people (or their companies) are happy to pay it.

Ryanair, meanwhile, offers minimal customer service. It is a no-frills airline based on low costs and low prices. There is no free food or drinks on board, and rarely a smile from staff. Yet if all you want is to get to Spain and back cheaply, quickly and efficiently, Ryanair may be ideal, as you can see in Figure 46.1 below.

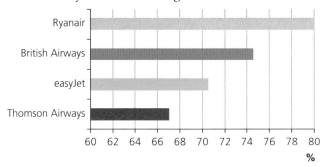

Figure 46.1 Percentage of flights arriving on time at British airports (Source: www.flightontime.info, 12 months to March 2016)

> Being on par in terms of price and quality only gets you into the game. Service wins the game.
>
> *Tony Alesandra, US entrepreneur*

Customer engagement

In the world of social media, it becomes possible to try to keep customers engaged with the business on a semi-permanent basis. This is exactly what happens with football supporters. They go to the ground to see a match once every fortnight, but may receive half a dozen Tweets a day from the club, telling of a new player signed, or the result of the Man of the Match vote. These are engaged customers. It may never be possible for an ordinary business to stimulate the fervour of the football supporter, but customer engagement is an important idea. Here are some examples:

◆ A customer at Burberry is sent regular updates on new fashion styling, images from the latest fashion shoot with Brooklyn Beckham and occasionally a free ticket to a Burberry event at London Fashion Week. The hope is that the customer feels 'part of' Burberry, rather than just a customer.

◆ Milkshake chain Shakeaway has 68,000 Facebook likes and many Twitter followers – all encouraged to post selfies taken with Shakeaway staff. The company manages to communicate its new

'Smoothies Re-invented' product launch – but again the key is to get people to feel part of something rather than being outsiders.

Shakeaway focusses on customer engagement

◆ Customer engagement existed long before social media, of course. For decades, people round the world have wanted a Hard Rock Cafe (a US hamburger chain) London/Miami/Tokyo T-shirt. In this case the customer engagement came first – by word-of-mouth. Only later did the company see the chance to turn this into revenue and profit.

Responses to customer feedback

Years ago, customer feedback meant two things: feedback to the business ('I thought the steak was a bit tough') and word-of-mouth, that is, telling friends and family. Even though bad news can spread pretty quickly, the power of word-of-mouth was a relatively slow burner. By comparison, a post on TripAdvisor is much more powerful – and worrying. Well-run restaurants or hotels post replies to the customers who have left comments. This is especially worthwhile if the comment was critical. Apologising for a dripping tap or lukewarm lasagne makes sense, especially if you – the boss – follow up the complaint and make sure it doesn't happen again.

For a business, the reason to provide great customer service is because it keeps customers coming back. It can cost a lot of money to persuade new customers to come: advertisers believe that people need to see a TV commercial at least five times before it has any effect, and five national TV commercials on ITV can easily cost £600,000. So, it is madness to risk losing these people through poor service.

> Profit in business comes from repeat customers; customers that boast about your product and service, and that bring friends with them.
>
> *W. Edwards Deming, the business guru's guru*

● Drawing the right conclusions

However good the customer service was at the time, poor after-sales service can ruin the effect. You paid £2,000 to a plumber just two months ago, but there's a small leak from the sink's waste pipe. You phone to ask for a speedy visit to sort the problem. Promises aren't kept and weeks go by. It is clear that, with the money banked, the plumber can't be bothered with your little problem. You're furious and take back the nice things you said to neighbours about the plumber – but the plumber may know that there are always other customers out there. In a small town a plumber can't get away with this, but in Birmingham or London, it is no problem.

For a well-run business that cares about its long-term reputation, good after-sales service is vital. It is reasonable to say that it is important in life to make a good impression when you say hello, as well as when you say goodbye.

Revision essentials

Customer engagement: the attempt to make a customer feel part of something rather than an outsider.

Customer feedback: comments, praise or criticisms given to the company by its customers.

Post-sales service: service received after the purchase is completed, perhaps because something has gone wrong or as a way of promoting customer engagement.

Product knowledge: how well staff know all the features of the products and the service issues surrounding the products, such as the precise terms of Kia's seven-year warranty on its new cars.

End of chapter exercises

1 Explain the importance of staff product knowledge for a customer going to buy their first new car.

2 Why may speed of service matter more to some customers than others?

3 Suggest two ways in which customer engagement might be promoted by a local kebab shop.

4 Explain the damage that might be caused to a company's profits if it responds bitterly to customer feedback.

5 Explain how a low-cost airline might benefit from improving its post-sales service.

Practice questions

Ipswich cruise ship firm Fred.Olsen could face compensation claims worth over £1 million after hundreds of passengers fell ill after a norovirus outbreak, a law firm has claimed.

Some 252 of the 919 passengers on board *Balmoral* fell ill after it left Southampton on April 16, according to the US Centers for Disease Control and Prevention (CDC). The ship's owner, Fred.Olsen Cruise Lines, said it undertook 'extensive sanitisation measures' and cleaned the ship. It said *Balmoral* has not been quarantined in any port and is continuing the 34-night 'Old England to New England' cruise 'as planned'.

Yesterday, seven passengers were required to remain in their cabins in a bid to stop the spread of the virus. All other passengers had recovered. The majority of those affected were British. Specimens collected when the ship docked in the US city of Baltimore between April 30 to May 1 tested positive for norovirus, CDC said. The ship has suffered from previous outbreaks of norovirus, which can cause projectile vomiting and diarrhoea.

Ciaran McCabe, a solicitor at law firm Moore Blatch, said: 'At this stage we don't have the full details, but it would be reasonable to assume that Fred.Olsen could be facing claims from affected travellers of in excess of £1 million. Typically, a passenger who has suffered for around two weeks from symptoms such as vomiting and diarrhoea would be entitled to between £2,000 and £3,000 each. If the illness is much more severe, the compensation can be significantly higher.'

A Fred.Olsen spokesman said: 'Fred.Olsen Cruise Lines can confirm that a gastroenteritis-type illness has affected a number of guests … There are currently just seven guests who have been required to remain in their cabins, out of a total of 1,434 guests and crew on board … Twenty additional professional cleaning staff are also being sent out to the ship.'

Fred.Olsen also said that it 'believes that it is unique amongst cruise lines in providing immediate compensation to any guest who is required to remain in isolation.'

Source: *Ipswich Star*, 11 May 2016

Total: 15 marks

1 Analyse whether Fred.Olsen Cruise Lines seems to be focused sufficiently on providing good customer service. (6)

2 The management at Fred.Olsen is considering two options for refreshing their service:
   - Option 1: Set up a new customer service department for dealing with customer complaints more quickly.
   - Option 2: Spend longer in dock between cruises, making sure that cleaning is more thorough.

Justify which **one** of these two options Fred.Olsen should choose. (9)

Exam-style questions on Topic 2.3

Don't rush; check your answers carefully.

Questions 1, 2 and 3 are based on Figure 46.2, the bar gate stock graph for JB Grocers.

Bar gate stock graph for JB Grocers

1 Which **one** of the following seems to be JB Grocers' maximum stock level for baked beans? (1)
   (a) 100 tins
   (b) 500 tins
   (c) 300 tins
   (d) 9 tins

2 How many tins are delivered to the shop every two weeks? (1)

3 Which **two** of the following statements are reasons why JB Grocers might want a delivery every two weeks instead of once a week? (2)
   (a) To lower their average stock levels.
   (b) To make sure the maximum stock capacity is fully used.
   (c) There may be a large delivery charge per order.
   (d) So that stocks don't fall below the buffer level.

(e) Bigger orders may mean bigger discounts from suppliers.

4 Which **one** of these is a definite result of using a system of quality control? (1)
   (a) It guarantees that every customer enjoys products of the highest quality.
   (b) It ensures that everyone in the business cares about quality.
   (c) It keeps the costs of quality management down to the minimum.
   (d) It ensures that products are inspected at the end of the production line.

5 Which **one** of the following is a reason why good quality management might provide a business with a competitive advantage? (1)
   (a) Higher quality may cost more, but the business doesn't *have* to push the price up.
   (b) Customers might come to see the product as superior to rivals.
   (c) Your high-quality products might worry competitors, making them back away.
   (d) Using quality assurance systems provides more paperwork and, therefore, better record keeping.

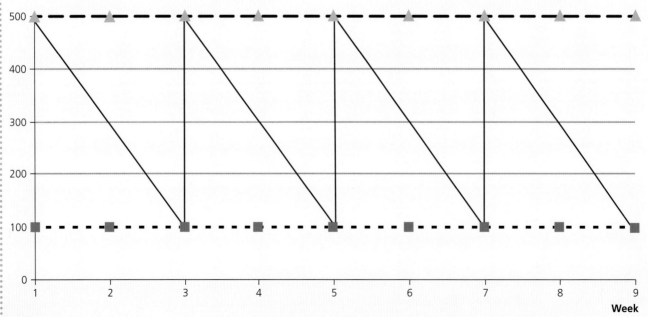

Questions 6, 7 and 8 are based on this information about BMax Ltd.

Between them, the 20 staff at BMax Ltd produce 600 chairs a week. The productivity level of the staff is twice as high as that at Balex, a major competitor.

6 Which **one** of the following is the productivity level of the BMax workforce? (1)

(a) 30 chairs per person per week

(b) 600 chairs per person per week

(c) 300 chairs per person per week

(d) 12,000 chairs per week

7 Which **two** of the following reasons might explain why BMax has higher productivity than Balex? (2)

(a) Better management at BMax may mean their staff are more motivated.

(b) BMax may make more use of job production than at Balex.

(c) Balex managers are more reluctant to spend on new technology.

(d) Balex managers may be better at procuring on-time supplies than BMax.

(e) Balex managers may use mass production methods to good effect.

8 Which one of the following is a problem Balex will have in competing with BMax? (1)

(a) It will struggle to produce enough to meet customer demand.

(b) Balex may lack the reliability BMax shows to its customers.

(c) Low productivity at Balex will mean a lower break-even point.

(d) Balex will have much higher labour costs per chair than BMax.

Now try this discussion question.

9 Discuss the importance to a growing business of keeping productivity up. (6)

47 Business calculations

When BHS collapsed in 2016, there were huge arguments about who or what was to blame, including about excessive dividends and low contributions to the pension scheme. At the heart of the matter, though, was that BHS was no longer a profitable business. The numbers no longer added up. It had to close.

Starting and running a business is a fascinating mix of problem solving, decision making, dealing with people and dealing with numbers. Even businesspeople who dislike calculations soon learn that some key calculations are critical. Among the most important are:

◆ **gross profit margin**
◆ **net profit margin**
◆ **average rate of return**.

It is important for businesses to make the right calculations

● Gross profit margin

Gross profit is the difference between a product's selling price and what it cost the business. A jacket bought for £100 from Superdry cost the business £35 to buy from the factory. So, Superdry's gross profit is £65. That profit figure may sound greedily high, but remember that gross profit doesn't include the background running costs of the business – fixed costs such as shop rents, staff salaries, spending on advertising, on heating, lighting and much more.

The following formula is used to calculate gross profit margin:

$$\text{gross profit margin} = \frac{\text{gross profit}}{\text{revenue}} \times 100$$

So, in the case of the Superdry jacket, a £65 gross profit on a £100 selling price means a gross profit margin of:

$$\text{gross profit margin} = \frac{£65}{£100} \times 100 = 65\%$$

Of course, even if individual Superdry clothes have a 65 per cent gross margin, it doesn't mean that the whole business achieves 65 per cent. Not everything is sold at full price, or else there wouldn't be January and July sales. As Table 47.1 shows, in 2016 SuperGroup plc (owner of Superdry) achieved a gross margin of 61.5 per cent. Comparable figures for clothing groups Ted Baker and French Connection show how well SuperGroup did. The higher the gross profit margin, the easier it should be to achieve a satisfactory net profit margin.

Table 47.1 Gross profit margins at selected UK clothing companies

	SuperGroup plc (Superdry) Year end 30/04/16	Ted Baker plc (Ted Baker clothing) Year end 30/01/16	French Connection plc (French Connection) Year end 31/01/16
Sales revenue	£598 million	£470 million	£164 million
minus cost of sales	£230 million	£183 million	£88 million
equals gross profit	£368 million	£287 million	£76 million
Gross profit margin	$\frac{£368 \text{ million}}{£598 \text{ million}} \times 100 = \textbf{61.5\%}$	$\frac{£287 \text{ million}}{£470 \text{ million}} \times 100 = \textbf{61.1\%}$	$\frac{£76 \text{ million}}{£164 \text{ million}} \times 100 = \textbf{46.3\%}$

To improve a gross profit margin, a company has just two things to work with: either raise the price (charge £105 for that £35 item) or find a way to get the supplier price down (keep charging £100, but pay the supplier only £32 instead of £35).

◆ Increase the price: this is possible if the business has sufficiently distinctive brands to make people willing to pay the extra instead of switching to a rival. In the case of Superdry in 2015–16, the use of Idris Elba as the name behind the menswear range helped to firm up the brand image and, therefore, prices.

◆ Cut the price paid to the supplier: this can be done by:
  ◆ renegotiating with the existing supplier for a lower price, perhaps because good sales mean that you are buying more items per month
  ◆ getting a bidding war going between two suppliers, that is, get them to compete for your business; the lowest cost per unit wins
  ◆ rethinking the item, perhaps using slightly cheaper materials or redesigning it so that it is simpler and, therefore, cheaper to make.

◉ Net profit margin

Net profit is what's left after all the fixed running costs are taken away from gross profit. A jacket bought for £100 from Superdry may yield a £65 gross profit. But running a shop doesn't come cheap, and SuperGroup also has to pay for the fixed costs of running the head office. So, it may be that the company calculates that an item priced at £100 needs to pay £50 towards the fixed running costs, in which case the net profit on the jacket would be £65 × £50 = £15.

The following formula is used to calculate net profit margin:

$$\text{net profit margin} = \frac{\text{net profit}}{\text{revenue}} \times 100$$

So, for Superdry this £15 of net profit would mean a net margin of:

$$\text{net profit margin} = \frac{£15}{£100} \times 100 = 15\%$$

Even if individual Superdry clothes have a 15 per cent net profit margin, it doesn't mean that the whole business achieves 15 per cent. But as Table 47.2 (page 232) shows, in 2016 SuperGroup plc (owner of Superdry) achieved a net margin of 12 per cent. Comparable figures for Ted Baker make it look as if SuperGroup should be trying a bit harder, but they look wonderful against French Connection. In effect, French Connection's gross margin was too low to ensure that the fixed running costs of the business were covered – it made a loss. The higher the net profit margin, the happier the shareholders will be.

Table 47.2 Net profit margins at selected UK fashion clothing companies

	SuperGroup plc (Superdry) Year end 30/04/16	Ted Baker plc (Ted Baker clothing) Year end 30/01/16	French Connection plc (French Connection) Year end 31/01/16
Gross profit	£368 million	£287 million	£76 million
minus fixed running costs	£296 million	£228 million	£81 million
equals net profit	£72 million	£59 million	–£5 million
Net profit margin	$\dfrac{£72 \text{ million}}{£598 \text{ million}} \times 100 = \textbf{12.0\%}$	$\dfrac{£59 \text{ million}}{£470 \text{ million}} \times 100 = \textbf{12.6\%}$	$\dfrac{-£5 \text{ million}}{£164 \text{ million}} \times 100 = \textbf{–3.0\%}$

To improve a net profit margin, a company has just two things to work with: raise the gross profit or find a way to cut the fixed running costs (perhaps move head office somewhere cheaper, or sell off that corporate jet the directors love to fly around in). Other ways to cut the fixed running costs include:

◆ Consider whether the business might be quicker on its feet if there were fewer layers of management, either in-store or at head office. Fewer layers means faster decision making, and a lower salary bill.

◆ Cut back on that sponsorship of Formula 1 motor-racing. Does it really generate enough sales to be worth the cost? Isn't it a bit of an expenses-paid jolly for directors and senior managers?

◆ And does pay have to be quite so generous for directors? The directors of SuperGroup plc received £5,095,051 in 2015–16. Did they really need £5 million?

Talking point

Red Bull spends more than $100 million a year sponsoring its Formula 1 racing team. Can it really generate enough sales to cover the cost?

●Average rate of return

For senior managers, a regular part of the job is making decisions. Should we invest £50,000 on an automated car wash at our petrol station? Should we spend £12,000 on a forklift truck to save staff having to carry so much (and speed things up)?

To help make these decisions, a useful tool is average rate of return (ARR). It is a calculation of the average yearly profit on an investment as a percentage of the **sum invested**. So, if it is the car wash, we'd work out the average yearly profit (let's say £5,000) and calculate that as a percentage of the £50,000 set-up cost. In this case the ARR would work out as:

$$\frac{£5,000}{£50,000} \times 100 = 10\% \text{ a year}$$

That figure could then be compared with other possible investments of the petrol station's cash. If opening a Krispy Kreme doughnut franchise could generate an ARR of 15 per cent a year, the higher profitability would mean you'd choose it in preference to the car wash. Of course, if you had the cash and the space to do both, you might do that.

In an exam, the figures for ARR would be presented to you in a table, as shown in Table 47.3. This sets out:

◆ the initial outlay (the cash the investment costs the business)

◆ an estimate of the net yearly profit generated by the investment

◆ it may also provide you with a column showing the accumulated profit the key figure there is the bottom right hand corner, which shows everything that is expected to happen over the lifetime of the investment.

Table 47.3 shows the estimated annual profits from an £80,000 investment in a four-year Krispy Kreme franchise.

Table 47.3 The first stage in calculating average rate of return

Time period	Yearly profit	Accumulated profit
NOW: the initial investment	−£80,000	−£80,000
Year 1	+£10,000	−£70,000
Year 2	+£35,000	−£35,000
Year 3	+£45,000	+£10,000
Year 4	+£38,000	+£48,000

If the investment makes £48,000 profit over a four-year period, it has made an average of £12,000 profit per year. Therefore, the formula used to calculate ARR is:

$$\text{average rate of return} = \frac{\text{average yearly profit}}{\text{initial investment}} \times 100$$

So, for the Krispy Kreme franchise:

$$\text{average rate of return} = \frac{£12,000}{£80,000} \times 100 = \textbf{15\% a year}$$

The ARR is 15 per cent a year. This figure can be compared with other uses of cash, whether by leaving it in the bank (which might only earn three per cent interest a year) or by investing it elsewhere in the business.

Drawing the right conclusions

Below is a summary of ARR. Make sure you can recall what it is and how you calculate it.

1 What is ARR? It is a calculation of average yearly profit expected as a percentage of the sum invested.

2 Why do it? To make it easy to compare different investment options – to see which is the most profitable.

3 How do you do it?
 ◆ Identify the total profit over the lifetime of an investment, for example £48,000.
 ◆ Calculate the average yearly profit by dividing by the number of years, for example £48,000 / 4 years.
 ◆ Use the ARR formula to calculate the average yearly profit as a percentage of the sum invested, for example, (£12,000 / £80,000) × 100 = 15 per cent.

4 How do you evaluate the result? It is a measure of profitability, so the higher the better. The least you'd want from a business investment is that it must provide a higher percentage than keeping the money safe in a bank account, that is, it must make a better return than the interest rate.

Revision essentials

Average rate or return (ARR): average yearly profit as a percentage of the sum invested. This shows profitability and can be compared with the interest rates available on bank deposit accounts.

Gross profit margin: gross profit as a percentage of sales revenue (or, for an individual item, gross profit as a percentage of the selling price).

Net profit margin: net profit as a percentage of sales revenue (or, for an individual item, net profit as a percentage of the selling price).

Sum invested: the cash put at risk when investing in new equipment or a new product.

End of chapter exercises

1 Look again at Table 47.1 on page 231. Explain one possible reason why French Connection's gross profit margin was so much lower than that of SuperGroup and Ted Baker.

2 Outline what would happen to profits if a business allowed its fixed running costs to grow too fast.

3 Look at this data from Ryanair.

Table 47.4 Revenue and profit at Ryanair

	2015	2016
Sales revenue	£5,654 million	£6,536 million
Net (operating) profit	£1,043 million	£1,460 million

(a) Calculate Ryanair's net profit margin for 2015 and 2016.

(b) Comment on whether 2016 was a good or bad year for Ryanair.

4 Annual profits on an investment of £600,000 are shown in Table 47.5.

Table 47.5 Forecast annual profits

	Annual profits (£ thousands)
Year 1	+100
Year 2	+400
Year 3	+400
Year 4	+180

(a) Calculate the average rate of return.

(b) The company has another investment possibility that could yield a 25 per cent return a year. Should it go ahead with both?

Practice questions

As Figure 47.1 shows, companies in different markets can end up making very different profit margins. In this graph, Ted Baker and Burberry can be compared directly, as they are both in the luxury clothing sector. Sainsbury's and Ryanair are in very different sectors.

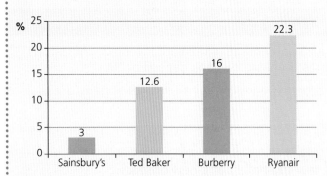

Figure 47.1 Net profit margins in 2016

Total: 15 marks

1 Analyse whether Burberry's higher net profit margin proves that it is better managed than Ted Baker. (6)

2 Having seen this graph, Sainsbury's senior management is determined to improve the company's net profit margin. It has identified two methods:

- Option 1: Moving the company's head office from central London to central Bristol, to cut the property rental costs in half.
- Option 2: Making all staff and managers earning more than £120,000 redundant.

Justify which **one** of these two options Sainsbury's should choose. (9)

48 Understanding business performance

Managers use quantitative data on a daily basis to support, inform and justify decisions. Teachers do this to check on student progress and decide whether to push for A*s or Bs. Companies use data to:

◆ check whether sales are rising in line with the market as a whole

◆ check whether staff 'illness' is consistently higher in some departments than in others

◆ help decide whether to promote Karen or Carl to the position of area manager

◆ help decide whether or not to keep the Northampton branch of a bakery open

◆ help decide whether to launch Smarties in China.

> There are lies, damned lies and statistics.
>
> *Benjamin Disraeli, former prime minister*

> The statistics on sanity are that one of every four Americans is suffering from some form of mental illness. Think of your three best friends. If they're OK, it's you.
>
> *Rita Mae Brown, author*

●Information from graphs and charts

A **line graph** is hugely important in business because it shows trends over time. All businesspeople know that China and India are two of the fastest-growing countries on the planet but, if you're a top manager at Jaguar Land Rover, the graph shown in Figure 48.1 holds crucial information. Back in 2001, China and India had similar-sized car markets. Added together they were smaller than the UK. Fast-forward to

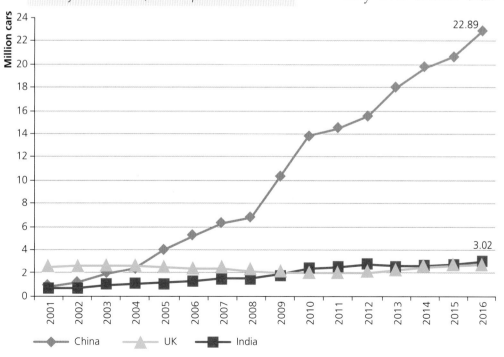

Figure 48.1 Yearly global sales of passenger cars, 2001–16 (Source OICA and press releases)

2016 and you can see the transformation. India's is now bigger than the UK, with 3.02 million cars, and China's is by far the biggest on the planet. Luckily for Britain, Jaguar Land Rover made a big push into China in 2010, which has been very successful. They saw what was happening and acted.

Business decisions are about the future, so line graphs are hugely helpful. By looking at the sales growth in China between 2001 and 2010, Jaguar Land Rover was able to anticipate that there was more growth to come. In 2010, Jaguar Land Rover sold 25,000 cars in China. In 2016, it was 130,000; that growth represented thousands more jobs in the UK.

A **bar chart** can be presented horizontally or vertically. It is a useful way to present different sets of data in a way that makes them understandable. In the bar chart presented in Figure 48.2, a comparison is made between Russia, India, China and the UK. The data shows the biggest problems faced by managers working in those countries. For the UK, 'access to finance' is the biggest problem, mentioned by 14.1 per cent of respondents. For Russia, corruption is the biggest issue at 14.3 per cent; happily, none of the businesspeople said that corruption was the biggest issue they face in the UK.

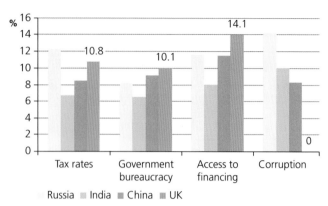

Figure 48.2 Biggest problems faced by businesspeople in different countries (Source: Global Competitiveness Report 2015–16)

A **pie chart** gives a simple look at proportions, such as market share. In Figures 48.3 and 48.4 the share of world sales of passenger aircraft is easy to take in at a glance (there are only two producers: America's Boeing and Europe's Airbus). In 2006, Boeing was boss with a 56 per cent share; by 2015 the Europeans were on top with 57 per cent: it is an extraordinary turnaround in a market worth hundreds of billions of pounds a year – and worth tens of thousands of jobs in the UK.

Table 48.1 Advantages and disadvantages of line graphs, bar charts and pie charts

	Line graphs	Bar charts	Pie charts
Advantages	Good for data shown over many time periods ... and for looking at how one factor affects another, e.g. sales in pounds and money spent on advertising	Good for data shown over two or three time periods Good for comparing the size of several different items, e.g. populations of the ten biggest countries	Good for showing proportions, e.g. Cadbury's share of the UK chocolate market Size of the circle can be made proportional to the quantity it represents
Disadvantages	Too many lines can be confusing, so it can only be used to compare two or three series of data A risk of oversimplifying in assuming that an upward line will stay upward in the future	Cannot easily be used to compare data over many time periods If there's too much data it get confusing to the eye	Pies show big differences clearly, but for small differences a bar chart can be clearer Cannot shows trends over a number of years

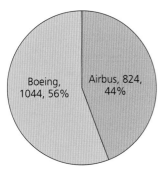
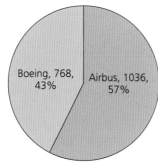

Figure 48.3 Global orders for large passenger planes in 2006

Figure 48.4 Global orders for large passenger planes in 2015

The different ways to present data have different advantages and disadvantages. They are presented in Table 48.1 on the previous page.

Financial data

Important business measures of financial data were dealt with in the previous chapter: profit margins and average rate of return (ARR). Decisions can also be made using the following calculations:

◆ Measuring the profit or loss on a specific deal, or the profit/loss made by one part of the business. When Theo Paphitis bought the struggling retail chain Robert Dyas for £10 million, he estimated that he could achieve annual profits of £2.5 million a year. In fact, within one year he'd pushed the profits up from £186,000 to £3.2 million.

◆ Measuring the break-even point. If one shop in a chain is making losses, the owner might set the store manager the goal of achieving a break-even level of sales. After reviewing how difficult it was to achieve that goal, the owner can then decide whether to try harder to achieve profits, or whether it is time to close down that shop.

◆ Forecasting cash flow. When a successful fashion designer decides to expand by taking on more staff and moving to bigger premises, the key problem is likely to be short-term cash flow. Expansions such as this cause huge extra cash outflows that occur before extra cash inflows can start to be generated.

In business, before every decision the effect on profit and the effect on cash flow should be calculated. When both look OK, the decision can go ahead.

Marketing data

Marketing data includes a company's own figures on sales and marketing spending, and the results of primary market research. Secondary market research would usually come under the heading of market data.

To help inform a decision on whether or not to go ahead with a new product launch, a business might get an independent survey done. A research company would go out with a sample of the product and a bank of questions about likes and dislikes. If a high enough percentage of people in your target market say yes, you'll go ahead and launch. As the launch might easily cost £5 million (and might fail), it makes to spend perhaps £50,000 on some serious primary research.

> **Talking point**
>
> If evidence shows only one in five new products succeeds in the long term, should Cadbury give up on producing new chocolate bars? Justify your answer.

Market data

Table 48.2 (page 238) shows spending on disposable nappies in the UK and China. It provides a clear idea of the UK market size (£642.9 million in 2015) and trends in the UK market – weak in terms of spending per person. By contrast, China's figures show huge growth, with sales per person rising by 164 per cent between 2009 and 2015. As people become wealthier in China, convenience becomes a greater priority. Knowing the size of China's population (1.376 billion at the time of writing), one can even work out the total size of the Chinese nappy market from China's 2015 figure:

£3.41 per person × 1.376 bn = £4,692 m

This is about seven times the size of the UK market.

Table 48.2 Sales of disposable nappies in the UK and China, 2009–15

	UK		China
	Total sales (£ millions)	£ per person	£ per person
2009	572.7	9.23	1.29
2010	593.0	9.49	1.56
2011	614.3	9.75	1.95
2012	638.3	10.05	2.28
2013	644.6	10.09	2.64
2014	643.9	10.01	3.09
2015	642.9	9.64	3.41

Data such as this enables the managers of a global brand such as Pampers to choose their priorities. If they have £50 million to spend advertising the brand worldwide, perhaps it is more sensible to support the growth in China than to try to sell more in the UK. Businesses collect market data such as this from secondary sources such as Euromonitor, or public sources such as government statistics.

⬤The use and limitations of financial information

To know what to do next, managers need to be clear on what's going right and wrong currently. To understand the company's current business performance, the manager may analyse:

◆ current trends in market share; are we beating or being beaten by our rivals?

◆ current trends in profit; are we making more or less per month than last year?

◆ current trends in our cash balances at the bank. Are our cash flows pulling the business down or pushing it up?

But there are limitations to the value of all this data. A manager is quite likely to assume that, if things are going well, it is because of brilliant management decisions.

But if things are going badly it is for some outside reason, such as bad weather or the uncertainties caused by Brexit. Collecting good data is not enough. It must be evaluated rigorously and, perhaps, independently. Data is only as good as the person using it.

The other key use of data is for making business decisions. Clearly the same applies: if calculations are misinterpreted, or key warning signs ignored, the result will be awful. Interestingly, this doesn't always hurt the decision maker. Some decisions take so long to evaluate that the manager responsible is long gone: promoted or off to a rival. In 2006, Tesco announced an exciting investment of £1.5 billion in a start-up grocery chain in America. After years of struggle the business finally admitted in 2013 that it was a disaster and gave away the remains of Tesco USA. In the intervening seven years, the directors involved in Tesco USA had been very well paid.

The limitations of using financial data to make business decisions include:

◆ The raw figures may be unreliable or even biased; a good example is market research data if the questions have been written too positively.

◆ Talking to staff can reveal insights that figures can't capture; there may be losses at the Barnsley branch because the manager is a bully and staff keep leaving. Closing the branch down might seem right according to the financial data, but a day spent talking to staff would reveal a different, better decision.

◆ Sometimes a business needs to be patient. Although the iPhone and iPad were overnight successes, the original Apple iPod was a sleeper. Look at Figure 48.5 to see how weak the sales were in the first two years, from Q1 2002 to Q1 2004. When making decisions, it is vital to bear in mind that new products, in particular, can take time to bed in (the iPod only took off after the launch of iTunes in late 2004).

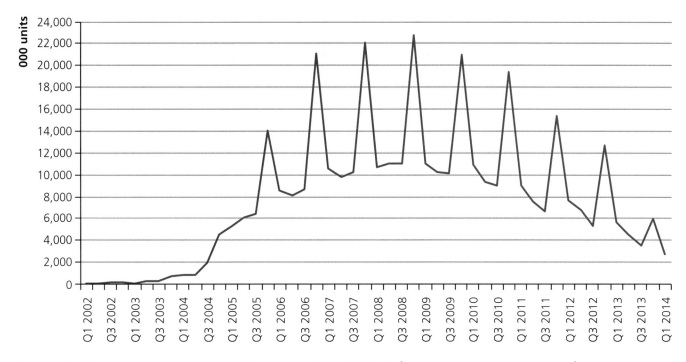

Figure 48.5 Global quarterly sales of the Apple iPod, 2002–14 (Source: Apple Inc. accounts)

◉ Drawing the right conclusions

To understand business performance it is important to be able to read columns of figures and interpret graphs and charts. Companies use graphs to make their performance look impressive, so it is a useful skill to be able to see when there's a degree of exaggeration.

◉ Quantitative skills

As you will have gathered from this chapter, managers employ a range of quantitative skills to make business decisions. In your exams you too will be required to apply quantitative skills to business contexts. The specific skills you will be expected to be able to apply can be found in Appendix 2 on page 31 of the Edexcel GCSE Business specification. They comprise calculations including:

◆ Percentages and percentage changes
◆ Averages
◆ Revenue, costs and profit
◆ Gross margin and net profit margin ratios
◆ Average rate of return
◆ Cash-flow forecasts

You will also be required to interpret quantitative data relating to business contexts and use it to inform business decisions. This includes:

◆ Interpreting graphs and charts
◆ Profitability ratios
◆ Financial data (profit/loss/average rate of return/ cash flow forecasts)
◆ Marketing data
◆ Market data (market share/changes in costs/ changes in prices)

All of these skills are covered in this book and if you answer the 'Exercises' and 'Practice questions' at the end of each chapter there are plenty of opportunities to practice applying them.

Revision essentials

Bar chart: data presented so that the height of the bar represents the quantity involved; good for making comparisons.

Line graph: data presented as lines, making it easy to identify trends, especially if time is on the horizontal axis.

Pie chart: data presented in a circle, with each slice of the pie representing a proportion of the whole; good for proportions of a total, for example market share.

End of chapter exercises

1 In the year to 26 March 2016 Lucozade retail sales were £463.8 million out of total sales of £1,300 million in the UK market for sports and energy drinks.

   (a) Calculate Lucozade's sales as a percentage of the whole market for sports and energy drinks.

   (b) State whether a bar chart, a pie chart or a line graph would be the best way of showing this.

2 Outline one possible reason why Airbus was able to move from a 44 per cent share of sales in 2006 to 57 per cent in 2015.

3 Given that spending per person on nappies was £9.64 in the UK and £3.41 in China in 2015, how is it possible for China's market size to be seven times that of the UK?

4 Explain why financial data might not help a business make a decision about whether to spend £5 million on a sponsorship deal with a successful Olympic athlete.

Calculation exercises

1 Percentage and percentage change

   1.1 A business has total weekly sales of £15,000. One of its products sells £10,500 a week. Calculate the percentage that one product represents as a percentage of the total.

   1.2 A company's profits fall from £42,000 last year to £29,400 this year. Calculate the percentage change.

   1.3 Last year a company had 60 staff. This year it employs 81. Calculate the percentage change in its staffing.

2 Averages

   2.1 In the past three years a company's profits have been: £42,000, £12,000 and £66,000. What has been the average level of profit per year?

   2.2 In a warehouse employing 50 people, actual attendance at work has varied as follows:
- 4 weeks ago: 44
- 3 weeks ago: 46
- 2 weeks ago: 39
- 1 week ago: 34
- Calculate the average weekly attendance

3 Revenue, costs and profit

   3.1 A hamburger stall sells burgers for £5. Each one costs £2 to make and running the stall costs £400 a week. Its weekly sales are 500 burgers.
     a) Calculate the revenue.
     b) Calculate the total costs.
     c) Calculate the profit.

   3.2 A company sells 200 items a week at £12 each. Its variable costs per unit are £4 and weekly fixed costs are £1,200.
     a) Calculate the profit.
     b) Calculate the break-even point.
     c) Calculate the new profit if sales rise by 50%

4 Gross and net profit margins

   4.1 In the past six months a company has £90,000 of revenue, with £40,000 cost of sales. After taking away other operating expenses and interest, the business was left with £12,000 of net profit.
     a) Calculate the gross margin.
     b) Calculate the net margin.

   4.2 A business with revenue of £200,000 has a gross profit margin of 40 per cent. Calculate its cost of sales.

Questions 3 and 4 are based on the following table of figures.

	Last year	This year
Sales revenue	£140,000	£165,000
Cost of sales	£70,000	£80,000
Cost of fixed overheads	£50,000	£55,000
Net profit	£20,000	£30,000

3 Which **one** of the following is a correct statement based on the figures? (1)

(a) The net profit margin this year is 10 per cent.

(b) The net profit margin last year was 14.29 per cent.

(c) Managers should have to answer for the serious rise in 'cost of sales' this year.

(d) The net profit margin this year is an increase of 50 per cent.

4 Which **one** of the following is the correct figure for the gross profit margin last year? (1)

(a) £85,000

(b) 100 per cent

(c) £70,000

(d) 50 per cent

5 Which **one** of the following are all needed to calculate the average rate of return (ARR)? (1)

(a) The number of years, the sales revenue, the net profit and the total cash inflows.

(b) All net cash flows over the investment's life, the initial outlay and the number of years.

(c) The initial outlay, the gross profit, the fixed overhead costs and the number of years.

(d) The initial outlay, the break-even point and the number of sales made.

6 ABC Ltd and BFG Ltd are direct rivals in the market for publishing computer games magazines. The figures given in the table show the latest position for each business.

Which **two** of the following are conclusions that can be taken from these figures? (2)

	ABC Ltd (£ millions)	BFG Ltd (£ millions)
Sales this year	£12.5	£16.0
Market size this year	£50.0	£50.0
Sales last year	£12.0	£14.4
Market size last year	£48.0	£48.0

(a) ABC's sales have risen by 20 per cent this year.

(b) The market hasn't been growing, which makes it hard to succeed.

(c) BFG's sales are rising faster than ABC's.

(d) BFG's share of the market has risen from 30 per cent last year to 32 per cent this year.

(e) The total publishing market seems to be worth £98 million.

Now try this discussion question.

7 Discuss whether a growing business could ever have a net profit margin that is too high. (6)

Topic 2.5 Making human resource decisions

49 Organisational structures

Is there a 'pecking order' among your group of friends? Is there someone who makes the decisions for your group, or who tells the others what to do? You might have someone who is in charge, who makes the final decisions. You might have a newer member of the group who is always the person told to go and make the drinks! If there is, you probably have what is called an informal hierarchy within your group. Without this structure and defined roles, you might never get anything organised and get together for any nights out!

In businesses it is no different: they have structures too. For a small firm there may just be the owner/boss and a few staff working for him/her. In a large company, the structure will be more complex. It will help identify who does what job and who is in charge of whom.

An **organisation chart** is a diagram showing the structure of a business. Let's take the example of a small business employing five workers. The structure will be straightforward, as shown in Figure 49.1.

There may be a pecking order among your group of friends

The chart shows that there is one person at the top of the organisation, who makes all the decisions, and there are five workers below who follow the instructions given.

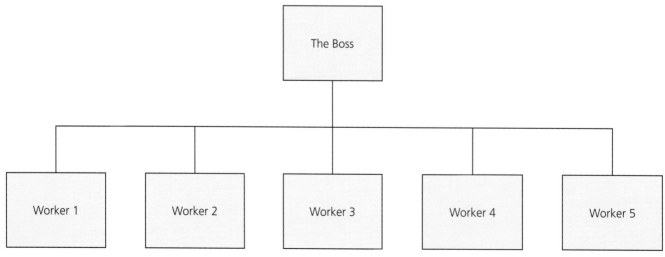

Figure 49.1 Simple organisational chart

Let's look consider the structure for a large organisation like the Metropolitan Police Service. The Met has a complex command structure that reflects its wide range of activities and 45,000 staff.

The purpose of an organisation chart is to show the shape of the hierarchy and who answers to whom within the organisation. In the small firm with five employees we looked at in Figure 49.1 on the previous page, there were two layers in the hierarchy and each worker was answerable to 'The Boss'.

> Every company has two organisational structures: the formal one is written on the charts; the other is the everyday relationship of the men and women in the organisation.
>
> *Harold Geneen, business boss and author*

Talking point

What problems may arise if decisions take a long time to reach the workers?

◉ Hierarchical and flat structures

Hierarchy refers to the levels of responsibility in an organisation. It is the formal structure of responsibility and authority, and is usually shown in vertical layers. The further up the hierarchy somebody is, the more important they tend to be and the more power they have. A **hierarchical organisation** is one in which individuals have relatively little room to make decisions for themselves. They have to do what the boss says.

Large organisations, like public limited companies or multinationals, have complex management structures. Such an organisation would be very hierarchical and would perhaps look like the Metropolitan Police chart shown in Figure 49.3.

The chart is like a pyramid, with the people with the most responsibility at the top. The layers form a pyramid structure as there are fewer people at the top than at the bottom. The management structure has several clear levels of responsibility. The people they are responsible for are on the next line down on the chart. This structure is called a tall structure because there are so many layers (Figure 49.2).

Advantages include the following:
◆ promotion opportunities should come up regularly; there's a clear career path
◆ it is easy to maintain standards across an organisation, since authority is strictly passed down the line
◆ it is easier to check everybody's work because there are managers and supervisors at each level.

Disadvantages include:
◆ people's position in the management structure shows their level of responsibility and authority; it is often seen as a status symbol with clear divisions between managers and the workers
◆ it is very hard for the person at the top to communicate with those at the bottom
◆ there can be too many layers of management, which slows down decision making.

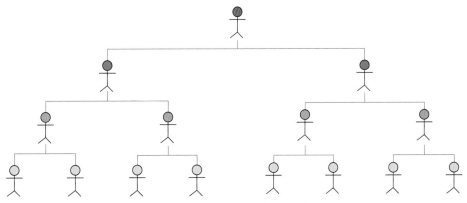

Figure 49.2 Sample organisational pyramid – tall structure

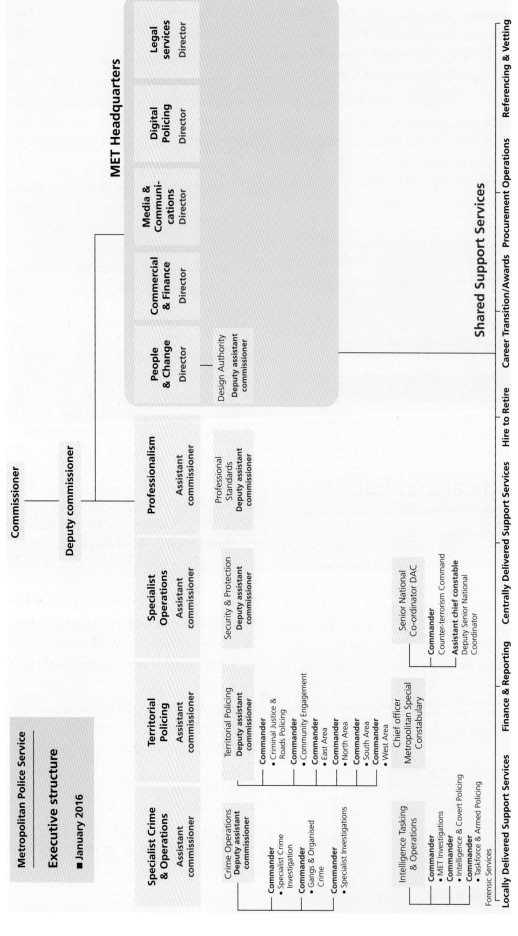

Figure 49.3 Metropolitan Police organisational chart

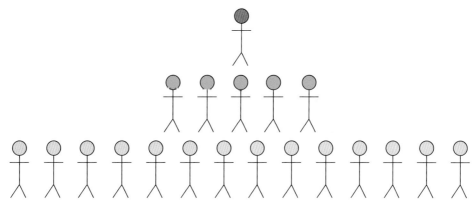

Figure 49.4 Sample organisational pyramid – flat structure

To overcome the problem of so many management layers, some businesses prefer a flatter structure, with fewer layers of management (Figure 49.4).

> In a hierarchy, every employee tends to rise to his level of incompetence.
>
> *Laurence J Peter, author of The Peter Principle*

In a **flat organisation** each manager is directly responsible for more people. People on the lower levels have more responsibility than those on the lower levels in a tall organisation. Managers therefore need to have confidence in their staff. They also need to be happy delegating work to junior staff.

Advantages include:
◆ fewer managers are needed, which saves money
◆ managers give more responsibility to the workers
◆ more responsibility leads to more job satisfaction for the workers
◆ there is faster, more efficient communication between staff and management
◆ it can lead to greater job satisfaction.

Disadvantages can be:
◆ each manager is responsible for more people
◆ managers have to rely on junior staff much more to work efficiently and safely
◆ managers may lose control of subordinates as there are so many people to supervise
◆ it can lead to overwork and stress
◆ there are fewer opportunities for promotion.

Centralised and decentralised organisations

Banks such as Lloyds TSB and supermarket chains such as Sainsbury's are examples of businesses that are normally **centralised**. Local branch managers have little decision-making power: they are strictly controlled by head office and they have to follow the instructions they are given so that each branch operate in the same way. Managers are expected to send regular reports to head office. Head office will also arrange orders of supplies for all the branches; the branches have no control over finance.

Advantages of centralisation are:
◆ decisions can be taken with an overview of the whole company
◆ central managers are able to make sure that policies and decisions are followed consistently across the whole organisation
◆ decision making and communication can be quick.

Drawbacks of centralisation are:
◆ it reduces delegation; this may reduce a company's ability to respond rapidly to changes in the market, since local managers have to refer to head office for decisions
◆ business opportunities may be lost because people are not allowed to make any decisions
◆ job satisfaction may be lost as staff are not able to feel involved.

A **decentralised organisation** is one that shares out the power of decision making to more people. Important decisions are made locally, perhaps by a store manager. Head office will make the policy and still have overall control, but important decisions about the running of the branch will be made by the branch manager. For example, a Tesco Express store manager near Trafford might stock Manchester United programmes on match days. A decentralised approach to management encourages involvement in decisions from those further down the hierarchy.

Talking point

What might be the effect of a manager losing control of junior staff?

> Each branch is now like its own business, responsible for its own profit and loss account. This has built the confidence of the people and the branches.
>
> *David Williams, technical director at AXA UK*

●Drawing the right conclusions

When companies hit problems, perhaps because of falling profits or because of a crisis, such as Samsung's exploding Galaxy Note 7 phones, senior managements regularly blame the organisational structure. They may decide that it is time for a change, perhaps to a more centralised system in which all significant decisions are made by the directors. This is why the subject of organisational structure comes up frequently in business exam papers.

Revision essentials

Centralised organisation: an organisation in which most decisions are made at head office.

Decentralised organisation: an organisation that allows staff to make decisions at a local level.

Flat structure: an organisation with few layers of hierarchy – presumably because each manager is responsible for many staff.

Hierarchical structure: an organisation with many layers of management, therefore creating a tall organisational pyramid.

Organisation chart: a diagram that shows the internal structure of an organisation.

End of chapter exercises

1 Outline the differences between a hierarchical and a flat organisational structure.

2 Identify the benefits to a business such as Topshop of having local managers with the power to make decisions about their local branch.

3 Explain the implications to a large firm of having too many layers in its hierarchy.

4 (a) Draw an organisation chart to show the structure of your school.

(b) Give reasons to explain why the structure is designed as it is.

(c) Evaluate the effectiveness of the school's structure.

Practice questions

In 2014, Simon Kossoff, chief executive of the Carluccio's Italian restaurant chain, agreed to take part in the Channel 4 TV series *Undercover Boss*. He was about to recommend a £50 million expansion of the chain and thought it would be useful to check on what was happening on the shop floor first. The series gives each boss a cover story and a physical disguise, and then places him or her in a variety of low-level jobs within the business. This cuts through the layers of management that separate the boss from the day-to-day experience of staff and customers.

David Kossoff found problems in the business when he went on Undercover Boss

Kossoff found problems with:

◆ Quality: the Peterborough site had not replaced its head chef and general manager since they left six months before. Unsurprisingly, problems were arising: messy kitchen (not something customers would appreciate on screen), equipment malfunctions (a faulty food lift, resulting in cold food), and so on.

◆ Efficiency: in the Bicester outlet, inadequate systems meant that staff were queuing to place orders, customers were waiting for their food, stress was rising and staff were dissatisfied.

◆ Business decision-making: the opening of a site in Trinity Leeds shopping centre proved too close to their first site in the city, causing a significant decline in custom. What had been done to boost marketing and recover sales?

◆ Management feedback: Kossoff often found that heroic efforts being made by junior staff received little or no recognition or thanks from middle managers. This was a huge disappointment.

As usual with these programmes, Kossoff ended up handing out rewards, praise and promotions to several of the individuals he had come across. But there was less evidence of wider concern about that huge vertical gap between the top and bottom of the Carluccio's hierarchy. One week 'going undercover' was not going to solve that problem.

Total: 20 marks

1 Outline one problem that might arise from not replacing the head chef in Peterborough. (2)

2 Outline how the use of quantitative data might have helped Carluccio's avoid its mistake with the Trinity Leeds store opening. (2)

3 Define the term 'organisational structure'. (1)

4 Analyse how Mr Kossoff might try to solve the problem of the 'huge vertical gap' between the top and bottom at Carluccio's. (6)

5 Mr Kossoff is still determined to expand Carluccio's, and sees two ways of doing it:

◆ Option 1: Expand in the UK, from 80 sites today to perhaps 120 in future.

◆ Option 2: Expand into Europe, especially France and Germany.

Justify which **one** of these two options Mr Kossoff should choose. (9)

50 The importance of effective communication

Imagine it is a Saturday afternoon and a group of you have gone into town shopping. You go into Frockshop and decide to try on some clothes. A couple of you try on the same style of jeans. Whichever size is tried, they come up a bit small. You have to buy a 30″ or even a 32″, even though your waist is 28″. Who wants to do that? As you leave the fitting room you mention it to the fitting room assistant.

Other customers do the same but nothing is done. Eventually the store decides to drop that range of jeans due to poor sales figures. Existing stock has to sold at 70 per cent off, and you start to shop at Lara where the jeans fit properly!

At Frockshop, the fitting room assistants were not involved in checking the quality or monitoring sales of clothes. Their job was to ensure the fitting room was run and managed well. The story would have ended differently if the store manager at Frockshop had taken the time to meet and talk with the fitting room assistants. The manager would have discovered that the batch of jeans was wrongly sized quite quickly.

◆ There are lots of different ways in which people can communicate. Even so, some managers only want to 'tell' and not 'ask'. Many employees in a business know and have an interest only in what their job is within their department. A really successful business has two-way **communication** with employees on a regular basis.

The purpose of communication

Why is communication so important to the success of a business? Managers need to communicate in a business in order to do the following:

◆ Provide and collect information about the business: the store manager in Frockshop did not communicate properly with the shop floor workers and, therefore, a potentially profitable product line was dropped due to poor communication. Staff were not motivated to say anything. Managers will have no idea how the business is performing or what staff are doing without communicating.

◆ Give instructions: it is important that staff understand what jobs they have to do. Once a manager has planned how the business' aims and objectives will be achieved, the next job is to put the plans into action. All managers in all organisations need to give workers instructions as to what task they are required to do, who is to do the task and when it should be done by.

◆ Ensure all workers are working towards the same goal: it is very important that all workers have knowledge of what the company is aiming towards. A business might have a goal of achieving more profit. It might intend to achieve this by launching a new product. But if the research and development department and the marketing department do not know about this planned course of action, the aim will probably not be achieved.

Without managers having this knowledge, the business cannot run smoothly.

What is effective communication?

It is quite easy to communicate simple instructions – as long as people are listening. To be effective, communication depends on the motivation of the receiver. Many a student teacher has found that saying things is not enough – not even shouting them! It only works if everyone listens. So the best way to ensure good, two-way communication is to have well-motivated staff (see Chapter 55).

The best way to find out whether the communication has been effective is to get feedback. This may mean asking each person individually, or requiring a text/email response from everyone.

To be effective, communications need to be:
◆ clear and easily understood
◆ accurate
◆ complete
◆ appropriate
◆ via the right medium
◆ with a chance for feedback.

> The greatest problem in communication is the illusion that it has been accomplished.
>
> *George Bernard Shaw, Nobel prize-winning playwright*

The process of effective communication

A business needs to make sure that it has effective communication channels to allow the flow of information around it. The communication process involves a sender, for example a 14-year-old boy; a message, 'Mum, can you come and pick me up?'; an appropriate medium, a text message; a receiver, Mum; and, most importantly, an opportunity for feedback, 'What time and where do you want me to pick you up from?'

It is not safe for anyone to assume that just because a message has been sent, that it has been received and understood. Some big mistakes have been made as a result of poor communication. The infamous Charge of the Light Brigade during the Crimean War happened because the instructions of an army commander were misunderstood by his commanding officer. It resulted in the death of over 100 men.

The impact of insufficient communication

Sometimes there may be too little communication in business. Some bosses tend to shut themselves away, communicating with only a small group of trusted managers and assistants directly. They end up cut off from the day-to-day reality of staff experience.
◆ There are some key consequences of **insufficient communication**:
◆ Misunderstandings and rumours: if staff are hearing little directly from the boss, the vacuum

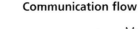

Figure 50.1 Communication model

may be filled with rumours. Whispers about possible redundancies can easily turn into 'certainties' in the minds of some. This could undermine staff morale.

◆ Inefficiency: sometimes workers in a particular area of a business may have an idea that could improve efficiency – they may be doing a job every day and have a suggestion as to how the job could be done better. If there is no opportunity to communicate their ideas, this could cost the business money.

◆ Low levels of motivation: if staff feel that their ideas are not listened to, they might feel that they are unimportant and have low self-esteem, which could lead to decreasing productivity levels. If workers are constantly getting things wrong because instructions are not clear and they have no opportunity to clarify their understanding, this will lead to low motivation and perhaps high levels of staff absences.

◆ Profits lost: if communication within the organisation is insufficient, this is ultimately going to affect levels of customer service or sales – think of the Frockshop example, where the customers turned to Lara. This will affect profits.

⬤The impact of excessive communication

Advances in technology today allow the same message to be sent to large numbers of people at the same time, for example using email. This could keep all the employees in a business informed of developments in the organisation. Unfortunately, there is often so much email every day that staff can become overwhelmed, or at least bored by it all. All the emails, texts, phone calls and voice mails can lead to information overload.

It is estimated that more than half of all managers struggle to deal effectively with the information they have to process. It can also mean that some people in business are working 24/7, constantly bombarded with information. To counteract this, some businesses in France ban emails after 5.30 p.m. – good for them.

Emails stop at 5.30 pm. in some French companies

◆ Research shows that middle managers in businesses receive about 10,000 emails a year. If an overloaded manager misses a key message from a customer ('We ordered 4,000 blue; please change to 2,000 red and 2,000 blue') the impact is obvious. The customer is disappointed and may, perfectly reasonably, refuse to pay. The business, having delivered 4,000 blue, may have to go and pick up 2,000 blue and replace them with red. Expensive! In this case **excessive communication** hits the efficiency of the business, and would have a negative effect on the confidence and motivation of the under-fire manager.

> In industry there's too much communication, and of course it's passive ... but if people are doing idiot jobs they really don't give a damn.
> *Professor Fred Herzberg, motivation guru*

⬤Barriers to effective communication

Business communication may be ineffective for a variety of reasons:

◆ the person sending the communication might not explain themselves properly

◆ the receiver of the information may not understand the message due to the technical language or 'jargon' used

◆ the receiver may not hear or receive the message due to a technical problem

◆ the message may get distorted in its transmission – especially if the message has to pass through many management layers in order to reach its target.

◆ All these **barriers** would be overcome if there was an opportunity for feedback to clarify the message.

contractors. So, good communication is a critical part of most successful people's skill set.

◉ Drawing the right conclusions

Research among managers shows that 'communicating' is the task that occupies more of their working day than any other. If they're not communicating with fellow staff, they may be communicating with customers or suppliers or

Revision essentials

Communication: the passing of information from one person or organisation to another.

Barrier to communication: something that prevents the flow of communication.

Insufficient communication: too little communication, which might leave some staff under-informed and demotivated.

Excessive communication: too much communication causing overload for staff – a particular problem with email.

End of chapter exercises

1 Use the chapter to identify three reasons why good communication is essential to any organisation.

2 Give two reasons why a business might experience barriers to effective communication.

3 Outline why it might be useful for a manager to arrange a regular meeting with staff.

4 Explain two problems that could arise as a result of poor communication between the sales department and the production department.

5 Each year the *Financial Times* carries out a survey of staff attitudes to find Europe's 'Best Workplaces'. A past winner was Microsoft. An article on why Microsoft did so well identified its communications as an exceptional strength. Below are some quotes about communications at Microsoft:

(a) 'At Microsoft employees spoke about the open communication with their leaders.'

(b) 'They (managers) share the goals and results without withholding any information.'

(c) 'Ask management any reasonable question and get a straight answer.'

(d) 'Microsoft is very transparent about its pay model and bonus plans.'

(e) 'The entire company holds a Happy Hour on the second Friday of the month ... a chance to eat and drink together.'

(f) 'Higher management is open for a talk when you need advice or feedback.'

Decide which two of these six statements are the most important ones for successful communications in a workplace. Explain why you have chosen them.

Practice questions

'The key thing I learned was the importance of good communication within any company. Without good communication on a day-to-day basis it can be very difficult to provide a good service.' This was the conclusion reached by Pickfords' director Grant Whitaker after spending a week on the removal vans in Birmingham. He was trying to find out how he could make the business better. Pickfords is a nationwide moving and storage company.

All removals depend on the salespeople, who visit the customers first to price the job and see how long it will take before letting the removal team know what they think. Often the drivers arrive late to jobs and find irate customers waiting for them. There seems to be a communications barrier between staff and customers. The reason for lateness is usually due to difficulties getting furniture up and down stairs and out of the houses.

One of the drivers showed Grant a set of aluminium ladders he had found that would make lifting the furniture much easier and quicker, but head office would not listen to his idea. The drivers often feel they are kept in the dark about the business. Grant took his findings back to the board of directors for discussion.

Total: 18 marks

1 Define the term 'communication barrier'.   (1)

2 Outline one piece of evidence that suggests poor communications at Pickfords.   (2)

3 Analyse the benefits to the business of solving these problems.   (6)

4 Pickfords is considering how to improve communications between management and the workforce. It sees two options:

   ◆ Option 1: Weekly video broadcasts given by Grant Whitaker, which every staff member must watch.

   ◆ Option 2: Weekly local meetings between staff and area managers, plus monthly meeting between area managers and head office.

Justify which **one** of these two options the company should choose.   (9)

51 Different ways of working

According to UK government figures, more than 2 million people have a job with no guaranteed minimum hours. In effect they have a zero-hours contract. At the end of this week they may be told they have no work next week – and therefore no pay. Awful if you're living at home with your parents; terrifying if you *are* a parent, needing to feed the kids.

There are three broad categories of employment:

◆ full time: usually between 35 and 40 hours a week, which entitles the employee to 28 days' paid holiday leave

◆ part time: for example three days a week, typically the same three days each week; this system gives predictable pay and holidays

◆ **flexible hours**: hours/days can vary within an agreed annual total, which helps the employer without affecting the employee's overall earnings; alternatively, the flexibility can be within a zero-hours framework, giving the employee no security at all.

In addition to employment there is **self-employment**, which includes entrepreneurs starting a business they hope will one day become a giant and people who are working for themselves. Those working for themselves would be the vast majority, such as cab, minicab and Uber drivers, who work from home. There are also many people pressed to be self-employed by companies that don't want responsibilities for sick or holiday pay. Millions of cleaners, care workers and others exist on low pay within the apparently glamorous self-employed sector.

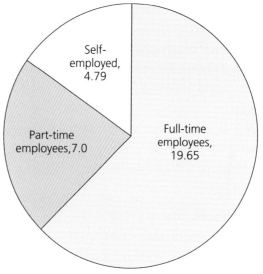

Figure 51.1 Ways of working, presented in millions (Source: ONS, April to June 2016)

● Permanent, temporary and freelance contracts

Permanent staff are employed on indefinite contracts, meaning that they are open-ended. By implication, you have a job until you retire. Such contracts can be full time or part time. The benefits of such a contract are that:

◆ You have stable earnings and a high degree of job security (though, of course, the company has the right to make you redundant if revenue falls or your skills are no longer needed).

◆ You will have regular contributions towards your pension and probably sick pay – providing still more financial security.

◆ Because you're permanent, you're worth investing in from the employer's point of view; so you'll be sent on training courses to improve your job and personal skills.

Temporary contracts offer a job for a set period of time, such as three months or a year. For an increasing number of new teachers, fresh from training, the best they can expect is a one-year contract. In the past they'd have been given a permanent job. Although most would prefer a permanent job, a temporary contract has some benefits:

◆ A young worker may be as keen for travel as for a career, so a one-year contract followed by a trip round the world might be perfect (but hard to finance).

◆ An employee with enough skills should always be demand; it might be interesting to work in several places for a short time before looking for a permanent job.

Freelance contracts offer no guarantees beyond a single task. Whereas a temporary contract might give you 35 hours a week for three months, freelance means one job today worth £80 but perhaps no more until next week, making it very insecure. It is the world of TV actors, many journalists and photographers, and also many lower-paid workers such as bricklayers' assistants.

> TV is a fickle business. I'm only good for the length of my contract.
>
> *Tom Brokaw, legendary US TV news anchor*

◉ The impact of technology on how we work

With fast broadband, smartphones, wi-fi and Facetime, it is increasingly easy to work with others while not being next to them physically. This is helpful for releasing key staff from the daily grind of commuting. Two days a week in the office and three working from home is realistic. The staff member has more flexibility for picking kids up from school, but can still keep on task. Many professionals are happy working through the night to get a task completed.

With this system they can have a day off when the sun's shining.

Sadly, it is not all like that. When conveyor-belt factory work took off in the early twentieth century, staff were monitored by supervisors. A trip to the toilet needed permission. Fierce protests by trade unions eventually led to workers having more control over their working lives. Now technology has turned the clock back for many. The modern equivalent of an old factory is a warehouse sending out thousands of Amazon or ASOS items to customers, but today technology is used to monitor the speed and accuracy of every aspect of the modern worker – sometimes in ten-minute segments. Trips to the toilet are recorded. Technology can be the snooper as easily as it can be the helper.

The impact of technology on efficiency

When you tap that Domino's app, it is not a drone that brings the pizza, it is a bloke on a wobbly moped with a red L-plate on the back. All the technology that goes into the app makes little difference to the efficiency of delivering your margherita. In this case, the technology has shifted business from Pizza Hut to Domino's, but not made much difference to efficiency.

In other situations technology may be very important. The London-based bicycle maker Brompton increased its output per worker from 140 bikes a year

Bicycle maker Brompton uses automation and robotics alongside skilled staff

to 200 between 2011 and 2016 – a key factor was buying in automation and robotics to work alongside the skilled staff.

What the above cases prove is that technology doesn't automatically improve efficiency; every case must be looked at on its own merits.

The impact of technology on remote working

Information technology makes it possible to work at home or abroad instead of in the office. This possibility needs to be managed with care. In 2015, the boss of IT giant Yahoo insisted that staff should stop all **remote working** and come back to the office. She was worried that the business would lose out if staff lacked the opportunity for natter and banter from which – occasionally – good ideas emerge.

> In teamwork, silence isn't golden, it's deadly.
>
> *Mark Sanborn, US business author*

Talking point

Would you like a job where you work entirely from home?

◉ Drawing the right conclusions

'Flexible' is a very positive word in many ways, implying a degree of freedom, especially from a humdrum 9–5 working life. And flexibility can be wonderful – for the black cab driver who can choose to go for a midweek seaside break without telling anyone, let alone asking permission. But flexibility can also be quite crushing for someone who has to jump to a boss's 'flexible' demands. One week with no work and no income; another week with two day shifts followed by four night shifts – and perhaps young children who need transport, food and the occasional hug. Suddenly flexibility becomes a form of control for the boss – and may leave the employee feeling out of control of their life. There's a clear trend towards different ways of working – but they won't work for everyone.

Revision essentials

Flexible hours: a contract between a company and an employee that doesn't specify how many hours of work will be provided.

Freelance contract: an agreement over one job between a company and self-employed worker.

Permanent contract: an agreement between a company and an employee that work and income will be provided constantly into the long-term future.

Remote working: working away from the office, typically from home.

Temporary contract: an agreement between a company and an employee that work and income will be provided for a specific time period, say six months.

End of chapter exercises

1 Identify two types of people who might welcome a job based on flexible rather than full-time hours.

2 Explain the downsides of a zero-hours contract from the employee's point of view.

3 Briefly explain whether 'remote working' would work well or badly for:

(a) the goalkeeper of a football team

(b) a specialist in creating and drawing the 'people' in computer games

(c) a primary school teacher.

4 Look at Table 51.1, then answer the questions below.

    (a) Outline two possible reasons why the trend towards self-employment was higher among ethnic minorities than the white majority.

    (b) Explain the possible effect on the Chinese community of the sharp rise in self-employment.

Table 51.1 Self-employment in the UK, broken down by ethnicity

	White	Ethnic minorities	Pakistani	Chinese	Afro-Caribbean
April–June 2013	3,761,000	425,000	86,000	14,000	66,000
April–June 2016	4,238,000	545,000	100,000	24,000	101,000
% increase	+12.7%	+28.2%	+16.2%	+71.4%	+53.0%

Deliveroo riders protest against changes to pay structure

Delivery riders are rebelling against plans to pay workers £3.75 per delivery instead of an hourly rate of £7 plus £1 per delivery. Outside the Deliveroo headquarters more than 100 self-employed workers gathered calling for the company to keep the hourly rate. Riders said they often earned less than the 'national living wage' (currently £7.20 an hour) once their expenses were taken into account.

Fahran, who delivers for the firm on his motorcycle, said removing the hourly rate would cause him to struggle. 'My phone contract is the same, insurance is the same – everything else is fixed,' he said. 'I have two children and I need to pay for them. They are forcing people to take benefits.'

Amir Ali started striking on Thursday. He said it had been a good place to work under the old pay terms.

Deliveroo's self-employed workers gather outside the company's headquarters

'£7 an hour was okay and if you worked hard, it was good. But now they are cutting it below the basic wage,' he said. 'We work in snow, we work in rain. They don't give you a place to sit down.'

One rider who covers central London said that he thought the company was trying to reduce its costs to boost profits. 'We risk our lives every day for the job. Deliveroo is a great start-up but without us it is nothing.' He said he believed he would earn less under the new rules. 'Sometimes you might be hanging round for an hour for a delivery,' he said. 'August is a really quiet month – in winter time, when people get lazy, you do better. It varies. We need something a bit more consistent, something more reliable. We have kids, we have rent, we can't deal with uncertainty.'

Deliveroo, which raised £212 million from venture capital investors this month, said it would roll out the pay terms from next week and claimed that couriers had responded positively in early trials.

Source: *The Guardian*, 11 August 2016

Within a week of this article being written, Deliveroo backed down on this new pay deal in the face of bad publicity about the way the company was pushing risk down to the riders.

Total: 15 marks

1 Define the term 'venture capital'. (1)
2 Outline one reason why the delivery riders disliked the new Deliveroo deal. (2)
3 Outline **one** benefit to the business of using self-employed riders instead of employing them permanently. (2)
4 State which month is the 'really quiet' one, according to delivery riders. (1)
5 Deliveroo is considering how to avoid such bad publicity in future. It sees two options:
   ◆ Option 1: Arrange weekly meetings with an elected representative of the delivery riders.
   ◆ Option 2: Tell the riders that they must sign zero-hours contracts instead of being self-employed from now on.

Justify which **one** of these two options the company should choose. (9)

52 Effective recruitment

Salvatore Falcone has run a bakery in Wimbledon for nearly 50 years. In that time he has built Panetteria Italiana into a terrific business. People drive 20 miles to buy armfuls of bread for their freezer. His Saturday morning queue is legendary. Yet in all these years he has rarely been able to find and keep staff. His business works because his wife and three children work there. When he tries to recruit someone, he usually finds the person too slow or too unconcerned to be worth having. He says, 'I take them on, I spend weeks training them up, then they decide to go elsewhere.'

For a small firm, recruiting staff is a worrying process. There is a huge amount that could go wrong. And a small business lacks the expertise to avoid some of the pitfalls. Is the job interview process unbiased? And does the person being interviewed really want the job, or are they just planning to use it as a stepping stone to something better?

For a large business, recruitment is an inevitable part of every week. Tesco employs 476,000 people worldwide and has to recruit around 1,000 staff every week. The recruitment method varies depending on the seniority of the job role. The next section considers job roles and responsibilities.

> The key for us, number one, has always been hiring very smart people.
>
> *Bill Gates, founder of Microsoft*

⬤ Key job roles and responsibilities

The following are key jobs that you might find in a big company.

Directors

Directors are members of 'the board', that is, the board of directors. They handle the most senior appointments, set out the main aims and objectives of the business, and discuss the key decisions faced by the business. Some board directors are executives working within the business, such as the marketing director. Others are outsiders, recruited to the board for their independent expertise; for example, a medium-sized clothes retailer might recruit a retired, former-director of Primark.

An interview enables the employer to judge the applicant's personality and attitude

Senior managers

A manager is a person responsible for organising others to carry out tasks. A senior manager will be involved in deciding what needs to be done, then finding the right middle manager to get the job done.

Senior managers need to communicate well with each other. For example, the head of marketing might discuss quality issues with the head of operations and the head of human resources.

Supervisors/team leaders

This junior management role is largely to do with ensuring that shop-floor staff do exactly what is asked of them. Do the checkout staff remember to greet each customer? Are there bare shelves in the store and, if so, why? Good team leaders make shop-floor staff want to meet the high standards asked of them.

Operational and support staff

Another important business issue is whether a job role is operational or support. An operational executive has direct responsibility for achieving a specific target, for example that sales will be up by at least four per cent on last year. The executive may get a bonus if the target is reached, but worry about their career prospects if it isn't. Support staff have no such pressures. They are employed to help the operational staff but don't have direct responsibility for achieving targets. The marketing director is held responsible for sales; the market research manager isn't.

> Hiring and training are costly – but it's infinitely more costly to have a barely average man on the company payroll for 30 years.
>
> *Gordon Wheeling, personnel manager*

◉ How businesses recruit people

There are nearly 5 million businesses in Britain, but fewer than 1.5 million have any employees. The vast majority are true sole traders: a business run by one person, perhaps helped by family members.

The star businesses are those that break away from being purely family firms. They need the courage to hire staff, despite the problems that may result. Every staff member causes a business to pay extra taxes, give four weeks' holiday pay and meet laws that cover health and safety, job security and conditions of work.

The breakthrough comes when employers gain the commitment and confidence to hire people and start treating them like adults. This requires skills that many entrepreneurs lack. They are often good at bossing people about, but poor at encouraging people to think for themselves.

Often small firms start by recruiting friends or former workmates. This gets round any concerns about whether the new recruit will prove unfriendly or work-shy. As a business grows, however, the boss will soon run out of friends to be brought in. Then the real process of judging people that you do not know begins. The keys to this process are:

◆ an **application form**, written well enough to provide useful, checkable information about the applicant, but not so detailed as to put potential applicants off

◆ a **CV (curriculum vitae)**, which sets out the person's qualifications, experience and any other relevant facts

◆ **references**, usually in the form of a letter from a named teacher or former boss, who will write about the applicant's qualities, strengths and weaknesses.

For bigger businesses, the recruitment process tends to start with two documents: the job description and the person specification.

> Hire character. Train skill.
>
> *Peter Schutz, former head of Porsche*

Job description and person specification

The recruitment process may be triggered by an existing employee finding a better-paid job elsewhere. Alternatively, additional workers may need to be recruited in order to support a firm's expansion strategies. Once the firm has established its requirements, the next step is to draw up a job description and a person specification.

A **job description** relates directly to the position itself, rather than the person required to fill it. Typically, a job description would contain the following information:

◆ the job title

◆ the main duties and tasks involved

◆ the person to whom the job holder reports and any employees for whom the job holder is responsible.

A **person specification** identifies the abilities, qualifications and qualities required of the job holder in order to carry out the job successfully. The main features of a person specification include:

◆ any educational or professional qualifications required

◆ necessary skills or experience

◆ suitable personality or character, for example the ability to work under pressure or as part of a team.

Internal and external recruitment

A business may choose to fill a vacancy internally, that is, from the existing workforce. This could be done either by redeploying a worker from elsewhere in the business or promoting someone. Although **internal recruitment** can have a number of benefits, it also has a number of disadvantages. It is of little use when a business needs to expand its workforce in order to respond to an increase in demand.

External recruitment means hiring someone from outside the business. This is likely to be more expensive than internal recruitment, as it will require one of the following approaches:

◆ media advertising: buying job ads in newspapers or specialist magazines, on the radio, TV, or by using dedicated employment websites such as www. monster.co.uk

◆ job centres: government-run organisations that tend to focus on vacancies for skilled and semi-skilled manual and administrative jobs

◆ commercial recruitment agencies, such as Alfred Marks or Reed, which recruit staff of all types in return for a (substantial) fee

◆ websites: in addition, many businesses have careers pages on their own websites, which are used to advertise vacancies.

Table 52.1 Advantages and disadvantages of internal recruitment

Advantages	Disadvantages
It is likely to be quicker and cheaper than external recruitment	Existing workers may not have the skills required, especially if the business wants to develop new products or markets
Greater variety of promotion opportunities may motivate employees	Relying on existing employees may lead to a stagnation of ideas and approaches within the business
The firm will already be aware of the employee's skills and attitude to work	Recruiting internally will create a vacancy elsewhere

Table 52.2 Advantages and disadvantages of external recruitment

Advantages	Disadvantages
It should result in a wider range of candidates than internal recruitment	It can be an expensive and time-consuming process, using up valuable resources
Candidates may already have the skills required to carry out the job in question, avoiding the need for (and cost of) training	It can have a demotivating effect on members of the existing workforce, who may have missed out on promotion

Drawing the right conclusions

Firms that aim to grow have no choice but to recruit staff, and it usually proves to be much harder than anyone expects. For small businesses, poor recruitment becomes a serious drag on the ability to develop and grow. In bigger businesses recruitment becomes a constant process, which in itself can help build a degree of expertise.

Perhaps the best approach is to always see internal recruitment as the priority. That gives a consistent message to staff that you trust them and want to give them every opportunity to succeed. In early 2016, Mark Price left Waitrose after a career that started as a graduate trainee for the business in 1982. He worked his way up from the bottom to the top of the organisation through a series of internal promotions. What a wonderful way to encourage every Waitrose employee.

Revision essentials

Application form: the series of questions a job-seeker must fill in when trying to get an employer interested in interviewing them.

CV (curriculum vitae): sets out the person's qualifications, experience and any other relevant facts (it literally means the 'story of life').

External recruitment: appointing from outside the existing staff.

Internal recruitment: appointing from within the existing staff.

Job description: a short account of the main features of the job.

Person specification: a description of the type of person who would best fit the job: their character, their experience and skills.

References: people such as teachers or previous bosses who are willing to answer questions about the qualities of a job applicant.

End of chapter exercises

1 Outline three reasons why a small business may need to take on additional staff.

2 Suggest two reasons why the owner of a small business might be reluctant to employ more staff.

3 Examine two advantages of recruiting part-time staff to a small, expanding business.

4 Suggest one suitable method of dealing with the following staff shortages:

(a) providing cover for a receptionist on two weeks' holiday

(b) providing extra sales assistance at a delicatessen on Saturdays

(c) providing additional waiters and kitchen staff at a restaurant over the busy Christmas period.

Practice questions

Graduate Leadership Development Programme (I.T.):

To be considered for this programme you will demonstrate a high level of energy in pursuing work objectives and a total commitment to achieving successful outcomes, as shown by your academic results and extra-curricular activities. You will have long-term ambitions with first class communication, planning and organisational skills.

We are looking to take on graduates who will develop into the company's leaders of the future. On joining Raytheon, you will undertake a structured two-year leadership development programme. You will be given a real job from day one and will be expected to start adding value immediately.

By joining Raytheon you will have the opportunity to work within a range of different areas of the IT function. Enthusiasm for a career in an innovative organisation is essential, as is the ambition to succeed.

Candidate requirements – Essential:

- You will have achieved (or be expected to achieve) at least a 2:1 in any IT, Business/ Project Management, Engineering, Maths, Physics or Humanities related degree discipline.
- A-levels (or equivalent) with a minimum of 300 UCAS points.
- Be a logical thinker with excellent problem solving ability.
- Have strong communication and presentation skills.
- Be methodical, hardworking, enthusiastic and able to work well under pressure.
- Self-motivated, energy and drive.
- Team player

Raytheon career development:

Raytheon has a wealth of resources available to help you develop your career from the moment you join. Activities range from online learning modules, to external training and support for taking professional qualifications relevant to your role.

About Raytheon:

Raytheon UK is a subsidiary of Raytheon Company. Raytheon Company, with 2015 sales of $23 billion and 61,000 employees, is a technology and innovation leader specialising in defence, civil government and cybersecurity solutions.

Standard benefits:

- £1,500 joining bonus
- 25 days holiday plus statutory holidays
- Contributory pension scheme, life assurance, flexible benefits and enhanced sick pay scheme

Diversity:

Diversity is a core business imperative at Raytheon. We are an equal opportunity employer that promotes inclusiveness and always employs the best professionals for the job. Having a diverse workforce allows Raytheon to draw upon a range of different ideas and experiences, which supports growing our business and creates an environment where everyone has an equal opportunity for success.

Source: Adapted from www.milkround.com

Total: 15 marks

1 Analyse whether a job description and a person specification would be enough to ensure that Raytheon recruits the right person for this job. (6)

2 The management at Raytheon is considering who best to recruit for this job:

- Option 1: A brilliant university student, predicted to get a 1st class degree, who started up and is now captain of the Oxford Football Club's women's team.
- Option 2: A graduate with a 2:1 degree who has spent the last year volunteering in Africa. She has been running a team designing and building a road bridge over a small river in Namibia.

Justify which **one** of these two options Raytheon should choose. (9)

53 Effective training and development

For many years productivity in the UK has been 25–30 per cent lower than in Germany. In other words, we take 25–30 per cent longer to complete a task than people working in Germany: building a wall, perhaps, or fitting doors to new cars. The reason for this is no mystery: German workers have higher skills because of better training. Most workers have been through an apprenticeship that lasts two to three years and gives solid grounding in details like how to mix cement perfectly for successful bricklaying. German workers not only start with better skills, their companies also invest more in ongoing training for staff. It seems time for UK firms to copy this approach.

◉ Different ways of training and developing employees

Here are some of the ways that employers can train and develop their employees.

Formal and informal training

Most trainee teachers go through a full programme of university-based sessions and formally measured teaching practice spells at schools. Most think this **formal training** programme is good, but often mention that the best bit of advice they received was in the staff room or pub from a random fellow-teacher. This would be classed as **informal training**, as would be the informal coaching that comes from a caring supervisor who just chips in occasional advice.

> Starbucks is not an advertiser; people think we are a great marketing company, but in fact we spend very little money on marketing and more money on training our people than advertising.
>
> *Howard Schulz, CEO of Starbucks*

Table 53.1 The benefits and costs to companies of providing training

Benefits of training	Costs of training
Increases the level and range of skills available to the business, leading to improvements in efficiency and quality	It can be expensive, both in hours spent providing the training and the cost of sending staff to outside courses
Increases the range of skills within a workforce, allowing it to respond quickly to changes in technology or demand	Production may be disrupted while training is taking place, leading to lost output
Can lead to a more motivated workforce by creating opportunities for development and promotion	Newly trained workers may be persuaded to leave and take up new jobs elsewhere (known as poaching), meaning the benefits of training are enjoyed by other businesses

Self-learning

There is no better way to learn than to push yourself. The most important part of **self-learning** is to learn from your mistakes. If you're not making mistakes, you're not trying hard enough; if you are making them, the key thing is to ask:

◆ What went wrong?

◆ Why did it go wrong?

◆ What could I have done differently?

◆ How should I avoid making that same mistake again?

> Insanity is doing the same thing over and over again but expecting a different result.
>
> *Usually attributed to Albert Einstein, all-round genius*

Ongoing training for all employees

When young people apply for a job they may be promised plenty of training in the early months, but what about the long-term future? According to recent research the average UK worker has only £700 a year spent on training them, and as many as a third of staff receive no **ongoing training** at all. The UK's output per person is as much as 30 per cent lower than America or Germany; this lack of efficiency could reasonably be blamed on insufficient training. In industries where technological progress is high especially, training seems essential.

Training is important to workers

Because it was worried about inadequate training from private companies, the government launched a new scheme. From 2016, every business with a pay bill of £3 million or more must pay one per cent of their pay bill to the government. Companies can apply to get the money back if they invest in an apprenticeship scheme. In effect that makes it free for companies to spend on apprenticeships, which may help those companies to improve their efficiency.

> Education is that whole system of human training within and without the school house walls, which moulds and develops men.
>
> *W.E.B. Du Bois, nineteenth-century civil rights activist*

Training is a way to keep people on top of a job

Use of target-setting and performance reviews

An ideal world might see staff organising their own careers. They might set themselves targets, arrange the training they need to help reach the target, then discuss personal progress in a **performance review** held by the operational manager. Many is the teacher who has asked a student to 'take control' of their own education. The same line is relevant at work, where managers want staff to set targets and find a way to achieve them.

While **target setting** is an important way to agree challenging goals for the coming year, performance reviews are an opportunity to discuss achievements. Part of the process is also to consider what future training needs the individual may have.

Human resource departments love setting up targets and performance reviews. They are a sign that something is happening to encourage staff development. However, most research shows that the most important thing is day-to-day contact between supervisor and employee. In other words, regular informal chats count for much more than six-monthly performance reviews. Supervisors who take the time to talk to their staff regularly could be termed **mentors**.

> The delicate balance of mentoring someone is not creating them in your own image, but giving them the opportunity to create themselves.
>
> *Steven Spielberg, Hollywood film director*

⬤ Why businesses train and develop employees

If a job was so simple that it required no training, it probably could – and would – be done by a robot. Yet there is much more to training than telling people how to do a job. Well-run organisations keep investing in staff training because there is no limit to the amount to be learned. Take, for example, the reasons why experienced teachers might need training:

◆ to know about a new GCSE course, or a change to an existing one
◆ to be kept up to date about the latest thinking in how the exams are to be set and marked
◆ to learn about new technology available for teaching, perhaps via an app.

In other words, things change, and training is a way to keep people on top of their job. This should ensure high-quality staff performance and also helps staff

feel properly looked after by the business, which in turn helps with motivation and staff **retention**.

The link between training and motivation is partly psychological ('they're spending money sending me on a course, so they like me') and partly practical. Motivation expert Professor Herzberg once said 'the more a person can do, the more you can motivate them'. In other words, we work more enthusiastically at the things we're good at. So, the employee trained in quality management is more likely to think about how to improve the standard of the goods produced.

If motivation can be boosted by more and better training, so too can labour retention. If an employee feels they're developing at work, they are far more likely to stay. There may be an employer down the road offering an extra 50p an hour, but the motivated staff member ignores that. They want to keep developing in the job they have.

This can create a hugely upward spiral for the business: good training boosting motivation, which boosts retention, which helps keep quality and efficiency high, which provides extra profit to pay for still more training. From a football point of view, welcome to FC Barcelona. From a business point of view, welcome to Jaguar Land Rover. Such a fast-growing, prestigious employer offers status but also a rising number of promotion possibilities. In 2015, the company boasted that the number of international assignments taken by UK-based staff rose by 33 per cent. Jaguar Land Rover's labour retention is one of the highest in the country, at around 95 per cent.

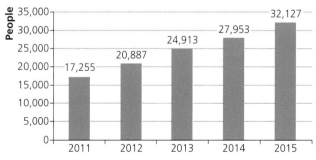

Figure 53.1 Jaguar Land Rover worldwide job growth (Source: JLR's annual report 2015)

Drawing the right conclusions

Training and developing employees could be seen by businesses as a moral duty. This has tended to be true in Germany, where many big businesses are family owned and take a broader view of their responsibilities. Many UK firms see training as a cost that must be tested like any other cost: 'is it value for money?' In this scenario, training is only worthwhile if it pays for itself (in better-quality output or in higher sales). Many organisations continue to view training as an avoidable expense; they cut training budgets when under pressure to cut costs or poach employees already equipped with the necessary skills from other firms. New employees can bring a number of benefits, including fresh ideas and approaches to work. However, such an approach fails to capture the long-term impact of training on labour retention, and the quality and motivation of the workforce.

Revision essentials

Formal training: the official training programme, for example a two-year graduate training programme.

Informal training: the unexpected, unplanned extra advice or demonstrations that come from colleagues or, occasionally, customers.

Mentor: someone in the workplace who gives you advice and help, officially or unofficially.

Ongoing training: regular, perhaps weekly, training sessions for all staff.

Performance reviews: discussion sessions between you and your boss (perhaps every six months) about how well you are doing against the targets set for you.

Retention: a calculation of how many staff stay loyal rather than leaving, for example staff staying as a percentage of all staff.

Self-learning: teaching yourself, perhaps by thinking why a problem occurred and making sure you learn from your mistakes.

Target-setting: when you are set goals by a manager and your job is to achieve them.

End of chapter exercises

1 Explain why informal training might be important to the development of someone starting their first job.

2 A small business owner has £40,000 of profit to reinvest in the business and is debating whether to invest this sum in new, faster computers or in staff training. Suggest two arguments in favour of each of the two options.

3 'Staff training is a waste of time as half my staff leave within a year.' Explain to this business owner why they should change this attitude to training.

4 Explain why a big business such as Google might provide a better formal training programme to new staff than a small business.

Practice questions

Just 25 per cent of small firm owners have invested in leadership training in the last year, according to new research by the Federation of Small Businesses (FSB), with price being cited as the biggest barrier to making such an investment. The survey also found that less than one-fifth of small business owners send their staff on external management development courses, even though 64 per cent think a lack of skills impedes business growth.

The cost of management training was the most important factor preventing business owners from providing it, with 43 per cent citing this as a key challenge. The availability of relevant training was also seen as an issue, with a third of respondents of the opinion that this held them back from providing it.

FSB policy director Mike Cherry said: 'The UK's 5.4 million small businesses boast some of the most dynamic and creative business leaders in the world. However, our research demonstrates how greater investment in management skills could significantly benefit start-ups and scale-ups (businesses attempting to grow) and help owners realise their growth ambitions.'

Source: businessadvice.co.uk, 3 March 2016

Total: 15 marks

1 Analyse why greater investment in management skills might 'benefit start-ups and scale-ups'. (6)

2 You have been appointed as the new boss of the FSB. You are looking at two ways to persuade more small companies to invest in leadership training:

- ◆ Option 1: Ask the potential leaders who are to receive this training to contribute half the cost.
- ◆ Option 2: Ask all FSB members to contribute two per cent of sales revenue then hand out the cash to those applying to do the course.

Justify which **one** of these two options you should choose. (9)

54 Motivation

Motivation matters. Motivation matters massively. On 27 June 2016, Iceland played England in the first knockout stage of the European Championships. It is the international equivalent of Brentford versus Barcelona. Iceland's population of 329,000 is 200 times smaller than that of the UK. And Wayne Rooney scores a penalty after four minutes. Playing with an incredible Icelandic noise behind them, Iceland match the Premier League's superstars – and more. The final score is 2-1 to Iceland, and England's most humiliating defeat in at least 50 years.

Motivation allows small companies to outperform large ones, and employees of average ability to outperform cleverer ones.

At 3.30 a.m. on a Saturday morning, 71-year-old Salvatore Falcone starts work at his bakery. He makes and bakes bread, pizzas, doughnuts, cakes and pastries until 11.30 a.m., then serves customers until 4.30 p.m. in the afternoon. On a Sunday evening he races stock cars at race tracks across the South East. In return for his amazing motivation, he has been able to afford houses in London and Italy, and is now eyeing a soft-top Ferrari Testarossa.

Entrepreneurs have motivation, but the big question is how to motivate staff who are not getting the direct financial reward from the success of the business.

● What is 'motivation' exactly?

To most people, motivation simply means having the commitment to do something. Within the home, it may be decorating the bathroom; at work, it may be working late to finish a job. However, Professor Herzberg says that motivation is doing something because you *want* to do it. In other words, motivation is not about whether you do it, it is why and how you do it. Motivation, he says, does not come from money or from threats – 'do this, or else' – it only comes from within.

There are many possible ways to motivate staff. Among them are:

◆ Give them a real sense of purpose. Staff on a hospital maternity ward should be fine, but in a profit-making business it may be harder. High quality standards can motivate people, as can success. Employees of Jaguar Land Rover have loved seeing their company's success since the dark days under previous owner Ford.

◆ Involve them in the decisions made by the business, for example getting shop-floor staff involved in deciding how to rearrange the shop to encourage higher sales.

◆ Give them meaningful, challenging tasks. An American TV station asked its staff to come up with a new schedule of programmes for a Friday night; the management followed the advice of staff and the viewing audience rose by 20 per cent. The staff then reorganised the rest of the week's programmes with equal success – and the number of staff days off 'sick' fell by 30 per cent.

● The importance of motivation in the workplace

Word of mouth matters everywhere. If staff enjoy working at the Warwick Zara but not at Topshop, word will spread. Staff will rarely leave Zara but, when they do, the best and brightest locally will apply for the jobs. The talented Zara store manager will find the job increasingly easy because of the quality and self-motivation of the staff. The warm, positive atmosphere at Zara make customers keen to come, stay and buy. The high motivation feeds directly through to higher sales and profits.

So, staff motivation is important for attracting employees, most notably attracting high-quality employees. Due to its rapid growth, each year Google employs 5,000 new staff. It has to select them from 2 million applicants! Although some applications can be rejected quickly, an amazing amount are very high quality indeed. And, of course, that's the point. A business as dependent on motivated brains as Google is needs to hire more motivated brains – the bigger the better.

Staff motivation is also important for retaining employees, that is, keeping them. Between 2009 and 2016 Google's worldwide workforce grew from 6,000 to 60,000. It is no good spending big on recruitment if the staff flowing in are balanced by lots of others pouring down the plughole. Keeping good staff is at least as important as recruiting them. The more motivated they are towards your company's goals and towards the job they do, the fewer will leave. That saves you:

◆ the cost of hiring new staff
◆ the cost of training new staff
◆ the lost efficiency – that is, productivity – in the time until the new staff have learned to do their jobs properly.

The important thing about productivity is that it relates to labour cost per unit. Bicycle manufacturer Brompton has 240 staff producing 48,000 bikes a year (200 bikes per worker per year). If Brompton workers earn an average of £30,000 a year each, than the labour cost per bike is £30,000 / 200 bikes = £150. If productivity rose to 300 bikes per worker per year, the labour cost per bike would fall to £30,000 / 300 = £100 per bike. From the company's point of view, the lower the labour cost per bike, the greater the chance of being able to make a profit from the bikes. From the worker's point of view, if we're now making 300 bikes a year each, how about a pay rise?

The important thing to remember, though, is that:
◆ high productivity means high efficiency
◆ the higher the productivity, the lower the labour cost per unit
◆ lower labour costs per unit should mean higher profits per unit.

> Motivation is the art of getting people to do what you want them to do because they want to do it.
>
> *Dwight D. Eisenhower, former US president*

How businesses motivate employees

Professor Herzberg's view is simple: motivation comes from within. Financial methods such as bonuses are nothing to do with motivation; they are ways to incentivise. In other words, a bonus may make you do something; it doesn't mean that you *want* to do it. Iceland's football team beat England because they had the fire from within: that's motivation.

The following financial methods can be used to incentivise staff.

Remuneration

Most people in the UK have full-time, permanent jobs for which they are paid a salary. In other words, their monthly pay is unrelated to their efforts or achievements. Your teacher receives the same pay in August (while swimming up to that pool bar) as they do in May (when sweating over last-minute GCSE revision). Salaries work on the assumption that pay is not there to motivate or even incentivise. It is there to keep the worker happy enough to keep doing the job with no reason to click through the job advertisements.

Employees in the private sector may benefit further from **fringe benefits** – non-monetary rewards given to staff. Often known as 'perks', these are benefits other than money, paid in addition to wages or salaries. Examples include a company car, health insurance, payments into a pension fund, free life assurance, discounts when buying the firm's goods, use of a company mobile phone, subsidised canteen and leisure facilities. These are all part of an employee's **remuneration**.

In addition to being paid by salary, many people are paid in relation to their specific efforts, be it by the hour (this week you've done 14 hours at £9.20, so it is £128.80) or in relation to the amount of work done (you've made 400 units at £1.10 a unit, so it is £440 for the week). The problem with variable incomes such as these is that mortgage payments or the electricity direct debit are constant sums. For some people, a few bad weeks of earning can put them in financial difficulties.

A company car can reinforce the status of a manager

Bonuses

Bonuses are extra payments over and above the basic wage or salary. They are often paid as a reward for reaching a target. In 2016, full-time staff at John Lewis received a ten per cent bonus, which represented five weeks' worth of pay. The company suggests every year that this bonus is an important incentive to work hard and that it adds to teamwork within the business.

In 2014, the EU placed a cap on the bonus level allowed within the banking sector of 100 per cent. This was to try to limit the distorting effect of bankers being able to earn such a vast amount in one year's bonus that it would be worth taking huge risks ('if I get this right, I'm made for life'). The UK protested about this cap, saying that it would force banks to push up fixed salaries to staff. A later report from the Bank of England admitted that this didn't happen. The lower bonuses simply led to lower total remuneration among the bankers.

Commission

Sales people may be paid a basic salary plus a **commission** (a percentage of the value of sales).

A&M Carpet and Bed Centre is a shop based in Wigan. Peter is the director of the business and is in charge of the day-to-day running of the shop. Tony is employed by the business as a salesman; he is paid a basic salary of £12,000 per year. Tony is also paid commission: he receives 2.5 per cent of the value of anything he sells. This means is that Tony will get paid the equivalent of £12,000 a year (roughly £1,000 per month) even if he sells nothing.

If Tony sells carpets to the value of £8,000 and beds to the value of £2,000 in one month, he will receive £1,250 for that month. How is this calculated? £8,000

Table 54.1 The advantages and disadvantages of awarding a bonus

Advantages of bonuses	Disadvantages of bonuses
An unpromised bonus might be a great reward for a worker who's achieved great things during the year	A bonus-driven business pushes staff to lower their ethical standards in pursuit of the money (the bankers' bonus problem)
If a company has made huge profits, staff would be thrilled to receive a payout	Firms can end up giving bonuses for staff completing ordinary tasks – such as footballers being paid 'appearance money'
Bonuses may be a help in getting staff to do the less pleasant part of their jobs, e.g. a bonus for getting dull paperwork tasks done on time	Once staff get used to bonuses, they can come to expect them rather than be thrilled by them; the 10 per cent bonus at John Lewis in 2016 was actually down sharply on 17per cent in 2013

added to £2,000 is £10,000; 2.5 per cent of £10,000 is £250; add this to the basic salary of £1,000 gives £1,250. This means the more Tony sells, the more money he earns.

Some sales people are paid on a commission-only basis. This is harsh to the point of cruelty. A bad week means zero income – and in industries such as double-glazing, a bad week is always a possibility.

> **Talking point**
>
> If working on a till paid £9 an hour and cleaning the toilets paid £14 an hour, which would you choose? Why?

Promotion

In the long term an employee's earnings are mainly going to be affected by promotion. Some will enjoy a steady rise up the career ladder, ending up with a big salary and a fat pension. Some may even deserve this. Unfortunately, many big businesses in the UK are famously badly run – and the heart of the problem is middle senior management. Both Morrisons and Tesco seemed to do significantly better after making substantial cutbacks to their senior management ranks.

The problem is that promotions often happen for the wrong reason. Employee A, who argues a lot (showing that they care), is cast aside for 'Mr Yes', who nods at the right time: in this way junior staff learn that promotions don't happen to the best staff, or even the brightest, but the 'yes-iest'. Of course, well-run businesses – such as Jaguar Land Rover,

James Dyson and Apple – are quite different, but they may be in the minority.

> Motivation is a fire from within. If someone else tries to light that fire under you, chances are it'll burn very briefly.
>
> *Stephen Covey, business writer*

Non-financial methods to motivate employees

Job rotation

Job rotation means that an employee does several tasks within the working day. It is intended to stop the boredom of doing one thing constantly. So, instead of sitting at the checkout all day, you might spend two hours refilling shelves and an hour on customer services. As motivation comes from within, this can only work if carrying out more tasks leads to a more stimulating working life. There is little evidence that this happens. For the most part, job rotation may help to relieve boredom, but it does little to motivate.

Job enrichment

Job enrichment is defined by Professor Herzberg as 'giving people the opportunity to use their ability'. It means giving more responsibility as well as more tasks. For job enrichment, perhaps the checkout worker should also spend time as a supervisor; for example, from a seven-hour day they might spend

Table 54.2 Looking further at promotions

Promotion: the way it should be	Promotion: the way it often is	Promotion: making it better
Promotions go to the best, the brightest, or those showing leadership potential	Promotions go to those whose face fits – and agree with management policies	Managers should learn that different viewpoints can lead to better decisions
Juniors showing leadership potential should get equal training for equal opportunity	Ethnic minority staff don't get put on the training courses that fit with a promotion push	Companies should check whether training opportunities are provided equally
Staff should all aspire to get promoted and therefore have the incentive to be their best	Seeing how things are, many staff don't look for promotion – they look to get out	If not many are applying for promotion, senior managers should investigate why

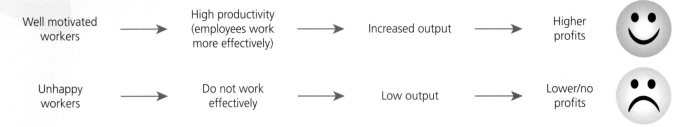

Figure 54.1 Motivation is vital to business success

two hours as the supervisor of all the checkout staff. That would represent a greater challenge, and also give the individual the opportunity to show their abilities to more senior staff. Herzberg suggested the following factors are needed for a job to be considered 'enriched':

◆ complete unit of work
◆ self-checking
◆ direct feedback.

Autonomy

Autonomy means independence, that is, power over your own life at work. Very few people have this absolutely; more have a degree of it. Teachers love a moan but speak most positively about their relatively independent life in the classroom. They decide what they're going to teach that day, and how they're going to do it. By contrast, a train driver has huge responsibility but little or no autonomy. Autonomy is potentially a huge contributor to motivation.

●Drawing the right conclusions

The most successful companies are usually those with the best-motivated staff. People who have started their own business can underestimate the importance of this. They often expect people to find the motivation from within, without doing enough to create a situation in which staff can easily be motivated. If the boss barks out orders and hands over a series of dull tasks, it is no surprise if staff dislike their work. Motivation requires a manager to think about how best to organise work so that staff feel that their intelligence is being used properly. This is where job enrichment and even autonomy should be considered.

Revision essentials

Autonomy: the independent power to decide on what you are going to do at work.

Commission: being paid a percentage of the value of a sale you have made, for example a ten per cent commission.

Fringe benefits: rewards you get from work other than pay, such as a company phone or car.

Job enrichment: being given a range of activities and responsibilities that enable the worker to learn and to grow.

Job rotation: having several tasks to do at work to relieve the boredom of doing the same thing all the time.

Remuneration: all the financial rewards received from work, whether direct, such as a salary, or indirect, such as free membership of a sports club.

End of chapter exercises

1 What is it called when employees are given perks in addition to their pay?

2 Identify three benefits that a highly motivated employee might bring to a business.

3 How might the store manager at a Costa Coffee boost staff motivation?

4 Should your teacher's salary be stopped and instead be paid solely on the basis of the coming year's GCSE results?

5 Read the following extract and answer the questions.

(a) Explain how staff motivation might affect customer service.

(b) Discuss whether the business would be better off using financial or non-financial methods to try to achieve the improved motivation.

Aston & Magill cafe employs two staff who are paid out of the quite satisfactory weekly takings. But now a Costa is to open 50 metres away – the first chain to open up nearby. Boss Cara Aston is worried about the new competitor and thinks that her staff need to be more motivated in order to give better customer service.

Practice questions

Morrisons is to invest £30 million into improving staff conditions across its 498 stores. It hopes that a more motivated workforce will help the company's turnaround from the falling market share it suffered 2-3 years ago.

The news comes following a company-wide consultation, in which employees were asked how stores could be improved. Cheaper coffee, free Wi-Fi and more comfortable rest areas are amongst the changes. This follows a recent announcement that staff will get a 20 per cent pay rise to £8.20 an hour from next month, beating the government's new 'national living wage' of £7.20.

The Morrisons plan is strikingly different to the approach by Asda, which recently announced a cutback on 'fringe benefits' such as staff canteens and free coffee – to cut costs. It is noticeable that Asda's market share has been falling while Morrisons has stabilised its market position.

'We asked our staff for their views about their stores and many commented about their restrooms saying they would like them to be more relaxing and offer a better food service,' said Morrisons' CEO David Potts. 'This investment will ensure they are provided with the facilities and food to help them recharge during their breaks.' Potts added that 'we are a business that listens hard to colleagues and responds wherever possible.'

Clare Grainger, Morrisons' head of human resources, said: 'We are also pleased that our retail management team is becoming more representative of our largely female colleague and customer base.' In the past Morrisons' senior management team was dominated by men.

Source: Various, February 2016

Total: 20 marks

1 Outline one reason why Asda might regret scrapping staff 'fringe benefits'. (2)

2 Analyse why Morrisons may benefit from a 'more representative' balance between men and women among its senior management. (6)

3 Evaluate whether the actions that Morrisons has taken will achieve a 'more motivated workforce'. You should use the information provided as well as your knowledge of business. (12)

Exam-style questions on Topic 2.5

Don't rush; check your answers carefully.

1 Which **one** of the following is the best explanation for a rise in the productivity of a UK car manufacturer? (1)

   (a) Recruiting more staff.

   (b) A rise in UK economic growth.

   (c) Higher investment in new technology.

   (d) More support staff to help operational staff.

2 Which **two** of the following are benefits to a business from decentralising? (2)

   (a) Helps maintain the consistency of customer experience.

   (b) Encourages junior staff to take more initiative.

   (c) Makes sure you get the best from high-paid senior staff.

   (d) Cuts down on management costs.

   (e) Makes sure decisions are taken closer to the customer.

Questions 3, 4 and 5 are based on the following bar chart.

Staff responses to survey at J.L. Biscuits; sample size was 119 out of 140 in Assembly and 110 out of 120 in Packing

3 Which **two** conclusions can be taken from this data? (2)

   (a) Jobs in Packing seem much better liked than jobs in Assembly.

   (b) Assembly workers were more likely to respond than those in Packing.

   (c) Twice as many in Packing said 'not keen on job' than said 'enjoy my job'.

   (d) Surveys such as this are pointless because not everyone answers them.

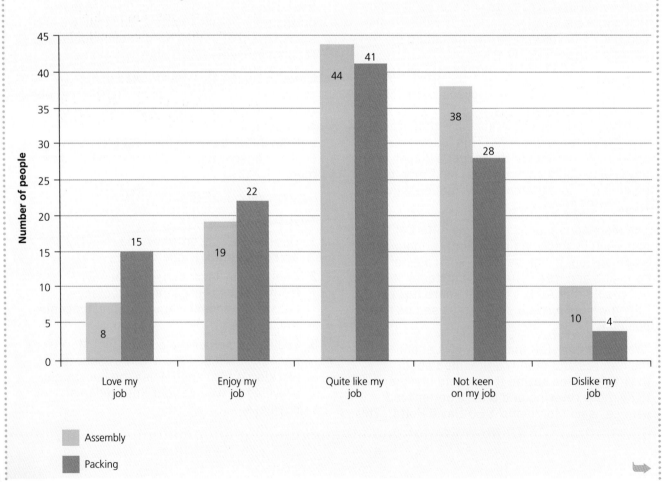

Assembly

Packing

(e) Bosses at J.L. Biscuits should look into how each of these departments is managed.

4 Which **one** of the following may be the approach taken by the Packing manager? (1)

(a) Paying staff on commission to give a bigger incentive.

(b) Using job rotation to give them a more challenging job.

(c) Enriching the jobs by giving staff more responsibility and challenge.

(d) Putting all staff on temporary contracts to force them to fight for their jobs.

5 Which **one** of the following is most likely to improve motivation in the Assembly section? (1)

(a) Setting targets to put pressure on staff to work faster.

(b) More training, both informal and through self-learning.

(c) Switching to a more hierarchical organisational structure.

(d) Communicating very often with staff, texting regularly to provide the latest company news.

6 Which **two** of the following are significant barriers to communication? (2)

(a) In a flat hierarchy there may be too many layers of management.

(b) Shop-floor workers rarely socialise with management.

(c) Lack of motivation on the part of the worker/listener: 'who cares?'

(d) A hierarchical structure may make communication too slow from bottom to top.

(e) The company has too high a level of labour retention.

7 Which **one** of the following is a reason why a worker may prefer permanent to temporary work? (1)

(a) Permanent jobs are more likely to be supported by investment in new technology.

(b) Temporary work may fit better with an individual's lifestyle.

(c) Permanent work ensures that the employee benefits from remuneration.

(d) Greater job security lowers the pressure adults can feel about family finances.

Now try this discussion question.

8 Discuss whether a new business could benefit from keeping a flat hierarchy as it grows. (6)

Glossary

Adapting existing products Finding new products that are based on the original one, such as Walls White Chocolate Magnum.

Aesthetics How things appeal to the senses: Do they look great, smell good, feel nice, sound solid (the 'ker-lunk' of a BMW door shutting) and taste great?

Aims A general statement of where you're heading; for example, 'to get to Uni'.

Autonomy The independent power to decide on what you are going to do at work.

Availability Knowing how to get the right supplies quickly – just when you need them.

Average rate of return (ARR) Average yearly profit as a percentage of the sum invested. This shows profitability and can be compared to the interest rates available on bank deposit accounts.

Bankrupt When an individual is unable to pay his/her debts, even after all personal assets have been sold for cash.

Bar chart Data presented so that the height of the bar represents the quantity involved; good for comparisons.

Barrier to communication Something that prevents the flow of communication.

Batch production Producing a limited number of identical products.

Branding Giving a product or service 'personality', with a name and logo that makes it stand out.

Break-even The level of sales at which total costs equals total revenue. At this point the business is making neither a profit nor a loss.

Break-even output = fixed costs / (price – variable costs per unit)

Break-even chart A graph showing a company's revenue and total costs at all possible levels of output.

Budget A ceiling on the amount of money that can be spent. So a marketing budget of £1 million means the marketing manager can spend up to that figure, but no more.

Buffer stock A minimum stock level to be held at all times, to avoid the risks involved if a supplier fails to deliver on time.

Business decisions Choices that have to be made, usually within a short time period.

Business failure The collapse of a business, probably leading to its closure.

Business growth Factors allowing a company to expand through higher sales and (usually) higher staff levels.

Business operations The section of an organisation concerned with making and delivering what the customer wants.

Business performance Ways of measuring how well a business has done in the recent past (often the basis for setting targets in the future).

Business plan A document setting out a new company's aims, plans and cash flow forecasts.

Cash The money the firm holds in notes and coins and in its bank accounts.

Cash flow The movement of money into and out of the firm's bank account.

Cash flow forecast Estimating the likely flows of cash over the coming months – and therefore the overall state of one's bank balance.

Centralised organisation An organisation in which most decisions are made at head office.

Choice Giving customers options and increasing the chance that a product will be available which is perfect for the tastes/habits of one type of customer.

Closing balance The amount of cash left in the bank at the end of the month.

Commission Being paid a percentage of the value of a sale you have made, for example, a '10% commission'.

Communication The passing of information from one person or organisation to another.

Competing internationally Finding a way to succeed against rivals from overseas.

Competition Companies operating in your market or market sector.

Competitive advantage Features of a product or service that make it stronger in the marketplace than its competitors.

Competitive environment The strength and number of the competitors operating in a market.

Consumer incomes   The amounts available to be spent by households after income taxes have been deducted.

Consumer rights   Laws that empower the consumer to demand certain minimum standards from every business supplier.

Consumer spending   The total spent by all shoppers throughout the country.

Convenience   Making life easier for customers, perhaps by a great location (next to the bus stop) or a product that saves time in preparation or consumption.

Crowdfunding   Raising capital online from many small investors (but not through the stock market).

Culture   'The way we do things round here'; in other words, the accepted attitudes and practices of staff at a workplace.

Curriculum vitae (CV)   A document which sets out the person's qualifications, experience and any other relevant facts (it literally means the 'story of life').

Customer engagement   The attempt to make a customer feel part of something rather than an outsider.

Customer feedback   Comments, praise or criticisms given to the company by its customers.

Customer needs   The products or services people have to have to make life comfortable.

Customer wants   What people choose to spend their money on, once the weekly bills have been paid.

Decentralised organisation   An organisation which allows staff to make decisions at a local level.

Demographics   A study of the statistical differences that exist within a population, both now and in the future.

Design   Deciding how something will look, both internally (the gearbox) and externally (the bonnet).

Design mix   Finding the right design balance between function, aesthetics and cost of manufacture.

Digital communication   Passing messages by email, smartphone or app (rather than by face-to-face conversation).

Dividends   Payments to shareholders from the company's yearly profits. The directors of the company decide how large a dividend payment to make; in a bad year they can decide on zero.

Dynamic nature of business   The idea that business is ever-changing because external factors such as technology are always changing.

E-commerce   Selling online rather than in a physical one-to-one transaction. An important part of e-commerce is m-commerce, meaning commerce using apps/phones rather than websites/PCs.

Economic climate   Taking the temperature of the broader economy, to see whether it is unhealthy or well and therefore whether the government is likely to need to change its economic policy.

Economic manufacture   Whether the product be made cheaply enough to make it profitable.

E-newsletters   Regular updates on the activities of a business, sent electronically to actual or potential customers.

Entering markets   When a company decides to open up in a market it hasn't been in before, for example, Walkers making cereal bars.

Enterprise   The personal characteristics of questioning and initiative that can be shown by an employee or an entrepreneur.

Entrepreneurs   Businesspeople who see opportunities and are willing to take risks in making them happen.

Environment   The condition of the natural world that surrounds us, which is damaged when there is pollution.

Environmental considerations   Factors relating to 'green' issues, such as sustainability and pollution.

E-tailer   An electronic retailer; in other words, one from whom purchasing is done electronically, either by e-commerce or, more likely these days, mobile commerce ('m-commerce').

Ethical considerations   Thinking about ethics, which may lead to morally valid decisions, or may lead to the manipulation of customer attitudes, that is, pretending to be ethical.

Ethics   Weighing up decisions or actions on the basis of morality, not personal gain.

Excessive communication   Too much communication causing overload for staff – a particular problem with email.

Exchange rates   The value of one currency measured by how much it will buy of other currencies.

Exiting markets   Choosing to leave a market, probably because it was loss-making.

Exports   Goods produced in one country but sold to buyers overseas, for example, a British-made Mini sold in France.

Glossary

Extension strategy An attempt to prolong sales of a product for the medium-long term and prevent it from entering its decline stage.

External influences Factors and changes from outside that might prevent a business achieving its objectives, for example, sales being hit by a sudden recession.

External recruitment Appointing from outside the existing staff.

Fairtrade An organisation that buys directly from suppliers in, say, Africa, ensuring that the price paid is high enough to allow fair wages to be paid to the farmworkers. The Fairtrade brand can be found on many products, including KitKat.

Fixed costs Costs that don't vary just because output varies, for example, rent.

Fixed premises Buildings that have to be where they are, for example, the high street; e-commerce buildings can be moved anywhere.

Flat structure An organisation with few layers of hierarchy – presumably because each manager is responsible for many staff.

Flexibility The ability to switch quickly and easily from one task to another.

Flexible hours A contract between a company and an employee that doesn't specify how many hours of work will be provided.

Flotation Listing company shares on the stock market, therefore allowing the price to float freely (up and down).

Flow production Continuous production of identical products, therefore giving scope for high levels of automation.

Focus group A group discussion among people selected from the target market. It draws upon psychology to provide qualitative insights into consumer attitudes.

Formal training The training programme put on by the company.

Formulae Plural of formula; a way of showing how the components of a calculation can be turned into an answer, for example, 'revenue – total costs = profit'.

Franchising Paying a franchise owner for the right to use an established business name, branding and business methods.

Free trade Trade between countries with no barriers, for example, no tariffs.

Freelance contract An agreement over a single job between a company and self-employed worker.

Fringe benefits Rewards you get from work other than pay, such as a company phone or car.

Function How well the product or service works for the customer, for example, for a hotel: comfortable bed; for a smartphone: sharp photos.

Gap in the market An area on a market map where few or no existing brands operate, implying a business opportunity to fill an unmet consumer need.

Globalisation The increasing tendency for countries to trade with each other and to buy global goods such as Coca-Cola, or services such as Costa coffee.

Goods Products that can be grown (cabbages) or manufactured (Mars Bars and cars).

Graph Data presented as lines, making it easy to identify trends, especially if 'time' is shown on the horizontal axis.

Gross profit margin Gross profit as a percentage of sales revenue or, for an individual item, gross profit as a percentage of the selling price.

Hierarchical structure An organisation with many layers of management, therefore creating a tall organisational pyramid.

Identifying customers Finding out who they are: their age, gender, incomes, where they live and what they want.

Imports Goods or services bought from overseas.

Independence The need of many business owners to make their own decisions; be their own boss.

Inflation The rate of rise in the average prices of goods and services.

'Inform' decisions Evidence that can be used to make a better decision. Through the 4Ps a company can gain an understanding of its customers that helps in decision-making.

Informal training Learning on the job, usually through advice and tips from colleagues.

Innovation Bringing a new idea to the market, such as Warburton's clever idea of an extra-large crumpet.

Innovative A new, perhaps original, product or process.

Inorganic (external) growth Growing by buying up other businesses or by merging with a business of roughly equal size.

Insufficient communication Too little communication, which might leave some staff under-informed and demotivated.

Interest The regular charges made by banks for the cash they have lent to a business, for example, '6 per cent per year'.

Interest rates The annual cost of a loan to the borrower.

Internal recruitment Appointing from within the existing staff.

Job description A short account of the main features of the job.

Job enrichment Being given a range of activities and responsibilities that enable the worker to learn and to grow.

Job production Production of a one-off item for a single customer.

Job rotation Having several tasks to do at work to relieve the boredom of doing the same thing all the time.

Lack of security Uncertainty for the business owner about day-to-day family income and assets.

Legislation Laws passed by Acts of Parliament; breaking those laws may result in a fine or even a prison sentence.

Lifestyle Grouping people by common characteristics based on how they live, from sports and leisure to views regarding the environment, interest in music festivals or nerdier things such as a passion for trains.

Limited liability Restricting the losses suffered by owners/shareholders to the sum they invested in the business.

Location The extent to which consumers identify with the place where they were born, or grew up.

Logistics ensuring that the right supplies will be ordered and delivered on time.

Managing quality Choosing the right method for achieving high-quality results, then supervising what workers actually do, day by day.

Manufacturing Turning raw materials into finished products ready for sale; usually takes place in a factory.

Margin of safety The amount by which demand can fall before the business starts making losses.

Margin of safety = sales – break-even output

Marketing mix The blend between product, price, promotion and place that can help a business achieve its revenue targets.

Market map Measuring where existing brands sit on a two-factor grid, for example, young/old compared with high price/low price.

Market segments The subsets within a market that have been identified as a result of market segmentation.

Market share The percentage of a market held by one company or brand.

Mentor Someone in the workplace who gives you advice and help, officially or unofficially.

Merger When two businesses of roughly equal size agree to come together to form one big business.

Negative cash flow When cash outflows are greater than cash inflows.

Net cash flow Cash in minus cash out, over a month.

Net profit margin Net profit as a percentage of sales revenue or, for an individual item, net profit as a percentage of the selling price.

Objectives A clear goal that is measurable, so success or failure is clear to see.

Obsolete A product with sales that have declined or come to an end as customers find something new.

Ongoing training Regular, perhaps weekly, training sessions for all staff.

Opening balance The amount of cash in the bank at the start of the month.

Operational decisions Deciding on key production factors, such as how to manage quality or how much stock to order.

Organic (internal) growth Growth from within the business, such as creating and launching successful new products.

Organisation chart A diagram that shows the internal structure of an organisation.

Original ideas Ideas that have not been done before.

Overdraft The amount the business uses of the facility provided by the Bank for short-term borrowing.

Overdraft facility An agreed maximum level of overdraft.

Payment systems Ways of paying electronically, such as PayPal.

Performance reviews Discussion sessions between the employee and their boss (perhaps every six months) about how well the employee is doing against the targets set for them.

Permanent contract An agreement between a company and an employee that work and income will be provided constantly into the long-term future.

Glossary

Person specification   An account of the type of person who would best fit the job: their character, their experience and skills.

Pie chart   Data presented in a circle, with each slice of the pie representing a proportion of the whole; good for representing proportions of a total, for example, market share.

Place   How and where the supplier is going to get the product or service to the consumer; it includes selling products into retailers and getting the products displayed in prominent positions.

Post-sales service   Service after the purchase is completed, perhaps because something has gone wrong or as a way of promoting customer engagement.

Pressure group   An organisation founded to achieve a specific objective, for example, Surfers Against Sewage.

Price   Setting the price that retailers must pay, which in turn affects the consumer price.

Primary research   Research conducted first hand; tailored to a company's specific needs, for example, a quantitative sales estimate for a brand new chocolate bar.

Private limited company   A small family business in which shareholders enjoy limited liability.

Procurement   Obtaining the right supplies from the right supplier.

Product   Targeting customers with a product that has the right blend of functional and aesthetic benefits, without being too expensive to produce.

Productivity   A measure of efficiency, usually output per person per time period, for example, Nissan UK's 98 cars per worker per year.

Product knowledge   How well staff know all the features of the products and the service issues surrounding the products, such as the precise terms of Kia's seven-year warranty on its new cars.

Product life cycle   The theory that every product goes through the same stages, of introduction, growth, maturity and decline.

Product range   The number of different product types, sizes, colours and brands offered by a company.

Profit   The difference between revenue and total costs. If the figure is negative the business is making a loss.

Profit margins   Profit as a percentage of the selling price (one unit) or as a percentage of total sales revenue (for the business as a whole).

Promotion   Within the 4Ps, promotion refers to all the means a business uses to persuade customers to buy, for example, branding, packaging, long-term image-building advertising and short-term offers.

Promotional strategy   A medium-to long-term plan for communicating with your target customers.

Proximity   Nearness; whether or not a business wants to be close to a factor such as 'materials'.

Public limited company (plc)   A company with at least £50,000 of share capital that can advertise its shares to outsiders and is therefore allowed to float its shares on the stock market.

Qualitative data   In-depth research into a small group of potential or actual customers – to provide insight into why consumers buy what they buy.

Quality   To a customer, quality means getting what they want – or perhaps better than expected; some companies use the term 'customer delight'.

Quality control   Putting measures in place to check that the customer receives an acceptable level of quality.

Quantitative data   Results from research among a large enough sample of people to provide statistically reliable results, for example, a survey of 500 15–24 year olds.

Recession   A downturn in sales and output throughout the economy, often leading to rising unemployment.

Red tape   The term given to laws that (some people say) tie the hands of businesspeople, making it hard to act entrepreneurially.

Remote working   Working away from the office, typically from home.

Remuneration   All the financial rewards received from work, whether direct, such as a salary, or indirect, such as free membership of a sports club.

Research and development   The scientific research and technical development needed to come up with successful new products.

Resources   Things or people that can be used to help build and run the business.

Retailer   A shop or chain of shops, probably selling from a building in a high street or shopping centre.

Retained profit   Profit kept within the business (not paid out in dividends); this is the best source of finance for expansion.

Retention   A calculation of how many staff stay loyal rather than leaving, for example, staff staying as a percentage of all staff.

Risk and reward   The balance between the worst that can happen and the best that can happen.

Risk-taking   Making decisions where unknown factors or chances of failure loom large in the decision maker's mind.

Robots   Machines that can be programmed to do tasks that can be done by humans, such as welding, spray painting and packing.

Role of business enterprise   What business organisations are for, such as to meet consumer needs and wants.

Royalties   A percentage of the sales revenue to be paid to the overall franchise owner.

Sales process   All the factors required to ensure that an interested customer becomes a buyer.

Sales revenue   The total value of the sales made within a period of time, such as a month.

Secondary research   When a company taps into research that has already been carried out for general purposes, for example, using a document like 'Trends in the UK market for chocolate'.

Self-learning   Teaching yourself, perhaps by thinking why a problem occurred – and making sure you don't do that again.

Services   Doing work for people other than by producing goods, for example, by running a shop or running an airline.

Share capital   Raising finance by selling part-ownership in the business. Shareholders have the right to question the directors and to receive part of the yearly profits.

Shareholders   Those who have bought shares in the business, giving them part-ownership and therefore, potentially, part-control.

Social media   Interactive channels of communication, via words, photos or videos, such as blogs, Facebook and Instagram.

Social objectives   The possible goals of a business based on its contribution to society.

Sole trader   A business run by one person; that person has unlimited liability for any business debts.

Sources of business finance   Places where finance might be found, for example, banks or individuals.

Sponsorship   When companies pay to have a brand associated with an iconic individual or event (usually connected with sports or the arts).

Stakeholders   All those groups with an interest in the success or failure of a business.

Stock(s)   Items held by a firm for use or sale, for example, components for manufacturing, or sellable products for a retailer.

Sum invested   The cash put at risk when investing in new equipment or a new product.

Survival   Keeping the business going – which ultimately depends on grit plus cash.

Sustainability   Whether or not a resource will inevitably run out in the future. A sustainable resource will not.

Takeover   Obtaining control of another business by buying more than 50 per cent of its share capital.

Target-setting   When you are set goals by a manager, and your job is to achieve them.

Tariffs   Taxes charged only on imports.

Taxation   Charges placed by government on goods, imported goods and the incomes of individuals and companies.

Technology   Hardware and software that can help people be more productive.

Temporary contract   An agreement between a company and an employee that work and income will be provided for a specific time-period, say, six months.

Total costs   All the costs for a period of time, such as a month.

Trade bloc   A group of countries that has agreed to have free trade within external tariff walls.

Trade credit   When a supplier provides goods but is willing to wait to be paid, for perhaps three months. This helps with cash flow.

Trade-offs   How having more of one thing may force you to have less of another, for example, higher ethical standards may mean less profit.

Trust   Building a business relationship in which both sides know that the other won't let them down.

Understanding customers   Learning why customers do what they do – making it easier to understand how to make a product that better suits them.

Unemployment   When someone of working age wants a job but cannot get one.

Glossary

Unethical A decision or action that offends against a moral approach to business; that is wrong from a moral standpoint.

Unique Selling Point (USP) An original feature of a product that rivals aren't offering.

Unlimited liability Treating the business and the individual owner as inseparable, therefore making the individual responsible for all the debts of a failed business.

Value added The difference between selling price and the cost of bought-in goods and services (the difference that creates the possibility of profit).

Variable costs Costs that vary as output varies, such as raw materials.

Venture capital A combination of share capital and loan capital, provided by a bank that is willing to take a chance on the success of a small to medium-sized business.

Viral advertising When people start to spread your message for you, through social means, be it word of mouth or via social media.

Warranty The guarantee by the producer that it will repair any faults in a product for a specific period of time, often one year.

Working with suppliers Building a business relationship so that your suppliers can be trusted to deliver high quality materials on time.

Index

Index

Index

Photo credits